DIRECTORY

P9-DMB-738

RESEARCH

MLA DOCUMENTATION

APA, CM, CSE, AND COS DOCUMENTATION

DOCUMENT AND WEB DESIGN

GRAMMAR BASICS

TIPS FOR MULTILINGUAL WRITERS

PUNCTUATION AND MECHANICS

SPECIAL KINDS OF WRITING

TERMS GLOSSARY AND INDEX

RESPONSE SYMBOLS AND PROOFREADING MARKS

Your instructor might use correction symbols to show where writing should be edited or revised. You can use proofreading symbols to mark hard copy for editing or revision.

Correction Symbols

ab	abbreviation error
ad	adjective or adverb error
ca	pronoun case error
cap	needs a capital letter
cl	revise a cliché
coh	needs coherence
coord	faulty coordination
cs	comma splice
dev	needs development
dm	dangling modifier
e	needs exact language
emph	needs emphasis
frag	sentence fragment
hyph	hyphen needed
inc	incomplete sentence
ital	italics error
k	awkward
lc	needs lowercase letter
mixed	mixed construction
mm	misplaced modifier
¶	new paragraph
no ¶	no new paragraph
//	faulty parallelism
pl	faulty plural
pro agr	pronoun agreement error
pro ref	pronoun reference error
p	punctuation error
,/	comma error
;/	semicolon error
:/	colon error
’	apostrophe error
“ / ”	quotation marks error
rep	too much repetition
shift	sentence shift
sl	revise slang
sp	spelling error
subord	subordination error
sxt	sexist language
t, tense	verb tense error
trans	needs transition
u	needs unity
us	usage error
v	verb form error
v agr	verb agreement error
var	needs sentence variety
w	wordy
wc	word choice error
ww	wrong word

Proofreading Marks

Mark	Meaning	Example
℘	delete	take ~~this~~ this out
¶	new paragraph	This is the end. ¶ This is a new beginning.
∽	transpose letters	transpoes letters
⊔⊓	transpose words	words transpose
∧	insert	A ∧ signals an addition (caret)
#	add space	add#space
⁀	close up space	clo se up space
(SP)	spell out	They live in (AB.) SP
rom	use roman type	That sounds *silly.* rom
ital	use italic type	Vancouver Sun ital
(cap)	use capital letters	(m)argaret (a)twood cap
(lc)	use lowercase letters	Drive (N)orth and then (E)ast. lc

Quick ACCESS

Simon & Schuster Reference for Writers

Second Canadian Edition

Lynn Quitman Troyka

with the assistance of Cy Strom

Toronto

National Library of Canada Cataloguing in Publication

Troyka, Lynn Quitman, 1938–
Quick access : Simon & Schuster quick access reference for writers / Lynn Quitman Troyka ; with the assistance of Cy Strom.—2nd Canadian ed.

Includes index.
ISBN 0-13-139906-3

1. English language—Rhetoric—Handbooks, manuals, etc. 2. English language—Grammar—Handbooks, manuals, etc. 3. Report writing—Handbooks, manuals, etc. 4. Academic writing—Handbooks, manuals, etc.—I. Strom, Cy, 1954– II. Title.

PE1408.T75 2003 808'.042 C2003-900218-7

Copyright © 2004, 2000 by Lynn Quitman Troyka
Original edition published by Prentice-Hall, Inc., a Pearson Education Company, Upper Saddle River, New Jersey, USA. Copyright © 2004 by Lynn Quitman Troyka.
This edition is authorized for sale in Canada only.

All Rights Reserved. This publication is protected by copyright, and permission should be obtained from the publisher prior to any prohibited reproduction, storage in a retrieval system, or transmission in any form or by any means, electronic, mechanical, photocopying, recording, or likewise. For information regarding permission, write to the Permissions Department.

ISBN 0-13-139906-3

Grateful acknowledgment is made to all the copyright holders for permission to use copyrighted material.

p. 7: Excerpt from "Sports Only Exercise Our Eyes," from *The Best of Sydney J. Harris*. Copyright © by Sydney J. Harris. Reprinted by permission of Houghton Mifflin Company. All rights reserved.

p. 40: Arthur Andrew, excerpt from *The Rise and Fall of a Middle Power*. © 1993 Arthur Andrew. By permission of James Lorimer & Company Ltd., Publishers.

pp. 40–41: Excerpt from "Safe Lifting Technique," by John Warde, *The New York Times*, March 11, 1990. Copyright © by The New York Times Company. Reprinted by permission.

p. 111: Dictionary entry from *Webster's New World™ College Dictionary, Third Edition*. Copyright © 1996 Wiley Publishing, Inc. All rights reserved. Reproduced here by permission of Wiley Publishing Company, Inc.

p. 141: Screen capture from University of Alberta Libraries reproduced with permission from the University of Alberta Library.

p. 153: Screen capture from Google Canada reproduced with permission of Google.

p. 155: Screen capture of Yahoo! Science reproduced with permission of Yahoo! Inc. © 2003 by Yahoo! Inc.YAHOO! and the YAHOO! Logo are Trademarks of Yahoo! Inc.

p. 305: Screen capture of Edwin Jahiel's movie review page reproduced with the permission of Edwin Jahiel, Professor of French, Comparative Literature and Cinema, Film Critic, Founder and Director, Unit for Cinema Studies at the University of Illinois.

p. 464: "Blackberries," by Yusef Komunyakaa, from *Pleasure Dome: New and Collected Poems*, Middletown, CT: Wesleyan University Press, 2001, pp. 280–81. Reproduced with the permission of Wesleyan University Press.

p. 475: Canada Post guidelines for business envelope format reproduced by permission of Canada Post Corporation.

Vice President, Editorial Director: Michael Young
Acquisitions Editor: Marianne Minaker
Marketing Manager: Toivo Pajo
Supervising Developmental Editor: Suzanne Schaan
Supervising Production Editor: Avivah Wargon
Copy Editor: Cy Strom
Proofreaders: Stephanie Fysh, Susan Ginsberg, Marie Graham
Senior Production Coordinator: Peggy Brown
Permissions Research: Susan Wallace-Cox
Art Direction: Julia Hall
Cover Design: Amy Harnden
Interior Design: Amy Harnden
Page Layout: B.J. Weckerle

4 5 6 08 07 06 05 04

Printed and bound in Canada.

For David,
my husband and sweetheart

HOW TO USE QUICK ACCESS

Your *Simon & Schuster Quick Access Reference for Writers*, Second Canadian Edition, is a reference book, like a dictionary or an encyclopedia. To find information, use the steps below. At each step, choose the options that help *you* the most.

STEP 1 Scan the following lists to decide where to start looking.

- Scan the Divider Directory inside the front cover.
- Scan the Table of Contents starting on p. viii.
- Scan the detailed contents on the back of each divider.
- Scan the Index at the back of the book for an alphabetical list of all topics.
- Scan the list of 90 *Quick Access* boxes on pages xvi–xviii.

STEP 2 Find a number tied to the information you want.

- Find the number of the chapter you want.
- Find the number-letter combination of the question you want answered.
- Find the numbers of the pages you need.
- Find the page number of a box that has information you need.

STEP 3 Check page elements, illustrated on the opposite page, to be sure you're where you want to be.

- Check for the chapter number in the blue square on the top outside corner of each page.
- Check for the number-letter combination and its question.
- Check the top of right-hand pages for the subject discussed in the section.
- Check for the page number on the top of each page.
- Check for a box number and/or title.

STEP 4 Read the information you need. Use the following special features, illustrated on the opposite page, to help you.

- Read any cross-references to related key concepts.
- Read terms in SMALL CAPITAL LETTERS as being defined in the "Terms Glossary" on pages 497–517.
- Read Alerts ❶, Computer Tips 💻, and other notes as needed.

Question to be answered

Chapter number

Page number

Icon shows this is a summary box

Box title and number

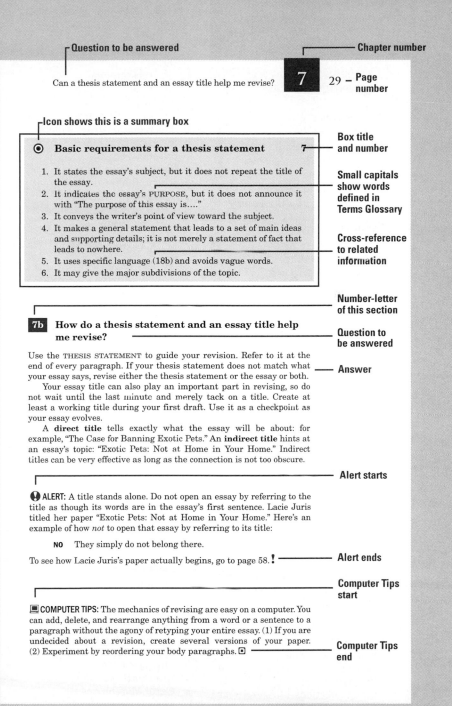

◉ Basic requirements for a thesis statement 7

1. It states the essay's subject, but it does not repeat the title of the essay.
2. It indicates the essay's PURPOSE, but it does not announce it with "The purpose of this essay is…."
3. It conveys the writer's point of view toward the subject.
4. It makes a general statement that leads to a set of main ideas and supporting details; it is not merely a statement of fact that leads to nowhere.
5. It uses specific language (18b) and avoids vague words.
6. It may give the major subdivisions of the topic.

Small capitals show words defined in Terms Glossary

Cross-reference to related information

Number-letter of this section

7b How do a thesis statement and an essay title help me revise?

Question to be answered

Use the THESIS STATEMENT to guide your revision. Refer to it at the end of every paragraph. If your thesis statement does not match what your essay says, revise either the thesis statement or the essay or both.

Answer

Your essay title can also play an important part in revising, so do not wait until the last minute and merely tack on a title. Create at least a working title during your first draft. Use it as a checkpoint as your essay evolves.

A **direct title** tells exactly what the essay will be about: for example, "The Case for Banning Exotic Pets." An **indirect title** hints at an essay's topic: "Exotic Pets: Not at Home in Your Home." Indirect titles can be very effective as long as the connection is not too obscure.

Alert starts

ALERT: A title stands alone. Do not open an essay by referring to the title as though its words are in the essay's first sentence. Lacie Juris titled her paper "Exotic Pets: Not at Home in Your Home." Here's an example of how *not* to open that essay by referring to its title:

NO They simply do not belong there.

To see how Lacie Juris's paper actually begins, go to page 58. **!**

Alert ends

Computer Tips start

COMPUTER TIPS: The mechanics of revising are easy on a computer. You can add, delete, and rearrange anything from a word or a sentence to a paragraph without the agony of retyping your entire essay. (1) If you are undecided about a revision, create several versions of your paper. (2) Experiment by reordering your body paragraphs. ▣

Computer Tips end

Contents

WORDS

RESEARCH

TIPS FOR MULTILINGUAL WRITERS

SPECIAL KINDS OF WRITING

TERMS GLOSSARY AND INDEX

Quick Access Boxes

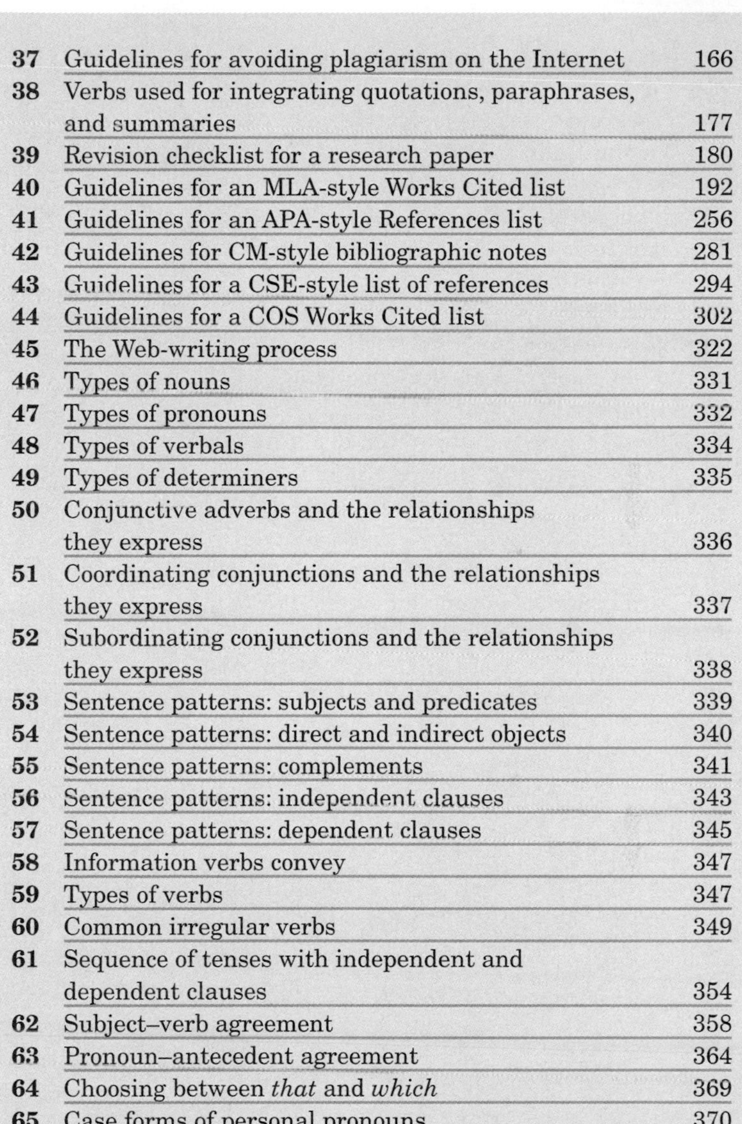

A PERSONAL MESSAGE FROM LYNN TROYKA TO STUDENTS

Many of you as writers have much in common with me. Sure, I've been at it longer, so I've had more practice, and lots of rules are cemented in my head by this time (though some stubbornly refuse to stick, and I still need to look them up). Rather, our shared experiences during the act of writing define our commonalities. After all, we're each trying to put into words ideas worthy of someone else's time to read.

When I write, I'm often unsure of how to begin (starting in the middle and then working back and ahead usually helps). Not infrequently, I'm stuck for examples sufficiently effective to get my point across (running my thoughts past my friends can often get me going). Somewhat regularly, the precise expression that I'm looking for eludes me as I rummage through the clutter of words in my mind (using a thesaurus commonly helps me sort things out, as long as I attend to the subtle differences in meanings of synonyms). I offer this book to you as my partners in the processes of writing, hoping that its pages suggest strategies that enhance your abilities to give voice to your thoughts. You're always welcome to write me at <LQTBook@aol.com> to share your reactions to my book and your own experiences as writers.

I'd like to end this message with a personal story. When I was an undergraduate years ago, handbooks weren't as common as they are now. Questions about writing nagged at me. No one seemed to have the answers I sought. One day, browsing through the library, I found a dust-covered book sitting on a wrong shelf. Its title included the words "handbook" and "writers." I read that book hungrily and often. Back then, I could never have imagined that someday I might write such a book myself. Now that I've completed the *Simon & Schuster Quick Access Reference for Writers,* Second Canadian Edition, I'm amazed that I ever had the nerve to begin. What this proves to me—and I hope to you—is that anyone can write. Students don't always believe that. I hope you will.

With cordial regards,

Lynn Troyka

PREFACE

Welcome to the Second Canadian Edition of *Quick Access Reference for Writers*. This handbook gives you Quick Access to information about the writing process, grammar, punctuation, thinking and reading critically, writing argument essays, writing research papers and documenting them, writing for the Web, designing documents, writing about literature, writing for business, and creating oral presentations.

Quick Access to Contents

The Divider Directory inside the front cover gives you a brief list of the contents of *Quick Access*. Simply open the book to see instantly which divider—one of the 13 pages with a tab sticking out—you need. Or, for a more detailed overview of the contents, go to the Table of Contents on pages viii–xv. Or, to find a specific topic, use the Index (pages 519–550) that follows the last divider.

Quick Access to All Topics

Thirteen dividers separate major topics into sections. Glance over the tabs sticking out from the dividers to find your topic. Then with a flip of your finger, you're where you want to be. On the back of each divider, you'll find a detailed list of the contents of that section. Numbered chapters contain uncomplicated discussions in small "chunks" of information. Every chunk is identified by its chapter number plus a letter in alphabetical order within the chapter. To get back quickly to a page that you consult frequently, personalize your book by placing a sticky note over the edge of the page and writing your individualized label on both sides of the note.

Quick Access to Every Page's Information

The spiral binding lets you open the book flat and fold it over flat. You'll never lose your place. All major headings resemble FAQs (Frequently Asked Questions) to match the questions you're likely to ask when you consult *Quick Access*. Look for the FAQ repeated in a "running head" at the top of each right-hand page to help you navigate smoothly through the book. Skim through the pages to spot FAQs easily. Also, use the blue flag at the top-outside corner of each page to check what chapter you're in.

Quick Access to Special Elements Throughout

Each of the 90 Quick Access boxes is a special element providing a thumbnail sketch of key information. The icon at each box carries a message: ⦿ means the box is a summary; ⌘ says the box shows a pattern; and ☰ tells that the box is a checklist. Also, ❶ signals an Alert to remind you about a related rule or other relevant information so that you can easily cope with "juggling" different rules and ideas at the same time—a common condition for writers. For example, in a discussion of sentence style, an Alert might remind you of a comma rule to apply.

Quick Access to Documentation Styles

When you look for MLA documentation, locate the MLA divider. On the divider's back is a directory telling you where you can find out how to document books, articles, nonprint media, and electronic sources. When you look for APA documentation, locate the APA divider, which has its directory on the back. When you look for the documentation style of the *Chicago Manual* (CM) or of the Council of Science Editors (CSE), or for Columbia online style (COS), locate them all in one section immediately after the divider for the APA listings.

Quick Access to Sample Research Papers

Quick Access contains five complete examples of student writing. Of these, three are student research papers: at the end of Chapter 10 ("Writing to Argue"); of Chapter 30 ("A Student's MLA Research Paper"); and of Chapter 33 ("A Student's APA Research Paper"). The other two are student essays: at the end of Chapter 9 ("Writing to Inform") and of Chapter 62 ("Writing About Literature").

Quick Access to Help for Native Speakers and Multilingual Students

Whether English is your only language or you're multilingual, you'll find quick answers in *Quick Access* to your questions about standard Canadian English grammar, punctuation, and sentence correctness and style. Additionally, there's an entire section devoted to questions of special concern to multilingual students.

New Features of the Second Canadian Edition

NEW **COMPANION WEBSITE** at **<www.pearsoned.ca/troyka>** offers:

- ***Quick Access* E-Book available online,** 24 hours a day, in a searchable format that enables you to find information quickly and easily.
- **A diagnostic test for you to grade yourself** so that you can identify your specific problem areas.
- **Hundreds of interactive, text-tied, and self-graded exercises,** including editing activities.
- **Access to Research Navigator™,** designed especially to help you use your research time efficiently and effectively. It facilitates your research process and offers three exclusive databases full of relevant and reliable source material, including EBSCO's ContentSelect Academic Journal Database, The New York Times Archive, and the Best of the Web Link Library.

NEW **Discussion of the research process increased to six chapters.** You now have the latest information in separate chapters about developing a research project, building a search strategy, finding and evaluating library resources, finding and evaluating online resources, avoiding plagiarism, and writing the research paper.

NEW **More highly developed discussion of practical ways to avoid plagiarism,** with an emphasis on your position as a student scholar.

NEW **Up-to-date, expanded coverage of MLA (6th edition, 2003) and APA documentation guidelines.** Each documentation section now ends with a complete student research paper based on print and online sources.

NEW **Chapter on Columbia online style of documentation (COS).**

NEW **MLA research paper with greatly expanded writing guidance.** Annotations run along the sides of the paper to describe technical aspects of the writing, and opposite each page of the research paper is a page of commentary that tells you about the student's writing and thinking processes.

NEW **Full coverage of document design.** Computer-based, it tells you how to incorporate graphics into papers, how to write and format business letters, and how to design a résumé.

NEW **All sentence topics in one divider section.** You can look up topics without having to decide if they relate to sentence style and effectiveness or sentence errors.

NEW **Chapter (3) on the connections between thinking, reading, and writing. Chapter (64) on oral presentations,** explaining how to plan, create, and deliver an oral presentation.

NEW **Chapter (10) on writing argument,** ending with a complete source-based student essay.

NEW **Chapter (62) on writing about literature,** ending with a student essay that analyzes a poem.

SUPPLEMENTS

RESOURCES FOR STUDENTS

- **Companion Website** at <www.pearsoned.ca/troyka> offers an E-Book available online, 24 hours a day, that contains the entire *Quick Access* in a searchable format; a **self-graded diagnostic test** to assist students in identifying their specific problem areas; **hundreds of interactive exercises,** text-tied and self-graded; and access to **Research Navigator™.**
- **Exercise Booklet** (ISBN 0-13-139907-1), which can be packaged with *Quick Access*, contains exercises and activities to help students improve their writing skills.
- **Additional Reference Tools** are available. Choose a high-quality **thesaurus** or **dictionary** that can be packaged at a special price with *Quick Access*. Contact your Pearson Education sales representative for ordering information.

RESOURCES FOR INSTRUCTORS

- **Answer Key** (ISBN 0-13-141462-3) provides answers to the exercises in the student Exercise Booklet.

ACKNOWLEDGMENTS

Each person I mention here shares in my writing by transforming an intensely personal activity into dynamic occasions of interaction. Thank you to my students who taught me much about writing and learning; colleagues across the United States and Canada who share their expertise generously; and family and friends who give me safe harbour and the chance to cherish them each day.

Three colleagues contributed significantly to this edition of *Quick Access.* Carolyn Calhoun-Dillahunt, English instructor/Writing Center Director, Yakima Valley Community College, shared with me her extraordinary talent as a writer and teacher by drafting the new chapter on writing essays of argument and by finding its accompanying student paper. Doug Hesse, Director of the Center for the Advancement of Teaching and Professor of English at Illinois State University, honoured me with his skill, insight, and grace as he drafted the new chapter on writing about literature and found the accompanying student paper. Additionally, he brought his impressive experience to expanding my discussion of plagiarism and helping with updates and new information for research writing. Kip Strasma, Professor of English, Illinois Central College, contributed his considerable expertise to the new chapter on Web-based writing.

In preparing the Second Canadian Edition of *Quick Access,* I was privileged to draw on the trenchant comments of these Canadian colleagues: Kathy Cocchio, Northern Alberta Institute of Technology; Arlene Davies-Fuhr, Grant MacEwan College; Karen Manarin, Mount Royal College; and Ilona Ryder, Grant MacEwan College.

In my work on the U.S. editions of *Quick Access,* I heartily thank the Southeast Regional Editorial Advisory Board for Prentice Hall and Lynn Troyka: Peggy Jolly, University of Alabama, Birmingham; Steve Prewitt, David Lipscomb University; Maryanne Reis, Elizabethtown Community College; Mike Thro, Tidewater Community College, Virginia Beach; and Sally Young, University of Tennessee, Chattanooga. Equally, I'm grateful to the Southwest Regional Editorial Advisory Board for Prentice Hall and Lynn Troyka: Jon Bentley, Albuquerque Technical–Vocational Institute; Kathryn Fitzgerald, University of Utah, Salt Lake City; Maggie Smith, University of Texas, El Paso; Martha Smith, Brookhaven College; and Donnie Yeilding, Central Texas College. Many other colleagues have written helpful reviews of my earlier works, and I thank each one of them most sincerely for their wisdom and practical advice.

At Prentice Hall/Simon & Schuster, outstanding people facilitated my work on this new edition of *Quick Access*. Elizabeth Morgan, Development Editor, improved each chapter with her indispensable ability to read perceptively and organize a multivariate project patiently. The vision and energy of the following people were invaluable as I was writing: Leah Jewell, Editor in Chief for English; Corey Good and Stacy Best, Senior Acquisitions Editors for English Composition; and Brandy Dawson, Senior Marketing Manager for English Composition. Shelly Kupperman, Senior Production Editor, yet again was a major partner with me in seeking to realize our vision for this book.

In the preparation of the Canadian edition, Cy Strom, of Colborne Communications Centre in Toronto, once again improved on my work with his penetrating intelligence and talented pen, helping especially by adapting samples to a Canadian context. At Pearson Education Canada, Marianne Minaker, Acquisitions Editor, and Suzanne Schaan, Supervising Developmental Editor, brought vigour and talent to the project; Avivah Wargon steered us all expertly and graciously through the maze of book production; and Peggy Brown made production coordination look easy.

My family and friends nourish my spirit and enrich my days. Ida Morea, my Administrative Assistant and friend, daily enhances my work with her excellence. With love, I salute and thank Susan Bartlestone; Kristen Black, together with Dan, Lindsey, and Ryan Black; Florence Bolden; Rita and Hy Cohen; Alan, Lynne, Adam, and Joshua Furman; Elaine Gilden Dushoff; Elliott Goldhush; Warren Herendeen; Cynthia Lester; Brenda and John Lovas; Edith Klausner, my wonderful sister; Jo Ann and Tom Lavery; Betty Renshaw; Magdalena Rogalskaja; Shirley and Don Stearns; Marilyn and Ernest Sternglass; Douglas Young III; Lisa and Nathaniel Wallace; Muriel Wolfe; and Tzila Zwas. Above all, I am grateful for the loving encouragement of my husband and sweetheart, David Troyka.

ABOUT THE AUTHOR

Photo by Ida Morea

Lynn Quitman Troyka earned her Ph.D. at New York University and taught for many years at the City University of New York (CUNY), including Queensborough Community College, the Center for Advanced Studies in Education at the Graduate School, and in the graduate program in Language and Literacy at City College. She served also as Senior Research Associate in the Office of Academic Affairs, CUNY.

Dr. Troyka is an author in composition/rhetoric for the *Encyclopedia of English Studies and Language Arts* (Scholastic, 1993), and in basic writing for the *Encyclopedia of Rhetoric* (1994). Former editor of the *Journal of Basic Writing*, she publishes in journals such as *College Composition and Communication, College English,* and *Writing Program Administration* and in books from Southern Illinois Press, Random House, the National Council of Teachers of English (NCTE), and Heinemann/Boynton/Cook. She often conducts seminars at numerous colleges, universities, and national and international meetings. She has received many honours, most recently the 2001 Exemplar Award from the Conference on College Composition and Communication (CCCC), its highest award given for scholarship, teaching, and service.

Dr. Troyka is the author of the *Simon & Schuster Handbook for Writers,* Sixth U.S. Edition and Third Canadian Edition (Prentice Hall, 2002); the *Simon & Schuster Concise Handbook* (Prentice Hall, 1992); *Structured Reading,* Sixth Edition, co-authored with Joseph Wayne Thweatt (Prentice Hall, 2002); and *Steps in Composition,* Seventh Edition, with Jerrold Nudelman (Prentice Hall, 1999). She is co-author with Richard Lloyd-Jones, John Gerber, et al. of *A Checklist and Guide for Reviewing Departments of English* (Associated Departments of English of the Modern Language Association, 1985).

The first elected Chair of the Two-Year College English Association of the National Council of Teachers of English (NCTE), Dr. Troyka is also a past chair of CCCC, of the College Section of NCTE, and of the Writing Division of the Modern Language Association.

"All this information," says Dr. Troyka, "tells what I've done, not who I am. I am a teacher. Teaching is my life's work, and I love it."

The Pearson Education Canada **COMPANION WEBSITE**

A Great Way to Learn and Instruct Online

The Pearson Education Canada Companion Website is easy to navigate and is organized to correspond to the chapters in this textbook. Whether you are a student in the classroom or a distance learner you will discover helpful resources for in-depth study and research that empower you in your quest for greater knowledge and maximize your potential for success in the course.

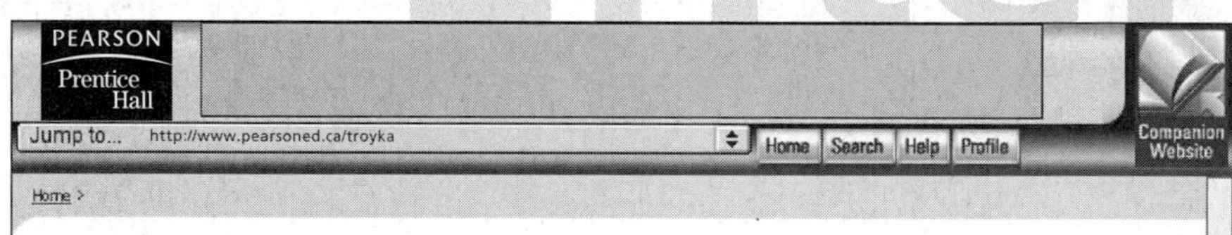

PEARSON Prentice Hall

Jump to... http://www.pearsoned.ca/troyka

Home Search Help Profile

Companion Website

Home >

Companion Website

Quick Access Reference for Writers, Second Canadian Edition, by Lynn Quitman Troyka

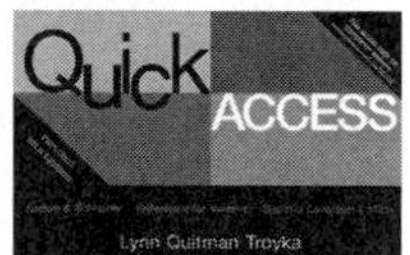

Student Resources

The modules in this section provide students with tools for learning course material. These modules include:

- Online Study Guide
- Web Destinations
- Writing Tutor
- Diagnostic Test
- Quick Access E-Book

In the quiz modules students can send answers to the grader and receive instant feedback on their progress through the Results Reporter. Coaching comments and references to the textbook may be available to ensure that students take advantage of all available resources to enhance their learning experience.

Instructor Resources

This module links directly to additional teaching tools. Downloadable PowerPoint Presentations and an Instructor's Manual are just some of the materials that may be available in this section.

Why begin a book about writing for college or university with chapters on critical thinking and reading? The answer is simply this: Being successful in your university or college career and beyond involves your developing a careful mind and a clear eye. You pause to examine ideas. You challenge ideas instead of passively accepting them. You question conclusions instead of agreeing with them without reflecting on them. By thinking and reading critically, you move beyond the obvious toward an understanding that goes below the surface to deeper meanings.

1 THINKING CRITICALLY

1a What is critical thinking?

Thinking is not something you choose to do, any more than a fish chooses to live in water. To be human is to think. Yet, while the process of thinking may come naturally, awareness of how you think does not. Thinking about thinking is how you think critically.

1b What steps do I use to think critically?

Critical thinking is a process of contemplation and deliberation. It begins with understanding and progresses to reaction. Critical thinking is something you do every day. It applies to what you read, hear, and see. For example, when you picked a postsecondary institution, you reflected on the information you gathered about the school. When you start a new job, you engage in critical thinking to learn and master the work, to decide whether the job is in line with your abilities, and to form your opinion of the job.

The steps of the critical thinking process rarely proceed in a rigid order. I discuss each step separately, but in reality, the steps interweave and loop back and forth. As you work through the process, you can expect to combine steps, reverse their order, or return to earlier parts of the process when you get to the end.

Steps in the critical thinking process: SASE 1

1. **S = Summarize:** Extract and restate the material's main message or central point (4a). Use only what you see on the pages. Add nothing.
2. **A = Analyze:** Examine the material by breaking it into its component parts. By seeing each part of the whole as a distinct unit, you discover how the parts interrelate. Consider the line of reasoning as shown by the evidence offered (27b) and the logic used (10f). Read "between the lines" to draw inferences about information that is implied but not stated (2b). When reading or watching a performance, notice how the writing style and choice of words work together to create a tone (2b).
3. **S = Synthesize:** Pull together what you have summarized and analyzed by connecting it to your own experiences, such as reading, talking with others, watching TV and films, and so on (4b). In so doing, you create a new whole that reflects your newly acquired knowledge and insights combined with your prior knowledge.
4. **E = Evaluate:** Judge the quality of the material now that you have become informed by the activities of analysis and synthesis (2b). Resist the very common urge to evaluate before you summarize, analyze, and synthesize.

2 READING CRITICALLY

2a What is critical reading?

To read critically is to think about what you are reading—while you're reading and afterward. Critical reading is similar to critical thinking (1b). As you read, you actively think about the material. Reading is an active process, a dynamic interaction between the page and your brain. Understanding how this interaction works can help you become a better reader.

2b What steps do I use to read critically?

As you read, you make split-second predictions. Your mind is constantly guessing what ideas and words are coming next. When you do see what has come next, you instantly confirm or revise your prediction and move on. For example, if you encounter the title "The Heartbeat," you start guessing: Is this a love story? Or is this about how the heart pumps blood? Or maybe it tells the story of someone who had a heart attack? As you read the first few sentences, your mind confirms which guess was correct. If you see words like *romance* and *kisses,* you know that the material involves a human relationship. On the other hand, if you see words like *electrical impulse, muscle fibres,* and *contraction,* you know instantly that you're in the realm of physiology. As you read further, you narrow your predictions to the heart as pump, or a heart suffering an attack, or a related topic.

To make predictions efficiently, determine in advance your PURPOSE* for reading. People generally read for two reasons: to relax or to learn, though the two often go together. Both types of reading are enjoyable, but they involve different approaches. Reading a popular novel or current biography usually helps you relax—and possibly learn. Reading for college and university courses calls for you to understand and remember the material—and possibly enjoy it. When you read to comprehend and retain information, you can rarely read

Steps in the critical reading process 2

1. Read for *literal meaning:* Read "on" the lines to see what is stated. Be sure not to stop here. Steps 2 and 3 give you a complete understanding of the material.
2. Read to draw *inferences:* Read "between" the lines to analyze the material. Figure out what is implied but not stated. See how the writer uses language and style to create a tone. Assess the reasoning to check whether it is faulty (10f).
3. Read to *evaluate:* Read "beyond" the lines to mould your informed opinion about the material.

*Words printed in small capital letters (such as PURPOSE) are defined in the Terms Glossary on pages 497–517.

something just once. Most students repeatedly reread sections of textbooks, lab manuals, research sources, and lecture notes.

What role does reading speed play in critical reading? That depends on what you want to accomplish. If you are hunting for a particular fact, you skim until you find it. If you are reading about a subject you know well, you might read reasonably rapidly, although you would slow down when you encounter material that's new to you. If you don't know a subject well, you would proceed more slowly, to give your mind time to understand and absorb the new material. No matter what your reading speed in each situation, you need to be critical as you read. Therefore, you want to attend to the LITERAL MEANING of the material, to make **inferences** about the material, and to **evaluate** it.

Determining literal meaning

Reading for literal meaning involves reading to comprehend. Your goal is to discover the main ideas and supporting details or, in a work of fiction, the central details of plot and character. If you find reading on the literal level difficult, the cause might be a writer's complex style. Try breaking the sentences into shorter units or rewording them in a simpler style. Think about the vocabulary used and what the words mean. Resist the temptation to add your own interpretation. Take your time. Rushing through material to cover it, rather than to understand it, wastes your valuable time.

SUGGESTIONS FOR IMPROVING YOUR READING COMPREHENSION

- Associate new material with what you already know, especially when you're reading about an unfamiliar subject. Many readers locate an easier book on the subject and read it before they tackle the more complex material.
- Remain fiercely determined to concentrate, especially if your mind tends to wander. Arrange for silence or music, for being alone or with others in the library. Try to complete your reading at your best time of day. Do whatever it takes.
- Allow sufficient time to read, reflect, reread, and study. Discipline yourself to balance your time for reading and studying with time for classes, working, socializing, and family activities. Reading and studying take time. Nothing prevents your success as much as poor time management.
- Keep an up-to-date college edition dictionary at hand or on your hard disk. As you encounter new words, try to figure them out from the context in which they appear. You'll find that the rest of the sentence, or a nearby sentence, often cues you to what the words mean. If the context doesn't hint at a word's meaning, see if your

textbook has a glossary at the end of each chapter or in the back of the book.

- Work efficiently. Don't waste time looking up a word more than once. Tape a list of new words into each textbook, inside your dictionary, or into a document you create on your computer for that purpose. Take time as often as possible to look over the list to remind yourself of the meanings. This is a quick, easy way to build your vocabulary.

Making inferences

Making **inferences** is something you do all the time. For example, if you see a large crowd at a bus stop and many of the people look annoyed, you can infer that the bus is late. To make inferences, you need to read "between the lines," a central concept in reading critically. This process involves detecting a writer's **assumptions;** telling the difference between **fact** and **opinion;** discovering a writer's **bias;** and recognizing a writer's **tone.**

A WRITER'S ASSUMPTIONS

All writers make **assumptions** about the readers who will be reading their material. Writers suppose that readers bring a certain level of knowledge to the subject, ranging from zero to advanced. In addition, some writers take for granted that readers already know certain facts about them: their background, beliefs, or point of view. To read critically, you need to sort out a writer's assumptions. Once you do, you can read with greater understanding of the writer's approach to the subject—and greater insight into how the writer expects you to react. Most importantly, you can resist being manipulated, if that is the writer's intention.

FACT VERSUS OPINION

Some writers intentionally blur the difference between fact and opinion. **Facts** are statements that people can verify objectively by observation, experiment, or research. Critical readers know the difference between a fact and an **opinion**—a statement with which people may or may not agree.

In judging facts, remember that they sometimes change as time passes. For example, a person once thought to be a hero might later turn out to be a criminal. As facts change, knowledge grows. Always use current knowledge to assess the accuracy of facts.

To differentiate between fact and opinion, think beyond the obvious. For example, is the following statement a fact or an opinion? "Some scientific puzzles can never be solved." Though this statement carries the ring of truth, it actually implies a prediction that is beyond our ability to demonstrate. It is, therefore, an opinion.

A WRITER'S BIAS

You may encounter viewpoints based on **bias** rather than facts or evidence. If a writer makes rude or cruel remarks, you can infer that the author is swayed by certain dislikes. Be critical of such bias and **prejudice,** because it slants the material toward the writer's beliefs and attitudes and away from facts or evidence. You might find that the author uses positive language to cover up prejudice. For example, in the statement "Most women are too nice to succeed in business," *nice* sounds complimentary, but the underlying assumption is negative and prejudicial.

A WRITER'S TONE

By recognizing the **tone** that emerges from a writer's use of words and ways of presenting ideas, you're making inferences. Reading with an ear for tone is a major critical reading skill. Tone can be serious, respectful, friendly, humorous, slanted, sarcastic, or angry. Most writers of textbooks and academic journals choose language that is neutral, direct, and neither overly relaxed nor stiff. When the tone doesn't fit the occasion, the writer may be seeking to manipulate readers rather than to influence their reasoning. Critical readers view such writing with suspicion.

Making evaluations

Critical readers evaluate what they've read only after dealing with the literal and inferential meanings in the material. Making evaluations calls for reading "beyond the lines," to come to conclusions about whether a writer's reasoning is sound and the presentation and word choice are balanced.

2c How do close reading and active reading work?

The secret to reading closely and actively is **annotating.** When you annotate, you write notes to yourself in a book's margins, occasionally underlining or highlighting major passages or using asterisks and other special marks to focus your attention.

Close reading means annotating for content and meaning. You might, for example, number and briefly list the steps of a process or summarize major points in the margin. Where you underline or highlight, also jot key words or phrases in the margin. When you review, these marginal notes will jog your memory. Your goal is to extract meaning on the literal, inferential, and evaluative levels (2b).

Active reading means annotating to make connections between what you already know or have experienced and the material you're reading. This is your chance to converse on paper with the writer. See what associations arise between what you know and what you are learning. Consider yourself a partner in the making of meaning, a full participant in the exchange of ideas.

Here is an example that shows annotations for both close reading and active reading.

Although I like to play, and sometimes like to watch, I cannot see what possible difference it makes which team beats which. The tactics are sometimes interesting, and certainly the prowess of the players deserves applause—but most men seem to use commercial sports as a kind of narcotic shutting out reality, rather than heightening it.

There is nothing more boring, in my view, than a prolonged discussion by laymen of yesterday's game. These dreary conversations are a form of social alcoholism, enabling them to achieve a dubious rapport without ever once having to come to grips with a subject worthy of a grown man's concern.

It is easy to see the opiate quality of sports in our society when tens of millions of men will spend a splendid Saturday or Sunday fall afternoon sitting stupefied in front of the TV, watching a "big game," when they might be out exercising their own flaccid muscles and stimulating their lethargic corpuscles.

Doesn't matter who wins, but tactics and prowess can be admired.
Sports talk is boring.
Other examples include soap operas and sitcoms.
When my son and husband watch together, the rapport is very real.
Instead of watching men should exercise.

Annotations for close reading (content) and active reading (synthesis). Active reading notes are circled.

The act of annotating pages has a proud history that dates back to the Middle Ages. However, if you can't bring yourself to write in a book, design for yourself a "double-entry notebook." On one side of each sheet of paper, write close-reading notes on the content; on the other side, enter active-reading notes on your thoughts as you synthesize the material.

2d How does systematic reading work?

When you **read systematically,** you follow the structured plan of **PRR.**

- **P = Preview:** Before you start reading, look over the assignment or the chapter's list of contents to get an idea of what is ahead. This activity helps you make efficient predictions and ask yourself questions that engage you to think about the material (2b). You won't have answers at this point, but the questions prepare your mind to learn actively. To preview a textbook chapter, begin by reading the summary at the end of the chapter, if there is one. Then skim through the chapter, reading all the headings, large and small. Read any words in boldface, because they're the key terms in the chapter. Next, look at all figures, tables, charts, drawings, and photographs—always reading the captions. Think about what the summary covers. Finally, read the first and last paragraphs of the major sections of the chapter.
- **R = Read:** Read the chapter closely and actively. Seek meaning at all three levels: literal, inferential, and evaluative (2b). Always expect to reread. College- or university-level material is rarely understood fully and absorbed in one reading. Budget your time accordingly.
- **R = Review:** To review, repeat the preview process by looking at the chapter summary, the headings, the boldface terms, the first and last paragraphs of major sections, and once again, the chapter summary. Ask yourself the same questions that you asked during your preview, but this time answer your questions. If you have trouble with an answer, reread that section of the chapter and try again.

For best success, review in chunks—small sections that you can capture comfortably. Don't try to cover too much at once. Give your mind a chance to absorb the new material. Repeat your review the next day, again about a week later, and at frequent intervals during a course. This process reinforces your learning and makes it yours forever. Another system for reinforcing your learning is to work collaboratively with a friend or classmate. When you've reached the same knowledge level, test each other orally. An equally effective strategy is to teach the material to someone who needs help understanding it.

3 CONNECTING THINKING AND READING TO WRITING

3a How will other people read my writing?

The following statement might seem obvious, but it carries a message that goes beyond its simple words: *When you write for college or university, one or more readers will read your material carefully and think about it critically.* This statement explains why the first two chapters of this writer's reference cover the topics of critical thinking and critical reading.

When you write, you're writing for people—no matter what their backgrounds or your topic—who will read your material

- at the literal, inferential, and evaluative levels (2b);
- closely and actively (2c);
- systematically (2d); and
- while thinking critically about it, by going through the steps of summary, analysis, synthesis, and evaluation (1b).

Because the people who read your writing—whether your peers, your instructor, specialized experts on your topic, or all of these—use these processes of critical reading and thinking, you want to keep the steps of each process in mind as you write. Use Chapters 1 and 2 to help you read your writing as others will.

3b Who are the people who will read my writing?

The people who read your writing are your AUDIENCE. These people read your writing in the light of their own backgrounds and prior knowledge of your topic. When you write for yourself, you're free to focus only on what matters to you. Often, in such situations, this includes what you're writing about (your topic) as well as your choice of words and stylistic techniques (your writing style). If, however, you're writing for a specific audience, you need to maintain a keen awareness of their presence as you focus on your topic and writing style. Section 5c suggests how you can determine the characteristics of your audience in each of your specific writing situations.

4 DISTINGUISHING BETWEEN SUMMARY AND SYNTHESIS

As a person with a reflective mind, you need to recognize the difference between summary and synthesis. Box 1 on page 2 gives steps in the critical thinking process, known for short as SASE. In the process, summary always comes before synthesis. They are two different steps, but it is easy to confuse them. Be careful not to.

4a What is summarizing?

Summarizing extracts the main message or central point of a passage. A **summary** tells what is written or said, without any additions from your personal thinking and reacting.

4b What is synthesizing?

Synthesizing weaves ideas together. When you synthesize, you connect ideas from what you have read, listened to, and experienced. In so doing, you create a new whole that is your own. To synthesize, you have first to set your mind on making connections. Avoid the fear of some students who assume that what they think has no value. **Synthesis** is a form of thinking that is creative and challenging. With practice, you will become increasingly adept at it. The only way to learn how to synthesize is to get started.

TECHNIQUES FOR SYNTHESIZING MULTIPLE SOURCES

- Wrap your mind around the multiple sources you have just encountered. Then work toward synthesis by making connections among concepts, ideas, and information that you have read, heard, and experienced. Synthesized ideas and information become threads woven into a tapestry that creates a new whole. By synthesizing, you show evidence of your ability to tie ideas together in the tapestry of what you learn and know and experience.
- Find comparisons among concepts, ideas, and information.
- Think of contrasts between concepts, ideas, and information.
- Create definitions that combine and extend definitions you encounter in the separate sources.
- Apply examples or descriptions from one source to illustrate ideas in another.
- Use processes described in one source to explain those in others.

ALERT: Do not do "synthesis by summary." This is a mere listing of who said what about a topic. It is not synthesis. It does not create new connections among ideas.

If you have read or seen only one source, you need to rely even more on what you remember, your prior knowledge. Try the following techniques for stimulating your mind toward creating a synthesis. Use all that you have read, heard, and experienced.

TECHNIQUES FOR SYNTHESIZING WITH ONE SOURCE

- Use your powers of play. Mentally toss ideas around, even if you make connections that seem outrageous. Try opposites (for example, read about athletes and think about the most unathletic person you know). Try turning an idea upside down (for example, if you have read about the value of being a good sport, list the benefits of being a bad sport). Try visualizing what you are reading about, and then tinker with the mental picture (for example, picture two people playing tennis, and then substitute dogs playing Frisbee or seals playing Ping-Pong).
- Use the technique of clustering (5g) to lay out visually relationships among elements in your source and other ideas that come to mind.
- Make word associations, think up song lyrics, draft a TV commercial. Your goal is to jump-start your thinking so that you see ideas in new ways.
- Discuss the source with another person. Summarize its content and elicit the other person's opinion or ideas. Debate that opinion or challenge those ideas. Discussions and debates can get your mind moving.
- Write a critical response to the material. Summarize its content and then write your personal response to it. Explain whether you agree or disagree and also the reasons you respond as you do. Connect your reasons with your prior knowledge and experiences so that the synthesized material becomes your own.

5 GETTING STARTED

5a What is the writing process?

Many people assume that a real writer can magically write a finished product, word by perfect word. Experienced writers know better. They know that *writing is a process,* a series of activities that starts the moment they begin thinking about a topic and ends when they complete a final draft. In addition, experienced writers are aware that good writing is actually rewriting—again and yet again. Their drafts contain additions, deletions, rewordings, and rearrangements. For a real-life example, see how this paragraph was drafted and then revised (page 14).

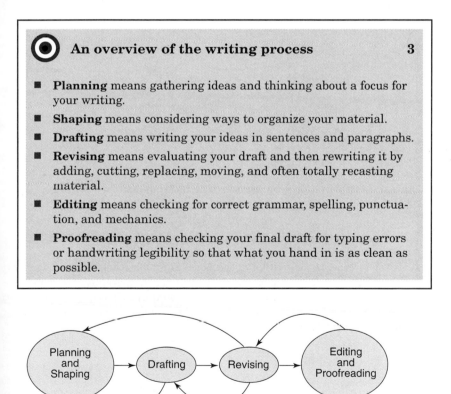

An overview of the writing process 3

- **Planning** means gathering ideas and thinking about a focus for your writing.
- **Shaping** means considering ways to organize your material.
- **Drafting** means writing your ideas in sentences and paragraphs.
- **Revising** means evaluating your draft and then rewriting it by adding, cutting, replacing, moving, and often totally recasting material.
- **Editing** means checking for correct grammar, spelling, punctuation, and mechanics.
- **Proofreading** means checking your final draft for typing errors or handwriting legibility so that what you hand in is as clean as possible.

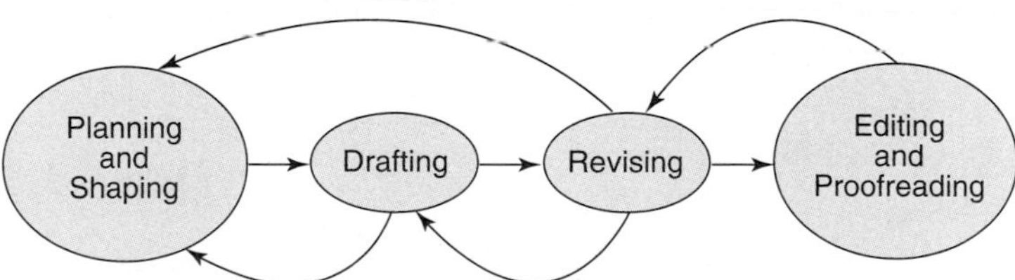

Visualizing the writing process

As you work through the writing process, remember that writing is a *recursive* activity, which means that writers often move back before moving ahead, skip a step and go back to it later, or finish a section but then return to it. As the circles and arrows in the diagram of the writing process show, planning is not over when drafting begins; drafting is not over when revising begins; and editing might take you back to revising. Paths differ for each writer and for the same writer in each new WRITING SITUATION.*

Here's my personal advice from one writer to another: Most writers struggle with ideas that are difficult to express, sentences that won't take shape, and words that aren't precise. Be patient with yourself; writing takes time. The more you write, the easier it will become—though writing never goes easily for anyone. Here is how I revised and edited the opening paragraph of this chapter.

magically
Many people assume that a real writer can ^ write a
word by perfect word.
finished product, ~~easily.~~ Experienced writers know better ⊙
They know that
~~than that;~~ ^ writing is a process, ~~that involves~~ a series
the moment they begin
of activities that starts ~~when the writers start~~ ^ thinking
about a topic when they complete
^ and ends ~~with~~ ^ a final draft.

Draft and revision of first paragraph in 5a by Lynn Quitman Troyka

5b What are the purposes of academic writing?

A writer's **purpose** for writing is the motivating force behind what that writer wishes or is assigned to write. You need, therefore, to choose among the four major purposes of writing, listed in Box 4.

In this book, I concentrate on the two major purposes of most academic writing: to inform a reader and to persuade a reader.

*Words printed in small capital letters (such as WRITING SITUATION) are defined in the Terms Glossary on pages 497–517.

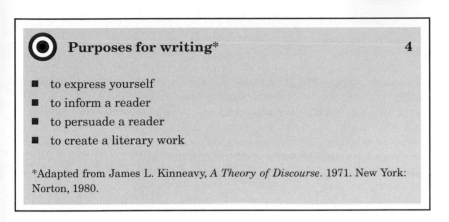

Purposes for writing* 4

- to express yourself
- to inform a reader
- to persuade a reader
- to create a literary work

*Adapted from James L. Kinneavy, *A Theory of Discourse*. 1971. New York: Norton, 1980.

Informing a reader

Informative writing, also called *expository writing,* seeks to present and explain information. It expounds on—that is, systematically tells about—observations, ideas, and facts. Typically, you can find informative writing in textbooks, encyclopedias, technical and business reports, nonfiction books, newspapers, and many magazines. Paragraph 2 in Chapter 8 (see page 35) is an example of an informative paragraph.

Persuading a reader

Persuasive writing, also called *argumentative writing,* seeks to convince readers about a matter of opinion. Examples of persuasive writing include newspaper editorials, letters to the editor, opinion essays in newspapers and magazines, reviews, sermons, books that argue a point of view, and business proposals. Chapter 10 covers the specific requirements of persuasive writing. Paragraph 11 in Chapter 8 (see page 41) is an example of a persuasive paragraph.

5c What does "audience" mean for writing?

Your **audience** consists of everyone who will read your writing. After you have graduated, your audience will be readers of your business, professional, and public writing. When you are in college or university, you address a mix of audiences, each of which expects to read **academic writing**—the writing assigned in your courses. These audiences may include

- your peers (fellow students)
- a general audience (educated, experienced readers without specialized knowledge of your topic)

- a specialized audience (experts on your topic)
- your instructor

The more specifics you can assume about the audience for your academic writing, the better are your chances of reaching it successfully. For example, if you're writing a sales report for your supervisor, you can use terms such as *product life cycle, breakeven quantity, nonprice competition,* and *markup*. In contrast, if general readers were your audience for this information, you would want to avoid specialized, technical vocabulary—or if you had to use some essential specialized terms, you would want to define them in a non-technical way. Ask yourself the questions in Box 5 to pinpoint the characteristics of your audience.

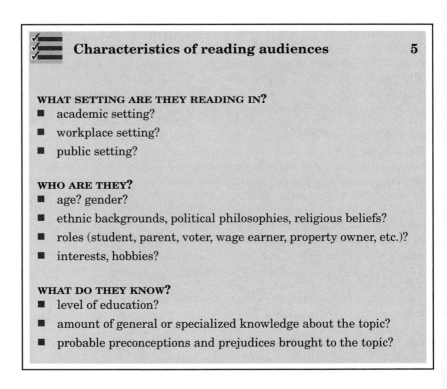

Characteristics of reading audiences **5**

WHAT SETTING ARE THEY READING IN?
- academic setting?
- workplace setting?
- public setting?

WHO ARE THEY?
- age? gender?
- ethnic backgrounds, political philosophies, religious beliefs?
- roles (student, parent, voter, wage earner, property owner, etc.)?
- interests, hobbies?

WHAT DO THEY KNOW?
- level of education?
- amount of general or specialized knowledge about the topic?
- probable preconceptions and prejudices brought to the topic?

ESL NOTE: If you come from outside North America, you may be surprised by the directness with which people speak and write in Canada. If so, I hope you'll read my open letter to multilingual students about honouring one's own culture (see page 381). Your own tradition may expect elaborate or ceremonial written language that does not introduce the central point immediately and that prefers tactful, indirect discussion. In contrast, Canadian writing contains language and style that are direct, straightforward, and without digressive embellishments. Canadian college and university instructors expect academic writing to contain a thesis statement (usually at the end of the introductory paragraph); to demonstrate a tightly organized presentation of information from one paragraph to the next; to back up generalizations with strong supporting details; and to end with a logical concluding paragraph. In addition, you are expected to use "standard" English grammar that follows the rules used by educated speakers. !

Writing for a peer-response group

Instructors sometimes divide the students in a class into small **peer-response groups.** Participating in a peer-response group makes you part of a respected tradition of colleagues helping colleagues. Professional writers often seek comments from other writers to improve their rough drafts. As a member of a peer-response group, you're not expected to be a writing expert. Rather, you're expected to offer responses as a practised reader and a student writer who knows the difficulties of writing well. Hearing or reading comments from your peers can be very informative, surprising, and helpful.

As you work with your peers, you'll face the sometimes sticky issue of how to take criticism of your writing. Here's my personal advice as a writer for being able (or at least appearing able) to take constructive criticism gracefully. First, know that most students don't like to criticize their peers. They worry about being impolite, being inaccurate, or losing someone's friendship. Try, therefore, to cultivate an attitude that encourages your peers to respond as freely and as helpfully as possible. Show, also, that you can listen with an open mind, without getting angry or defensive.

Second, realize that most people tend to be a little (or quite a bit) defensive about even the best-intentioned and tactful criticism. Of course, if a comment is purposely mean or sarcastic, you and all others in your peer-response group have every right to reject it. Third, if you don't understand a comment fully, ask for clarification. Finally, no matter what anyone says about your writing, never forget that it remains yours alone. You retain "ownership" of your writing, so use only those comments that can move you closer to reaching your intended audience.

Writing for an instructor

As your audience, your instructor plays three roles. An instructor (1) represents either general or specialized readers; (2) acts as your writing coach; and (3) becomes the eventual evaluator of your final drafts.

Instructors know that few students are experienced writers or experts on their topics. Still, instructors expect your writing to show that you took serious time to learn something worthwhile about a subject, and then to write about it clearly. Instructors are experienced readers; they recognize a minimal effort almost at once. In addition, instructors are people whose professional lives centre on intellectual endeavours. You want, therefore, to write within the constraints of academic writing, and to write on topics that have built-in intellectual interest.

If you're a relatively inexperienced college or university writer, you might wrongly assume that your instructor can mentally fill in what you haven't bothered to say fully. On the other hand, you might think incorrectly that you are wrong to extend your discussion beyond simple statements. Instructors—indeed, all readers—are not mind readers, and they become annoyed if you don't write fully on a topic. It's never wrong to go beyond stating the obvious or to show that you know how to develop your material beyond bare-bones basics.

5d How does the tone of my writing affect my audience?

Tone is more than what you say; tone is how you say it. Tone in writing operates like tone of voice in speaking, except that in writing, you can't rely on your facial expressions and vocal intonations to communicate your meaning. If your tone is inappropriate for your audience or your topic, it can ruin your essay, no matter how well you handle other matters.

Your choice of words, level of formality, and writing style create your tone. You can use slang and other highly informal language in a note to your roommate, but not in academic writing or business writing. When you write for audiences such as instructors or supervisors, use more formality. "More formality," however, doesn't mean dull and drab. In fact, in a serious discussion, lively language can enhance your message and strike the right tone.

Academic writing almost always calls for a medium-to-formal tone. For details about how to achieve such a tone, see the discussions of word meanings (Chapter 19) and gender-neutral language (Chapter 20).

5e How do I work with a writing topic?

Situations vary. Some assignments are very specific about your topic. For example, "Explain how oxygen is absorbed in the lungs" leaves no room for choice. You would need to write about that topic precisely, without going off the topic. However, only rarely are class assignments as specific as this.

More often, your instructor will ask you to select your own topic, to narrow a broad topic, or to broaden a narrow topic. As you do this, the overriding principle always is this: **What separates most good writing from bad is the writer's ability to move back and forth between general statements and specific details.**

Selecting your own topic

If you need to choose a topic, don't rush. Take time to think through your ideas. Avoid getting so deeply involved in one topic that you can't change to a more suitable topic in the time allotted. Not all topics are suitable for academic writing. Your topic needs to allow you to demonstrate your intellectual thinking and writing abilities.

Think through potential topics by breaking each into logical subsections. Then make sure you can supply specific details to back up each general statement. Make sure you don't drown your essay with so many details your readers can't figure out what generalizations these details are supporting. Work toward balance by finding a middle ground. Beware of topics so broad that they lead to vague generalizations (for example, *Education is necessary for success*). Also, beware of topics so narrow that they lead nowhere after a few sentences (for example, *Wilfrid Laurier was the first French-speaking prime minister*).

Narrowing or broadening an assigned topic

Suppose that "marriage" is your assigned topic for a 1000-word essay. You'd be thinking too broadly if you chose "What makes a successful marriage?" Conversely, you'd be thinking too narrowly if you came up with "Alexandra and Gavin were married by a Justice of the Peace." You'd probably be on target with a topic such as "In successful marriages, husbands and wives learn to accept each other's faults." A thousand words should allow you to explain and give concrete examples of typical faults and discuss why accepting them is important.

Carol Moreno, the student whose essay appears in 9b, knew that her assigned topic—"Write about a challenge you faced and tried to meet"—was too broad. She had to be specific. She wanted to write about having faced the challenge of how to become physically fit. She realized that "getting physically fit" or even "women's fitness" was still too broad. She thought of some narrower topics, such as "organized sports," "power walking," and "weight training." In the end, she chose "weight training" because she knew about it from personal experience and could think of both generalizations and specific details to use in her essay. In addition, Moreno knew that if her assignment called for research, she could find many sources on weight training in books and magazines and on the Internet.

5f What is a "writing situation"?

The **writing situation** of each assignment involves four elements: *topic, purpose, audience*, and *special requirements*. Use the questions in Box 6 to analyze each element.

5g How can I find ideas for writing?

Do you worry that you have nothing to write about? You are not alone. Most people know more than they give themselves credit for. The techniques listed here can help you uncover ideas and details to use in your writing. If one technique does not provide enough useful material, try another.

Keeping a journal

Writing in a journal is like having a "conversation on paper" with yourself. You can write about anything you like—your experiences, observations, dreams, creative ideas, reactions to your reading.

Why do it? First, writing every day gives you the habit of productivity. The more you write, the more you get used to the feeling of expressing yourself on paper. Second, writing regularly in a journal helps you think through ideas that need time to develop. Third, your journal becomes a source of ideas when you need to choose your own writing topic (5e).

Freewriting

Freewriting means writing down whatever comes to mind about whatever topic surfaces, without stopping to worry about whether ideas are good or spelling is correct. You allow your thoughts to emerge as the physical act of writing is under way. **Focused freewriting** means starting with a favourite word or sentence from your journal, a quotation you like, or perhaps a topic you are studying for a course.

When you freewrite, do not interrupt the flow. Keep writing. Do not censor thoughts or flashes of insight. Do not review or cross out. Sometimes, when you are finished and read over your freewriting, it might seem mindless. But other days it might startle you to discover interesting ideas.

Guidelines for analyzing each writing situation: TPAS **6**

- **T = Topic:** What is the topic you'll be writing about? (5e)
- **P = Purpose:** Is your purpose to be INFORMATIVE or PERSUASIVE? (5b)
- **A = Audience:** Who are your readers? (5c)
- **S = Special requirements:** How much time do you have to complete the assignment? What is the length requirement?

COMPUTER TIP: When you write at a computer, dim the screen so that you cannot see what you are writing. This way, you record your thoughts, but you resist the temptation to censor yourself. When you brighten the screen, your freewriting will be visible.

Brainstorming

Brainstorming means listing everything you can think of about a topic. Let your mind range freely, generating quantities of ideas before analyzing them. After you have brainstormed, look for patterns and ways to group your ideas. Discard items that do not fit into any group. Groups with the most items are likely to be topics you can write about successfully.

Here is brainstorming by student writer Carol Moreno, whose essay on women lifting weights appears in 9b. Moreno grouped the items marked with an asterisk and used them in her third paragraph.

```
safety with free weights (barbells)*
don't bend at the waist*
don't hold your breath
use leg strength to straighten up*
don't allow a twist*
concentrate on each move
```

Asking and answering questions

Try exploring your topic by asking questions that journalists use.

- Who?
- What?

- When?
- Why?
- Where?
- How?

Here is how Carol Moreno used these questions: *Who* was in my first weight-lifting class? *What* reasons did other women have for taking the class? *Why* did I get interested in weight lifting? *When* did I realize that weight lifting wasn't just an activity for guys? *How* do I feel about weight lifting now?

Here is another useful list of questions:

- What is it?
- How is it the same as other things?
- How is it different from other things?
- Why or how does it happen?
- How is it done?
- What does it look, smell, taste, sound, feel like?

Clustering

Clustering, also called *mapping,* is a visual form of brainstorming. Write your topic in the middle of a sheet and put a circle around it. Now, moving out from the centre, use lines and circles to record your ideas, as the example shows. Continue using this method to subdivide and add details. Here is part of Carol Moreno's clustering for the fifth paragraph of her essay in 9b.

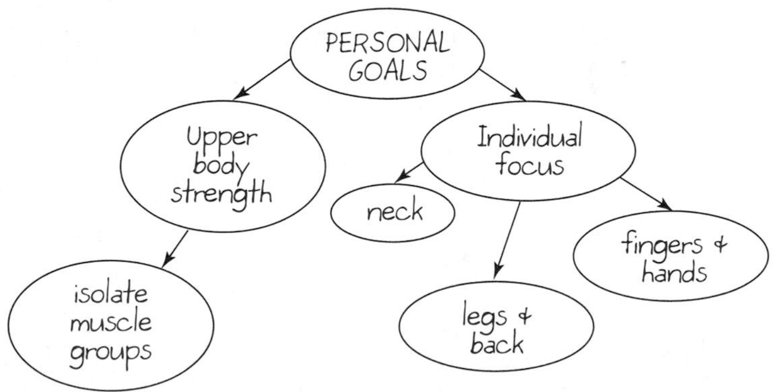

Clustering that became Carol Moreno's fifth paragraph

5h What is a thesis statement?

A **thesis statement** is the central message of an essay. Your thesis statement both reflects the content of your essay and guides your writing. To compose a thesis statement, first write a simple statement that makes an **assertion.** Writing an assertion focuses your thinking as you progress toward a fully developed thesis statement. As you are writing, if you find that your thesis statement and the content of your essay do not match, revise one or the other—or both.

Here is student writer Carol Moreno's assertion for her essay about women lifting weights (9b), followed by her progression toward a final version of her thesis statement.

- I think women can pump iron like men. [This assertion is a start.]
- If she is trained well, any woman can pump iron well, just like a man. [This statement is more developed because it mentions training, but the word *well* is used twice and is vague, and the word *any* is inaccurate.]
- Most people think only men can pump iron, but women can also do it successfully with the right training. [This statement is closer to a thesis statement because it is more specific. However, men are not part of Moreno's topic. Also, the concept of building strength, a major aspect of Moreno's final draft, is missing.]
- With the right training, women can "pump iron" to build strength. [This final version serves as Moreno's thesis statement, except for one further change: She added a transitional word—*also*—to connect the thesis statement to what comes before in her introductory paragraph.]

Moreno's final version fulfils the basic requirements for a thesis statement.

Basic requirements for a thesis statement 7

1. It states the essay's subject, but it does not repeat the title of the essay.
2. It indicates the essay's PURPOSE, but it does not announce it with "The purpose of this essay is. . . ."
3. It conveys the writer's point of view toward the subject.

→

Basic requirements for a thesis statement *(continued)*

4. It makes a general statement that leads to a set of main ideas and supporting details; it is not merely a statement of fact that leads nowhere.
5. It uses specific language and avoids vague words.
6. It may give the major subdivisions of the topic.

5i How might outlining help me write?

An **outline** is a structured, sequential list of the contents of an essay. Some writers always use outlines, while others never do. Some instructors require an outline with an essay, while others don't. Find what works best for you personally as well as what your assignment calls for.

In some writing situations, writers like to outline before they begin an essay. In other situations, they prefer to outline after they've written a first draft. In addition, some writers like to outline during the WRITING PROCESS, especially at two distinct points: before DRAFTING, to flesh out, pull together, and arrange material; and while REVISING, to check the logic and flow of thought of the essay. Outlines are excellent tools for revealing where information is missing, repeated, or off the topic.

An **informal outline** doesn't follow any of the numbering and lettering conventions of a formal outline. It often looks like a BRAINSTORMING list, with ideas jotted down in a somewhat random order. Here is part of an informal outline for the second paragraph of Carol Moreno's essay (9b).

SAMPLE INFORMAL OUTLINE

Need the right training
Muscle building
Biology
Hormones and longer muscles
Anaerobic exercise
Aerobic workout

A **formal outline** follows certain conventions in numbering and lettering to show relationships among ideas. A formal outline can be a **topic outline,** composed of words and phrases, or a **sentence outline,** composed entirely of complete sentences. Never mix the two styles.

Requirements of formal outlines 8

FORMAL OUTLINE FORM

Thesis statement

I. First main idea
    A. First subordinate idea
        1. First reason or example
        2. Second reason or example
            a. First supporting detail
            b. Second supporting detail
    B. Second subordinate idea
II. Second main idea

SAMPLE OF A FORMAL SENTENCE OUTLINE

This outline is based on the third paragraph of Carol Moreno's essay (9b). Essay's thesis statement: With the right training, women can also "pump iron" to build strength.

I. The right training shows women how to use weights safely to prevent injury.
    A. Free weights require special precautions.
        1. Bending at the waist and jerking a barbell up is unsafe.
        2. Squatting and using leg and back muscles to straighten up is safe.
            a. The head is held erect and faces forward.
            b. The neck and back are aligned and held straight.
    B. Weight machines make it easier to lift safely because they force proper body alignment.

GUIDELINES

- Use at least two subdivisions at each level—no I without a II, no A without a B, and so on. If a level has only one subdivision, either integrate it into a higher level or expand it to at least two subdivisions.
- Keep all subdivisions at the same level of generality (do not pair a main idea with a supporting detail).
- Use PARALLELISM for entries on the same level.

6 DRAFTING

6a What strategies can I use to write a first draft?

A first draft is always rough. It is not meant to be perfect; it is meant to give you something to improve by revising. Here are three alternatives for writing a first draft:

- Put aside all the notes you made to get started. Write a **discovery draft:** This means using focused freewriting (5g) to find ideas and make connections that spring to mind as you write.
- Or, keep at hand your notes from getting started (5e) and write a structured first draft by working through all your material.
- Or, combine the first two approaches. When your notes can guide you, use them to write. When you do not know what to say next, switch to writing a discovery draft.

The direction of drafting is forward: Keep pressing ahead. If you wonder about the spelling of a word or a point in grammar, underline it and check it later. If you cannot think of an exact word, use a SYNONYM and mark it to change later. If you are worried about your sentence style or the order in which you present details, note *Style?* or *Order?* in the margin and return to it later. If you begin to run dry, reread what you have written to propel yourself to further writing; do not begin revising too early.

6b What strategies can I use to overcome writer's block?

Writer's block means the writer cannot think of ideas or get words onto paper. Experienced writers often use strategies to overcome writer's block.

COMPUTER TIPS: (1) When you draft on a computer and have questions but need to keep moving ahead, insert a symbol. Later, search for the symbols and then make your changes. (2) If you print out your first draft, resist any urge to consider it final merely because it looks neatly typed.

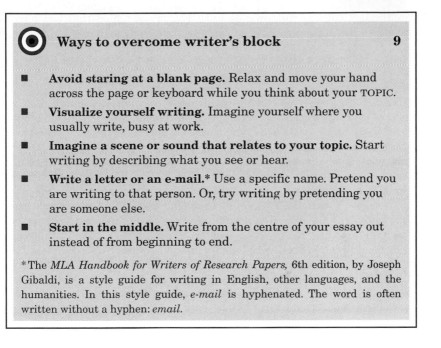

Ways to overcome writer's block **9**

- **Avoid staring at a blank page.** Relax and move your hand across the page or keyboard while you think about your TOPIC.
- **Visualize yourself writing.** Imagine yourself where you usually write, busy at work.
- **Imagine a scene or sound that relates to your topic.** Start writing by describing what you see or hear.
- **Write a letter or an e-mail.*** Use a specific name. Pretend you are writing to that person. Or, try writing by pretending you are someone else.
- **Start in the middle.** Write from the centre of your essay out instead of from beginning to end.

*The *MLA Handbook for Writers of Research Papers,* 6th edition, by Joseph Gibaldi, is a style guide for writing in English, other languages, and the humanities. In this style guide, *e-mail* is hyphenated. The word is often written without a hyphen: *email.*

7 REVISING, EDITING, AND PROOFREADING

Once you have finished your first DRAFT, you begin to revise. Then you edit and proofread.

7a What strategies can I use to revise?

When you **revise,** you take a draft from first to final version by evaluating, adding, cutting, replacing, and moving material. In other words, you need to shift from suspending judgment to making judgments.

At the same time that you want to be critical, do not be overly harsh on yourself. Most early drafts provide sufficient raw material for you to revise. Do, however, be systematic in evaluating your draft. Use the questions in Box 10 or guidelines supplied by your instructor. Evaluate every change alone and in the context of the surrounding material. Continue this process until you are satisfied that you have made all the improvements you can and your essay is in its final form.

7b How do a thesis statement and an essay title help me revise?

Use the THESIS STATEMENT to guide your revision. Refer to it at the end of every paragraph. If your thesis statement does not match what your essay says, revise either the thesis statement or the essay or both.

Your essay title can also play an important part in revising, so do not wait until the last minute and merely tack on a title. Create at least a working title during your first draft. Use it as a checkpoint as your essay evolves.

A **direct title** tells exactly what the essay will be about: for example, "The Case for Banning Exotic Pets." An **indirect title** hints at an essay's topic: "Exotic Pets: Not at Home in Your Home." Indirect titles can be very effective as long as the connection is not too obscure.

ALERT: A title stands alone. Do not open an essay by referring to the title as though its words are in the essay's first sentence. Lacie Juris titled her paper "Exotic Pets: Not at Home in Your Home." Here's an example of how *not* to open that essay by referring to its title:

NO They simply do not belong there.

To see how Lacie Juris's paper actually begins, go to page 58.

COMPUTER TIPS: The mechanics of revising are easy on a computer. You can add, delete, and rearrange anything from a word or a sentence to a paragraph without the agony of retyping your entire essay. (1) If you are undecided about a revision, create several versions of your paper. (2) Experiment by reordering your body paragraphs, splitting or joining paragraphs, or moving your last paragraph to the very beginning. (3) Resist the temptation to revise endlessly. (4) Delete cautiously. If you think you want to drop material, save it in a new document so that you can put it back in your essay if you wish.

7c How can a revision checklist help me revise?

Use a revision checklist to focus your attention as you evaluate your writing. But do not let a checklist overwhelm you. Adjust it to each writing situation so that your checklist works for you.

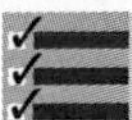

Revision checklist 10

In the format of this checklist, if an answer is "no," you need to revise. The section numbers in parentheses tell you where in this book to look for help.

THE WHOLE ESSAY AND PARAGRAPHS

1. Is your essay topic suitable and sufficiently narrow? (5d, 5e)
2. Does your thesis statement communicate your topic, focus, and purpose? (5h, Box 7)
3. Does your essay show that you are aware of your audience? (5c, Box 5)
4. Is your essay arranged effectively? (5i)
5. Have you checked for material that strays off the topic? (7b)
6. Does your introduction prepare your reader for the rest of the essay? (8b)
7. Do your body paragraphs express main ideas in topic sentences as needed? (8c) Are your main ideas clearly related to your thesis statement? (5h)
8. Do your body paragraphs provide specific, concrete support for each main idea? (8d, 8f)
9. Do you use transitions and other techniques to connect ideas within and between paragraphs? (8e)
10. Does your conclusion give your essay a sense of completion? (8g)

SENTENCES AND WORDS

1. Are your sentences concise? (Ch. 15)
2. Do your sentences show clear relationships among ideas? (Ch. 16)
3. Do you use parallelism, variety, and emphasis correctly and to increase the impact of your writing? (Ch. 17)
4. Have you eliminated sentence fragments? (Ch. 11) Have you eliminated comma splices and run-on sentences? (Ch. 12)
5. Have you eliminated confusing shifts? (Ch. 13)
6. Have you eliminated disjointed sentences? (Ch. 13)
7. Have you eliminated misplaced and dangling modifiers? (Ch. 14)
8. Have you used exact words? (19a, 19b)
9. Is your usage correct and your language appropriate? (Ch. 18, 19d)
10. Have you avoided sexist language? (Ch. 20)

On page 31, see part of a paragraph from student writer Lacie Juris's paper on keeping wild animals as pets. Using a revision checklist, Juris made several changes and added more specific, concrete details. (For the final draft, see paragraph 2 of her essay on pages 58–59.)

7d What strategies can I use to edit?

Editing means finding and fixing errors in grammar, spelling, punctuation, capitals, numbers, italics, and abbreviations. You edit when the content and organization of your paper are set. Edit slowly and methodically. Editing takes concentration and time to look up advice and rules in this handbook. You may also want to ask a friend with a good editing "eye" to read your paper and circle anything that you should check for correctness.

7e How can an editing checklist help me edit?

An editing checklist can help you systematically focus your attention on everything you need to be concerned about when you edit your writing. Adjust this checklist to each writing situation so that the questions work for you.

Editing checklist 11

In the format of this checklist, if an answer is "no," you need to edit. The section numbers in parentheses tell you where in this book to look for help.

1. Is the grammar correct? (Chs. 39–49)
2. Are the sentences correct? (Chs. 11–17)
3. Are commas used correctly? (Ch. 50)
4. Are all other punctuation marks used correctly? (Chs. 51–56)
5. Are hyphens, capital letters, italics (or underlining), abbreviations, and numbers used correctly? (Chs. 57–61)
6. Are all words spelled correctly? (Ch. 21)

My topic sentence needs work

Wild animals are dangerous. Wild animals have inborn behaviour patterns and instincts, such as stalking prey, attacking, and self-defence. ~~including violent patterns.~~ Such patterns remain no matter where or how ~~they~~ the animals grow up, no matter how well the owners train them for domesticated living. This is what makes the animals ~~authentically~~ truly wild. Humans cannot influence, change, or even predict ~~these.~~ an animal's wild behaviours. An attack can occur without warning when an animal's wild instincts take over without warning (repetitive) ("Wild Animals Are Not"). In addition, wild pets can cause property damage, as illustrated by the case of Stoli, a tiger who caused $20 000 worth of damage to his owner's Mercedes ~~car~~ in less than five minutes ("Stoli and Lil" 1). Zoocheck Canada, an advocacy group for animals in captivity, writes about (revise) both the humane treatment of animals and the dangers that some exotic pets can pose ("About Zoocheck Canada").

Confirm spelling & mandate

Here is the introductory paragraph from Lacie Juris's essay showing her edits. Her complete final draft is on pages 58–63.

Tiger cubs look and behave like kitten. Baby chimps look almost human and sometimes act like precocious human infants. For many Canadians owning one of these as a pet, to play with and show off to nieghbours, sounds like a childhood fantasy come true yet for many, it is no fantasy: Tigers can cost as little as $200 ~~dollars.~~ (Nikolovsky A18) Animal-rights advocates estimate that as many tigers are kept as pets in the ~~U S~~ as exist in the ~~world~~ worldwide (Boehm B1). Unfortunately, these exotic dreams can turn deadly at any moment. Because wild animals owner ship comes under a confusion of federal, provincial, and local laws, there ~~are~~ little effective regulation (Nikolovsky A18). To eliminate dangerous situations for both people and animals alike, lawmakers need to ban private ownership of wild animals as pets.

7f What strategies can I use to proofread?

Proofreading is a careful, line-by-line reading of a final, clean version of your essay. You always proofread before you hand in your paper. Correct any errors you find, but if a page has numerous errors, recopy it or print out a corrected page. A neat, accurate paper conveys your positive attitude toward your course, your teacher, and yourself.

PROOFREADING STRATEGIES

- Proofread with a ruler so that you can focus on one line at a time.
- Start at the end of a paragraph or the end of your essay and read each sentence in reverse order or word by word to avoid being distracted by the content.
- Read your final draft aloud so that you see and hear errors; look carefully for omitted letters and words as well as for repeated words.

COMPUTER TIPS: (1) Try editing and proofreading by highlighting a small section of your writing. This separates it visually from the rest of the screen and helps reduce your tendency to read too quickly and overlook errors. (2) Create your personal spell-check or a style checker by keeping a file of the errors you have made in the past. Access it each time you revise and edit. Also, if you use a word-processing program's spell-check, proofread for words that are misused rather than misspelled (for example, *it's* for *its*) and words that cannot be identified by a spell-check because the errors are real words (for example, *form* for *from*). ▣

8 COMPOSING PARAGRAPHS

8a What is a paragraph?

A **paragraph** is a group of sentences that work together to develop a unit of thought. Paragraphing permits writers to divide material into manageable parts and arrange the parts in a unified whole. Much of your academic writing will typically consist of an introductory paragraph, a group of body paragraphs, and a concluding paragraph. (Your instructors may call such writing essays, compositions, themes, reports, or papers.)

8b How can I write effective introductory paragraphs?

An introductory paragraph prepares the reader for what lies ahead by giving background information or setting the stage in some other way. It also tries to arouse interest so the reader will want to read on. You may be required to include a THESIS STATEMENT in the introductory paragraph (5h, 7b). Usually, the thesis statement appears in the last sentence or two of the introductory paragraph, as shown in paragraphs 1 and 3. (Experienced writers sometimes diverge from this basic pattern, depending on their writing PURPOSE.)

1 Alone one is never lonely, May Sarton says in her essay "The Rewards of Living a Solitary Life." Most people, however, are terrified of living alone. They are used to living with others—children with parents, roommates with roommates, friends with friends, husbands with wives. When the statistics catch up with them, therefore, they are rarely prepared. Chances are high that

Introductory paragraphs 12

STRATEGIES FOR INTERESTING YOUR READER

- Provide relevant background information about your topic.
- Relate a brief, interesting anecdote that applies to your topic.
- Give pertinent, perhaps surprising statistics about your topic.
- Ask a provocative question or questions to lead into your topic.
- Use a quotation that relates closely to your topic.
- Draw an analogy to clarify or illustrate your topic.
- Define a key term you use throughout your essay.

STRATEGIES TO AVOID

- Avoid obvious statements about the essay's topic or purpose: Do not say, "I am going to discuss why women can learn to lift weights."
- Avoid apologizing, as in "I am not sure I'm right, but this is my opinion."
- Avoid overworked expressions, such as "Haste really does make waste, as I recently discovered."

most adult men and women will live alone, briefly or longer, at some time.

—Tara Foster, student

COMPUTER TIP: Few writers are able to draft a perfect introductory paragraph before moving on to the body of an essay. Remember that writing is a *recursive* process (5a). Writing on a computer gives you a great deal of flexibility in DRAFTING and REVISING your work (Chapters 6 and 7). It allows you to start drafting your body paragraphs and developing your ideas before returning to the introductory paragraph that, in turn, helps put the rest of your essay in focus.

8c How do topic sentences work?

A **topic sentence** contains the main idea of a body paragraph. The topic sentence controls what the paragraph can include.

Start with a topic sentence

When a topic sentence starts a paragraph, readers immediately know what topic will be discussed.

The cockroach lore that has been daunting us for years is mostly true. Roaches can live for twenty days without food, fourteen days without water; they can flatten their bodies and crawl through a crack thinner than a dime; they can eat huge doses of carcinogens and still die of old age. They can even survive as much radiation as an oak tree can, says William Bell, the Uni-
2 versity of Kansas entomologist whose cockroaches appeared in the movie *The Day After.* They'll eat almost anything—regular food, leather, glue, hair, paper, even the starch in book bindings. (The New York Public Library has quite a cockroach problem.) They sense the slightest breeze, and they can react and start running in .05 seconds; they can also remain motionless for days. And if all this isn't creepy enough, they can fly too.

—Jane Goodman, "What's Bugging You"

End with a topic sentence

When a topic sentence ends a body paragraph, readers sometimes feel more eager to read on to the next paragraph.

When he was ten years old, Lester taught himself to windsurf by hanging around the European and Canadian tourists who
3 rented boards on the beach at Varadero. "If you made friends with them, they would sometimes let you use their equipment," he says. As he grew older and got better at the sport, he found he

liked the isolation and freedom of the sea. "Sometimes I would sail for eight hours without stopping, and go very far out," he says. His windsurfing to freedom seemed destined.

—Sam Moses, "A New Dawn"

Imply a topic sentence

Some paragraphs convey a main idea without a specific topic sentence. Writers carefully construct these paragraphs so that details add up in such a way that the main idea is clear even though it is not explicitly stated.

Annie was a compact, gray-haired woman whose carriage
belied a strength acquired from many years of work. She
mounted the hall stairs and opened a door to the left to show
4 me a small, modest one-bedroom apartment. "I clean on Tues-
days and Fridays. Just leave the trash outside in the hall," she
said. I liked the soft resonance of her voice. She took my check
and gave me the key.

—Bob Akin, "Out of Their Element"

8d How can I use details to develop body paragraphs?

Use specific, concrete details to develop body paragraphs that support the generalization in the TOPIC SENTENCE. What separates most good writing from bad is the writer's ability to move back and forth between generalizations and specific details. To check that you have enough detail, try using **RENNS** as a memory device to guide you.

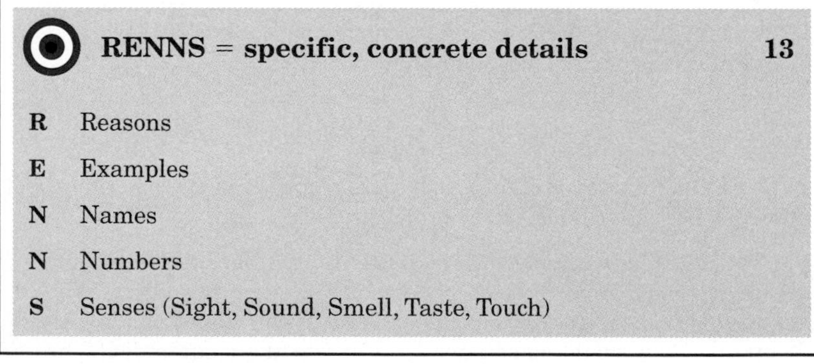

RENNS = specific, concrete details 13

R Reasons

E Examples

N Names

N Numbers

S Senses (Sight, Sound, Smell, Taste, Touch)

You do not have to use details in the order of the letters in RENNS. Neither do you have to use all the RENNS. For example, paragraph 5 uses three RENNS. See if you can identify them.

> Whether bad or good, in tune or not, whistling has its practi-
> cal side. Clifford Pratt is working with a group of speech therapists
> to develop whistling techniques to help children overcome speech
> problems through improved breath control and tongue flexibility.
> 5 People who have a piercing whistle have a clear advantage when
> it comes to hailing cabs, calling the dog or the children, or indicat-
> ing approval during a sporting event. And if you want to leave the
> house and can't remember where you put your keys, there's a key
> chain on the market now with a beep that can be activated by a
> whistle: You whistle and the key chain tells you where it is.
>
> —Cassandra Tate, "Whistlers Blow New Life into a Forgotten Art"

Paragraph 5 uses several examples (E) of how whistling can be helpful: overcoming speech problems, hailing cabs, calling dogs and children, cheering at sporting events, and finding keys. Also, it uses specific names (N): *Clifford Pratt* (not the general term *researcher*), *children* (not the general term *people*), and *dogs* (not the general term *animals*). In addition, the paragraph uses sensory description (S): the feeling of breath control and tongue flexibility, the sounds of whistles at a sporting event and of a beeping key chain.

8e What strategies can I use to create coherent paragraphs?

A paragraph shows **coherence** when its sentences are connected in content and relate to each other in form and language. Coherence creates a smooth flow of thoughts.

Coherence applies to each paragraph as well as to the progression from one paragraph to another. A coherent work results when you use transitional words and expressions, deliberate repetition, and parallelism.

Transitional words and expressions

Transitional words and expressions help connect ideas within and between paragraphs by showing relationships. Box 14 lists frequently used transitional words and the relationships they show. In paragraph 6, transitional words and expressions are in boldface type.

> **Equally important,** when a writer reads her work in public, she
> 6 has the opportunity to gauge the audience reaction. Do listeners
> shift uneasily in their seats? Or do they **instead** lean forward

attentively? If audience members come back to her with interesting and relevant questions, **of course,** she will know that she has hit the mark. **In addition to** discovering how she herself hears her own spoken words, **therefore,** an author who gives a public reading can learn how other people hear them.

—Kerry Liu, student

Do not overuse transitional expressions.

- Also, we were served ice cream ~~in addition~~.

Be sure the transitional word you choose fits your intended meaning. For example, use *on the other hand* for contrast, not for summary. Also, vary the transitional expressions you use. Avoid *for example* every time you give an example; try *for instance.*

ALERT: Within a sentence, a transitional expression is usually set off with commas (50h). However, between INDEPENDENT CLAUSES, a semicolon must come before the transitional expression (51b).!

Transitional words and expressions and the relationships they signal — 14

ADDITION	in addition, also, too, besides, equally important, furthermore, moreover
COMPARISON	in the same way, likewise, similarly
CONCESSION	granted, naturally, of course
CONTRAST	in contrast, however, instead, on the contrary, on the other hand, at the same time, despite the fact that, otherwise, nevertheless, still
EMPHASIS	of course, certainly, indeed, in fact
EXAMPLE	for example, for instance, as an illustration, a case in point, namely, specifically
RESULT	as a result, consequently, hence, then, therefore, thus, accordingly
SUMMARY	finally, in conclusion, in short, in summary
TIME SEQUENCE	today, tomorrow, yesterday, once, now, next, then, eventually, meanwhile, subsequently, finally

Deliberate repetition and parallelism

You can also achieve coherence through **deliberate repetition** of key words. Key words can be introduced in the topic sentence, or they may appear in the supporting sentences, where they refer to major details. Use repetition sparingly or your writing will become monotonous. Paragraph 7 shows effective use of deliberate repetition.

You can also use **parallelism** to link ideas and thereby achieve coherence. Sentences are parallel when they repeat a grammatical structure. Notice, for example, that in paragraph 7, the middle supporting sentences all open with the same structure: *It was work.* Notice, too, the parallelism within the fourth sentence—*to swing, to tighten,* and *to walk.*

7 The world of *work* into which Jacinto and the other seven-year-olds were apprenticed was within sight and sound of the pueblo. **It was *work*** under blazing suns, in rainstorms, in pitch-black nights. **It was *work*** that you were always *walking to* or *walking from, work without wages* and *work without end.* **It was *work*** that gave you a bone-tired feeling at the end of the day, so you learned **to swing** a machete, **to tighten** a cinch, and **to walk** without lost motion. Between seven and twelve you learned all this, each lesson driven home when your *jefe* said with a scowl: "*Así no, hombre; así.*" And he showed you how.

—Ernesto Galarza, *Barrio Boy*

8f What strategies can I use to develop body paragraphs?

As you develop the supporting body paragraphs in your writing, you will use various rhetorical strategies. **Rhetorical strategies** are patterns and techniques for presenting ideas clearly and effectively. The specific rhetorical strategies you use depend on what you want to accomplish.

Rhetorical strategies are presented one at a time in this section. When you write, however, no paragraph is isolated, so techniques often overlap in one paragraph. For example, in a paragraph explaining how to prepare a slide to study under a microscope, you would likely use the process pattern along with definition and description.

Narration

Narrative writing tells what is happening or what has happened—it is storytelling. Narration is usually organized chronologically—first this, then that.

8 The significance of General de Gaulle's famous "*Vive le Québec libre*" spoken from a balcony in Montreal in 1967 was debated in the Department as it was throughout the country. Mr. Pearson declared the general's utterance to be unacceptable, and de Gaulle promptly left the country without completing his visit. Although there were some dissenting voices, particularly to the effect that the government had overreacted, there was general agreement that the General's statement was not a slip of the tongue. After General de Gaulle's visitation, the government could not longer assume that the influence of France would always be benign so far as Canada was concerned. Now one thing had become clear: Canada's relations with France had become a matter of prime concern not just within the Department, but at all its diplomatic posts.

—Arthur Andrew, *The Rise and Fall of a Middle Power* (James Lorimer & Company Ltd., Publishers)

Description

Descriptive writing paints a picture in words. It usually calls on the five senses. It may be organized spatially (from top to bottom, or left to right, or inside to outside, and so on). Paragraph 9 is organized spatially. Description can also be organized from general to specific and from least to most important, building to a climax.

9 The old store, lighted only by three fifty-watt bulbs, smelled of coal oil and baking bread. In the middle of the rectangular room, where the oak floor sagged a little, stood an iron stove. To the right was a wooden table with an unfinished game of checkers and a stool made from an apple-tree stump. On shelves around the walls sat earthen jugs with corncob stoppers, a few canned goods, and some of the two thousand old clocks and clockworks Thurmond Watts owned. Only one was ticking; the others he just looked at.

—William Least Heat Moon, *Blue Highways*

Process

Process writing tells how to do something. It gives instruction or advice. Most process writing is organized chronologically because sequence is very important, and it must include all the steps of the process.

10 Carrying loads of equal weight like paint cans and toolboxes is easier if you carry one in each hand. Keep your shoulders back and down so that the weight is balanced on each side of your body, not suspended in front. With this method, you will be able to lift

heavier loads and also to walk and stand erect. Your back will not be strained by being pulled to one side.

—John Warde, "Safe Lifting Techniques"

Example or illustration

Writing developed with **examples** provides concrete, specific representations of the main idea. A single extended example is often called an **illustration.** Examples may be arranged from least to most important or the other way around, depending on your purpose and the impact you desire.

11 One major value of rain forests is biomedical. The plants and animals of rain forests are the source of many compounds used in today's medicines. A drug that helps treat Parkinson's disease is manufactured from a plant that grows only in South American rain forests. Some plants and insects found in rain forests contain chemicals that relieve certain mental disorders. Discoveries, however, have only begun. Scientists say that rain forests contain over a thousand plants that have great anticancer potential. To destroy life forms in these forests is to deprive the human race of further medical advances.

—Gary Lee Houseman, student

Definition

When you **define** something, you give its meaning. Definition is often used with process or other rhetorical strategies. You can also develop an entire paragraph by definition.

12 Chemistry is that branch of science which has the task of investigating the materials out of which the universe is made. It is not concerned with the forms into which they may be fashioned. Such objects as chairs, tables, vases, bottles, or wires are of no significance in chemistry; but such substances as glass, wool, iron, sulfur, and clay, as the materials out of which they are made, are what it studies. Chemistry is considered not only with the composition of such substances, but also with their inner structure.

—John Arrend Timm, *General Chemistry*

Comparison and contrast

Writing developed by **comparisons** deals with similarities. Writing developed by **contrasts** deals with differences. Comparison and contrast writing is usually organized one of two ways: **Point-by-point organization** moves back and forth between the items being compared, as in paragraph 13 (Mark, Wayne, Mark, Wayne). **Block organization** discusses one item completely before discussing the next, as in paragraph 14 (games are discussed completely before anything is said about business).

13 My husband and I constantly marvel at the fact that our two sons, born of the same parents and only two years apart in age, are such completely opposite human beings. The most obvious differences became apparent at their births. Our firstborn, **Mark,** was big and bold—his intense, already wise eyes, broad shoulders, huge and heavy hands, and powerful, chunky legs gave us the impression that he could have walked out of the delivery room on his own. Our second son, **Wayne,** was delightfully different. Rather than having the football physique that Mark was born with, Wayne came into the world with a long, slim, wiry body more suited to running, jumping, and contorting. Wayne's eyes, rather than being intense like Mark's, were impish and innocent. When **Mark** was delivered, he cried only momentarily, then seemed to settle into a state of intense concentration, as if trying to absorb everything he could about the strange, new environment he found himself in. Conversely, **Wayne** screamed from the moment he first appeared. There was nothing helpless or pathetic about his cry either—he was darn angry!

—Roseanne Labonte, student

14 **Games** are of limited duration, take place on or in fixed and finite sites and are governed by openly promulgated rules that are enforced on the spot by neutral professionals. Moreover, they are performed by relatively evenly matched teams that are counseled and led through every move by seasoned hands. Scores are kept, and at the end of the game, a winner is declared. **Business** is usually a little different. In fact, if there is anyone out there who can say that the business is of limited duration, takes place on a fixed site, is governed by openly promulgated rules that are enforced on the spot by neutral professionals, competes only on relatively even terms, and performs in a way that can be measured in runs or points, then that person is either extraordinarily lucky or seriously deluded.

—Warren Bennis, "Time to Hang Up the Old Sports Clichés"

Analysis

Analysis examines and discusses separate parts of a whole. For example, the next paragraph identifies a new type of zoo design and then analyzes why this new kind of design has developed, specifying three reasons for "the landscape revolution."

The current revolution in zoo design—the landscape revolution—is driven by three kinds of change that have occurred during this century. First are great leaps in animal ecology, veterinary medicine, landscape design, and exhibit technology, making pos-
15 sible unprecedented realism in zoo exhibits. Second, and perhaps most important, is the progressive disappearance of wilderness—the very subject of zoos—from the earth. Third is knowledge derived from market research and from environmental psychology, making possible a sophisticated focus on the zoo-goer.

—Melissa Greene, "No Rms, Jungle Vu"

Classification

Classification groups items according to a shared characteristic. Then each category is discussed or clarified.

Many different kinds of signals are used by the coaches. There are flash signals, which are just what the name implies: The coach may flash a hand across his face or chest to indicate a bunt or hit-and-run. There are holding signals, which are held in one position for several seconds. There might be the clenched fist,
16 bent elbow, or both hands on knees. Then there are the block signals. These divide the coach's body into different sections, or blocks. Touching a part of his body, rubbing his shirt, or touching his cap indicates a sign. Different players can be keyed to various parts of the block so the coach is actually giving several signals with the same sign.

—Rockwell Stensrud, "Who's on Third?"

Analogy

Analogy is a kind of comparison, identifying similarities between objects or ideas that are not usually associated with each other.

Casual dress, like casual speech, tends to be loose, relaxed, and colorful. It often contains what might be called "slang words": blue jeans, sneakers, baseball caps, aprons, flowered cotton housedresses, and the like. These garments could not be worn on a formal occasion without causing disapproval, but in ordinary
17 circumstances they pass without remark. "Vulgar words" in dress, on the other hand, give emphasis and get immediate attention in almost any circumstances, just as they do in speech. Only the skillful can employ them without some loss of face, and even then they must be used in the right way. A torn, unbuttoned shirt, or wildly uncombed hair can signify strong emotions: passion, grief, rage, despair. They are most effective if people already think of you as

being neatly dressed, just as the curses of well-spoken persons count for more than those of the customarily foul-mouthed.

—Alison Lurie, *The Language of Clothes*

Cause and effect

Causes lead to an event or an effect; effects result from causes. Writing that shows **cause and effect** examines outcomes and reasons for outcomes.

Because television is so wonderfully available as child amuser
and child defuser, capable of rendering a volatile three-year-old
harmless at the flick of a switch, parents grow to depend upon it
in the course of their daily lives. And as they continue to utilize
television day after day, its importance in their children's lives increases. From a simple source of entertainment provided by par-
18 ents when they need a break from child care, television gradually
changes into a powerful and disruptive presence in family life. But
despite their increasing resentment of television's intrusions into
their family life, and despite their considerable guilt at not being
able to control their children's viewing, parents do not take steps
to extricate themselves from television's domination. They can no
longer cope without it.

—Marie Winn, *The Plug-In Drug*

8g How can I write effective concluding paragraphs?

The concluding paragraph of an essay brings the writing to a smooth end. The conclusion needs to follow logically and from your THESIS STATEMENT and body paragraphs. Do not merely tack on a conclusion. Use it to provide a sense of completion, a finishing touch that adds to the whole essay.

Concluding paragraphs **15**

STRATEGIES FOR INTERESTING YOUR READER

- Use one of the strategies suggested for introductory paragraphs (see Box 12), but not the same one in both the introduction and the conclusion.
- Ask the reader for awareness, action, or a similar outcome.

Concluding paragraphs ***(continued)***

- Project ahead to the future.
- Summarize the main points, but only if the essay is longer than three pages.

STRATEGIES TO AVOID

- Avoid introducing new ideas or facts that belong in the body of the essay.
- Avoid merely rewording the introduction.
- Avoid announcing what you have done, as in "In this paper, I have explained the problems associated with owning exotic pets."
- Avoid making absolute claims, as in "In this essay, I have proved that keeping wild animals as pets must be outlawed."
- Avoid apologizing, as in "Even though I am not an expert, I feel the points I have made are accurate."

The conclusion that follows poses a challenging question and asks the reader to be prepared to face living alone. (For the introduction to this essay, see paragraph 1 on page 34.)

> You need to ask yourself, "If I had to live alone starting to-
> 19 morrow morning, would I know how?" If the answer is "No," you need to become conscious of what living alone calls for. If you face up to life today, you will not have to hide from it later on.
>
> —Tara Foster, student

9 WRITING TO INFORM

To deliver your message most effectively, you want to arrange all elements of your essay for the greatest clarity and impact. No one arrangement fits all essays. But all arrangements are based on the ancient principles of storytelling: that is, every essay should have a beginning, a middle, and an end. In this chapter, you can see how such an arrangement works in INFORMATIVE WRITING, by studying the final draft of an essay by student writer Carol Moreno. In Chapter 10 you can find a full discussion of arrangement in PERSUASIVE WRITING.

9a How is an informative essay usually arranged?

1. **Introductory paragraph:** captures the reader's interest and leads into the subject of the essay (8b).
2. **Thesis statement:** states the central message of the essay (5h, 7b). In academic essays the thesis statement usually appears at the end of the introductory paragraph.
3. **Background information:** provides context for the ideas that will be presented in the essay. Depending on its complexity, background information may be presented in the introductory paragraph or given its own paragraph.
4. **Body paragraphs:** explain and expand on the message of the essay. They form the core of the essay. Body paragraphs usually open with a TOPIC SENTENCE (general statement) and are backed up by specific details. Generalizations come to life with RENNS (8d). Each paragraph should be unified and coherent (8e).
5. **Concluding paragraph:** ends the essay smoothly and flows logically from the rest of the essay (8g).

9b Carol Moreno's essay

Women Can Pump Iron, Too

TITLE

When my grandmother fell and broke her hip last summer, I wanted to help take care of her. Because she was bedridden, she needed to be lifted at times, but I was shocked to discover that I could not lift her without my mother's or brother's help. My grandmother does not weigh much, but she was too much for me. My pride was hurt, and even more important, I began to worry about my plans to be a nurse specializing in the care of elderly people. What if I were too weak to help my patients get around? When I realized that I could satisfy one of my Physical Education requirements by taking a weight-lifting course for women, I decided to try it. Many people think only big, macho men want to lift weights, but times have changed. With the right training, women can also "pump iron" to build strength.

INTRODUCTION: Gets reader's attention with personal anecdote

Question to add sentence variety

THESIS STATEMENT: Focus of essay

Women who lift weights, I was happy to learn from my course, can easily avoid developing overly masculine muscle mass. Women can rely on their biology to protect them. Women's bodies produce only very small amounts of the hormones that enlarge muscles in men. With normal weight training, women's muscles grow longer rather than bulkier. The result is smoother, firmer muscles, not massive bulges. Also, women benefit most when they combine weight lifting, which is a form of anaerobic exercise, with aerobic exercise. Anaerobic exercise strengthens and builds muscles, but it does not make people breathe

BODY PARAGRAPH ONE: Gives background information

Refutes possible objection

Transition to signal additional point

→

Specific details of two types of conditioning

harder or their hearts beat faster for sustained periods. In contrast, aerobic exercises like running, walking, and swimming build endurance, but not massive muscles, because they force a person to take in more oxygen, which increases lung capacity, improves circulatory health, and tones the entire body. Encouraged by my instructor, I balanced my weight-lifting workouts by swimming laps twice a week.

BODY PARAGRAPH TWO: Describes safe use of equipment and lifting techniques

Striving for strength can end in injury unless weight lifters use free weights and weight machines safely. Free weights are barbells, the metal bars that round metal weights can be attached to at each end. To be safe, no matter how little the weight, lifters must never raise a barbell by bending at the waist, grabbing the barbell, and then straightening up. Instead, they should squat, grasp the barbell, and then use their leg muscles to straighten into a standing position. To avoid a twist that can lead to serious injury, lifters must use this posture: head erect and facing forward, back and neck aligned. The big advantage of weight machines, which use weighted handles and bars hooked to wires and pulleys, is that lifters must use them sitting down. Therefore, machines like the Nautilus and Universal actually force lifters to keep their bodies properly aligned, which drastically reduces the chance of injury.

Transition to show contrast

BODY PARAGRAPH THREE: Describes and explains the design and purpose of weight-training programs

Once a weight lifter understands how to lift safely, she needs a weight-lifting regimen personalized to her specific physical needs.

→

Because benefits come from "resistance," which is the stress that lifting any amount of weight puts on a muscle, no one has to be strong to get started. A well-planned progressive weight-training program begins with whatever weight a person can lift comfortably and gradually adds to the base weight as she gets stronger. What builds muscle strength is the number of repetitions, or "reps," the lifter does, not necessarily an increase in the amount of resistance from adding weight. Our instructor helped the women in the class, who ranged from 18 to 43, scrawny to pudgy, and couch potato to superstar, develop a program that was right for our individual weights, ages, and overall level of conditioning. Everyone's program differed in how much weight to start out with and how many reps to do for each exercise. Our instructor urged us not to try more weight or reps than our programs called for, even if our first workouts seemed too easy. This turned out to be good advice because those of us who did not listen woke up the next day feeling as though our bodies had been twisted by evil forces.

Specific details for reader to visualize a class

In addition to fitting a program to her physical capabilities, a weight lifter needs to design an individual routine to fit her personal goals. Most students in my group wanted to improve their upper body strength, so we focused on exercises to strengthen arms, shoulders, abdomens, and chests. Each student learned to use specific exercises to isolate certain muscle groups. Because muscles strengthen and grow when

BODY PARAGRAPH FOUR: Explains the need for developing a program to fit individual needs

→

Specific examples to add interest

they are rested after a workout, our instructor taught us to work alternate muscle groups on different days. For example, a woman might work on her arms and abdomen one day and then her shoulders and chest the next day. Because I had had such trouble lifting my grandmother, I added exercises to strengthen my legs and back. Another student, who had hurt her neck in a car crash, added neck-strengthening exercises. Someone else, planning to be a physical therapist, added finger- and hand-strengthening exercises.

CONCLUSION: Reports writer's personal progress

At the end of our 10 weeks of weight training, we had to evaluate our progress. Was I impressed! I felt ready to lift the world. When I started, I could lift only 10 pounds over my head for 3 reps. By the end of the course, I could lift 10 pounds over my head for 20 reps, and I could lift 18 pounds for 3 reps. Also, I could swim laps for 20 sustained minutes instead of the 10 I had barely managed at first. I am so proud of my weight-training accomplishments that I still work out three or four times a week. I am proof that any woman can benefit from "pumping iron." Not only will she become stronger and have more stamina, she will also feel energetic and confident. After all, there is nothing to lose--except maybe some flab.

10 WRITING TO ARGUE

10a What is an argument?

A written **argument** consists of two elements:

- The **claim** states the issue and then takes a position on a debatable topic (the taking of a position reads somewhat like a THESIS STATEMENT).
- **Support** for the claim consists of EVIDENCE, reasons, and examples presented factually and logically.

In academic writing, arguments are ways of demonstrating critical thinking. Arguments involve making and defending a position, proposal, or interpretation on a topic open to debate. Arguing your position effectively requires you to examine critically all sides of the topic. Your goal is to persuade an audience to accept your position, which means that your audience's viewpoints and values need to influence your decisions about content, organization, and style.

10b How do I choose a topic and develop a claim for an argument?

When you choose a topic for written argument, be sure that it is open to debate. An essay becomes an argument when it makes a claim—that is, takes a position on information. An effective way to develop a position on a topic is to ask a question about it or to identify a controversy surrounding it.

FACTS	Students are required to study a foreign language.
DEBATABLE QUESTION	Should students be required to study a foreign language?
ONE SIDE:	Students should not be required to study a foreign language.
OTHER SIDE:	Students should be required to study a foreign language.

Though you need to select one side of a debatable question to defend, keep the other side(s) in mind as you develop your argument. Mentioning viewpoints that are different from your own shows that you are well informed and fair-minded. As you refute these opposing positions, avoid insults, abstain from exaggerations, and resist sarcasm.

Often, instructors assign an argument topic, including the claim to make. In such cases, you need to argue in support of that position. Even if you personally disagree with the position, readers expect you to reason logically about it. Experienced debate teams practise arguing all sides of an issue—in competition, a debate team may have to argue either the "pro" or the "con" position.

If you can choose your own topic, choose one that is suitable for academic writing. Your readers expect you to select a topic of substance and to argue convincingly and reasonably about it. Also, so that you choose a claim sufficiently narrow for the practical situation, consider the length and time frame mentioned in your assignment.

Lacie Juris, the student who wrote the argument essay shown in section 10h, chose her own topic. Lacie was thinking about a career as a zookeeper, which led to her interest in issues concerning wild animals. In her career research, especially when she looked for the latest information on the Web, she discovered a major concern: the problem of private ownership of wild animals. Her curiosity aroused, Lacie read a number of sources and then found that she had a topic appropriate for her assignment to write an argument essay for her English class. Next, she worked on developing a claim about that topic that would then evolve into the thesis statement for her essay. Here's how Lacie progressed from topic to thesis statement.

Topic: Private ownership of wild animals

My claim: I think private ownership of wild animals should not be allowed.

Thesis statement (first draft): It is bad for private citizens to own wild animals as pets. [This is a preliminary thesis statement. It states the writer's position and gives reason for that position, but the word "bad" is vague, and the writer does not address how to stop private ownership of wild animals.]

Thesis statement (second draft): To eliminate what few people realize are increasingly dangerous situations for people and animals alike, ownership of wild animals as pets needs to be made completely illegal. [This revised thesis statement of the writer's position is better because it states not only the writer's claim but also a reason for the position. However, it suffers from lack of conciseness in wording and from the presence of the PASSIVE CONSTRUCTION "needs to be made."]

Thesis statement (final draft): To eliminate dangerous situations for both people and animals alike, lawmakers need to ban private ownership of wild animals as pets. [This final version of the thesis statement is improved and ready to use. It not only states the writer's claim clearly, but the language is concise and all verbs are in the ACTIVE VOICE. The writer now has a thesis statement that is narrow enough for an effective argument and suitable for the time and length given in her assignment.]

10c How do I support my argument?

Use evidence, reasons, and examples to support an argument's claim. Evidence needs to be sufficient, representative, relevant, accurate, and reasonable (see section 27b for complete explanations of these terms). Specifically, evidence consists of facts, statistics, expert testimony, personal experience, and so on. One good method for developing reasons for an argument is to ask yourself why you believe your claim. Another is to list "pros" and "cons" about your claim.

If you consult SOURCES to find supporting evidence, reasons, or examples, be sure to use correct DOCUMENTATION (23e, 28) within the text of your essay and in your bibliography. By doing this, you avoid engaging in PLAGIARISM, the attempt to pass off someone else's ideas as your own—a form of stealing. Take the time to master the concept and applications of documentation. Faculty can use Internet sites that scan student writing for plagiarized material; academic institutions treat plagiarism as a serious offence.

10d How do I structure an argument?

The two most frequently used structures for organizing an argument are **classical argument** and the **Toulmin model for argument.** Whatever structure you choose, readers expect your argument essay to have a clear introduction, body, and conclusion.

The ancient Greeks and Romans developed the structure for the **classical argument.** The student essay in 10h uses this structure. Box 16 lists its parts.

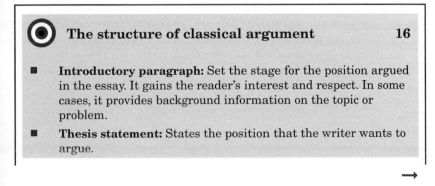

The structure of classical argument — 16

- **Introductory paragraph:** Set the stage for the position argued in the essay. It gains the reader's interest and respect. In some cases, it provides background information on the topic or problem.
- **Thesis statement:** States the position that the writer wants to argue.

→

The structure of classical argument ***(continued)***

- **Evidence and reasons:** Supports the position that the writer wants to argue. Each piece of evidence or reason usually consists of a general statement backed up with specific details, including examples. Evidence and reasons presented in logical sequences reach audiences most successfully. Common sequences include most familiar to least familiar, least important to most important.
- **Rebuttal—objections and responses to them:** Presents the opposition's position, and then argues against it. Writers can position this information in one of three ways: after the introduction, before the conclusion, or in a point-counterpoint format throughout the essay's body.
- **Concluding paragraph:** Wraps up the essay, often with a summary of the argument, an elaboration of the argument's significance, or a call to action for the readers.

The **Toulmin model,** developed by philosopher Stephen Toulmin, is another common argument method. Box 17 presents the elements in Toulmin's system for mounting an argument.

The Toulmin model for argument **17**

- The **claim,** which is a variation of a thesis statement. (If needed, the claim is qualified or limited.)
- The **support** of the claim with EVIDENCE and reasons, moving from broad reasons to specific data and details.
- The **warrants,** which are the writer's underlying assumptions, and are often implied rather than stated. Warrants may also need support (also called *backing*).

10e How do I convince my audience?

The PURPOSE of written argument is to convince your readers, known as your **audience,** either that they should agree with you or be open to your position. Therefore, you want to consider the characteristics of your audience. What do your readers already know about your topic? What are their values, viewpoints, and assumptions? Always use this information to develop your strategy for being persuasive in an argument essay.

Do you think that your audience is likely to read your point of view with hostility? If so, you might consider using a **Rogerian argument.** Based on psychologist Carl Rogers's communication principles, Rogerian argument looks for **common ground.** In many instances, of course, you can't expect to change your reader's mind, which means that your goal is to demonstrate that your point of view has merit.

An effective argument relies on three types of persuasive appeals: **logical appeals, emotional appeals,** and **ethical appeals.** The relative importance you decide to give these three types of appeals will help you decide on the relative weight to give different kinds of evidence. Therefore, your decision will also influence the sources you use and your search strategy (Chapter 23).

When you use **logical appeals,** called *logos* by the ancient Greeks, you allow your readers, whether they agree or disagree with you, to respect your position on the topic. Sound reasoning involves using effective evidence (10c) and reasons, an organized and well-structured argument (10d), and clear distinctions between fact and opinion. Equally important, you want to avoid using logical fallacies (10f) in your reasoning.

When you use **emotional appeals,** or *pathos,* you try to persuade your readers by appealing to their hearts more than their minds. Note, however, that academic writing requires you to combine emotional appeals with solid logical arguments. Emotional appeals can use descriptive language and concrete details or examples that lead readers to feel or understand the importance of your claim. Never manipulate your readers with biased, slanted language, and never lecture them on how they "should" feel. Readers see through such tactics and resent them.

When you use **ethical appeals,** or *ethos,* you establish your personal credibility with your audience. One effective way to make an ethical appeal is to draw on personal experience that relates directly to your argument. (Check first to see if your instructor allows first-person writing in essays.) Demonstrating—not merely claiming—that you are well informed about your topic also establishes your credibility. Considering a variety of perspectives and using reliable SOURCES for evidence communicate that you are arguing fairly and honestly. Equally important is a reasonable TONE.

10f What are logical fallacies?

Logical fallacies are flaws in reasoning that lead to faulty, illogical statements. They represent either a writer's attempt to manipulate readers or errors in the writer's reasoning process.

- **Hasty generalization** occurs when someone draws a conclusion based on inadequate evidence. Stereotyping is a common example of hasty generalization.
- The **either-or fallacy,** also called *false dilemma,* limits the choices to only two alternatives when more exist. For example, *Either get your diploma or forget about getting a job* falsely implies that a diploma is a prerequisite for all jobs.
- **False analogy** claims that two items are alike when actually they are more different than similar. The statement *If we can put a man on the moon, we should be able to find a cure for cancer* is faulty because space science is very different from biological science.
- **False cause** asserts that one event leads to another when, in fact, the two events may only be related. A common type of false cause is called *post hoc, ergo propter hoc,* which in Latin means *after this, therefore because of this*.
- **Slippery slope** arguments suggest that one event will cause a "domino effect," a series of uncontrollable consequences.
- **Personal attack,** also known as *ad hominem,* attacks a person's appearance, personal habits, or character instead of dealing with the merits of the individual's argument.
- **Bandwagon,** also known as *ad populum,* implies that something is right because everyone else is doing it.
- **False authority** means citing the opinion of an "expert" who has no claim to expertise on the subject at hand. Using celebrities to advertise products unrelated to their careers is a common example of this tactic.
- **Irrelevant argument** is also called *non sequitur* in Latin, which means *it does not follow*. This flaw occurs when a conclusion does not follow from the premises: *Ms. Sih is a forceful speaker, so she will be an outstanding mayor*. Ms. Sih's forceful speaking style does not mean that she has outstanding political skills.
- **Red herring** sidetracks an issue by bringing up unrelated matters that distract the audience. The following question diverts attention from the issue being argued rather than arguing it: *Why worry*

about pandas becoming extinct when we should be concerned about the plight of the homeless?

- **Begging the question** is also called *circular reasoning*. The supporting reasons only restate the claim—for example, *Wrestling is a dangerous sport because it is unsafe. Dangerous* and *unsafe* essentially have the same meaning, so the reason simply restates the claim rather than supporting it.
- **Emotional appeals,** such as appeals to fear, tradition, or pity, substitute emotions for logical reasoning. These appeals attempt to manipulate readers by reaching their hearts rather than their minds.
- **Slanted language** involves biasing the reader by using word choices that have strong positive or negative connotations. Calling a group of people involved in a protest rally a *mob* attempts to provoke a negative response, whereas referring to the group as *active citizens* seeks to provoke a positive response.

10g What guidelines do I use to revise my argument essays?

You revise your argument essay as you would any essay (see Boxes 10 and 11). In addition, check the elements listed in Box 18.

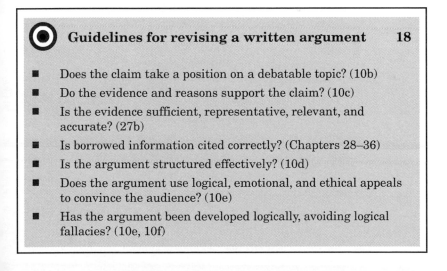

Guidelines for revising a written argument 18

- Does the claim take a position on a debatable topic? (10b)
- Do the evidence and reasons support the claim? (10c)
- Is the evidence sufficient, representative, relevant, and accurate? (27b)
- Is borrowed information cited correctly? (Chapters 28–36)
- Is the argument structured effectively? (10d)
- Does the argument use logical, emotional, and ethical appeals to convince the audience? (10e)
- Has the argument been developed logically, avoiding logical fallacies? (10e, 10f)

10h The final draft of a student's argument essay

Juris 1

Lacie Juris

Professor Calhoon-Dillahunt

English 101

16 June 2002

TITLE

Exotic Pets: Not at Home in Your Home

INTRODUCTION: Gets reader's attention with examples

Tiger cubs look and behave like kittens. Baby chimps look almost human and sometimes act like precocious human infants. For many Canadians, owning one of these as a pet, to play with and show off to neighbours, sounds like a childhood fantasy come true. Yet for many, it is no fantasy: Tigers can cost as little as $200 in Canada (Nikolovsky A18). Animal-rights advocates estimate that as many tigers are kept as pets in the United States as exist in the wild worldwide (Boehm B1). Unfortunately, these exotic dreams can turn deadly at any moment. Because wild animal ownership comes under a confusion of federal, provincial, and local laws, there is little effective regulation (Nikolovsky A18). To eliminate dangerous situations for both people and animals alike, lawmakers need to ban private ownership of wild animals as pets.

IN-TEXT CITATION: MLA style

THESIS STATEMENT: Focus of essay

BODY PARAGRAPH ONE: Gives background information

Wild animals are dangerous to humans, both owners and nearby residents. Wild animals have inborn behaviour patterns and instincts, such as stalking prey, attacking when threatened, and

→

Juris 2

self-defence. Such patterns remain no matter where or how the animals grow up, no matter how well the owners train them for domesticated living. This is what makes the animals truly wild. Humans cannot influence, change, or even predict an animal's wild behaviours. An attack can occur at any time when an animal's wild instincts take over without warning ("Wild Animals Are Not Pets"). In addition, wild pets can cause tremendous property damage, as illustrated by the case of Stoli, a tiger who caused $20 000 worth of damage to his owner's Mercedes in less than five minutes ("Stoli and Lil" 1). Zoocheck Canada, an advocacy group for animals in captivity, realistically puts emphasis both on the humane treatment of animals and on the dangers that some exotic pets can pose ("About Zoocheck Canada").

BODY PARAGRAPH TWO: Anecdote to support thesis

Many animal owners teach their young exotic pets little games and tricks. Owners do not realize, however, that when the wild animals have grown to three or four times the strength of most people, the "pets" still expect to take part in the same games and tricks. Take, for example, the story of a pet African serval named Kenya. Servals are known as "leaping cats," able to jump four metres straight up and run 70 kilometres an hour. The woman who purchased Kenya believed that the tiny cub would make the perfect "exotic pet." However, no one told the woman about servals' amazing jumping abilities--or about their becoming extremely territorial as adults. At

→

Juris 3

home, the woman taught the cub to leap onto her shoulder, without realizing that she was actually teaching him to leap onto people in general. In addition, as he grew, he became so territorial that he attacked anyone who would come to her house ("Kenya").

BODY PARAGRAPH THREE: Presents evidence—logical appeal

Transition to signal additional point

Another little-realized fact is that wild animals greatly endanger owners and people in the surrounding areas by transmitting diseases. Few purchasers of exotic animals know if their animals are carrying diseases. Wild animals can host internal parasites and other pathogenic organisms that can be debilitating or even fatal to their human caretakers--especially small children (Laidlaw).

BODY PARAGRAPH FOUR: Presents evidence—logical appeal

Transition to show contrast and signal additional point

While the risk to humans of exotic pet ownership is very high, domestication is hazardous to the animals themselves. After all, wild animals need specific and natural environments to survive. Such settings do not include humans, houses, or backyard kennels. Owners of wild animals usually lack the knowledge and funds to recreate the animal's environment or to provide proper nutrition, let alone care for the animals if they were to become sick or injured (Boehm B1). Very few professional veterinarians are trained or willing to work on wild animals.

BODY PARAGRAPH FIVE: Presents evidence—emotional appeal

Usually, infant wild animals are stolen from their parents at only a few weeks, or even days, of life. Their capture robs the babies of the chance to learn skills necessary for survival if

→

Juris 4

they are ever abandoned or re-released into the wild. These animals often develop stress and behaviour disorders, because they have never experienced social interaction with their own species ("Wild Animals Are Not Pets"). Eventually, many owners become frightened or confused by sudden behaviour problems with their "little babies," and they decide to leave the animals in remote places to fend for themselves. These animals that never learned how to survive on their own often starve to death. Some seek out food near rural homes or suburbs, which frequently ends in their death at the hands of frightened people ("Wild Animals Do Not Make Good Pets" 2).

BODY PARAGRAPH SIX: Rebuttal of possible objections

Some people may argue for the benefits of personal ownership of wild animals. It allows ordinary people to enjoy exotic pets in their own homes. These people insist that they can safely restrict their wild animals' movements to their own property. Further, defenders of the private possession of wild animals argue that owners can help preserve endangered species. Increasingly, however, exotic pet owners' fantasies turn into nightmares as the wild animals become adults increasingly controlled by their basic instincts and inbred behaviours. Owners often expect local animal control agencies or animal sanctuaries to deal with their problems, even though such facilities are already over capacity or are staffed by people unequipped to deal with undomesticated animals (Milloy A19).

Transition to show contrast

→

Juris 5

CONCLUSION: Call to action and emotional appeal

Keeping wild animals as pets must be outlawed. Though exotic creatures may look like Simba or Tigger, they are still completely wild, and it is in the wild that they belong. As pointed out in "Wild Animals Are Not Pets," "The only ones who benefit from the practice of sales of exotic animals as pets are the breeders and sellers. These people make an enormous amount of money by exploiting these animals once they are sold" (1). Poachers also profit when they capture baby wild animals from their native habitats and sell them as pets to the highest bidder. The best way for humans to see and experience wild animals in safe environments is to visit and support zoos and wildlife parks that specialize in providing professionally constructed natural habitats for animals. In such settings, people can enjoy the beauty and behaviours of wild animals without putting humans and the animals at risk.

→

Juris 6

WORKS CITED LIST: MLA style

Works Cited

"About Zoocheck Canada." Zoocheck Canada. 2002. 19 Apr. 2002 <http://www.zoocheck.com/about/>.

Boehm, Ted. "A New Local Worry: Exotic Cats--Lion and Tiger Prices Fall, and Once Rare Pets Become a Costly Menace." Wall Street Journal 30 June 2000: B1.

"Kenya." Cat Tales Zoological Park. 1999. 19 Apr. 2002 <http://cattales.org/kenya.html>.

Laidlaw, Rob. "Salmonella, Captivity-Related Stress and the Human Health Implications of Pet Reptiles." 2002. 25 Apr. 2002 <http://www.wspa.ca/reptiles/reports/zoonoses/report.html>.

Milloy, Ross E. "Banning Lions and Other Large Pets." New York Times 10 Dec. 2001: A19.

Nikolovsky, Boris. "Critics Growl over Keeping of Exotic Pets: Zoo Animals Live in Basements and Backyards." Toronto Star 11 Aug. 1994: A18.

"Stoli and Lil." Cat Tales Zoological Park. 1999. 19 Apr. 2002 <http://cattales.org/stolilil.html>.

"Wild Animals Are Not Pets." The Wild Animal Orphanage. 2001. 19 Apr. 2002 <http://www.wildanimalorphanage.org/wild.html>.

"Wild Animals Do Not Make Good Pets." Cat Tales Zoological Park. 1999. 19 Apr. 2002 <http://cattales.org/notapet.html>.

11 SENTENCE FRAGMENTS

11a What is a sentence fragment?

A **sentence fragment** looks like a sentence but isn't one. It is punctuated like a sentence, but it is only a part, not a whole. Fragments are incomplete because of faulty structure or grammar. Watch out for errors like these:

- When winter comes early. [fragment]
- Whales in the Arctic Ocean. [fragment]
- Stranded in the Arctic Ocean. [fragment]

11b How can I recognize fragments?

You will find it easier to recognize fragments once you can recognize complete sentences. Get to know the basic pattern of an INDEPENDENT CLAUSE* (Box 56, p. 343). When you read your own writing, ask yourself the questions in Box 19 on page 66. If any answer is yes, you are looking at a sentence fragment. To eliminate the fragment, follow the advice in 11c, 11d, or 11e.

11c How can I correct a fragment that starts with a subordinating word?

Start by recognizing SUBORDINATING CONJUNCTIONS (39h). You can choose between two methods to correct a fragment that starts with a subordinating conjunction.

FRAGMENT **Because** the ship had to cut a path through the ice.

CORRECT BY JOINING TO AN INDEPENDENT CLAUSE

Because the ship had to cut a path through the ice, the rescue effort took time.

CORRECT BY DELETING THE SUBORDINATING CONJUNCTION

The ship had to cut a path through the ice.

* Words printed in small capital letters (such as CLAUSE) are defined in the Terms Glossary on pages 497–517.

How to identify sentence fragments **19**

Note: When any answer here is yes, you have a sentence fragment.

Does a word group that starts with a SUBORDINATING WORD stand alone rather than being joined to a complete sentence?

FRAGMENT **When** winter comes early.

CORRECT **When winter comes early,** many whales are stranded in the Arctic Ocean.

Does a word group lack a VERB, and the words are not joined to a complete sentence?

FRAGMENT Whales in the Arctic Ocean.

CORRECT Whales **live** in the Arctic Ocean.

Does a word group lack a SUBJECT, and the words are not joined to a complete sentence?

FRAGMENT Stranded in the Arctic Ocean.

CORRECT **Many whales** were stranded in the Arctic Ocean.

Some fragments start with the subordinating words *who* or *which*. Either join the fragment to an independent clause or rewrite the idea in an independent clause.

FRAGMENT The ship's noisy motor worried the scientists. **Who feared the whales would panic.**

CORRECT BY JOINING TO AN INDEPENDENT CLAUSE

The ship's noisy motor worried the scientists, who feared the whales would panic.

CORRECT BY REWRITING AS AN INDEPENDENT CLAUSE

The ship's noisy motor worried the scientists. They feared the whales would panic.

11d How can I correct a phrase fragment?

To start, learn to recognize a PHRASE (39m). A phrase that begins with a capital letter and ends with a period (or question mark or exclamation point) is a fragment. In the following five examples, the phrase fragments are in bold type.

The crew played classical music. **To calm the whales.** [infinitive phrase]

The crew chose classical music. **Hoping for success.** [present-participle phrase]

The whales began to panic. **Trapped by the ice.** [past-participle phrase]

The ship moved slowly. **Toward the whales.** [prepositional phrase]

An enormously powerful icebreaker. The ship arrived to free the whales. [appositive phrase]

To correct a phrase fragment, you can choose between two methods:

CORRECT BY JOINING TO AN INDEPENDENT CLAUSE

The crew played classical music **to calm the whales.**

The crew chose classical music, **hoping for success.**

The whales began to panic, **trapped by the ice.**

The ship moved slowly **toward the whales.**

An enormously powerful icebreaker, the ship arrived to free the whales.

CORRECT BY REWRITING INTO AN INDEPENDENT CLAUSE

The major concern was how **to calm the whales.**

The crew was **hoping for success** and willing to try an unusual strategy.

No one knew whether whales **trapped by the ice** would cooperate with a rescue attempt.

A slow approach **toward the whales** was the method they used.

An enormously powerful icebreaker arrived to free the whales.

11e How can I correct a fragment that is a part of a compound predicate?

In a complete sentence, a **compound predicate** contains two or more verbs connected by a COORDINATING CONJUNCTION such as *and*. In the example here, the boldface type shows a fragment that is half of the compound predicate. You can choose between two methods to correct such fragments.

FRAGMENT The ship reached the whales. **And led them to freedom.**

CORRECT BY JOINING TO AN INDEPENDENT CLAUSE

The ship reached the whales **and led them to freedom.**

CORRECT BY REWRITING WITHOUT A COMPOUND PREDICATE

The crew cheered **as the whales were led to freedom.**

11f What are intentional fragments?

Professional writers sometimes intentionally use fragments for emphasis and effect. The ability to judge the difference between acceptable and unacceptable sentence fragments comes from much exposure to the works of skilled writers. Many instructors, therefore, consider sentence fragments errors. A few instructors occasionally allow well-placed intentional fragments after a student has shown the consistent ability to write well-constructed complete sentences.

12 COMMA SPLICES AND RUN-ON SENTENCES

12a What are comma splices and run-on sentences?

Comma splices and run-on sentences (also called run-together or fused) are errors that look almost alike. They incorrectly join two INDEPENDENT CLAUSES. A **comma splice** is created when only a comma separates independent clauses. A **run-on sentence** is created when no punctuation at all separates independent clauses.

COMMA SPLICE The hurricane **intensified, it** turned toward land.

RUN-ON SENTENCE The hurricane **intensified it** turned toward land.

ALERT: Occasionally, experienced writers use a comma to join short independent clauses: *Mosquitoes do not bite, they stab.* Your instructor may consider this punctuation an error, so check before you use it.

12b How can I recognize comma splices and run-on sentences?

Watch out for the four major causes of comma splices and run-on sentences.

How to identify comma splices and run-on sentences — 20

1. Watch out for a second INDEPENDENT CLAUSE that starts with a pronoun.

COMMA SPLICE Grey Owl was an author and conservationist**, he lived** in northern Ontario and the Prairies.

RUN-ON SENTENCE Grey Owl was an author and conservationist **he lived** in northern Ontario and the Prairies.

CORRECT Grey Owl was an author and conservationist**. He lived** in northern Ontario and the Prairies.

2. Watch out for a CONJUNCTIVE ADVERB that joins two sentences.

COMMA SPLICE He passed himself off as a North American Indian**, however,** he was born Archibald Belaney in England.

RUN-ON SENTENCE He passed himself off as a North American Indian **however,** he was born Archibald Belaney in England.

CORRECT He passed himself off as a North American Indian**; however,** he was born Archibald Belaney in England.

3. Watch out for a TRANSITIONAL EXPRESSION that joins two sentences.

COMMA SPLICE Grey Owl served as a conservation officer**, in addition,** he lectured and wrote bestselling books.

RUN-ON SENTENCE Grey Owl served as a conservation officer **in addition,** he lectured and wrote bestselling books.

CORRECT Grey Owl served as a conservation officer**. In addition,** he lectured and wrote bestselling books.

→

How to identify comma splices and run-on sentences *(continued)*

4. Watch out when a second independent clause explains or gives an example of the information in the first independent clause.

COMMA SPLICE	Belaney appeared to be expert in First Nations **traditional lore, most of the traditions** he knew he learned from his Iroquois wife and his Ojibway friends.
RUN-ON SENTENCE	Belaney appeared to be expert in First Nations **traditional lore most of the traditions** he knew he learned from his Iroquois wife and his Ojibway friends.
CORRECT	Belaney appeared to be expert in First Nations **traditional lore. Most of the traditions** he knew he learned from his Iroquois wife and his Ojibway friends.

12c How can I correct comma splices and run-on sentences?

You have many choices for correcting comma splices and run-on sentences.

Using punctuation

You can use a period or a semicolon to separate independent clauses in a comma splice or run-on sentence. Notice that all these errors are like item 1 in Box 20.

COMMA SPLICE	A shark's skeleton is all cartilage**,** the shark does not have a bone in its body.
RUN-ON SENTENCE	A shark's skeleton is all cartilage the shark does not have a bone in its body.
CORRECT	A shark's skeleton is all cartilage**.** The shark does not have a bone in its body.
CORRECT	A shark's skeleton is all cartilage**;** the shark does not have a bone in its body.

Using a coordinating conjunction

If the ideas in your independent clauses relate closely in meaning and are grammatically equivalent, you can connect them with a comma followed by a coordinating conjunction (*and, but, for, nor, or, so, yet*).

COMMA SPLICE Every living creature gives off a weak electrical charge in water**,** special pores on a shark's skin can detect these signals.

RUN-ON SENTENCE Every living creature gives off a weak electrical charge in water special pores on a shark's skin can detect these signals.

CORRECT Every living creature gives off a weak electrical charge in water**, and** special pores on a shark's skin can detect these signals.

Revising an independent clause into a dependent clause

If one of two independent clauses expresses information that can be subordinated logically to the other independent clause, start it with a SUBORDINATING CONJUNCTION or a RELATIVE PRONOUN and join it correctly to the independent clause.

COMMA SPLICE Costa Rica's Cobos Island harbours more sharks than anywhere else on earth**,** it is paradise to underwater filmmakers.

RUN-ON SENTENCE Costa Rica's Cobos Island harbours more sharks than anywhere else on earth it is paradise to underwater filmmakers.

CORRECT **Because** Costa Rica's Cobos Island harbours more sharks than anywhere else on earth**,** it is paradise to underwater filmmakers.

COMMA SPLICE Some sharks have large, triangular teeth**,** these teeth can tear flesh.

RUN-ON SENTENCE Some sharks have long, large, triangular teeth these teeth can tear flesh.

CORRECT Some sharks have long, large, triangular teeth **that** can tear flesh.

ALERT: When a conjunctive adverb or transitional expression falls between spliced or run-on independent clauses, you must use a period or semicolon to correct the error. (CONJUNCTIVE ADVERBS include such words as *however, therefore, also, next, then, thus, furthermore,* and *nevertheless.* TRANSITIONAL EXPRESSIONS include *for example, for instance,* and others. For a list of conjunctive adverbs, see Box 50 on page 336.)!

COMMA SPLICE Some sharks cannot bite**, for example,** the basking shark can only filter plankton through its small mouth.

RUN-ON SENTENCE Some sharks cannot bite **for example,** the basking shark can only filter plankton through its small mouth.

CORRECT Some sharks cannot bite**. For example,** the basking shark can only filter plankton through its small mouth.

CORRECT Some sharks cannot bite**; for example,** the basking shark can only filter plankton through its small mouth.

13 PROBLEMS WITH SENTENCE SHIFTS

A correct sentence does not "shift." To avoid writing sentences that shift, be consistent in the four areas covered in 13a–13d.

13a What is being consistent in person and number?

In this context, **shifts** are grammatical changes for no reason. Shifts in person and number often occur together, causing confusion.

Person tells who or what is acting or being acted upon. **First person** (*I, we*) focuses attention on the writer or speaker: *I see a field of fireflies.* **Second person** (*you*) focuses attention on the reader or listener: *You see a shower of sparks.* **Third person** focuses attention on the subject that is being discussed: *The physicist sees a cloud of cosmic dust.* All NOUNS and many PRONOUNS are in the third person.

Number refers to singular (one) or plural (more than one). Do not mix singular and plural unless your meaning calls for it.

CONFUSING **I** enjoy reading forecasts of the future, but **you** never know which ones will never happen. One recent prediction claimed that **car buyers** will pay twice today's price for a car, but **you** will get twice the gas mileage. [This short passage shifts from first to second to third person and back to second, which is very confusing. Is this an informal first-person report? a piece of advice addressed directly to readers? an impersonal piece of informative writing?]

REVISED Although forecasts of the future make enjoyable reading, it is impossible to know which ones will never happen. One recent prediction claimed that **car buyers** will pay twice today's price for a car, but **they** will get twice the gas mileage. [The revisions here make the third-person perspective consistent. Revising in other ways would bring other perspectives into focus.]

ALERTS: (1) Watch out for shifts from nouns (third person) to the second-person pronoun *you*.

- By the year 2020, most people will live longer, and ~~you~~ they will have to work longer, too.

(2) Watch out for shifts between singular and plural in third person.

- The longer ~~a person stays~~ people stay in the workforce, the more competition they will face from younger job seekers. **!**

13b What is being consistent in subject, voice, and mood?

Sometimes a shift in SUBJECT within or between sentences is justified to convey meaning. More often, though, a shift in subject makes your writing drift out of focus. An unnecessary shift in subject goes along with a shift in voice—from active to passive voice. In **active voice,** the subject does the acting; in **passive voice,** the subject receives the action.

SHIFT IN SUBJECT AND VOICE People complain about sugary, high-fat foods, but donuts by the millions are eaten for breakfast every day. [The subject shifts from *people* to *donuts,* and the verb voice shifts from active *complain* to passive *are eaten.*]

REVISED People complain about sugary, high-fat foods, but **they eat** donuts by the millions for breakfast every day.

Similarly, an unnecessary shift often happens when MOODS shift (40e). Avoid combining statements or questions (INDICATIVE MOOD) and commands (IMPERATIVE MOOD) in one sentence.

SHIFT IN MOOD Breakfast is the most important meal of the day. Eat cereal, not donuts. [The first sentence is a statement, but the second sentence shifts unnecessarily to a command.]

REVISED Breakfast is the most important meal of the day. Cereal may be a better breakfast choice than donuts.

13c What is being consistent in verb tense?

Unnecessary tense shifts create illogical time sequences. Some shifts in verb tense, however, are necessary to show time passing (Box 61, p. 354).

SHIFT IN VERB TENSE Canada **gave** its music industry a boost in the 1970s when government regulations **require** AM radio stations to play a minimum of 30 percent Canadian content. [The tense shifts from past to present, even though the action of both verbs occurred in the past.]

REVISED Canada **gave** its music industry a boost in the 1970s when government regulations **required** AM radio stations to play a minimum of 30 percent Canadian content.

SHIFT IN VERB TENSE Pop music **was** the greatest beneficiary of the new Canadian content regulations. However, the artists rushing into production with their recordings in the 1970s **include** a large number of failures as well as many well-known stars. [The illogical tense shift here occurs between sentences.]

REVISED Pop music **was** the greatest beneficiary of the new Canadian content regulations. However, the artists rushing into production with their recordings in the 1970s **included** a large number of failures as well as many well-known stars.

13d What is being consistent in direct and indirect discourse?

Direct discourse repeats someone's words exactly, and the quoted words are enclosed in quotation marks. **Indirect discourse** reports someone's words but is not enclosed in quotation marks. The grammatical patterns of direct and indirect discourse differ.

SHIFT BETWEEN DIRECT AND INDIRECT DISCOURSE

He asked did we enjoy the movie. [The verb *did* implies direct discourse, but quotation marks are missing. The PRONOUN *we* shifts away from direct discourse.]

CORRECT DIRECT DISCOURSE

He asked, "Did you enjoy the movie?" [The quotation marks indicate that this is direct discourse. The speaker's words are repeated exactly. The sentence ends correctly with a question mark.]

CORRECT INDIRECT DISCOURSE

He asked whether we had enjoyed the movie. [The statement indicates that words are being reported, not quoted. The verb *had enjoyed* clarifies the time relationship between the enjoyment and the asking. The sentence ends correctly with a period.]

13e What happens in sentences with mixed parts?

A sentence with mixed parts starts in one direction but goes off in a different direction. Its meaning is therefore unclear. To revise such errors, think through exactly what you want to say.

Mixed clauses

In a sentence containing a DEPENDENT CLAUSE and an INDEPENDENT CLAUSE, the clauses need to carry meaning in one direction, not in two directions. Otherwise, the meaning is unclear.

MIXED CLAUSES Because television's first transmissions in the 1920s included **news, programs** were popular. [The dependent clause talks about the news, but the independent clause goes off in another direction by talking about the popularity of programs in general. What exactly does the writer mean?]

CORRECT Television's first transmissions in the 1920s included **news programs, which** were popular. [Dropping *Because,* putting *news* and *programs* together, and adding *which* solves the problem by keeping the focus on news programs throughout.]

Mixed phrase-clause

In a sentence containing a PHRASE and part of an independent clause, the meaning gets lost.

MIXED PHRASE-CLAUSE **By doubling the time allotment** to thirty minutes **increased** the prestige of news programs. [This sentence uses a PREPOSITIONAL PHRASE, *By doubling the time allotment,* but the sentence does not hold to its meaning with *increased the prestige.*]

CORRECT **Doubling** the time allotment to thirty minutes **increased** the prestige of news programs. [Dropping the preposition *By* clears up the problem; now *Doubling* is the SUBJECT of the sentence.]

CORRECT **By doubling the time allotment** to thirty minutes, **network executives increased** the prestige of news programs. [Inserting a logical subject, *network executives,* clears up the problem, creating an independent clause preceded by a modifying prepositional phrase.]

Faulty predication

Faulty predication results when the subject and PREDICATE of a sentence do not make sense together. You can correct the error by revising one part or the other so that they work together.

FAULTY PREDICATION The purpose of television was invented to entertain. [The subject is *purpose.* The predicate is *was invented to entertain.* They do not make sense together.]

CORRECT **Television** was invented to entertain. [This sentence revises the subject and keeps the original predicate.]

CORRECT The purpose of television **was to entertain.** [This sentence keeps the subject and revises the predicate.]

FAULTY PREDICATION Lloyd Robertson's outstanding characteristic as a newscaster is believable. [The predicate, *is believable,* is about Lloyd Robertson, but the subject of the sentence is *characteristic.*]

CORRECT Lloyd Robertson's outstanding characteristic as a newscaster is **believability.** [*Believability,* a noun, acts as a COMPLEMENT renaming *characteristic,* and the sentence now makes sense.]

CORRECT Lloyd Robertson has one outstanding characteristic as a newscaster: He is believable. [The information is divided into two sentences separated correctly by a colon.]

13f How should I use elliptical constructions and comparisons?

An **elliptical construction** deliberately leaves out, rather than repeats, one or more words that appear earlier in a sentence. Here is a correctly written elliptical sentence:

- I have my book and Joan's. [The writer is expressing this thought: *I have my book and Joan's book.*]

An elliptical sentence is correct only when it contains exactly the same words that are omitted.

- In the 1980s, software expertise and communications equipment ~~were becoming~~ became two major Canadian exports, and comedy talent a third.

  [The plural verb *were becoming* cannot take the place of *was becoming,* which the singular subject *comedy talent* requires. *Became* works because it goes with both singular and plural subjects.]

in

- Talented expatriates have appeared ^ and written for *Saturday Night Live, SCTV, David Letterman,* and other shows that revolutionized television comedy.

  [*Appeared* must be followed by *in,* not *for,* as implied.]

In writing a comparison, you can omit words as long as it is clear what the missing words are. That is, the relationship between the compared items must be clear even when words are omitted.

than low achievers do

- High achievers make better business executives ^.

  [*Better* implies a comparison, but none was stated.]

they value

- Most stockholders value high achievers more than ^ risk takers.

  [Who values whom most? The revised sentence reflects one clear meaning. Another clear revision, with a different meaning, is *Most stockholders value high achievers more than risk takers do*.]

from that of a high achiever

- A risk taker's ability to manage long-term growth is very different ^.

  [Different from what? Both items being compared must be expressed.]

ALERT: When you write *as much as, as . . . as . . . than . . . ,* and similar comparisons (for example, ***as** pretty **as,** if not prettier **than***), be sure to state the second *as.*

as

- High achievers value success as much ^, if not more than, high salary. !

14 PROBLEMS WITH MISPLACED MODIFIERS

A **modifier** is a word, PHRASE, or CLAUSE that describes or limits other words, phrases, or clauses. Place modifiers carefully so that your intended meaning is clear.

14a How should I correct misplaced modifiers?

Usually, the correct placement for a modifier is next to the word it is meant to modify. Modifiers placed elsewhere in the sentence can confuse your readers. Sometimes, as the example shows, **misplaced modifiers** provide unintended humour.

MISPLACED MODIFIER Nicholas Cugnot built the first self-propelled vehicle, determined to travel without horses. [The modifier *determined to travel without horses* is meant to describe *Nicholas Cugnot*. But it is placed next to *vehicle,* so the sentence says that the vehicle was determined to travel without horses.]

CORRECT Determined to travel without horses, Nicholas Cugnot built the first self-propelled vehicle.

Adverbs such as *only, just, almost, hardly, scarcely,* and *simply* always limit the word they immediately precede. Placed anywhere else in the sentence, they change the meaning. Notice how various placements of *only* affect the meaning of the sentence *Professional coaches say that high salaries motivate players.*

- **Only** professional coaches say that high salaries motivate players. [No one else says that.]
- Professional coaches **only** say that high salaries motivate players. [The coaches don't believe it.]
- Professional coaches say that **only** high salaries motivate players. [The coaches think nothing else works.]
- Professional coaches say that high salaries motivate **only** players. [No one else is motivated by high salaries.]

14b How should I correct squinting modifiers?

A **squinting modifier** appears to apply to what comes before it as well as to what comes after it. Revise so that the modifier applies to only one word.

- While Karl Benz watched, the vehicle he had built ~~noisily~~ announced its arrival ^noisily^.

  [Before the revision, the car seems to be both noisily built and noisily announcing its arrival.]

14c How should I correct split infinitives?

A **split infinitive** occurs when a modifier separates *to* and the verb that completes the infinitive. (*To plan* is an infinitive. *To originally plan* is a split infinitive.) In general, place modifiers before or after the complete infinitive phrase.

SPLIT INFINITIVE Orson Welles's radio drama *War of the Worlds* managed **to,** on October 30, 1938, **convince** listeners that they were hearing an invasion by Martians.

CORRECT On October 30, 1938, Orson Welles's radio drama *War of the Worlds* managed **to convince** listeners that they were hearing an invasion by Martians.

Sometimes a modifier seems awkward in any position except between *to* and the verb.

- Welles wanted **to** realistically **portray** a Martian invasion for the radio audience.

If, however, you are required never to split an infinitive, you can usually revise the sentence to avoid the split.

- Welles wanted his "Martian invasion" **to sound** realistic to the radio audience.

14d How can I keep modifiers from disrupting a sentence?

Watch out for complex descriptive PHRASES or CLAUSES that separate the subject and verb of a sentence. They make a sentence hard to understand and overly complicated, disturbing its smooth flow.

- ~~The invention of the automobile, if~~ If we consider the complete history of many people working independently in different countries, the invention of the automobile should probably be credited to Nicholas Cugnot in 1769.

Also, interrupting a VERB PHRASE with modifiers makes a sentence lurch instead of flow. Observe the general rule to put modifiers next to the word they modify.

- Karl Benz has~~, by most automobile historians,~~ been given
  by most automobile historians
  credit ^ for the invention of the automobile.

14e How should I correct dangling modifiers?

A **dangling modifier** is an introductory phrase that hangs (dangles) helplessly because the NOUN it modifies is not the intended subject. Introductory phrases attach their meaning to the first noun after the phrase. That noun is the sentence's subject. If some other word falls in that position, the result is confusing and may be humorous.

DANGLING MODIFIER While participating in a revolution in the Caribbean, terrible events overtook the novel's heroine. [The *terrible events* did not participate in the revolution.]

CORRECT **While the novel's heroine was participating** in a revolution in the Caribbean, terrible events overtook her.

DANGLING MODIFIER Reading Margaret Atwood's novel *Bodily Harm,* the ending was shocking. [The *ending* did not read the novel.]

CORRECT Reading Margaret Atwood's novel *Bodily Harm,* **I was shocked** by the ending.

CORRECT **I read** Margaret Atwood's novel *Bodily Harm* and was shocked by the ending.

15 CONCISENESS

Concise writing is direct and to the point. Wordy writing is filled with unnecessary words. Readers must clear away the excess words before the sentence can deliver its message.

15a How can I eliminate unnecessary words?

Wordy writing is padded with deadwood—empty words and phrases that increase the word count but do not contribute meaning. Prune your sentences of deadwood.

- The local
  ~~In fact, the~~ ^ television station ~~which was situated in the local area~~
  for
  had won ~~a great~~ many awards ~~as a result of~~ ^ its ~~having been~~
  ~~involved in the~~ coverage of ~~all kinds of~~ controversial issues.

Eliminating unneeded words 21

EMPTY WORDS	WORDY EXAMPLES REVISED
as a matter of fact	~~As a matter of fact, s~~Statistics show that many marriages end in divorce.
at the present time	The bill is being debated ~~at the present time~~ now.
because of the fact that, in light of the fact that, due to the fact that	Because ~~of the fact that~~ a special exhibit is scheduled, the museum is open late.
by means of	We travelled by ~~means of~~ car~~s~~.
factor	The project's final cost was an essential ~~factor to consider~~ consideration.
that exists	The crime rate ~~that exists~~ is unacceptable.
for the purpose of	A work crew arrived ~~for the purpose of~~ to fix~~ing~~ the pothole.
have a tendency to	The mixture ~~had a tendency~~ tended to evaporate.
in a very real sense	~~In a very real sense, d~~Drainage problems caused the house to flood.
in the case of	~~In the case of t~~The proposed tax~~,~~ angered residents. ~~were angry.~~
in the final analysis	~~In the final analysis, n~~No observer described the apparent thief accurately.

→

Eliminating unneeded words ***(continued)***

EMPTY WORDS	WORDY EXAMPLES REVISED
in the event that	~~In the event that~~ If you are late, I will buy your tickets.
in the process of	We are ~~in the process of~~ reviewing six sites.
it seems that	~~It seems that the~~ The union struck over wages.
manner	Most people looked at the snake ~~in a fearful manner~~ fearfully.
nature	The review was ~~of a~~ sarcastic ~~nature~~.
the point I am trying to make	~~The point I am trying to make is that news~~ News reporters should not invade people's privacy.
what I mean to say	~~What I mean to say is that~~ I expect a bonus.
type of	Gordon took a relaxing ~~type of~~ vacation.

15b How can I avoid redundancies?

Redundant writing delivers the same message more than once, but in slightly different words. Unlike planned repetition, which can create a powerful rhythmic effect, unplanned repetition can be irritating.

- ~~People anesthetized~~ Anesthetized people ~~for surgery~~ can remain semiconscious during surgery but may still feel no pain.

  [*Surgery* is used twice, but it is implied in *anesthetized.* The revision is concise.]

- Completing ~~Bringing~~ the project ~~to final completion~~ three weeks early, the new manager earned our respect. ~~respectful regard~~

  [*Completion* implies *final,* and *regard* implies *respect*. The concise revisions eliminate redundancy.]

- The rectangular package~~, rectangular in shape,~~ lay on the counter.

  [*Rectangular* is a *shape*. The concise revision eliminates redundancy.]

15c How can I eliminate wordy sentence structures?

Two sentence structures often cause wordiness problems: expletive constructions and passive voice.

Expletive constructions

An **expletive construction** places *it* or *there* and a form of *be* before the subject of the sentence. Remove the expletive and revise to make the sentence more direct.

- ~~It is necessary for~~ S~~s~~tudents must ~~to~~ fill out both registration forms.

- ~~There are three majors offered by~~ T~~t~~he computer science department offers three majors.

Passive voice

The PASSIVE VOICE is less lively and concise than the ACTIVE VOICE. Unless your meaning justifies using the passive voice, prefer the active voice.

PASSIVE Volunteer work was done by the students for credit in sociology. [The passive is unnecessary. The students are the ones doing the action, so *students,* not *volunteer work,* should be the subject of the sentence.]

ACTIVE The students did volunteer work for credit in sociology.

ACTIVE Volunteer work earned the students credit in sociology. [Here, *volunteer work* can be the subject because it performs the action of the verb *earned*.]

Be particularly alert for passive-voice constructions that intend to mislead readers by not disclosing who is doing the action: *Cracks in the foundation of the structure had been found, but they were not considered serious.* Who found cracks and who decided that they were not serious could be important information.

15d How else can I reduce the number of words in my sentences?

You can try to combine and simplify sentences. Start by looking at them two at a time. See if you can reduce a sentence to a group of words that can be included in another sentence.

- ~~The *Titanic* was discovered~~ S~~s~~eventy-three years after being sunk by an iceberg~~.~~, ~~T~~the Titanic ~~wreck~~ was located in the Atlantic by a team of French and American scientists.

Within a sentence, try to shorten longer structures to a phrase or even to a single word.

- The *Titanic,* ~~which was~~ a huge ocean liner, sank in 1912.
- The scientists held a memorial service for the dead passengers and crew members. ~~who had died.~~
- ~~Loaded with luxuries, the~~ The luxury liner was thought to be unsinkable.

15e How do verbs affect conciseness?

ACTION VERBS are strong verbs. *Be* and *have* are weak verbs that lead to wordy sentences.

WEAK VERB	The plan before the city council has to do with tax rebates.
STRONG VERB	The plan before the city council proposes tax rebates.

ALERT: When you revise, look for the pattern *be* + ADJECTIVE + *of* (such as *be aware of, be capable of*). These phrases can often be replaced with one-word verbs: *I envy* [not *am envious of*] *your ability as a public speaker.* Use *appreciate,* not *be appreciative of; illustrate,* not *be illustrative of;* and *support,* not *be supportive of.* **!**

When you revise, look for NOUNS that are derived from verbs. They usually end with *-ance, -ment,* and *-tion.* Turning these nouns into verbs gives you the chance to be more concise.

NO The accumulation of paper went on for more than thirty years.

YES The paper **accumulated** for more than thirty years.

16 COORDINATION AND SUBORDINATION

COORDINATION and SUBORDINATION help writers communicate relationships between ideas.

TWO IDEAS The sky turned brighter.

The wind calmed down.

COORDINATED VERSION The sky turned brighter, and the wind calmed down. [Here, *sky* and *wind* get equal emphasis.]

SUBORDINATED VERSIONS As the sky turned brighter, the wind calmed down. [Here, *wind* is the subject and main focus of the sentence.]

As the wind calmed down, the sky turned brighter. [Here, *sky* is the subject and main focus of the sentence.]

16a How does coordination show that ideas are equivalent?

COORDINATION gives you a grammatical strategy to show that ideas are equal or balanced. A **coordinate** (or **compound**) **sentence** has INDEPENDENT CLAUSES joined by a semicolon or by a coordinating conjunction (*and, but, for, or, nor, yet, so*).

- The sky turned brighter, and the wind calmed down.
- The sky turned brighter; the wind calmed down.

ALERT: Use a comma before a coordinating conjunction that joins two independent clauses (50c). **!**

16b How can I avoid problems with coordination?

Two problems can occur with coordination. First, when unrelated or nonequivalent ideas are joined with a coordinating conjunction, the result is an illogical sentence.

NO Computers came into common use in the 1970s, and they sometimes make costly errors. [The statement in each INDEPENDENT CLAUSE is true, but the ideas are not logically connected and therefore should not be coordinated.]

YES Computers came into common use in the 1970s, and now they are indispensable business tools.

A second problem is overused coordination. Stringing sentences together with coordinating conjunctions (*and, but, for, or, nor, yet, so*) does not make the relationships among ideas clear.

NO Dinosaurs could have disappeared for many reasons, and one theory holds that the climate suddenly became cold, and another suggests that a sudden shower of meteors and asteroids hit the earth, so the impact created a huge dust cloud that caused a false winter. The winter lasted for years, and the dinosaurs died.

YES Dinosaurs could have disappeared for many reasons. One theory holds that the climate suddenly became cold, and another suggests that a sudden shower of meteors and asteroids hit the earth. The impact created a huge dust cloud that caused a false winter. The winter lasted for years, killing the dinosaurs.

16c How does subordination show relationships of nonequivalent ideas?

Subordination gives you a grammatical strategy to show that one idea in a sentence is more important than another. The more important idea goes in an INDEPENDENT CLAUSE; the less important (subordinate) idea goes in a DEPENDENT CLAUSE. The information you choose to subordinate depends on the meaning you want to deliver.

UNCLEAR RELATIONSHIPS

- In 1911, two ranchers had to fight a dangerous Alberta snowstorm. They were looking for cattle. They came to a canyon. They saw outlines of buildings through the snow. Survival then seemed certain.

CLEAR RELATIONSHIPS

- In 1911, two ranchers had to fight a dangerous Alberta snowstorm while they were looking for cattle. When they came to a canyon, they saw outlines of buildings through the snow. Survival then seemed certain.

A subordinating word at the start of a clause makes the clause dependent. SUBORDINATING CONJUNCTIONS, listed in Box 22, start ADVERB CLAUSES. RELATIVE PRONOUNS (*who, which, that*) and RELATIVE ADVERBS (such as *where* or *why*) start ADJECTIVE CLAUSES.

Subordination patterns 22

Sentences with Adverb Clauses

- **Adverb clause,** independent clause.
  - **After the sky grew dark,** the wind died suddenly.
- Independent clause, **adverb clause.**
  - Birds stopped singing, **as they do during an eclipse.**
- Independent clause, **adverb clause.**
  - The stores closed **before the storm began.**

Sentences with Adjective Clauses

- Independent clause, **restrictive (essential)* adjective clause.**
  - Weather forecasts warned of a storm **that might bring a 45-centimetre snowfall.**
- Independent clause, **nonrestrictive (nonessential)* adjective clause.**
  - Spring is the season for tornadoes, **which may have wind speeds over 350 kilometres an hour.**

→

Subordination patterns ***(continued)***

- Beginning of independent clause, **restrictive (essential)* adjective clause,** end of independent clause.
    - Anyone **who lives through a tornado** remembers the experience.
- Beginning of independent clause, **nonrestrictive (nonessential)* adjective clause,** end of independent clause.
    - The sky, **which had been clear,** turned greenish black.

*For an explanation of restrictive and nonrestrictive elements, see (50f).

16d How can I avoid problems with subordination?

Two problems can occur with subordination. The first, **illogical subordination,** occurs when a SUBORDINATING CONJUNCTION does not communicate a sensible relationship between the INDEPENDENT CLAUSE and the DEPENDENT CLAUSE (Box 52).

NO Because Beethoven was deaf when he wrote them, his final symphonies were masterpieces. [*Because* is illogical. It conveys that the masterpieces resulted from the deafness.]

YES Although Beethoven was deaf when he wrote them, his final symphonies were masterpieces. [*Although* is logical. It conveys that Beethoven wrote masterpieces despite being deaf.]

A second problem is **overused subordination,** which crowds too many images or ideas together. It causes readers to lose track of the message. Always check carefully to see whether the meaning of a sentence with two or more dependent clauses is clear.

NO A new technique for eye surgery, which is supposed to correct nearsightedness, which previously could be corrected only by glasses, has been developed, although many doctors do not approve of the new technique because it can create unstable vision.

YES A new technique for eye surgery, which is supposed to correct nearsightedness, has been developed. Previously, nearsightedness could be corrected only by glasses. Many doctors do not approve of the new technique, however, because it can create unstable vision. [In the revision, one long sentence is broken into three sentences, making the material easier to read and the relationships among ideas clearer.]

17 SENTENCE STYLE

To develop your writing style, experiment with the techniques described in this chapter—parallelism, sentence variety, and emphasis.

17a What is parallelism?

When words, phrases, or clauses within a sentence grammatically match, the result is **parallelism.** Parallelism serves to emphasize information or ideas. Also, balance and rhythm in parallel structures add grace to your writing.

PARALLEL WORDS Recommended exercise includes running, swimming, and cycling.

PARALLEL PHRASES Exercise helps people maintain healthy bodies and handle mental pressures.

PARALLEL CLAUSES Many people exercise because they want to look healthy, because they need to increase stamina, and because they hope to live longer.

17b How can I avoid faulty parallelism?

You can avoid faulty parallelism by checking that words, PHRASES, or CLAUSES occur in the same grammatical form.

NO The strikers had tried shouting, threats, and pleading.

YES The strikers had tried shouting, threatening, and pleading.

YES The strikers had tried shouts, threats, and pleas.

NO The strikers read the offer, were discussing it, and the unanimous decision was to reject it.

YES The strikers read the offer, discussed it, and unanimously decided to reject it.

17c How should I use parallelism with conjunctions?

Words, phrases, or clauses joined with coordinating conjunctions (*and, but, for, or, nor, yet, so*) usually deliver their message most clearly and concisely when put in parallel form.

> You come to understand what to expect when you tease a cat, or toss a pebble in a pool, or touch a hot stove.
>
> —Ann E. Berthoff, *Forming, Thinking, and Writing*

Parallel forms are also usually called for when you link elements of a sentence with CORRELATIVE CONJUNCTIONS (such as *either . . . or* and *not only . . . but also*).

> Differing expectations for marriage can lead not only to disappointment but also to anger.
>
> —Norman DuBois, student

ALERT: A VERB or a PREPOSITION immediately *before* the first correlative conjunction in a pair carries its meaning to both pairs: *Look **in both** the encyclopedia **and** the dictionary.* That same verb or preposition positioned *after* the first conjunction must be repeated—or another verb or preposition must be used—after the second conjunction in the pair: *Look **both in** the encyclopedia **and in** the dictionary.* **!**

17d How does parallelism intensify my message?

Deliberate repetition of word forms, word groups, and sounds creates a rhythm that intensifies a sentence's message. Repetition is a highly effective technique if not overused.

> Travel a thousand miles by train and you are a brute; pedal five hundred on a bicycle and you remain basically a bourgeois; paddle a hundred in a canoe and you are already a child of nature.
>
> —Pierre Elliott Trudeau, "The Ascetic in a Canoe"

Balanced sentences use parallel structures to intensify ideas that you compare or contrast.

> By night, the litter and desperation disappeared as the city's glittering lights came on; by day, the filth and despair reappeared as the sun rose.
>
> —Jennifer Kirk, student

17e What is sentence variety?

Sentence variety results when you use sentences of various lengths and structures, communicating distinctions among ideas and helping your readers understand your main idea. Sentence variety also avoids monotonous rhythm in writing.

Revising strings of short sentences

Sometimes, several short sentences in a row can create impact. But unplanned strings of many short sentences are boring and do not establish relationships among ideas. Vary sentence length to distinguish the major points of your essay from its minor points.

NO There is a problem. It is widely known as sick-building syndrome. It is really indoor air pollution. It causes office workers to suffer. They have trouble breathing. They have painful rashes. Their heads ache. Their eyes burn.

YES Widely known as sick-building syndrome, indoor air pollution causes office workers to suffer. They have trouble breathing. They have painful rashes. Their heads ache. Their eyes burn. [Many revisions are possible; this one uses a long sentence to introduce the idea of indoor air pollution and its victims and then uses a series of short sentences to emphasize each problem it causes. The revised version is also more concise, reducing 38 words to 28.]

Revising for a mix of sentence lengths

To emphasize one idea among many others, express it in a sentence that is noticeably different in length or structure from the sentences surrounding it.

> Today is one of those excellent January partly cloudies in which light chooses an unexpected landscape to trick out in gilt, and then shadow sweeps it away. **You know you are alive.** You take

huge steps, trying to feel the planet's roundness arc between your feet.

—Annie Dillard, *Pilgrim at Tinker Creek*

17f How does the subject of a sentence affect emphasis?

The SUBJECT of a sentence establishes the focus for that sentence. You want the subject to correspond to the emphasis you intend to communicate. The following sentences all contain the same information. Notice how changing each subject (and VERB) affects meaning and emphasis.

- Our study showed that 25 percent of undergraduates' time is spent eating or sleeping. [Focus is on the study.]
- Undergraduates eat or sleep 25 percent of the time, according to our study. [Focus is on the students.]
- Eating or sleeping occupies 25 percent of undergraduates' time, according to our study. [Focus is on eating and sleeping.]
- Twenty-five percent of undergraduates' time is spent in eating or sleeping, according to our study. [Focus is on the percentage of time.]

17g How does adding modifiers affect variety and emphasis?

You can add richness and variety to your writing with MODIFIERS. For example, try beginning a sentence with a modifier. This pattern attracts attention because it is different from the SUBJECT-first pattern of most English sentences.

How you expand a sentence with modifiers depends on the focus you want and the way the sentence works with surrounding sentences. Position modifiers carefully so that meaning attaches where it belongs (Chapter 14).

BASIC SENTENCE	The river rose.
ADJECTIVE	The **swollen** river rose.
ADVERB	The river rose **dangerously.**
PREPOSITIONAL PHRASE	**In April,** the river rose **above its banks.**
PARTICIPIAL PHRASE	**Swelled by melting snow,** the river rose, **flooding the farmland.**
ABSOLUTE PHRASE	**Trees swirling away in the current,** the river rose.

ADVERB CLAUSE	**Because the snows had been heavy that winter,** the river rose.
ADJECTIVE CLAUSE	The river, **which runs through vital farmland,** rose.

17h How does inverting standard word order affect variety and emphasis?

Standard word order in English sentences places the SUBJECT before the VERB: *The mayor* [subject] *walked* [verb] *into the room.* Because this pattern is so common, any variation from it creates emphasis. **Inverted word order** places the verb before the subject: *Into the room walked* [verb] *the mayor* [subject]. Used sparingly, inverted word order creates both variety and emphasis.

18 USAGE GLOSSARY

This usage glossary presents the customary manner of using particular words and phrases. "Customary manner," however, is not as firm in practice as the term implies. Usage standards change. If you think a word's usage might differ from what you read here, consult a dictionary published more recently than this book.

As used here, *informal* and *colloquial* indicate words or phrases that occur commonly in speech but should be avoided in academic writing. *Nonstandard* indicates words or phrases that should not be used in either standard spoken English or writing.

This glossary also includes some of the most commonly confused words that are listed on pages 122–28 (Box 24). Parts of speech, sentence structures, and other grammatical terms mentioned below are defined in the Terms Glossary, which starts on page 497.

a, an Use *a* before words that begin with a consonant (*a dog, a grade, a hole*) or a consonant sound (*a one-day sale, a European*). Use *an* before words or acronyms that begin with a vowel sound or a silent *h* (*an owl, an hour, an MRI*). Most North American English uses *a,* not *an,* before words starting with a pronounced *h: a* [not *an*] *historical event.*

accept, except The verb *accept* means "agree to; receive." As a preposition, *except* means "leaving out." As a verb, *except* means "exclude, leave out."

- The workers were ready to **accept** [verb] management's offer **except** [preposition] for one detail: They wanted the no-smoking rule **excepted** [verb] from the contract.

advice, advise *Advice,* a noun, means "recommendation." *Advise,* a verb, means "recommend; give advice."

- I **advise** [verb] you to follow your car mechanic's **advice** [noun].

affect, effect As a verb, *affect* means "cause a change in; influence." (*Affect* also functions as a noun in the discipline of psychology.) As a noun, *effect* means "result or conclusion"; as a verb, it means "bring about."

- Because loud music **affects** people's hearing, many bands have **effected** quieter concerts. Many fans, however, happily ignore the harmful **effects** of high decibel levels.

aggravate, irritate *Aggravate* is used colloquially to mean "irritate." In formal writing, use *aggravate* to mean "intensify; make worse." Use *irritate* to mean "annoy; make impatient."

- The coach was **irritated** by her assistant's impatience, which **aggravated** the team's inability to concentrate.

ain't *Ain't* is a nonstandard contraction. Use *am not, is not,* or *are not* instead.

all ready, already *Already* means "before; by this time." *All ready* means "completely prepared."

- The team was **all ready** to play, and the manager had **already** given the lineup card to the umpire.

all right *All right* should be written as two words, never one (not *alright*).

all together, altogether *All together* means "in a group, in unison." *Altogether* means "entirely, thoroughly."

- The judge decided it was **altogether** absurd to expect the jurors to stay **all together** in one hotel room.

allude, elude *Allude* means "refer to indirectly." *Elude* means "escape notice."

- The detective **alluded** to budget cuts when she said, "Events beyond our control enabled the suspect to **elude** us."

allusion, illusion An *allusion* is an indirect reference to something. An *illusion* is a false impression or idea.

- The applicant's casual **allusions** to many European tourist attractions created the **illusion** that he had seen them himself.

a lot *A lot* is informal for *a great deal* or *a great many;* avoid it in academic writing. Write it as two words [not *alot*] when you do use it.

a.m., p.m. These may also be written as A.M., P.M. Use these abbreviations only with numbers, not as substitutes for *morning, afternoon,* or *evening.*

- We will arrive **in the afternoon** [*not* in the p.m.], and we have to leave no later than **8:00 a.m.**

among, amongst, between Use *among* for three or more items and *between* for two items. Canadian English prefers *among* to *amongst.*

- My roommates and I discussed **among** [*not* between *or* amongst] ourselves the choice **between** staying in school and getting full-time jobs.

amoral, immoral *Amoral* means "neither moral nor immoral"; it can also mean "not concerned with right or wrong." *Immoral* means "morally wrong."

amount, number Use *amount* for uncountable things (*wealth, work, corn, happiness*). Use *number* for countable items.

- The **amount** of rice to cook depends on the **number** of dinner guests.

an See *a, an.*

and/or This term is appropriate in business and legal writing when either or both of two items can apply: *The process is quicker if you have a modem and/or a fax machine.* In the humanities, usually express the alternatives in words: *This process is quicker if you have a modem, a fax machine, or both.*

anymore Use *anymore* with the meaning "now, any longer" only in negations or questions.

- No one knits **anymore.**

In positive statements, use an adverb such as *now.*

- Summers are so hot **now** [*not* anymore] that holding yarn is unbearable.

anyone, any one *Anyone* is a singular indefinite pronoun meaning "any person at all." *Any one* (two words), an adjective modifying a pronoun, means a member of a group.

- **Anyone** could test-drive **any one** of the display vehicles.

anyplace *Anyplace* is informal. Use *any place* or *anywhere* instead.

anyways, anywheres *Anyways* and *anywheres* are nonstandard. Use *anyway* and *anywhere* instead.

apt, likely, liable *Apt* and *likely* are used interchangeably. Strictly, *apt* indicates a tendency or inclination. *Likely* indicates a reasonable expectation or greater certainty than *apt. Liable* denotes legal responsibility or implies unpleasant consequences.

- Alan is **apt** to leave early on Friday. I will **likely** go with him to the party. [Some authorities in Canada do not allow this use of *likely* and prefer to use *probably* here.] Maggy and Gabriel are **liable** to be angry if we do not show up.

as, as if, as though, like Use *as, as if,* or *as though,* but not *like,* to introduce clauses.

- This hamburger tastes good, **as** [*not* like] a hamburger should. It tastes **as if** [*or* as though *but not* like] it was grilled by a chef.

Both *as* and *like* can function as prepositions in comparisons. Use *as* to indicate equivalence between two nouns or pronouns. Use *like* to indicate similarity but not equivalence.

- Beryl acted **as** [*not* like] the moderator in our panel.

- Mexico, **like** [*not* as] Argentina, belongs to the United Nations.

assure, ensure, insure *Assure* means "promise, convince." *Ensure* and *insure* both mean "make certain or secure," but *insure* is reserved for financial or legal certainty, as in insurance.

- The agent **assured** me that he could **insure** my inline skates but that only I could **ensure** that my elbows and knees would outlast the skates.

as to *As to* is nonstandard. Use *about* instead.

awful, awfully Do not use *awful* or *awfully* in place of *terribly, extremely,* or *very.*

a while, awhile As two words, *a while* (an article and a noun) can function as a subject or object. As one word, *awhile* is an adverb; it modifies verbs. In a prepositional phrase, the correct form is *a while: for a while, in a while, after a while.*

- The seals basked **awhile** in the sun after they had played for **a while** in the sea.

backup, back up As a noun, *backup* is a copy of electronic data. *Backup* can also be used as an adjective. *Back up* is a verb phrase.

- Many people recommend that you **back up** even your **backup** disks and protect all your **backups** from heat.

bad, badly *Bad* is an adjective; use it after linking verbs. (Remember that verbs like *feel* and *smell* can function as either linking verbs or action verbs.) *Badly* is an adverb and is nonstandard after linking verbs (43d).

- Farmers feel **bad** because a **bad** drought has **badly** damaged the crops.

been, being *Been* is the past participle of the verb *be; being* is the present participle of *be.* As main verbs, *being* and *been* must be used with auxiliary verbs.

- You **are being** [*not* being] silly if you think I believe you **have been** [*not* been] to Sumatra.

being as, being that *Being as* and *being that* are nonstandard. Use *because* or *since* instead.

- We forfeited the game **because** [*not* being as *or* being that] our goalie has appendicitis.

beside, besides *Beside* is a preposition meaning "next to, by the side of."

- She stood **beside** the new car, insisting that she would drive.

As a preposition, *besides* means "other than, in addition to."

- No one **besides** her had a driver's licence.

As an adverb, *besides* means "also, moreover."

- **Besides,** she owned the car.

better, had better Used in place of *had better, better* is informal.

- We **had better** [*not* We better] be careful.

between See *among, amongst, between.*

breath, breathe *Breath* is a noun; *breathe* is a verb.

- Don't take a **breath** [noun] or you will **breathe** [verb] diesel fumes.

bring, take Use *bring* to indicate movement from a distant place to a near place or to the speaker. Use *take* to indicate movement from a near place or from the speaker to a distant place.

- If you **bring** a leash to my house, you can **take** the dog to the vet.

but, however, yet Use *but, however,* or *yet* alone, not in combination with each other.

- The economy is strong, **but** [*not* but yet *or* but however] unemployment is high.

calculate, figure, reckon These are colloquial regional terms for *estimate, imagine, expect, think,* and similar, more formal words.

can, may *Can* signifies ability or capacity; *may* requests or grants permission. In negations, however, *can* is acceptable in place of *may.*

- You **can** [*or* **may**] leave after lunch.

can't hardly, can't scarcely These double negatives are nonstandard (43c).

capitol, capital *Capitol* means "a building in which U.S. state legislators meet." *Capital* means either a city or wealth and resources.

- If they can generate enough **capital,** the residents of the state **capital** will build a new **capitol.**

censor, censure The verb *censor* means "delete objectionable material; judge." The verb *censure* means "condemn or reprimand officially."

- The town council **censured** the mayor for trying to **censor** a report.

chairman, chairperson, chair Many writers and speakers prefer the gender-neutral terms *chairperson* and *chair* to *chairman; chair* is more common than *chairperson.*

choose, chose *Choose* is the simple form of the verb. *Chose* is the past-tense form.

- I **chose** a movie last week, so you **choose** one tonight.

cite, site The verb *cite* means "quote by way of example, authority, or proof." The noun *site* means a particular place.

- The investigator **cited** evidence he had gathered from both the crime **site** and the defendant's personal Web **site.**

cloth, clothe *Cloth* is a noun meaning "fabric." *Clothe* is a verb meaning "cover with garments or fabric; dress."

- "**Clothe** me in red velvet," snapped the monarch, and servants scurried forward with **cloth.**

complement, compliment Both terms function as both nouns and verbs. As a noun, *complement* means "something that goes well with or completes." As a noun, *compliment* means "praise, flattery."

- The president's **compliment** was a fine **complement** to our celebration.

As a verb, *complement* means "bring to perfection, go well with; complete." As a verb, *compliment* means "praise, flatter."

- When the president **complimented** us, her praise **complemented** our joy.

conscience, conscious The noun *conscience* means "a sense of right and wrong." The adjective *conscious* means "being aware or awake."

- To live happily, be **conscious** of what your **conscience** tells you.

consensus of opinion This phrase is redundant; use *consensus* only.

continual(ly), continuous(ly) *Continual* means "occurring repeatedly." *Continuous* means "going on without interruption."

- Intravenous fluids were given **continuously** for three days after surgery, so nurses were **continually** hooking up new bottles of saline.

could care less *Could care less* is nonstandard; use *couldn't care less* instead.

could of *Could of* is nonstandard; use *could have* instead.

couple, a couple of These terms are nonstandard. Use *a few* or *several* instead.

- Rest for **a few** [*not* a couple *or* a couple of] minutes.

criteria, criterion A *criterion* is "a standard of judgment." *Criteria* is the plural form of *criterion.*

- Although charisma is an important **criterion** for political candidates to meet, voters must also consider other **criteria.**

data This is the plural of *datum,* a rarely used word. Informally, *data* is commonly used as a singular noun requiring a singular verb. In academic or professional writing, it is more acceptable to treat *data* as plural.

- The researchers' **data** suggest that some people become addicted to e-mail.

different from, different than *Different from* is preferred for formal writing, although *different than* is common in speech.

disinterested, uninterested *Disinterested* means "impartial, unbiased"; *uninterested* conveys the meaning "indifferent."

- Although jurors must be **disinterested,** justice cannot allow them to be **uninterested.**

don't *Don't* is a contraction for *do not,* but not for *does not* (*doesn't*).

- She **doesn't** [*not* don't] like crowds.

effect See *affect, effect.*

elude See *allude, elude.*

elicit, illicit The verb *elicit* means "draw forth or bring out." The adjective *illicit* means "illegal."

- The government's **illicit** conduct **elicited** mass protest.

emigrate (from), immigrate (to) *Emigrate* means "leave one country to live in another." *Immigrate* means "enter a country to live there."

ensure See *assure, ensure, insure.*

enthused *Enthused* is nonstandard. Use *enthusiastic* instead.

etc. *Etc.* is the abbreviation for the Latin *et cetera,* meaning "and the rest." For writing in the humanities, avoid using *etc.* other than in parentheses. Acceptable substitutes are *and the like, and so on,* and *and so forth.*

everyday, every day The adjective *everyday* means "daily." *Every day* is an adjective-noun combination that can function as a subject or an object.

- Being late for work has become an **everyday** occurrence. **Every day** that I am late brings me closer to being fired.

everyone, every one *Everyone* is a singular, indefinite pronoun. *Every one* (two words), an adjective modifying a pronoun, means each member in a group.

- **Everyone** enjoyed **every one** of the variety acts.

everywheres Nonstandard for *everywhere.*

except See *accept, except.*

explicit, implicit *Explicit* means "directly stated or expressed." *Implicit* means "implied, suggested."

- The warning on cigarette packs is **explicit:** "Smoking can kill you." The **implicit** message is "Don't smoke."

farther, further Many writers reserve *farther* for geographical distances and *further* for all other cases. Only *further* can be used to express *in addition*.

fewer, less Use *fewer* for anything that can be counted (with count nouns): *fewer dollars, fewer fleas, fewer haircuts.* Use *less* with collective or other noncount nouns: *less money, less scratching, less hair.*

finalize Academic audiences prefer *complete* or *make final* instead of *finalize.*

former, latter When two items are referred to, *former* signifies the first one and *latter* signifies the second. Avoid using *former* and *latter* when referring to more than two items.

- Brazil and Ecuador are South American countries. Portuguese is the most common language in the **former,** Spanish in the **latter.**

go, say *Go* is nonstandard when used to mean *say, says,* or *said.*

- After he stepped on my hand, he **said** [*not* he goes], "Your hand was in my way."

gone, went *Gone* is the past participle of *go; went* is the past tense of *go.*

- They **went** [*not* gone] to the concert after Ira **had gone** [*not* had went] home.

good, well *Good* is an adjective. Using it as an adverb is nonstandard. *Well* is the equivalent adverb.

- **Good** maintenance helps cars run **well.**

good and This phrase is a nonstandard intensifier; omit it.

- They were **exhausted** [*not* good and tired].

got, have *Got* is nonstandard in place of *have.*

- What do we **have** [*not* got] for supper?

hardly See *can't hardly, can't scarcely.*

have, of Use *have,* not *of,* after such verbs as *could, should, would, might,* and *must.*

- You **should have** [*not* should of] called first.

have got, have to, have got to Avoid using *have got* when *have* alone delivers your meaning.

- I **have** [*not* have got] two more sources to read.

Avoid using *have to* or *have got to* for *must.*

- I **must** [*not* have got to] finish this assignment today.

he/she, s/he, his/her To avoid sexist language, use *he or she* or *his or her*. A less wordy solution is to use plural pronouns and antecedents.

- The **mourners** bowed their heads.
- Everyone bowed **his or her** head. [*Not* Everyone bowed his head.]

hopefully An adverb meaning "with hope, in a hopeful manner," *hopefully* can modify a verb, an adjective, or another adverb: *They waited hopefully for the plane to land. Hopefully* is commonly used as a sentence modifier with the meaning "I hope," but you should avoid this usage in academic writing.

- **I hope** [*not* Hopefully] the plane will land safely.

humanity, humankind, humans, mankind To avoid sexist language, use *humanity, humankind,* or *humans* instead of *mankind.*

i.e. This abbreviation refers to the Latin term *id est.* Use a comma after it. In formal writing, use the English translation *that is.*

if, whether At the start of a noun clause, use either *if* or *whether.*

- I don't know **if** [*or* **whether**] I want to dance with you.

In conditional clauses, use *whether* (or *whether or not*) when alternatives are expressed or implied.

- I will dance with you **whether or not** I like the music. I will dance with you **whether** the next song is fast or slow.

In a conditional clause that does not express or imply alternatives, use *if.*

- **If** you promise not to step on my feet, I will dance with you.

illicit See *elicit, illicit.*

illusion See *allusion, illusion.*

immigrate See *emigrate, immigrate.*

immoral See *amoral, immoral.*

imply, infer *Imply* means "hint at or suggest." *Infer* means "draw a conclusion." A writer or speaker implies; a reader or listener infers.

- When the cabinet minister **implied** that she would be taking French lessons, reporters **inferred** that she was planning to run for her party's leadership.

incredible, incredulous *Incredible* means "extraordinary; not believable." *Incredulous* means "unable or unwilling to believe."

- Listeners were **incredulous** as the freed hostages described the **incredible** hardships they had experienced.

in regard to, with regard to, as regards, regarding Replace these wordy phrases with *about, concerning,* or *for.* Avoid the nonstandard *as regards to.*

inside of, outside of These phrases are nonstandard when used to mean *inside* or *outside.*

- She waited **outside** [*not* outside of] the dormitory.

In time references, avoid using *inside of* to mean "in less than."

- I changed clothes **in less than** [*not* inside of] ten minutes.

insure See *assure, ensure, insure.*

irregardless *Irregardless* is nonstandard. Use *regardless* instead.

is when, is where Avoid these constructions in giving definitions.

- Defensive driving **involves** [*not* is when] drivers' staying alert.

its, it's *Its* is a personal pronoun in the possessive case. *It's* is a contraction of *it is* or *it has.*

- The dog buried **its** bone.
- **It's** a hot day; **it's** seemed hotter than usual this summer.

kind, sort Use *this* or *that* with these singular nouns; use *these* or *those* with the plural nouns *kinds* and *sorts.* Also, do not use *a* or *an* after *kind of* or *sort of.*

- Drink **these kinds of** fluids [*not* this kind of fluids] on **this sort of** [*not* this sort of a] day.

kind of, sort of These phrases are colloquial adverbs. In formal writing, use *somewhat* instead.

- The campers were **somewhat** [*not* kind of] dehydrated after the hike.

later, latter *Later* means "after some time; subsequently." *Latter* refers to the second of two items.

- The college library stays open **later** than the town library; also, the **latter** is closed on weekends.

lay, lie *Lay* (*laid, laid, laying*) means "place or put something, usually on something else" and needs a direct object. *Lie* (*lay, lain, lying*), meaning "recline," does not take a direct object (40b). Substituting *lay* for *lie* is nonstandard.

- **Lay** [*not* lie] the blanket down, and then **lay** the babies on it so they can **lie** [*not* lay] in the shade.

leave, let *Leave* means "depart"; *let* means "allow, permit." *Leave* is nonstandard for *let.*

- **Let** [*not* Leave] me use your car tonight.

less See *fewer, less.*

lie See *lay, lie.*

like See *as, as if, as though, like.*

likely See *apt, likely, liable.*

lots, lots of, a lot of These are colloquial usages. Use *many, much,* or *a great deal* instead.

mankind See *humanity, humankind, humans, mankind.*

may See *can, may.*

maybe, may be *Maybe* is an adverb; *may be* is a verb phrase.

- **Maybe** [adverb] we can win, but our team **may be** [verb phrase] too tired.

may of, might of *May of* and *might of* are nonstandard. Use *may have* and *might have* instead.

media This word is the plural of *medium,* but common usage pairs it with a singular verb. In most cases, a more specific word is preferable.

- **Television reporters** offend [*not* The media offends] me by shouting personal questions at grief-stricken people.

morale, moral *Morale* is a noun meaning "a mental state relating to courage, confidence, or enthusiasm." As a noun, *moral* means an "ethical lesson implied or taught by a story or event"; as an adjective, *moral* means "ethical."

- One **moral** to draw from corporate downsizings is that overstressed employees suffer from low **morale.** Unhappy employees with otherwise high **moral** standards may steal from their employers.

most *Most* is nonstandard for *almost: Almost* [not *Most*] *all the dancers agree. Most* is correct as the superlative form of an adjective (*some, more, most*): *Most dancers agree.* It also makes the superlative form of adverbs and some adjectives: *most suddenly, most important.*

Ms. A women's title free of reference to marital status, equivalent to *Mr.* for men. For a woman who does not use *Dr.* or another title, use *Ms.* unless she requests *Miss* or *Mrs.*

must of *Must of* is nonstandard. Use *must have* instead.

nowheres Nonstandard for *nowhere.*

number See *amount, number.*

of Use *have* instead of *of* after the following verbs: *could, may, might, must, should,* and *would.* See *could of; may of, might of; must of; should of;* and *would of.*

off of *Off of* is nonstandard. Omit the *of.*

- Don't fall **off** [*not* off of] the piano.

OK, O.K., okay All three forms are acceptable in informal writing. In academic writing, try to express meaning more specifically.

- The weather was **satisfactory** [*not* okay] for the race.

on account of, owing to the fact that These phrases are wordy. Use *because* or *because of* instead.

- **Because** [not *owing to the fact that*] humidity was high, paper jammed in the photocopier.
- **Because of** [*not* On account of] the high humidity, paper jammed in the photocopier.

outside of See *inside of, outside of.*

percent, percentage Use *percent* with specific numbers: *two percent, 95 percent.* Use *percentage* to refer to less exact portions of a whole.

- Less than **six percent** of Canada's land is legally protected wilderness, a smaller **percentage** [*not* percent] than is commonly believed.

plus *Plus* is nonstandard as a substitute for *and, also, in addition,* or *moreover.*

- The band will give three concerts in Hungary, **and** [*not* plus] it will tour Poland for a month. **Also** [not *Plus*], it may perform once in Vienna.

precede, proceed *Precede* means "go before." *Proceed* means "advance, go on, undertake, carry on."

- **Preceded** by elephants and tigers, the clowns **proceeded** into the tent.

pretty *Pretty* is an informal qualifying word; use *rather, quite, somewhat,* or *very* in academic writing.

- The flu epidemic was **quite** [*not* pretty] severe.

principal, principle *Principle* means "a basic truth or rule." As a noun, *principal* means "chief person; main or original amount"; as an adjective, *principal* means "most important."

- During the assembly, the **principal** said, "A **principal** value in this society is the **principle** of free speech."

proceed See *precede, proceed.*

quotation, quote *Quotation* is a noun; *quote* is a verb. Do not use *quote* as a noun.

- The newspaper **quoted** the coroner's inquest, and the **quotations** (*not* quotes) quickly showed up in public health messages.

raise, rise *Raise* (*raised, raised, raising*) means "lift" and needs a direct object. *Rise* (*rose, risen, rising*) means "go upward" and does not take a direct object. Using these verbs interchangeably is nonstandard.

- If the citizens **rise** [*not* raise], they may **raise** the flag of liberty.

real, really These are nonstandard intensifiers.

reason is because This phrase is redundant; use *reason is that* instead.

- One **reason** we moved **is that** [*not* is because] we changed jobs.

reason why This phrase is redundant; use either *reason* or *why* instead.

- I still do not know the **reason that** [*or* **I still do not know why,** *not* the reason why] they left home.

regarding See *in regard to, with regard to, as regards, regarding.*

regardless See *irregardless.*

respective, respectively The adjective *respective* relates the noun it modifies to two or more individual persons or things. The adverb *respectively* refers to a second set of items in a sequence established by a preceding set of items.

- After the fire drill, Dr. Pan and Dr. Moll returned to their **respective** offices [that is, each to his or her office] on the second and third floors, **respectively.** [Dr. Pan has an office on the second floor; Dr. Moll has an office on the third floor.]

Do not confuse *respective* and *respectively* with *respectful* and *respectfully,* which refer to showing regard for or honour to something or someone.

rise See *raise, rise.*

scarcely See *can't hardly, can't scarcely.*

seen Past participle of *see* (*see, saw, seen, seeing*), *seen* is a nonstandard substitute for the past-tense form, *saw.* As a verb, *seen* must be used with an auxiliary verb.

- Last night, I **saw** [*not* seen] the show that you **had seen** in Halifax.

set, sit *Set* (*set, set, setting*) means "put in place, position, put down" and must have a direct object. *Sit* (*sat, sat, sitting*) means "be seated." Using these verbs interchangeably is nonstandard.

- Susan **set** [*not* sat] the sandwiches beside the salad, made Spot **sit** [*not* set] down, and then **sat** [*not* set] on the sofa.

shall, will, should *Shall* was once used with *I* or *we* for future-tense verbs, and *will* was used with all other persons: ***We shall*** *leave Monday, and* ***he will*** *leave Thursday. Will* is commonly used for all persons now.

Similarly, distinctions were once made between *shall* and *should. Should* is much more common with all persons now, although *shall* is used about as often as *should* in questions asking what to do: ***Shall*** [or ***Should***] *I get your jacket?*

should of *Should of* is nonstandard. Use *should have* instead.

sit See *set, sit.*

site See *cite, site.*

sometime, sometimes, some time The adverb *sometime* means "at an unspecified time." The adverb *sometimes* means "now and then." *Some time* is an adjective-noun combination meaning "an amount or span of time."

- **Sometime** next year we have to take qualifying exams. I **sometimes** worry about finding **some time** to study for them.

sort of See *kind of, sort of.*

stationary, stationery *Stationary* means "not moving." *Stationery* refers to paper and related writing products.

such *Such* is an informal intensifier; avoid it in academic writing unless it precedes a noun introducing a *that* clause.

- The play got **terrible** [*not* such bad] reviews. It was **such** a dull drama **that** it closed after one performance.

supposed to, used to The final *d* is essential in both phrases.

- We were **supposed to** [*not* suppose to] leave early. I **used to** [*not* use to] wake up as soon as the alarm rang.

sure *Sure* is nonstandard as a substitute for *surely* or *certainly.*

- I was **certainly** [*not* sure] surprised at the results.

sure and, try and Both phrases are nonstandard. Use *sure to* and *try to* instead.

than, then *Than* indicates comparison; *then* relates to time.

- Please put on your gloves, and **then** put on your hat. It is colder outside **than** inside.

that, which Use *that* with restrictive (essential) clauses only. *Which* can be used with both restrictive and nonrestrictive clauses; many writers, however, use *which* only for nonrestrictive clauses, using *that* for all restrictive clauses. (42h, 42j)

- The house **that** [*or* **which**] Jack built is on Beanstalk Street, **which** [*not* that] runs past the reservoir.

their, there, they're *Their* is a possessive. *There* means "in that place" or is part of an expletive construction (41h). *They're* is a contraction of *they are.*

- **They're** going to **their** accounting class in the building **there** behind the library. **There** are twelve sections of Accounting 101.

theirself, theirselves, themself These are nonstandard. Use *themselves* instead.

them Use *them* as an object pronoun only. Do not use *them* in place of the adjective *these* or *those.*

- Buy **those** [*not* them] strawberries.

then See *than, then.*

thusly *Thusly* is nonstandard. Use *thus* instead.

till, until Both are acceptable; except in expressive writing, avoid the contracted form *'til.*

to, too, two *To* is a preposition. *Too* is an adverb meaning "also; more than enough." *Two* is the number.

- When you go **to** Prince Edward Island, visit Green Gables. Go **to** one of the seaside restaurants for dinner, **too.** It won't be **too** expensive because **two** people can share a lobster.

toward, towards Both are acceptable; *toward* is somewhat more common in North America.

try and, sure and See *sure and, try and.*

type *Type* is nonstandard when used to mean *type of.*

- Use that **type of** [*not* type] glue on plastic.

uninterested See *disinterested, uninterested.*

unique *Unique* is an absolute adjective; do not combine it with *more, most,* or other qualifiers.

- Solar heating is **uncommon** [*not* somewhat unique] in northern latitudes. A **unique** [*not* very unique] heating system in one Quebec home uses hydrogen for fuel.

used to See *supposed to, used to.*

utilize Academic writers prefer *use* to *utilize.*

- The team **used** (*not* utilized) all its players to win the game.

wait on *Wait on* is an informal substitute for *wait for;* it is appropriate in the context of persons giving service to others.

- I had to **wait** half an hour **for** (*not* wait . . . on) that clerk to **wait on** me.

way, ways When referring to distance, use *way* rather than *ways.*

- He is a long **way** (*not* ways) from home.

well See *good, well.*

where *Where* is nonstandard when used for *that* as a subordinating conjunction.

- I read **that** [*not* where] Wayne Gretzky is the greatest hockey player ever.

whether See *if, whether.*

which See *that, which.*

who, whom Use *who* as a subject or a subject complement. Use *whom* as an object. (42q)

who's, whose *Who's* is a contraction of *who is* or *who has. Whose* is a possessive pronoun.

- **Who's** willing to drive? **Whose** truck should we take?

will See *shall, will*

-wise The suffix *-wise* means "in a manner, direction, or position." Be careful not to attach *-wise* indiscriminately to create new words rather than using good words that already exist. When in doubt, check your dictionary to be sure that a *-wise* word you want to use is acceptable.

would of *Would of* is nonstandard. Use *would have* instead.

your, you're *Your* is a possessive. *You're* is the contraction of *you are.*

- **You're** generous to volunteer **your** time at the elementary school.

19 WORD MEANINGS AND WORD IMPACT

19a How can I learn about words and their meanings?

A good dictionary tells you about the meaning and use of words. Three dictionaries intended for Canadian users are the *Gage Canadian Dictionary* (revised and expanded, 2000), the *ITP Nelson Canadian*

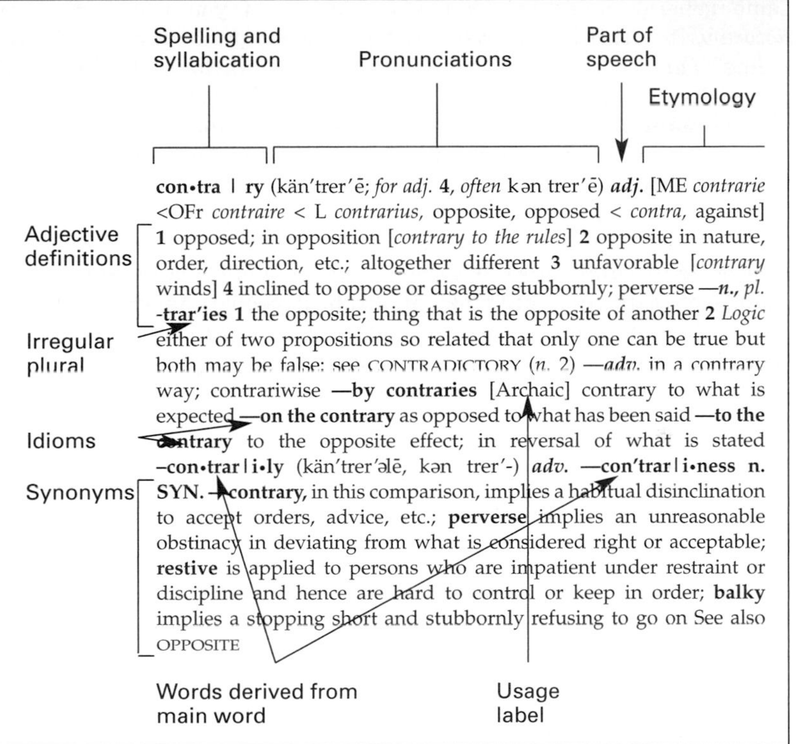

con•tra | ry (kän'trer'ē; *for adj.* **4**, *often* kən trer'ē) ***adj.*** [ME *contrarie* <OFr *contraire* < L *contrarius,* opposite, opposed < *contra,* against] **1** opposed; in opposition [*contrary to the rules*] **2** opposite in nature, order, direction, etc.; altogether different **3** unfavorable [*contrary* winds] **4** inclined to oppose or disagree stubbornly; perverse **—*n., pl.*** **-trar'ies 1** the opposite; thing that is the opposite of another **2** *Logic* either of two propositions so related that only one can be true but both may be false: see CONTRADICTORY (*n.* 2) **—*adv.*** in a contrary way; contrariwise **—by contraries** [Archaic] contrary to what is expected **—on the contrary** as opposed to what has been said **—to the contrary** to the opposite effect; in reversal of what is stated **–con•trar | i•ly** (kän'trer'əlē, kən trer'-) ***adv.*** **—con'trar | i•ness n.**
SYN.—contrary, in this comparison, implies a habitual disinclination to accept orders, advice, etc.; **perverse** implies an unreasonable obstinacy in deviating from what is considered right or acceptable; **restive** is applied to persons who are impatient under restraint or discipline and hence are hard to control or keep in order; **balky** implies a stopping short and stubbornly refusing to go on See also OPPOSITE

Dictionary of the English Language (1997), and the *Canadian Oxford Dictionary* (2002). For British style, Canadians usually consult the *Concise Oxford Dictionary;* some prefer an American dictionary such as *Webster's New World Dictionary*. Above is an annotated entry for the word *contrary* from *Webster's New World Dictionary,* Third College Edition, showing many of the kinds of information you can expect to find.

A dictionary's introductory pages describe the types of information found in word entries.

19b How can I choose exact words?

Diction—choice of words—affects the clarity and impact of your messages.

Denotation and connotation

Denotation is a word's explicit dictionary meaning—its definition. Interestingly, subtle shades of meaning differentiate words with the same general definitions. For example, would you use *famous* or *notorious* to describe a person well known for praiseworthy achievements? *Famous* is correct; *notorious* means "unfavourably known or talked about." Wilfrid Laurier is famous; Clifford Olson is notorious.

Connotation refers to ideas that a word implies. Connotations convey the associations and emotional overtones we bring to a word from our experiences. For example, the word *home* may evoke more emotion than does its denotation, "a dwelling place," or its synonym *house*. For some people, *home* may connote warmth, security, and the love of family. But for others, *home* may connote painful sights and sounds of institutionalized old or disabled people. As you write, be aware of the denotations and connotations of your words and of the special characteristics of your audience that may influence their reception of the words you choose (3b).

Specific and concrete language

Specific words identify individual items in a group (*Jeep, Honda*). **General words** relate to an overall group (*car*). **Concrete words** identify persons and things that can be perceived by the senses—seen, heard, tasted, felt, smelled (*black padded vinyl dashboard*). **Abstract words** denote qualities, concepts, relationships, acts, conditions, and ideas (*transportation*).

Specific and concrete words bring life to general and abstract words. As you write, try to supply specific, concrete details and examples to illustrate generalizations and abstractions. At the same time, keep in mind that most good writing combines general and specific with abstract and concrete.

- GENERAL SPECIFIC SPECIFIC SPECIFIC
My car, a 220-horsepower Trans Am, accelerates from 0 to 80
SPECIFIC SPECIFIC
kilometres per hour in 6 seconds but uses 13 litres of gas
per 100 kilometres.

- SPECIFIC ABSTRACT GENERAL
In contrast, the Dodge Lancer gets very good gas mileage: it uses
SPECIFIC GENERAL SPECIFIC
about 7 litres per 100 kilometres in highway driving and 8 litres
SPECIFIC
per 100 kilometres in stop-and-go traffic.

19c How can I increase my vocabulary?

The larger your vocabulary, the more you can understand, and the better you can express yourself in speaking and writing.

CHOOSING WHAT WORDS TO LEARN

- Mark unfamiliar words as you read. Underline or circle them, write them in the margin, or write them on index cards.
- Use context clues to figure out definitions, or look up the words in a dictionary. Write the definition in the margin or on an index card.
- Listen closely to speakers who know the language well. When you hear a new word, jot it down to look up later.

STUDYING NEW VOCABULARY WORDS

- Write each new word and its meaning on an index card, in a notebook, or on a computer list.
- Select eight to ten words to study each week.
- Set aside time each day to study your selected words. (Carry your cards, notebook, or computer printout to study in spare moments.)
- Try mnemonics—memory-jogging techniques—to help you memorize words. (*Desert* spelled with one *s* is filled with *s*and; *dessert* spelled with two *s*'s could stand for *s*trawberry *s*hortcake.)
- Use your newly learned vocabulary words in your writing and conversation.

Word roots, prefixes, and suffixes

Becoming aware of word parts can help you expand your vocabulary. **Prefixes** are syllables in front of a root word that modify its meaning. *Ante-* (*before*) before *room* refers to a waiting room leading to a larger room.

Suffixes are syllables added to the end of a word that modify its meaning. For example, *excite* plus *-able* means "able to be excited" and *excite* plus *-ment* means "the state of being excited."

19d What is appropriate language?

When you use **appropriate language,** your word choice suits your audience and purpose. Sometimes word choices are clearly appropriate or not. Often, the choices are subtle.

Levels of formality

Language has levels: highly informal, highly formal, and medium formal.

Certain word choices, including slang, colloquialisms, and regionalisms, create an informal tone. Informal tone also results from SENTENCE FRAGMENTS* and contractions. Language that is at a medium level of

* Words printed in small capital letters (such as SENTENCE FRAGMENTS) are defined in the Terms Glossary on pages 497–517.

formality uses standard vocabulary (for example, *learn,* not *wise up*), conventional sentence structure, and few or no contractions. Language that is highly formal is characterized by a Latinate vocabulary (*edify* for *instruct*) and, often, dramatic stylistic flourishes.

Appropriate language in academic writing uses language and sentence structure at a medium to somewhat formal level.

INFORMAL Ya know stars? They're a gas!

MEDIUM Gas clouds slowly changed into stars.

HIGHLY FORMAL The condensations of gas spun their slow gravitational pirouettes, slowly transmogrifying gas cloud into star.

—Carl Sagan, "Starfolk: A Fable"

Edited Canadian English

Academic writing in Canada uses edited Canadian English—the written language of a book like this one. Such language conforms to established rules of grammar, sentence structure, punctuation, and spelling. You often see English that varies from the standard, especially in advertisements. As a writer, do not think that because you see sentence fragments and slang in print, you can use them in academic writing.

You may find that early drafts of your academic writing contain slang or other informal language. There's nothing wrong with that, because you are getting your ideas down on paper. When you revise, however, check that your final draft is in edited Canadian English.

Slang, colloquialisms, and regionalisms

Slang, colloquial, and regional language are usually not appropriate for academic writing. **Slang** consists of new words (*phat* meaning "very good") or existing words that have new meanings (*wired* meaning "nervous"). Canadian slang borrows from that of the United States and Britain, but has also been enriched by our own special circumstances, including our obsession with hockey: *hat trick, deke,* and *rink rat*. Slang is appropriate only in very informal situations. **Colloquial language** is characteristic of casual conversation and informal writing: *The student flunked* [instead of *failed*] *chemistry.* **Regional** (also called **dialectal**) **language** is specific to a particular geographic area: *They have nary a cent.* (The term *idiom* may also be used to refer to regional or other dialects.)

Using slang, colloquial language, and regionalisms when writing for the general reading public tends to shut some people out of the communication. This is especially true of readers from other cultures and those whose first language is not English—an increasing number of your potential readers, given the global reach of communications today.

19e What is figurative language?

In **figurative language,** words are used for more than their literal meaning. There are various kinds of figurative language.

Analogy: comparing similar traits shared by dissimilar things. You can develop it in one, several, or many sentences.

- To understand the workings of a ball and socket joint, you can look at the movements of your own shoulder; the tool that you saw yesterday in the robotics laboratory was moved by a mechanical shoulder.

Irony: using words to suggest the opposite of their usual sense.

- Told that a minor repair would cost $2000 and take two weeks, she said, "Oh, how nice!"

Metaphor: creating images to compare otherwise dissimilar things. A metaphor does not use the words *like* or *as* to draw the comparison. (See below about not using mixed metaphors.)

- Rush-hour traffic in the city bled out through major arteries to the suburbs.

Overstatement (also called *hyperbole*): exaggerating deliberately for emphasis.

- If this paper is late, the professor will kill me.

Personification: assigning a human trait to something not human.

- The book begged to be read.

Simile: explicitly comparing dissimilar things. A simile uses the word *like* or *as*.

- Langston Hughes observes that a deferred dream dries up "like a raisin in the sun."

Understatement: emphasizing by using deliberate restraint.

- It feels warm when the temperature reaches 35 degrees.

Mixed metaphors

A **mixed metaphor** combines images that do not fit together: *Milking the workers without mercy, the supervisor barked orders at them.* The first image refers to taking milk from a cow, but the second image suggests a dog barking.

19f What is a cliché?

A **cliché** is an overused, worn-out expression. Clichés are once-clever phrases that have grown trite: *dead as a doornail, gentle as a lamb, straight as an arrow.* Sometimes a cliché is an action or idea such as "living happily every after." Rephrase a cliché, or delete it.

NO Needing to travel 800 kilometres before dark, we left at the crack of dawn.

YES Needing to travel 800 kilometres before dark, we left at dawn.

19g What is the effect of tone in writing?

Tone relates not so much to *what* you say as to *how* you say it. You want to control your choice of words so that they work with your message, not against it. Words are not just words. They need to fit your message and the audience you want to reach. In academic writing, you want to convey a reasonable tone in both content and choice of words. This calls for a medium to somewhat formal level of language (19d). Reject the misuses of word choice discussed below.

Slanted language

When you feel strongly about a topic, you might wrongly slip into biased or emotionally loaded language. Such slanted language does not persuade your readers to agree with you. Rather, it compromises your credibility. For example, suppose you are arguing against the use of animals in medical experimentation. If you refer to "laboratories where Frankensteins maim helpless puppies and kittens," you are using slanted language. Less loaded language would describe the "technicians who experiment on animals."

Pretentious language

Pretentious language draws attention to itself with big, unusual words and overly complex sentence structures. Overblown words usually obscure your message and damage your credibility with your reader.

NO The raison d'être for my matriculation in this institution of higher learning is the acquisition of an education.

YES My reason for being in college is to get an education.

Jargon

Every field—professions, academic disciplines, business, and sports—has its own specialized vocabulary. Specialized language can make communication clearer when your readers know what you mean. When your readers do not know what you mean, you are using **jargon.** If you need a special term when writing for a general audience, give the definition or revise into simpler terms.

> Eutrophic changes (or eutrophication) is the nutritional enrichment of the water, promoting the growth of aquatic plants.
>
> —Davis and Solomon, *The World of Biology*

Euphemisms

Euphemisms attempt to avoid unpleasant truths by substituting "tactful" words. When the truth is "My cousin lies," you should usually not write "My cousin has a wonderfully vivid imagination." Some euphemisms are properly tactful in social situations (using *passed away* instead of *died* when offering condolences).

20 GENDER-NEUTRAL LANGUAGE

20a What is gender in the English language?

Many languages assign gender (masculine, feminine, or neuter) to words. English, however, does not. Still, a few words in English have gender-specific meanings: *she, it, him, her, his, hers, its, man, boy, woman, girl, heiress.* When you use these words, you deliver gender information along with whatever other message you deliver.

20b What is gender-neutral language?

Using **gender-neutral language** means choosing words that do not carry a message of masculinity or femininity. Gender-neutral language is preferred over **sexist language,** which assigns roles or characteristics to people on the basis of gender. Sexist language unfairly discriminates against both sexes. It inaccurately assumes that all nurses and homemakers are female (calling them "she") and all physicians and car mechanics are male (calling them "he"). You can avoid sexist language. When you write, turn gender-specific words into gender-neutral words: use *police officer* instead of *policeman, people* or *humans* instead of *mankind,* and *salesperson* instead of *salesman* or *saleswoman.* Also eliminate your use of masculine pronouns in gender-neutral cases: *No one wants to lose his job.* The word *his* makes all females disappear.

Many writers avoid sexist pronouns by using a *he or she* construction rather than only *he* or only *she.* If you choose this method, remember that *he or she* acts as a singular pronoun, and as a sentence subject it calls for a singular verb. Be careful not to use too many *he or she* constructions in one sentence or in consecutive sentences. Revising the pronouns into the plural may be a better solution.

Also, gender-neutral language avoids demeaning stereotypes: *Women are bad drivers* or *Men can't cook.* Treat both sexes equally: If you describe a woman by her looks, clothes, age, or marital status, describe a man the same way in the same context. If you use the first name of one person in a partnership, use the first name of the other; if you use a title for one, such as *Mr., Dr.,* or *Mrs.,* use a title for both.

NO Mr. Miller and his wife, Jeannette, live in Regina.

YES Phil and Jeannette Miller live in Regina.

YES Mr. and Mrs. Miller live in Regina

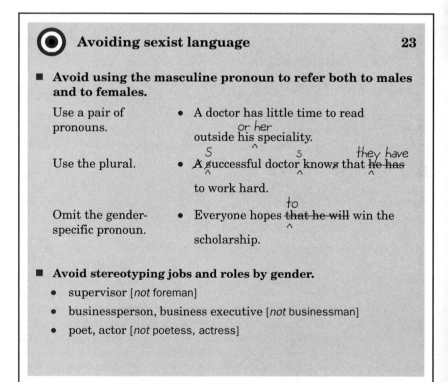

Avoiding sexist language 23

- **Avoid using the masculine pronoun to refer both to males and to females.**

Use a pair of pronouns.	• A doctor has little time to read outside his ^or her^ speciality.
Use the plural.	• ~~A~~ ^S^~~s~~uccessful doctor^s^ know~~s~~ that ^they have^ ~~he has~~ to work hard.
Omit the gender-specific pronoun.	• Everyone hopes ^to^ ~~that he will~~ win the scholarship.

- **Avoid stereotyping jobs and roles by gender.**
  - supervisor [*not* foreman]
  - businessperson, business executive [*not* businessman]
  - poet, actor [*not* poetess, actress]

→

Avoiding sexist language *(continued)*

- **Avoid expressions that exclude one sex.**
  - person [*not* man]
  - humanity, people [*not* mankind]
  - the average person [*not* the common man]
  - superstition [*not* old wives' tale]
- **Avoid demeaning and patronizing labels.**
  - nurse [*not* male nurse]
  - professional, executive, manager [*not* career girl]
  - My assistant will help you. *Or* Ida Morea will help you. [*not* My girl will help you.]

21 SPELLING

You might be surprised to learn that good spellers do not know how to spell every word they want to use. What they do know is to check if they are not sure of a word's spelling. If your inner voice questions a spelling, do what good spellers do—check your dictionary.

But how do you look up a word when you do not know how to spell it? If you know the first few letters, find them and then browse for the word. If you do not know the first few letters, think of a synonym and look it up in a thesaurus.

COMPUTER TIP: Computers usually have a spell-check. Use it with one caution: Spell-checks cannot identify words that are correctly spelled but not intended. For example, if you write *whole* for *hole* or *it's* for *its,* your spell-check will not catch the mistake.

Canadian spelling, because it has been influenced by both British and American spelling conventions, contains elements of both. The drift, however, is toward American conventions because of the influence of the media and new information technologies. Both American and British spellings may appear in any given piece of writing. Here are some examples:

labor	*or*	labour	humor	*or*	humour
theater	*or*	theatre	catalog	*or*	catalogue
check	*or*	cheque	realize	*or*	realise
defense	*or*	defence	program	*or*	programme

In both academic and business writing, your purpose for writing and the expectations of your audience may determine your choice of spelling conventions. Readers in the scientific and medical fields, and especially in information technologies, often expect American spellings to be used. Writing about Canadian history, government, and institutions usually uses a more British-oriented style—one that might be called a typically *Canadian* spelling style.

Whatever spelling you choose, aim for a logical and consistent style. If you use the spelling *labour* in a document, use *colour* as well; and if you spell *theatre,* use the spelling *centre.* Each of the Canadian dictionaries listed in section 19a has its own version of Canadian spelling that can guide you in finding a consistent spelling style. Journalists often follow the guidelines published by the Canadian Press in its handbooks *CP Caps and Spelling* and the *Canadian Press Stylebook*.

21a How are plurals spelled?

- **Adding *-s* or *-es*:** Plurals of most words are formed by adding *-s,* including words that end in "hard" *-ch* (sounding like *k*): *leg, legs; shoe, shoes; stomach, stomachs.* Words ending in *-s, -sh, -x, -z,* or "soft" *-ch* (as in *beach*) are formed by adding *-es* to the singular: *lens, lenses; beach, beaches; tax, taxes; coach, coaches.*
- **Words Ending in *-o*:** Add *-s* if the *-o* is preceded by a vowel: *radio, radios; cameo, cameos.* Add *-es* if the *-o* is preceded by a consonant: *potato, potatoes.* A few words can be made plural either way: *cargo, volcano, tornado, zero.*
- **Words Ending in *-f* or *-fe*:** Some *-f* and *-fe* words are made plural by adding *-s: belief, beliefs.* Others require changing *-f* or *-fe* to *-ves: life, lives; leaf, leaves.* Words ending in *-ff* or *-ffe* simply add *-s: staff, staffs; giraffe, giraffes.*
- **Compound Words:** For most compound words, add *-s* or *-es* at the end of the last word: *chequebooks, player-coaches.* In a few cases, the first word is made plural: *sister-in-law, sisters-in-law; kilometre per hour, kilometres per hour.* (For hyphenating compound words, see page 441 and Box 77 on page 442.)
- **Internal Changes and Endings Other Than *-s*:** A few words change internally or add endings other than *-s* to become plural: *foot, feet; man, men; mouse, mice; crisis, crises; child, children.*
- **Foreign Words:** The best advice is to check your dictionary. In general, many Latin words ending in *-um* form the plural by changing *-um* to *-a: curriculum, curricula; datum, data; medium,*

media; stratum, strata. Latin words that end in *-us* usually form the plural by changing *-us* to *-i: alumnus, alumni; syllabus, syllabi.* Greek words that end in *-on* usually form the plural with *-a: criterion, criteria; phenomenon, phenomena.*

- **One-Form Words:** Some words have the same form in both the singular and plural: *deer, elk, fish, quail.* Additional words indicate which form is meant: *one deer, nine deer; some rice.*

21b How are suffixes spelled?

A **suffix** is an ending added to a word to change the word's meaning or its grammatical function. For example, adding the suffix *-able* to the verb *depend* creates the adjective *depend**able.***

- ***-y* Words:** If the letter before the final *y* is a consonant, change the *y* to *i* and add the suffix. If, however, the suffix begins with an *i,* keep the *y: fry, fried, frying.* If the letter before the *-y* is a vowel, keep the final *y: employ, employed, employing.* These rules do not apply to irregular verbs (see Box 60 on p. 349).
- ***-e* Words:** Drop a final *e* when the suffix begins with a vowel unless this would cause confusion (*be + ing* does not become *bing*): *require, requiring; like, liking.* Keep the final *e* when the suffix begins with a consonant: *require, requirement; like, likely.* Exceptions include *argument,* and *truly.*
- **Words That Double a Final Letter:** If the final letter is a consonant, double it only if it passes these tests: (1) its last two letters are a vowel followed by a consonant; and (2) the suffix begins with a vowel: *drop, dropped; begin, beginning; forget, forgetful, forgettable.* (American spelling adds a third test. The word must have one syllable or be accented on the last syllable: *begin* [accent on last syllable], *beginning;* but *travel* [accent on first syllable], *traveling*. British spelling doubles the final consonant in many words even when the accent is not on the last syllable: *travel, travelling; worship, worshipper.*)
- ***-cede, -ceed, -sede* Words:** Only one word in the English language ends in *-sede: supersede.* Three words end in *-ceed: exceed, proceed, succeed.* All other words with endings that sound like "seed" end in *-cede: concede, intercede, precede.*
- ***-ally* and *-ly* Words:** The suffixes *-ally* and *-ly* turn words into adverbs. For words ending in *-ic,* add *-ally: logically, statistically.* Otherwise, add *-ly: quickly, sharply.*

21c What is the *ie, ei* rule?

The old rhyme for *ie* and *ei* is usually true:

- *I* before *e* [*believe, field, grief*],

  Except after *c* [*ceiling, conceit*],

  Or when sounded like "ay"

  As in *neighbour* and *weigh* [*eight, vein*].

Here are major exceptions (sorry!) to memorize:

- **ie:** conscience, financier, science, species
- **ei:** either, neither, leisure, seize, counterfeit, foreign, forfeit, sleigh, sleight (*as in* sleight of hand), weird

21d How are homonyms and other frequently confused words spelled?

Words that sound exactly like others (*to, too, two; no, know*) are called **homonyms.** They, as well as words that sound almost alike (*accept, except*), can be confusing.

"Swallowed" pronunciation—not pronouncing a letter or letters at the end of a word—can also cause misspellings. For example, the *-ed* endings in *used to* and *prejudiced* are often swallowed and pronounced as *use to* and *prejudice.* If you write what you hear, you will be incorrect.

Finally, some misspellings result from writing one word instead of two. The most common errors in this case are *all right* (not *alright*) and *a lot* (not *alot*).

Homonyms and other commonly confused words — 24

ACCEPT	to receive
EXCEPT	with the exclusion of
ADVICE	recommendation
ADVISE	to recommend

→

Homonyms and other commonly confused words *(continued)*

AFFECT	to influence [VERB]; emotion [NOUN]
EFFECT	result [NOUN]; to bring about or cause [VERB]
AISLE	space between rows
ISLE	island
ALL TOGETHER	everyone or everything in one place
ALTOGETHER	thoroughly
ALLUDE	to make indirect reference to
ELUDE	to avoid
ALLUSION	indirect reference
ILLUSION	false idea, misleading appearance
ALREADY	by this time
ALL READY	fully prepared
ALTAR	sacred platform or place
ALTER	to change
ARE	PLURAL form of *to be*
HOUR	sixty minutes
OUR	PLURAL form of *my*
ASCENT	the act of rising or climbing
ASSENT	consent [NOUN]; to consent [VERB]
ASSISTANCE	help
ASSISTANTS	helpers
BARE	nude, unadorned
BEAR	to carry [VERB]; an animal [NOUN]
BOARD	piece of wood
BORED	uninterested
BRAKE	device for stopping
BREAK	to destroy, make into pieces
BREATH	air taken in
BREATHE	to take in air

→

Homonyms and other commonly confused words *(continued)*

BUY	to purchase
BY	next to, through the agency of
CAPITAL	major city; money
CAPITOL	government building (U.S.)
CHOOSE	to pick
CHOSE	PAST TENSE of *choose*
CITE	to point out
SIGHT	vision
SITE	a place
CLOTHES	garments
CLOTHS	pieces of fabric
COARSE	rough
COURSE	path; series of lectures
COMPLEMENT	something that completes
COMPLIMENT	praise, flattery
CONSCIENCE	sense of morality
CONSCIOUS	awake, aware
COUNCIL	governing body
COUNSEL	advice [NOUN]; to advise [VERB]
DAIRY	place associated with milk production
DIARY	personal journal
DESCENT	downward movement
DISSENT	disagreement
DESERT	to abandon [VERB]; dry, usually sandy area [NOUN]
DESSERT	final, sweet course in a meal
DEVICE	a plan; an implement
DEVISE	to create

→

Homonyms and other commonly confused words *(continued)*

DIE	to lose life (dying) [VERB]; one of a pair of dice [NOUN]
DYE	to change the colour of something (dyeing)
DOMINANT	commanding, controlling
DOMINATE	to control
ELICIT	to draw out
ILLICIT	illegal
EMINENT	prominent
IMMANENT	living within; inherent
IMMINENT	about to happen
ENSURE	guarantee, protect
INSURE	buy or give insurance
ENVELOP	to surround
ENVELOPE	container for a letter or other papers
FAIR	light-skinned; just, honest
FARE	money for transportation; food
FORMALLY	conventionally, with ceremony
FORMERLY	previously
FORTH	forward
FOURTH	number four in a series
GORILLA	animal in ape family
GUERRILLA	soldier conducting surprise attacks
HEAR	to sense sound by ear
HERE	in this place
HOLE	opening
WHOLE	complete; an entire thing
HUMAN	relating to the species *Homo sapiens*
HUMANE	compassionate
ITS	POSSESSIVE form of *it*
IT'S	contraction for *it is* or *it has*

→

Homonyms and other commonly confused words *(continued)*

KNOW	to comprehend
NO	negative
LATER	after a time
LATTER	second one of two things
LEAD	heavy metal substance [NOUN]; to guide [VERB]
LED	PAST TENSE of *lead*
LIGHTENING	making lighter
LIGHTNING	storm-related electricity
LOOSE	unbound, not tightly fastened
LOSE	to misplace
MAY BE	might be [VERB]
MAYBE	perhaps [ADVERB]
MEAT	animal flesh
MEET	to encounter
MINER	a person who works in a mine
MINOR	underage
MORAL	distinguishing right from wrong; the lesson of a fable, story, or event
MORALE	attitude or outlook, usually of a group
OF	PREPOSITION indicating origin
OFF	away from, not on
PASSED	PAST TENSE of *pass*
PAST	at a previous time
PATIENCE	forbearance
PATIENTS	people under medical care
PEACE	absence of fighting
PIECE	part of a whole; musical arrangement
PERSONAL	intimate
PERSONNEL	employees

→

Homonyms and other commonly confused words ***(continued)***

PLAIN	simple, unadorned
PLANE	to shave wood [VERB]; aircraft [NOUN]
PRECEDE	to come before
PROCEED	to continue
PRESENCE	being at hand; attendance at a place or in something
PRESENTS	gifts
PRINCIPAL	foremost [ADJECTIVE]; school head [NOUN]
PRINCIPLE	moral conviction, basic truth
QUIET	silent, calm
QUITE	very
RAIN	water that falls to earth [NOUN]; to fall like rain [VERB]
REIGN	to rule
REIN	strap to guide or control an animal [NOUN]; to guide or control [VERB]
RAISE	to lift up
RAZE	to tear down
RESPECTFULLY	with respect
RESPECTIVELY	in that order
RIGHT	correct; opposite of *left*
RITE	ritual
WRITE	to put words on paper
ROAD	path
RODE	PAST TENSE of *ride*
SCENE	place of an action; segment of a play
SEEN	viewed
SENSE	perception, understanding
SINCE	measurement of past time; because

→

Homonyms and other commonly confused words *(continued)*

STATIONARY	standing still
STATIONERY	writing paper
THAN	in comparison with; besides
THEN	at that time; next; therefore
THEIR	POSSESSIVE form of *they*
THERE	in that place
THEY'RE	contraction for *they are*
THOROUGH	complete
THREW	PAST TENSE of *throw*
THROUGH	finished; into and out of
TO	toward
TOO	also; indicates degree (*too much*)
TWO	number following one
WAIST	midsection of the body
WASTE	discarded material [NOUN]; to squander, to fail to use up [VERB]
WEAK	not strong
WEEK	seven days
WEATHER	climatic condition
WHETHER	if, when alternatives are expressed or implied
WERE	PAST TENSE of *be*
WHERE	in which place
WHICH	one of a group
WITCH	female sorcerer
WHO'S	contraction for *who is* or *who has*
WHOSE	POSSESSIVE form of *who*
YORE	long past
YOUR	POSSESSIVE form of *you*
YOU'RE	contraction for *you are*

22 STARTING A RESEARCH PROJECT

22a What is research writing?

Every research project involves three processes: conducting research, understanding the results of your research, and writing an accurately documented paper based on your research. For some students, information comes from **primary sources**—from interviewing, reading diaries, and directly observing, measuring, or interpreting physical phenomena or social interactions. For most students, especially when writing college or university research papers, information comes from **secondary sources**—from reading, analyzing, discussing, and reviewing what people with respected academic and professional credentials have written.

Research writing can seem very intimidating, but if you follow a research plan (22e), the process is manageable. Keep in mind that the goal of every research project is to *attempt* to answer a question. Your first step is to choose a suitable research topic (22b). Because assignments rarely are phrased as questions, your next, crucial step is to think about, search for, and develop a research question (22c) that is suitable for a college- or university-level research paper.

22b How do I choose a research topic?

Some instructors assign a specific topic for research (for example, "the feasibility of making robots that act like humans"). Others assign a general subject ("artificial intelligence") and expect you to narrow it down to a manageable topic. Still other instructors expect you to choose a topic on your own ("Write a research paper on a topic of current importance").

A good research topic is narrow enough so that you can research and write about it within the time and length allowed in the assignment. Make sure that enough material has been published on the topic to offer you a sufficient number of sources and perspectives to answer your research question and write your paper.

A good topic generally allows you to demonstrate your critical thinking abilities. There are two broad ways of doing so. First, you might choose a topic on which intelligent people have formed different opinions. Then you might analyze your sources to decide which position appears most reasonable. Your paper might take the form of an argument (Chapter 10) that shows readers you have considered the various positions and reached a reasonable conclusion.

Second, you might choose to write an informative paper in which you *synthesize* several sources related to a complex subject. Writing a SYNTHESIS* means pulling together extensive information in an attempt to explain the essential points involved in a topic. For example, after you have read a dozen articles on the topic of artificial intelligence, you might try to identify three or four key points and then organize information from your reading around those points. Your goal is to clarify complicated or scattered information for your readers.

Finally, a good research topic is one that your readers will perceive as significant and worthwhile. That is, the topic is important or timely, your insights are fresh, or your synthesis is particularly clear and skilful.

To summarize, keep the following points in mind as you choose your topic:

- Select a topic that interests you. It will be your companion for quite a while, perhaps most of a semester.
- Choose a sufficiently narrow topic. Avoid topics that are too broad, such as *emotions*. A well-narrowed topic is *how people perceive and respond to anger in others*.
- Choose a topic that is worth researching. Avoid trivial topics that prevent you from doing what is expected of a student researcher: investigating ideas, analyzing them critically, and creating a synthesis of complex concepts.

NO Types of cars that are popular among teenagers.

YES The effect of SUVs on the environment.

The freedom to choose any topic you want sometimes creates what can be called a "research topic block." Don't panic. Instead, use some of these strategies for generating ideas:

- Browse through some textbooks in your area of interest. Read the table of contents and major headings. Scan the text for material that catches your eye. As you narrow your focus, note the names of important books and experts, often mentioned in reference lists at the end of the chapters or at the back of the book.
- Talk briefly with an instructor or another expert in your area of interest. Ask for the names of major books and authorities on the subject and for advice about subcategories related to your area of interest. Ask what issues currently seem important or "hot."

*Words printed in small capital letters (such as SYNTHESIS) are defined in the Terms Glossary on pages 497–517.

- Read an encyclopedia article about your area of interest and its subcategories. Never, however, stop with the encyclopedia—it is too basic for academic research, which demands a thorough search of a variety of sources.
- Browse through books and periodicals. Stroll through the open stacks of your library, if available, to find subjects that interest you, or spend some time in a good bookstore. Look at books as well as periodicals. Browse academic journals in fields that interest you. Thumb through more popular magazines as well.
- Browse the Internet. Many Web search engines provide a list of general categories on their opening screens (25b). Click on a general category to get subcategories. Browsing increasingly specific subcategories can turn up an interesting topic.

22c What is a research question?

A **research question** controls and drives your research. Without such a question, your research writing can become an aimless search for a haphazard collection of facts and opinions. Consider the difference between a paper on the topic "artificial intelligence" and a paper on the question "Does emotion have a place in the definition of artificial intelligence?" The question provides a clear focus for your research and a goal for your writing process. Depending on your question, you may write a successful paper even if your attempt to answer your research question is unsuccessful.

Attempt is an important word in research. Some research questions can lead to a final, definitive answer (for example, "How does penicillin destroy bacteria?"). Other research questions cannot (for example, "Is Parliament more responsible than the Supreme Court for setting social policy?"). When a question concerns a very recent or highly debatable topic, your answer calls for you to present a convincing, informed opinion. This means that you need to use sources that represent various viewpoints, and that your own position must take those viewpoints into account. In fact, all answers to research questions, whether definitive or not, need to be supported by thorough research that is based on (or supported by) reliable scholarly and expert sources.

As is true of the writing process for all essays and papers, your research writing often moves forward, loops back, and jumps ahead as you ask and refine your research question, read source material, take notes, SYNTHESIZE your findings, and support your findings with quotations, paraphrases, and summaries of your source materials. Consider the following example of refining a research question:

1. What is the future of computers?
2. Is it possible to create artificial intelligence?
3. What problems need to be solved in creating artificial intelligence?
4. Do computers need emotions to be considered intelligent?

From the first, very broad question, a succession of more specific questions emerges. The last one focuses on one issue out of many possible ones. Even this question is quite complicated, but at least it provides a clear direction for your writing.

The answer to your research question usually, but not always, appears in your thesis statement. Sometimes the thesis statement simply alludes to the answer, especially when the answer is long or complicated. Chandra Johnson's MLA research paper (30b) attempts to answer research question 4 above.

Research is an absorbing, creative activity. Developing a research question, gathering information about it, and creating a synthesis of what you've learned lets you come to know a subject deeply. It leads you to fresh insights. The entire process, especially when repeated in a number of courses of study, helps to shape you into a self-reliant learner with the discipline to pursue new and unfamiliar topics.

22d What is a research log?

A research log is a diary of your research process. Create a new computer file or folder for this log, or use a separate notebook. In your log, record

- each step in your search for information: enter the date of your work, your search strategies, the gist of the information you discover, and (1) the name, location, and other details of exactly where you found it and (2) exactly where you filed your detailed notes—for example, the exact file or folder name
- the next step you think you should take when you return to your research
- your plans for moving from gathering material to organizing it or writing about it
- your thoughts and insights as you move through the research and writing process

Although much of what you write in your research log will never find its way into your paper, what you read and reread in the log will greatly increase your efficiency as a researcher.

```
October 16: Went online to find sources for "artificial
intelligence" and was overwhelmed by the number of
hits. Gave up. Logged onto the library's Web site and
searched some databases there. PsycINFO turned up lots
of promising stuff. Chose several citations and
e-mailed full records to myself to check out later.
Readers' Guide Abstracts also had articles, and some
were available as full text. Printed out three of the
best ones. Need to start taking notes on them. Will go
to library tomorrow to find PsycINFO sources.
```

Excerpt from Chandra Johnson's research log

22e How do I plan a research project?

If you feel overwhelmed by the prospect of research writing, you are not alone. The best approach is to divide your project into a series of steps, which makes the process far less intimidating. Research projects take time, so plan your schedule realisticaly using the checklist in Box 25. Then add about 10 percent more time to your plan as a safety margin.

Sample research project plan 25

Assignment received (date) ________________

STARTING THE RESEARCH PROJECT	FINISH BY (DATE)
✓ Set up my research log	________________
✓ Choose a suitable topic	________________
✓ Draft my research question	________________

FINDING AND EVALUATING SOURCES

✓ Decide what documentation style to use	________________
✓ Decide the kinds of research I need to do	________________
Field research yes/no	
Library sources yes/no	
Online sources yes/no	

→

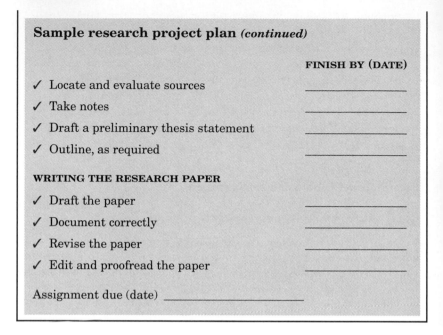

Sample research project plan ***(continued)***

	FINISH BY (DATE)
✓ Locate and evaluate sources	________
✓ Take notes	________
✓ Draft a preliminary thesis statement	________
✓ Outline, as required	________
WRITING THE RESEARCH PAPER	
✓ Draft the paper	________
✓ Document correctly	________
✓ Revise the paper	________
✓ Edit and proofread the paper	________

Assignment due (date) ________________

23 DEVELOPING A SEARCH STRATEGY

23a What is a search strategy?

A **search strategy** is an organized procedure for locating and assembling information for your research. A wealth of source material is available to researchers (23b). To find material that helps to answer your specific research questions, you need to search systematically and thoroughly. Using a search strategy guarantees that you'll work systematically rather than haphazardly and find what you're looking for more quickly. It will permit you to use what you learn at the early stages of your research to focus your search as you move through subsequent stages.

Following are three frequently used search strategies. If no one strategy quite fits your requirements, you can create one of your own that better meets your needs. As you work through useful sources, you can switch strategies or combine them. "Flexibility with focus" is the guiding principle for experienced researchers.

Expert method

This is a useful strategy when your topic is specific and narrow. Start with articles or books by an expert in the field, or interview an expert on the topic. If your topic calls for **field research,** such as direct observation, a survey, or personal visits to museums or events, build it into your plan.

Chaining method

This strategy is useful when your topic is a general one. Start with reference books and bibliographies you find in current articles or Web sites; use them to link to additional sources. Keep following these links until you reach increasingly specific sources by experts in the field. Alternatively, talk with people who have some general knowledge of your topic, and ask them to refer you to experts they might know.

Layering method

This is a useful method when you need to find your own topic. Start with general sources and gather layers of information that lead to increasingly specific topics and sources. If you need to conduct field research, such as interviews or observations, try to relate the information you gather to other studies or to scholarly sources on the same subject.

Start and complete your search as soon as possible after you get your assignment. Early in the process you may discover sources that take time to obtain (for example, through interlibrary loan) or are hard to locate (for example, certain business documents or government archives). One more piece of advice: Avoid getting too far along in your search until you're reasonably certain you are going in a useful direction. Rather than spending endless hours gathering sources, read and analyze some of your materials to make sure your topic is a good one. Your **research log** can be useful for this purpose.

23b What is a source?

A **source** can be either a **secondary source** that presents information at second hand, as reported or analyzed by an expert on the subject, or a **primary source.** Secondary sources are often found in the form of scholarly books, articles in a periodical or a compilation, or Web sites or other electronic media such as CD-ROMs, videotapes, and DVDs. Information that researchers gain at first hand comes from primary sources. One important category of primary sources includes original literary, scientific, autobiographical, or historical works, in print or electronic formats, and original works of art. Another major category includes performances, interviews, experiments, observation, and surveys. Your decision to use primary or secondary sources depends on your research question. Neither type of source is superior to the other.

As you locate, assemble, and evaluate sources related to your topic, expect to accumulate much more information than you will eventually use in your paper. In fact, the quality of your paper depends partly on your ability to eliminate inadequate or repetitive sources and recognize what is valuable material.

23c What is field research?

Field research is one type of primary research. Because it involves going into real-life situations to survey people, interview experts, or observe or participate in an activity, it yields original data. Allow extra time to conduct field research. Plan carefully to assure for yourself enough time to conduct your survey, interviews, or observations and to gather, ANALYZE, and SYNTHESIZE the information you collect.

A research assignment may state or imply that you need to do field research, or it may leave the decision up to you. If you have a choice, ask yourself whether field research on your topic would add useful information to your paper. If you're unsure, ask your instructor.

If you want to interview an expert on your topic, first schedule an appointment at the person's convenience. Then write, reflect on, and perhaps revise the questions you want to ask so that you feel confident about getting the information you seek. Perhaps the best place to look for an expert is on the faculty at your college or university. Your instructors are also scholars and researchers, who not only may provide information and insights but may suggest additional sources. Other experts might be businesspeople, government officials, religious leaders, or heads of local organizations and clubs. For example, for a paper on astronomy, you might interview a local amateur astronomer. You can conduct interviews by telephone as well as in person.

If you want to survey a group of people on an issue related to your topic, first write out your questions in full sentences. Then test the questionnaire on a few people who will not be in the group you intend to survey. Revise any questions that do not work well.

If you intend to observe an event such as a concert or a play, get tickets as soon as you receive your assignment. If you need to visit a museum or gallery, go as soon as possible to allow time for a follow-up visit if you need one.

Your success in doing field research depends on effective note-taking. Here are guidelines to follow for interviews and observations.

NOTETAKING GUIDELINES FOR FIELD RESEARCH

- For an interview:
  - Avoid using a tiny notebook or small sheets of paper. Standard-size paper (8 1/2 × 11 inches) allows you sufficient room to write without having to turn pages often.
  - Bring extra pens (in case yours runs out of ink) or pencils (in case yours breaks).
  - Before you go for the interview, practise asking your questions without reading them (perhaps highlight significant words).
  - During the interview, look your interviewee in the eye to put him or her at ease. If you are interviewing over the telephone, be organized and precise.
  - Create symbols or letters for key terms you expect to hear during the interview. This cuts down on your need to look away from the interviewee.
  - Take careful notes, listening especially for key names, books, or other print or online sources.
  - Never depend on a tape recording of an interview. In recent years, many people have become reluctant to permit anyone to record them. If you want to, ask permission to record the interview in advance, when you schedule the interview; or ask in person, when you arrive for the interview. Never imply that a recording is essential to you or your research, however. Some interviewees will cancel the appointment on the spot if a tape recording is even mentioned.
- For an observation:
  - Follow the guidelines for an interview.
  - For observations of behaviour (for example, an audience at a sporting event or school children at play during recess), plan to take notes during the activity. Permission to videotape is hard to get because of privacy concerns. If conditions make notetaking impossible, write detailed notes as soon afterward as you possibly can. Then go over and fill in your notes while your memory is fresh, to highlight major categories of information.

23d Where do I locate secondary sources?

The two best places to locate SECONDARY SOURCES are the library and the Internet. Your main goal in conducting **library research** is to identify source materials that exist in print: books, magazines, journals, microfilms, and so on. Some print sources exist also in electronic versions, on CD-ROMs, at Web sites, or in databases, although relatively few books are available in electronic formats. For detailed, practical strategies for finding and evaluating library sources, see Chapter 24. For strategies for finding and evaluating online sources, either on the World Wide Web or in the larger universe of the Internet, see Chapter 25.

23e What documentation style should I use?

A **documentation style** is a system for providing information about each source you have used in your research paper. Determine the documentation style you need to follow when you're developing your search strategy (23a). Doing so helps to guarantee that you'll write down the exact details you need to document your sources.

If you are doing field research, decide what you must document before you begin. Your instructor may have special requirements for such documentation, so be sure to ask for guidelines. Because your observations, questionnaires, surveys, or interviews produce primary data on your research topic, your instructor may expect you to submit these sources with your research paper. For example, you may need to hand in your filled-out questionnaires or provide background material on an interviewee you claim is an expert.

Documentation styles vary from one academic discipline to another. Modern Language Association (MLA) style is often used in the humanities (see Chapters 28–30). American Psychological Association (APA) style is used frequently in the social sciences (see Chapters 31–33). Chicago Manual (CM) style is used in various disciplines in the humanities, including English and history (see Chapter 34). Council of Science Editors (CSE) style is used in the biological and other sciences (see Chapter 35). Finally, Columbia online style (COS) includes format elements that are unique to electronic publications (see Chapter 36). If you don't know which style to use, ask your instructor. Never mix documentation styles; use only one style in each piece of writing.

23f What is a working bibliography?

A **working bibliography** is a preliminary list of the PRIMARY and SECONDARY SOURCES you gather in your research. Begin your working bibliography as soon as you start identifying sources. Compiling a working bibliography will help you find out what is available on a particular subject before you do extensive reading and notetaking. If your search turns up very few sources, you may want to change your topic. If it reveals a vast number of sources, you definitely want to narrow your topic, or even choose a different one. Expect to add and drop sources as you refine your research question and locate other sources.

You can record your working bibliography on note cards or on a computer. Note cards have the advantage of being easy to sift through and rearrange when you're adding or discarding sources. You can also carry them with you when you do library research. At the end of your writing process, you can easily sort and alphabetize them to prepare your final bibliography. Write only one source on each card.

On the other hand, putting your working bibliography on a computer saves you from having to type in your list of sources later. If you use a computer for this purpose, clearly separate one entry from another. You can organize the list alphabetically or by author, or group the entries according to your subtopics.

Whichever method you use, whenever you come across a source you think you might be able to use, write a card or computer entry for it immediately, while the source is in front of you. Record the information exactly as you need it to fulfil the requirements of the DOCUMENTATION STYLE that is required by the academic discipline, or that your instructor prefers. Spending a few extra moments at this stage can save you hours of work and frustration later on. Few things are as aggravating as having to return to the library merely to check the volume or page numbers of a source you recorded weeks earlier. (Besides, the book you need might not be available when you return.)

As a rough estimate, your working bibliography needs to be about twice as long as the list of sources you end up using. If your assignment asks for 10 to 12 sources, then at a mimimum you want your working bibliography to contain 20 to 25 entries.

24 FINDING, EVALUATING, AND USING LIBRARY SOURCES

24a What is library research?

Library research uses sources that are stored in the library or catalogued by librarians. Before the Internet, library research involved print sources (books, periodicals, microfiche) and portable electronic sources (CD-ROMs), which students could access by going to the library in person.

Now that the Internet has come into widespread use, some—but not nearly all—of what used to be located in a library building is available online. Similarly, researchers can now find many—but not all—library sources using computer-based searches, both inside and outside the library. The distinguishing characteristic of library research is that professional librarians or scholars have gathered, organized, and made available the sources. If you ever feel confused about how to find what you're looking for, ask a reference librarian. These professionals enjoy helping students master the art and science of research both in libraries and online.

24b What is a library search strategy?

A **library search strategy** leads you from general to specific sources to answer your research question (22c). Libraries contain several kinds of sources, including books, general reference works, specialized reference works, periodicals, and government documents. Each type of source is catalogued in a particular way, so you need to know how to identify and use the index or database appropriate to your topic and each type of source.

24c How do I find books on my topic?

A library's **book catalogue** lists all the holdings in its collection. The catalogue in almost every modern library exists in the form of a computer database. You can access it from computer terminals inside the library, and sometimes from outside the library, on the Internet. You find a book by searching the catalogue for the book's **author, title,** or **subject,** or a related **keyword.** When you search the book catalogue, some computer programs ask which of these four categories you would like to search. For instance, try searching the University of Alberta Libraries online.

Suppose you want to find a book by Naomi Klein, but you don't know its title. You can search the online catalogue for books by this author. In the space for "author" on the computer screen, you type in "klein, naomi." (Usually you enter the last name first, but check to see how your library's system works.) If your library owns any books by Naomi Klein, the catalogue will show you their titles and other information (24e). Among the books you might find is *No Logo: Taking Aim at the Brand Bullies* (Toronto: Knopf Canada, 2000). Or suppose you know this title and want to see if your library owns the book. In the space for "title," you type in "no logo." (Usually you do not need to include the full title or words like *the* or *a*.)

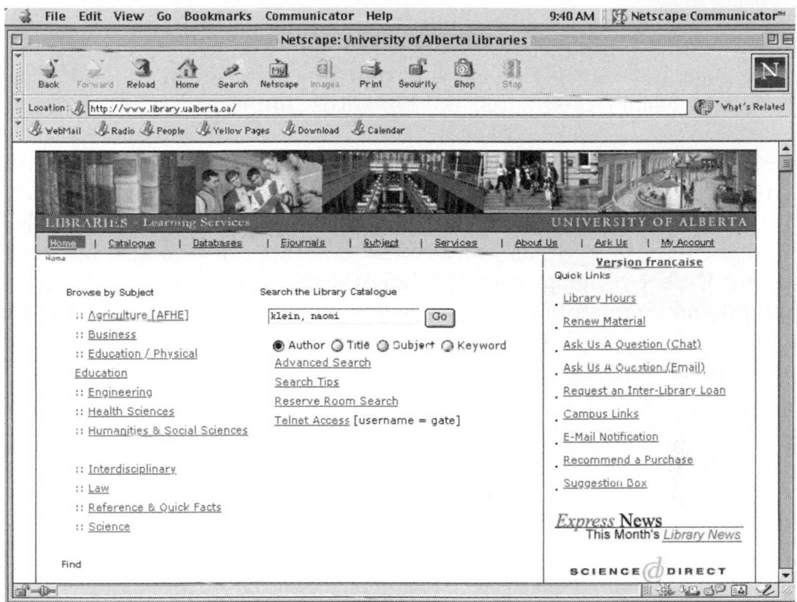

Search categories in an online library catalogue

Often you don't know an author's name or a book's title. Instead, you have a research topic and need to find sources. In this case you need to search by subject, using the terms listed in the *Library of Congress Subject Headings (LCSH)*. The *LCSH* is a multivolume catalogue available in the reference section of the library, that lists only subject headings, organized from most general to most narrow. If you are researching a Canadian topic, consult the National Library of Canada's *Canadian Subject Headings (CSH)* at <www.nlc-bnc.ca/cshweb-bin/search/>. Suppose you are researching the topic "brand name products—public opinion." If you enter that term in the space for subject searches, *No Logo: Taking Aim at the Brand Bullies* by Naomi Klein will be listed—if your library owns that book. Finally, you may wish to search by **keyword.**

24d What is a keyword?

Keywords are the main words that appear in a source's title, or that the author or editor has identified as central to that source. Keywords are sometimes called *descriptors* or *identifiers*. *LCSH* entries can serve as keywords, as can the important terms in your THESIS STATEMENT or research question. Keywords can help you search not only most book catalogues, but also periodical indexes (24i) and Web sites (25d). You could find Klein's book using the keywords "brand names," "logo," and so on.

In using keywords to search for sources, chances are you'll come up with a large or even overwhelming number of sources. Soon you'll discover that much of what turns up isn't relevant to your topic. You need to figure out which words best generate the sources you find useful. Expect to adopt an experimental approach. Keep a record of helpful and unhelpful keywords in your research log, so you don't have to retrace your steps. Don't get discouraged. If you're stumped, ask a research librarian for help.

24e What does a catalogue entry tell me about a book?

Each entry in the book catalogue contains a great deal of valuable information. Some libraries allow you to print out these entries, and some even let you send them to your e-mail account or download them to a disk. Whether you use any of these options or choose to copy the information directly into your working bibliography, be sure to record the call number exactly as it appears, with all its numbers, letters, and decimal points.

The call number tells where the book is located in the stacks (the shelves where the books are kept). If you are working in a library with open stacks (that is, if you can go where the books are shelved), the call number leads you to the area where all the books on your subject can be found. Simply looking at the books shelved next to the ones you have identified may yield additional useful sources. But keep in mind that in browsing the stacks, you are not seeing those sources that other students have checked out, or that librarians are holding at the reserve desk.

The call number is especially crucial if you are working in a library with closed stacks (that is, one where you fill out a call slip, hand it in, and wait for the book to be brought). In such libraries you aren't permitted to browse the stacks, so you have to rely entirely on the book catalogue. If you copy an incorrect or incomplete number onto the call slip, your wait will be in vain.

24f What are general reference works?

General reference works include encyclopedias, almanacs, yearbooks, fact books, atlases, dictionaries, biographical reference works, and bibliographies. A reference is said to be general if it provides limited information on a vast number of subjects.

Reference books and the CD-ROM reference collection are the starting point for many researchers—but only the starting point. Reference works summarize, so they are too general for use in academic research. Still, because general reference works give you an overall picture, they are a good place to find subject headings and keywords for online catalogue searches. In addition, general reference works are excellent sources for examples and facts. Most widely used reference works are available in electronic versions, usually CD-ROM. Some can be accessed on the Internet, either at the publisher's Web site or through an online database.

Using general encyclopedias

Articles in multivolume general encyclopedias, such as the *Encyclopaedia Britannica,* summarize information in a wide variety of subjects. The articles give helpful background information and the names of major figures and experts in many fields. Best of all, many articles end with a brief bibliography of major works on the subject. Remain aware that general encyclopedias don't include information on recent events or current research, although they sometimes cover ongoing controversies in a field up to the date of publication.

To locate information in a multivolume encyclopedia, start with the index volume, which lists the volume and page numbers for your topic. Be on the alert for a note, such as the letters *bib* at the end of an entry, indicating that the article contains a bibliography. The bibliography could be helpful in finding additional sources. If you can't locate an entry on your topic, try alternative keywords.

Using almanacs, yearbooks, and fact books

Almanacs, yearbooks, and fact books are huge compilations of facts in many subject areas. These books often appear both in print and online. They are excellent sources for verifying information from other sources and, in some cases, finding supporting facts and figures on a subject. *The Canadian Global Almanac* and *The World Almanac and Book of Facts* present capsule accounts of a year's events along with data on government, politics, economics, science and technology, sports, and many other topics. *Facts on File* covers world events in a weekly digest and an annual one-volume yearbook.

Sources of Canadian information include *Canada Year Book, Canadian Almanac and Directory,* and *Canadian News Facts*. The annual *Statistical Abstract of the United States,* the international *Demographic Yearbook,* and the *United Nations Statistical Yearbook* carry a wealth of data.

Using atlases and gazetteers

Atlases contain maps of our planet's continents, seas, and skies—and whatever we currently know about other planets. Gazetteers provide comprehensive geographical information on topography, climates, populations, migrations, natural resources, crops, and so on. Examples include *The Atlas of Canada, Canada Gazetteer Atlas,* the *Times Atlas of the World,* and *The Columbia Gazetteer of the World.*

Using dictionaries

Dictionaries define words and terms. Unabridged dictionaries contain hundreds of thousands of words, while abridged dictionaries, sometimes referred to as "college editions," are less comprehensive. Three abridged dictionaries intended for Canadian users are the *Gage Canadian Dictionary* (2000), the *ITP Nelson Canadian Dictionary of the English Language* (1997), and the *Canadian Oxford Dictionary* (2002). For British style, Canadians usually consult the *Concise Oxford Dictionary;* some prefer an American dictionary such as *Merriam-Webster's Collegiate Dictionary*. In addition to general dictionaries, you might want to consult specialized dictionaries, which define words and phrases specific to a particular academic discipline.

Using biographical reference works

Biographical reference books give brief factual information about famous people, including their accomplishments and pertinent events and dates in their lives. Biographical references include the *Who's Who* series, including *Canadian Who's Who, The Dictionary of Canadian Biography,* and many others. In most academic libraries, you can find specialized biographical reference books about people in various fields. Because so many different biographical sources are published, you may want to ask a reference librarian about the volumes that will help you most.

Using bibliographies

Bibliographies, available both in print and online, list books, articles, documents, films, and other resources, along with their publication information. Comprehensive bibliographies list sources on a wide range of topics. For example, the database WorldCat, available through First-Search, lists all the book holdings in thousands of libraries throughout the world. These listings don't describe a book's contents, but they do list the subject headings assigned to the book by librarians. Specialized bibliographies list sources on a particular subject. Annotated or critical bibliographies describe and evaluate the works they list.

24g What are specialized reference works?

Specialized reference works, which provide more authoritative and specific information than general reference works, are usually appropriate for postsecondary-level research. Box 26 lists some specialized reference works in several subject areas.

Some students mistakenly overlook specialized encyclopedias, moving from general references directly to books and articles. However, specialized encyclopedias are valuable for discovering the controversies in a subject area, or accumulating lists of experts on your topic and keywords that are useful in searching book and periodical catalogues and online resources.

Some specialized reference works 26

Encyclopedia of Banking and Finance
Handbook of Modern Marketing
New Grove Dictionary of Music and Musicians
Oxford Companion to Art
Dictionary of Canadian Biography
New Cambridge Modern History
Dictionary of Literary Biography
Oxford Companion to Canadian Literature
A Reference Guide to English, American and Canadian Literature
Encyclopedia of Philosophy
Encyclopedia of Religion
Political Handbook and Atlas of the World
The Canadian Annual Review of Politics and Public Affairs
Political Science Bibliographies
Encyclopedia of Chemistry
Encyclopedia of Computer Science and Technology
Encyclopedia of the Biological Sciences
Dictionary of Anthropology
Encyclopedia of Psychology
International Encyclopedia of Film
Oxford Companion to the Theatre

❗ **ALERT:** Hundreds of one-volume works are highly specific (for example, in the social sciences, *Encyclopedia of Divorce, Encyclopedia of Aging,* and *Encyclopedic Dictionary of Psychology*). Check to see what one-volume specialized reference books your own library has available. New special reference works are published throughout the year; you can use the general call number for your subject area to browse the reference collection. ❗

24h How do I use electronic databases?

Databases are indexes that contain electronic records of articles, reports, and books. Most databases are online; you access them through the World Wide Web. Some are distributed through CD-ROMs. Each entry in a database contains bibliographic information, including a title, author, date of publication, and publisher (for books or reports) or periodical (for articles). The entry might also provide an abstract, or summary, of the material.

Once you locate an entry that seems promising, you want to track down the source itself. Some databases, including ERIC (Educational Resources Information Center), provide the full texts of articles on microfiche. With this type of system, each citation contains an abstract as well as a catalogue number (for example, ERIC ED 139 580), which allows you to look up the microfiche that contains the article (ask a librarian where it is stored). ERIC is also available online at <www.eric.ed.gov>. Some databases allow you to purchase full copies of the sources you find, although that can become quite expensive.

You will find both general databases and specialized ones that concentrate on a single discipline or topic. Choose which databases will be most helpful before you begin to search, and restrict your search to one database at a time. Box 27 lists a few specialized databases.

A reference librarian can help you choose the databases best suited to your topic, if you provide a specific description of your research. Electronic databases are generally available in the library through a service like EBSCO, FirstSearch, or IBIS, or less frequently, on CD-ROM. Online databases require the library to pay a subscription fee, so your library may charge you when you use the system. Find out whether the service is free to students, and if not, what the charge is. Narrowing your search first with KEYWORDS (25d) can help you avoid paying for a list of useless sources.

24i How do I find periodicals for research?

Periodicals are newspapers, magazines, and journals that are published at set intervals during the year. To use periodicals efficiently,

Some specialized databases 27

Academic Search Elite
America: History and Life (U.S. and Canadian materials)
Children's Literature Comprehensive Database
Contemporary Women's Issues
Family Index Database
Lexis-Nexis Academic Universe
Medline
Statistical Universe
WilsonSelect Plus
World News Connection

consult an index to periodicals. These indexes allow you to search by subject and author. They're updated frequently, and are often available online as well as in print. Most databases also index periodicals.

ALERT: Use the correct periodical index for your research topic. If you are using the wrong index, you may miss some of the best sources for your paper. **!**

Using general indexes to periodicals

General indexes to periodicals list articles in journals, magazines, and newspapers that are published for general, non-expert readers. Headings and keywords vary from one index to another, so think of every possible way to look up the information you seek. Large libraries have many general indexes, including the following:

- The *New York Times Index* catalogues all articles printed in this newspaper since 1851.
- *The Readers' Guide to Periodical Literature* includes over 100 magazines and journals for general readers. Because this index doesn't include scholarly journals, its use in postsecondary-level research is limited. Nevertheless, you can use it to find topics, get a broad overview, and narrow a subject.

For research in Canadian periodicals, see *A Bibliography of Canadian Bibliographies, A Guide to Basic Reference Materials for Canadian Libraries, Canadian Newspaper Index,* and *Canadian Periodical Index*. Major newspapers have online archives that include articles from recent years. NewsBank (online) indexes over 500 U.S. newspapers.

Using specialized indexes to periodicals

Specialized indexes list articles in journals that are published for expert, academic, or professional readers. Each profession and field, and many subfields, have several specialized periodicals that are appropriate for postsecondary-level research. Many specialized indexes print an abstract, or summary, at the beginning of each article. Box 28 lists some specialized indexes.

Since the 1990s, many specialized indexes have appeared on CD-ROM and online. You can access them through your library's computer or on the Internet (24h). Check to see if your library has print, CD-ROM, or online versions of the indexes you wish to use.

Acquiring articles from periodicals

Indexes help you to identify specific articles on your topic. Once you have done so, how do you get your hands on an article? Sometimes you will find an online version of the article to read, download, or print. Frequently you will need to find a print copy of the periodical.

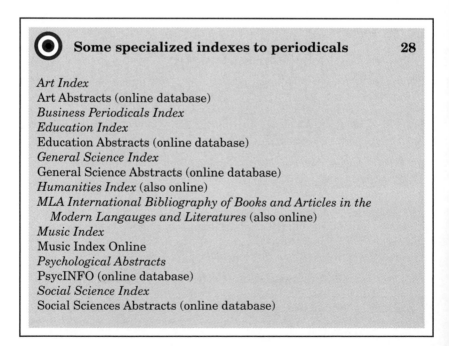

Some specialized indexes to periodicals **28**

Art Index
Art Abstracts (online database)
Business Periodicals Index
Education Index
Education Abstracts (online database)
General Science Index
General Science Abstracts (online database)
Humanities Index (also online)
MLA International Bibliography of Books and Articles in the Modern Langauges and Literatures (also online)
Music Index
Music Index Online
Psychological Abstracts
PsycINFO (online database)
Social Science Index
Social Sciences Abstracts (online database)

Most libraries include information about periodicals in their online catalogues, though many list periodicals separately. In either case, search for the periodical's name, not the title of the article or the name of the author who wrote it. If your library subscribes to that periodical, you can use its call number to find its location in the library. The citation you found in the index will then get you the article you are looking for.

24j How do I use government documents?

Canadian government publications are available in astounding variety. You can find information on laws, regulations, populations, weather patterns, agriculture, national parks, education, and health, and many other topics.

A federal government Web site known as the Canada Site <www.canada.gc.ca/> is an excellent starting point for online research into current Canadian government publications. It provides direct access to federal departments, boards, and agencies and their publications; to public records, including parliamentary debates and hearings; and to databases. You can also follow its links to provincial and territorial government sites. Statistics Canada <www.statcan.ca/> collects and analyzes a wide range of data.

24k What if my library doesn't have a source I need?

Almost no library owns every book or subscribes to every periodical on every topic. However, many libraries are connected electronically to other libraries, giving you access to additional holdings. The online TRACEit and AMICUS systems, which link the catalogues of university and other large libraries throughout Canada, are used for interlibrary loans. The Internet gives you access to the catalogues of many large libraries worldwide. Librarians can request materials from other libraries, including articles you have found in a periodical index, through interlibrary loan, which is generally free of charge. Alternatively, you may be able to use a different document delivery system (generally at some cost to you).

24l How should I evaluate print sources?

Sources are rarely of equal value. How do you know which are useful and reliable and which are not? First, decide whether the information in the source relates to your topic in more than a vague, general way. Check the table of contents, the introduction or preface, and as you narrow your search, the index for specific subtopics. Ask yourself how a source might help you to answer your research quetions. Finally, evaluate each source with a cold, critical eye using your critical thinking skills and the criteria listed in Box 29.

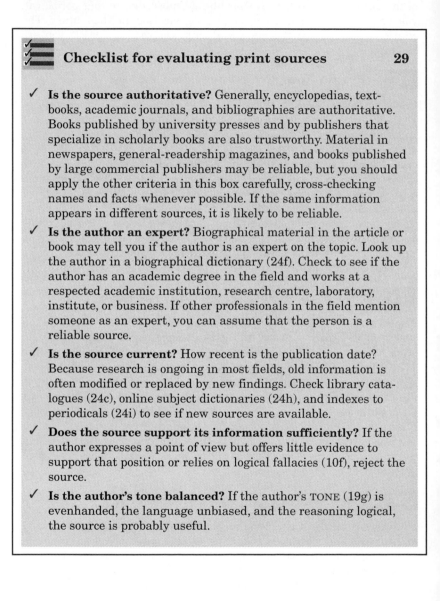

Checklist for evaluating print sources 29

- ✓ **Is the source authoritative?** Generally, encyclopedias, textbooks, academic journals, and bibliographies are authoritative. Books published by university presses and by publishers that specialize in scholarly books are also trustworthy. Material in newspapers, general-readership magazines, and books published by large commercial publishers may be reliable, but you should apply the other criteria in this box carefully, cross-checking names and facts whenever possible. If the same information appears in different sources, it is likely to be reliable.
- ✓ **Is the author an expert?** Biographical material in the article or book may tell you if the author is an expert on the topic. Look up the author in a biographical dictionary (24f). Check to see if the author has an academic degree in the field and works at a respected academic institution, research centre, laboratory, institute, or business. If other professionals in the field mention someone as an expert, you can assume that the person is a reliable source.
- ✓ **Is the source current?** How recent is the publication date? Because research is ongoing in most fields, old information is often modified or replaced by new findings. Check library catalogues (24c), online subject dictionaries (24h), and indexes to periodicals (24i) to see if new sources are available.
- ✓ **Does the source support its information sufficiently?** If the author expresses a point of view but offers little evidence to support that position or relies on logical fallacies (10f), reject the source.
- ✓ **Is the author's tone balanced?** If the author's TONE (19g) is evenhanded, the language unbiased, and the reasoning logical, the source is probably useful.

24m How do I extract information from library sources?

Taking good notes is essential to using source materials. The following guidelines suggest ways to make sure your notes are useful.

- Decide whether the source is reliable by using the checklist for evaluating print sources (Box 29).
- Decide whether to quote from, paraphrase, or summarize the source. On every note card or in every note in your computer file, do one of three things: (1) copy the exact words of the source as a QUOTATION, enclosing it in quotation marks (26f); (2) write a PARAPHRASE of the source (26g); or (3) write a SUMMARY of the source in your own words (26h). Record the page number(s) of the source that each of your notes refers to. Even if a source does not seem useful, record its title and location in your research log, along with a note about why you rejected it. What seems useless now might become useful as you revise.
- Decide what to put in your notes. Knowing how to select material for your notes comes with experience. Sort major points from minor points as they relate to your topic; leave out unimportant details. If you have only a general sense of your topic when you begin, read and take notes widely, but stay alert for ways to narrow your topic. Once you have narrowed your topic, focus your notetaking accordingly.
- Decide how to differentiate your sources' ideas from your own ideas and opinions as you read and think critically (Chapters 1–2). Doing so will help you avoid PLAGIARISM and put the information from your sources into a more useful form. Because your own ideas tend to pop in and out of mind during research, catch them on paper right away. You can use your research log to keep track of your thoughts on the direction and progress of your research. You might also record your own thoughts in a different colour of ink, on the back of your note cards, or in boldface type, if you are using a computer.

25 FINDING, EVALUATING, AND USING ONLINE SOURCES

25a What is online research?

Online research uses sources that exist in electronic form and that are available through the Internet. This chapter focuses on the sources available on one part of the Internet, the World Wide Web (often called *the Web*). The Web is organized around pages (called *Web pages*) that are linked together electronically. A group of pages that an individual or organization has created and linked together is called a *Web site*. The main page in a Web site (called the *home page*) acts as a table of contents.

25b How do I search the Web?

The principles for an online search strategy are very much like those for a library search (see Chapter 24). You start with a broad subject and narrow it to arrive at a suitable topic for an academic research paper. Before you can search the Web for sites that will help you answer your research question, you must get on the Web. You do this by means of a browser, a software program that gives you access to the Web and the search engines located there. Netscape Navigator and Microscoft Internet Explorer are two popular browsers. Once on the Web, you can search for sites by using a search engine or by typing an address into the locator box.

Using URLs

A **URL** is a Universal Resource Locator, a specific "address" on the Internet. Sometimes a URL will take you right to a site containing the information you need. To reach that site, type the URL into the locator box at the top of your screen.

PUNCTUATION ALERT: When you type a URL in your research paper, the MLA and APA suggest that you surround it with angle brackets. For example, <www.pearsoned.ca/troyka> is the URL for the Web site that accompanies this handbook. The brackets separate the URL from other sentence punctuation, which could be mistaken for part of the URL. However, never add angle brackets when you type a URL into the locator box on your computer screen. !

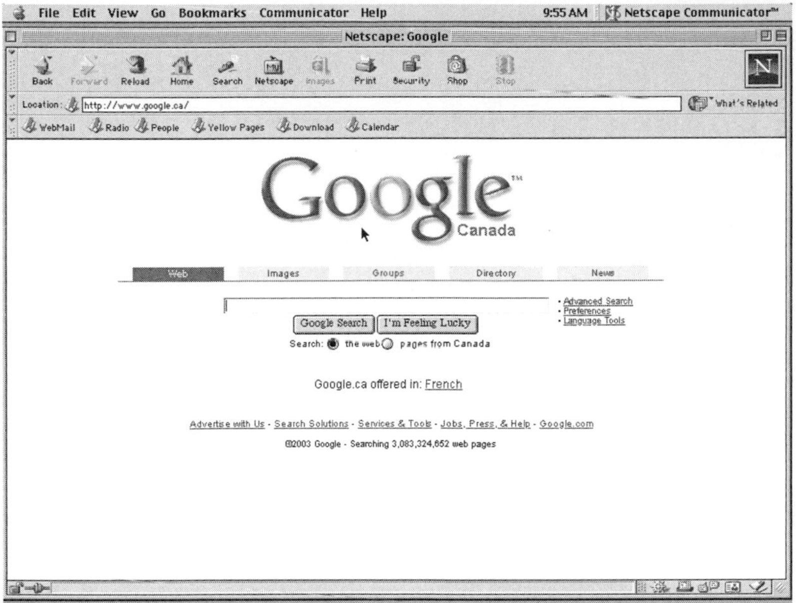

Opening page of the online search engine Google

Using search engines

Search engines are programs designed to hunt the Web for sources on specific topics that you identify. Box 30 lists the addresses of some useful search engines. When you start a search engine, you generally have two ways to access materials.

- You can see one or more **subject directories** on the home page. Subject directories are lists of topics (Education, Computing, Entertainment, and so on) or resources and services (Shopping, Travel, and so on), with links to Web sites on those topics and resources. For more advice on using subject directories, see 25c.
- You see a search box, or space for entering keywords. After you type a word or group of words into the box, you click on the Search or Enter button. The engine then lists Web sites that contain those keywords. For more advice on searching with keywords, see 25d.

Once you finish a search using one search engine, you might want to try another. Amazingly, different search engines yield somewhat—or even entirely—different lists of Web sites. This fact reflects the

Some online search engines and their addresses **30**

AltaVista	altavista.com
Excite	www.excite.com
HotBot	www.hotbot.lycos.com
Maple Square	maplesquare.ca
Yahoo!	www.yahoo.com

enormous number of choices on the World Wide Web. It is up to you to pick and choose from various search engines until you find the most useful sources.

COMPUTER TIP: **Metasearch engines** search other search engines for you. In other words, instead of using one search engine at a time to look for sources, you can use a metasearch engine to run simultaneous searches on several search engines. This lets you see at a glance which ones returned the best results. Examples of metasearch engines are AlltheWeb <www.alltheweb.com>, Ask Jeeves <www.ask.com>, Google <www.google.ca>, and MetaCrawler <www.metacrawler.com>.

25c How do I narrow my online search?

Because the Web has billions of pages, a search on even a moderately common topic may produce thousands of **hits**—sites listed or visited in a search. Not every hit will be what you are looking for. To help the search engine find the most relevant sites, you want to narrow your search as much as possible. Subject directories and keyword searches (25d) are good ways to begin narrowing your search.

Using a subject directory

A subject directory lists categories of information, with links to related Web sites. In this way, directories are similar to subject catalogues for print sources, like the *Library of Congress Subject Headings* (see 24c). Box 31 (p. 156) lists the Internet addresses of some useful subject directories.

Many search engine home pages have a subject directory that lists categories such as Government, Health, News, Science, and so forth. Clicking on a general category will take you to lists of increasingly specific categories. Eventually, you will get a list of Web pages on the most specific subtopic you select. These search engines also allow you to click on a category and enter keywords to search that category. For example, suppose that you are using Yahoo! to search for information on artificial intelligence. You would first go to the general category Science. Under Science you would find the category Computer Science, which contains a link to Artificial Intelligence, a page that lists more than 200 sources divided into different categories and types of

The Yahoo! Science directory

Some online subject directories and their addresses 31

AskERIC Virtual Library	ericir.syr.edu
Canadian Information by Subject	www.nlc-bnc.ca/caninfo/ecaninfo.htm
Infomine: Scholarly Internet Resource Collections	infomine.ucr.edu/
Internet Public Library	www.ipl.org
Librarians' Index to the Internet	www.lii.org
Library of Congress	lcweb.loc.gov
Search Canada	www.searchcanada.ca/
UBC Library Subject Guides	www.library.ubc.ca/home/subjects/
U of T Internet Resources, by Subject	www.utoronto.ca/subjects.html
Virtual Information Center	www.lib.berkeley.edu
Refdesk	www.refdesk.com

resources. You can copy down and use the subject headings and site links for future research on that topic. In this way, subject directories let you browse subjects and start narrowing your topic.

25d How do I conduct a keyword search?

To conduct a keyword search, go to the search engine and type your keyword (or a combination of keywords) into the search box on the opening page. The engine scans Web pages for keywords and lists Web sites that contain them. Very general terms may appear on thousands of Web sites. If a search engine produces thousands of hits for your keywords, do not give up. Instead, try more specific keywords. For example, a Google keyword search for the word *intelligence* yielded more than eight million hits, or links to Web sites containing that word. A search for the more specific keywords *artificial intelligence* yielded fewer than two million hits. Finally, a narrower search for the keywords *artificial intelligence computers emotion robots* yielded about 4000 hits.

As you become more adept at using keywords, your searches will become more directed and less time consuming. The further you are in the process of drafting a thesis statement or assertion, the more specific your searches become. In fact, the keywords in your thesis statement are likely to be good keywords for your searches. Most keyword search engines permit you to request very specific searches using Boolean expressions, quotation marks, and truncation.

Using Boolean expressions

Some search engines let you create keyword combinations that narrow and refine your search. These searches use **Boolean expressions**—the words AND, OR, and NOT, or symbols that represent those words. NEAR (which also may be represented by a symbol) is another expression used in structuring searches. You can also use parentheses to group expressions much as they group mathematical functions. When you use Boolean expressions between keywords, you are telling the search engine to list Web sites with your keyword specifications and to ignore others. When you group terms in parentheses, you direct or "force" the engine to look first at the grouped words and then at the words that follow.

A keyword search on the subject of artificial intelligence can show how Boolean expressions work. Without Boolean expressions, the keywords *intelligence computers emotions* would yield pages that include any of those words—and not necessarily in that order. Note the amount of weeding out that Boolean expressions allow.

- **AND** narrows the focus of your search to pages that contain both keywords. If you want to find information on the role of emotions in artificial intelligence, try the expression **artificial AND intelligence AND emotion.**
- **NOT** narrows your search by excluding texts that contain the specified word or phrase. If you want to eliminate *robots* from your search, type **artificial AND intelligence AND emotion NOT robots.** Sometimes you need to use NOT with another expression, such as AND—for example, **artificial AND intelligence AND emotion AND NOT robots.**
- **OR** expands a search to include more than one keyword. To expand your search to sources about artificial intelligence in either computers or robots, try the expression **artificial AND intelligence AND emotion AND computers OR robots.** Pages mentioning *artificial* and *intelligence* and *emotion* in connection with *computers* will be returned, as well as those mentioning *artificial* and *intelligence* and *emotion* in connection with *robots*.
- **NEAR** indicates that the keywords may be found in close proximity to each other. Depending on which search engine you are using, NEAR may produce hits that are found either in the same sentence or on the same page or site.

- **Parentheses ( )** can be used to group more than two expressions. For example, **(artificial intelligence AND emotions) AND (Turing Test OR Chinese Room)** would find documents about artificial intelligence and emotions and either the Turing Test or the Chinese Room Test (both, if possible). (These two tests are ways of judging whether a computer can be regarded as intelligent.)

These examples are not meant to be all-inclusive. Always review a search engine's search tips, since engines differ in the way they handle expressions and formats. For example, some search engines are **case sensitive,** which means that they look for keywords exactly as you type them, including capitals and lowercase letters. To be sure, check the Help box and/or Search Tips feature of any search engine you use.

Finally, many search engines have "advanced search" pages, which prompt you to enter search phrases in various spaces that function as Boolean expressions. Many also allow you to restrict sources to those created or updated within a specified period—for example, the last six months.

Using quotation marks in online searches

Enclosing your keywords in quotation marks directs the search engine to match your exact word order. For example, a search on Lycos for *"robots that think"* nets relatively few hits, each containing the title or phrase *robots that think*. This approach is helpful when you are searching for a name. If you search for *James Joyce* without using quotation marks, most engines will return pages containing *James* and *Joyce* anywhere in the document. However, a search using the keyword *"James Joyce"* will bring you closer to finding Web sites about the Irish author.

Using truncation

Truncation, sometimes called **wildcarding,** allows you to look for sites by listing only the first few letters of a keyword. You can also direct the search engine to search for variants of a keyword by using the wildcard symbol * in place of either the word ending or some of the letters in the word. For example, a truncated search for *wom*n* (or, in some cases, *wom#n*) would return hits for both *woman* and *women*. This approach is helpful when you do not want to exclude the plural form of a noun, or when a term comes in varying forms. Suppose you wanted to search for both *cognitive* and *cognition*. The search for *cogni** would turn up both forms. Most search engines recognize the symbol * for truncation, but a few use specialized symbols such as ?, : , or +. As always, check the Help screen of the engine you are using for specific details.

Box 32 offers some additional guidelines for using search engines.

Guidelines for using search engines 32

- Use keyword searches only when you have chosen a very specific, narrow topic with unique keywords. If you enter a general topic in most search engines, you will be overwhelmed by thousands of returns. If this happens, switch to a subject directory or see if you can restrict the number of hits by using additional keywords or Boolean expressions.
- Most search engines attempt to search as much of the Web as possible. But because the World Wide Web is vast and unorganized, different search engines will yield different results for the same search. Try using more than one search engine, or do a metasearch.
- Always check the Help screen in the search engine you use. As with the rest of the Web, search engines add or change features frequently.
- Ask the search engine to list results by ranking them according to their relevance. If you do not, the search results will be returned in random order, and the most important source may be last.
- If possible, limit the date range. For example, you might ask to see only pages that have been updated in the past six to twelve months.
- When you find a useful site, go to the toolbar at the top of the screen and click on Bookmark (or Favorites) and then click on Add. Doing so allows you to return to a good source easily by opening Bookmarks and double-clicking on the address.
- Use the History or Go function to track the sites you visit, in case you want to revisit one you initially thought wasn't helpful. If you want to, you can move a site from History to Bookmark.

25e How can I avoid plagiarizing from online sources?

Easy access to Web sources can be a tremendous help in your research. However, it can also cause problems if you aren't careful. Because downloading material from the Web is usually effortless, it is easy to PLAGIARIZE, or misrepresent the words of others as your own. Be very careful to avoid plagiarism while using online sources. Chapter 26 discusses plagiarism and its consequences in detail. The special risks of using online sources demand that you take the precautions described in 26c.

25f How do I evaluate online sources?

The unregulated nature of the Web creates special responsibilities for online researchers. You need to evaluate Web sources carefully, for two reasons. First, since anyone can post anything on the Web, some sources you find may well be plagiarized. Second, many sources on the Web are written by individuals who are posing as experts and giving out false or misleading information.

You are always accountable for the sources you choose. To evaluate an online source, use the checklist in Box 33. These criteria can help you separate sources that are worth a closer look from those that are not. Most reputable sites contain material that will help you to assess their credibility, such as a bibliography, links to the author or editor, or a description of the sponsoring organization. Discard sites that do not contain such information, however useful they may seem. To err on the side of caution is far better than to use a corrupt source.

An important question to ask about any Web site is why the information was put on the Internet. Be sure to question the motives of the site's author, especially if you are being asked to take a specific action.

For more help in evaluating online sources, try these Web sites:

Evaluating Internet Information (Industry Canada)
ln-rb.ic.gc.ca/e/training/eval.html

Thinking Critically About World Wide Web Resources
www.library.ucla.edu/libraries/college/help/critical/index.htm

Thinking Critically About Discipline-Based World Wide Web Resources
www.library.ucla.edu/libraries/college/help/critical/discipline.htm

Evaluating Web Resources
www2.widener.edu/Wolfgram-Memorial-Library/webevaluation/webeval.htm

25g How do I extract information from online sources?

You need to take notes from online sources just as you do from library sources (24m). You may take notes on cards or enter them in a carefully organized computer file. Be sure to record the exact source with each

Checklist for evaluating an online site 33

RELIABLE SITES ARE ...

✓ **From educational, not-for-profit, or government organizations.** Look for a URL ending in *.edu, .ac, .org, .gc, .gov*. These organizations should list their sources, however. If they fail to, don't use them. And be careful: Many colleges and universities now host student Web sites, which, in the United States, also end in *.edu*.

✓ **From expert authors.** Experts have degrees or credentials that you can check. See if their names appear in other reliable sources, in bibliographies on your topic, or in reference books in your college or university library. Check whether the site's author gives an e-mail address for questions or comments.

✓ **From reliable print sources.** Online versions of major newspapers, magazines, journals, and so on that are produced by the publisher or that appear in a full-text index are just as reliable as the print versions.

✓ **Supported by evidence and presented in a balanced, unbiased fashion.**

✓ **Current or recently updated.**

QUESTIONABLE SITES ARE ...

✓ **Sponsored by commercial organizations that are advertising a product or service *(.com)*. This category includes online advertisements, personal pages, and junk mail.** Such sites may or may not list their sources. If they fail to, don't use them. If they do, check that the sources are legitimate, not a front for the commercial enterprise.

✓ **Written by anonymous authors or authors who lack identifiable credentials.** Chat rooms, Usenet, discussion groups, bulletin boards, and similar networks are questionable for this reason.

✓ **Supported by second-hand excerpts and quotations.** Quotations that appear on a site that is not known to be reliable may have been edited in a biased or inaccurate manner. These sources may be incomplete and inaccurate.

✓ **Unsupported or biased.** These sites carry declarations and assertions that have little or no supporting evidence.

✓ **Old—that is, they have not been updated for a long time.**

note. Each source should have an entry in your working bibliography (23f).

Because Web pages can change and servers can go down, bookmark good online sources, print them out, or copy them onto your own computer. These steps ensure that you have ready access to the sources you need. However, the crucial work of moving from gathering sources to writing with sources requires that you take notes from the materials you have found. Unless you QUOTE (26f), PARAPHRASE (26g), or SUMMARIZE (26h) your sources effectively and accurately, writing a good SYNTHESIS will be very difficult. Not only do you risk PLAGIARISM (26a, 26c), you also risk compiling a choppy and ineffective paste-up of sources. The process of taking notes from your materials allows you to understand the sources better and begin seeing connections among them. Box 34 offers some guidelines for working with online sources.

Guidelines for using online sources **34**

- Immediately print out or download those sources that relate to your topic. Do this once you've narrowed your research focus, so that you have less information to keep track of. Keep your sources in separate files from your paper to avoid the risk of PLAGIARISM.
- Make sure each note shows the URL, the name of the source, and the date you accessed the source and printed it out (or the date you downloaded it).
- Check the documentation style you are required to use to see exactly what details you'll need to include in your in-text citations and final bibliography.
- Write down the exact reason you chose to print or download each source. Underline or highlight particular sections you think will be useful to you, and note why.

26 USING SOURCES AND AVOIDING PLAGIARISM

To use sources well, you need to learn three skills. First, you need to incorporate others' words or ideas into your own papers accurately. Second, you need to do so effectively. And third, you need to do so honestly. This last skill is especially important in order to avoid plagiarism.

26a What is plagiarism?

Plagiarism is presenting another person's words or ideas as if they were your own. Plagiarizing, like stealing, is a form of academic dishonesty or cheating. It's a serious offence that can be grounds for a failing grade or expulsion from a college or university. Beyond that, you're hurting yourself. If you're plagiarizing, you're not learning.

You're most definitely plagiarizing if you turn in a paper that someone else has written. This is true whether the paper comes from a friend, another student, the library, the Internet, or elsewhere. You're plagiarizing whether someone has "given" you the paper, you've found it in a file or on the Internet, or you've bought it. Furthermore, changing parts of an existing paper doesn't make it your work. Box 35 lists the major types of plagiarism.

Never assume that your instructor can't detect plagiarism. Instructors have a keen eye for writing styles that are different from those of students in general, and you in particular. Instructors can access Web sites that check your work against that of all online paper providers. Furthermore, sites exist that let instructors check your writing against hundreds of thousands of papers on the World Wide Web and the Internet. When instructors receive papers that they suspect contain

Types of plagiarism **35**

YOU'RE PLAGIARIZING IF YOU ...

- Buy a paper from an Internet site, another student or writer, or any other source.
- Turn in any paper that someone else has written, whether the person has given it to you, you have downloaded it from the Internet, or you have copied it from any other source.

→

Types of plagiarism ***(continued)***

- Copy or paste into your paper any *key terms, phrases, sentences,* or *longer passages* from another source without correctly citing that source (that is, without indicating precisely what you have used and listing the source in your References or Works Cited).
- Use *ideas* from another source without correctly citing and documenting that source, even if you put the ideas into your own words.
- Combine ideas from many sources and pass them off as your own without correctly citing and documenting the sources.

plagiarized passages, they can also check with other professors who may have seen the paper.

26b How do I avoid plagiarism?

The first step in avoiding plagiarism is to learn the techniques of QUOTING (26f), PARAPHRASING (26g), and SUMMARIZING (26h) source materials. The second step is to master how to DOCUMENT sources correctly, according to the DOCUMENTATION STYLE you're required to use. To do this, take advantage of the learning opportunities your instructor may build into research assignments. Many instructors require students to hand in a working bibliography (see 23f) or annotated bibliography (a list of sources that contains a brief summary of or commentary on each source). Your instructor may ask to see your research log (see 22d), your working notes, copies of your sources, or working drafts of your paper. Not only do such practices help you to avoid plagiarism, they also help you to plan your research project (see 22e) and move through the writing process. Box 36 suggests some practical steps you can take to avoid plagiarism.

26c How do I work with the Internet to avoid plagiarism?

As Chapter 25 explains, the Internet can both greatly help researchers and create potential problems. One of those problems is plagiarism. You might be tempted to download a paper from the Internet. Don't. That kind of intellectual dishonesty can get you into real trouble. Box 37

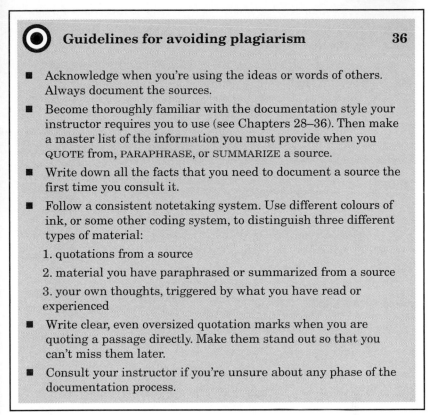

Guidelines for avoiding plagiarism 36

- Acknowledge when you're using the ideas or words of others. Always document the sources.
- Become thoroughly familiar with the documentation style your instructor requires you to use (see Chapters 28–36). Then make a master list of the information you must provide when you QUOTE from, PARAPHRASE, or SUMMARIZE a source.
- Write down all the facts that you need to document a source the first time you consult it.
- Follow a consistent notetaking system. Use different colours of ink, or some other coding system, to distinguish three different types of material:
  1. quotations from a source
  2. material you have paraphrased or summarized from a source
  3. your own thoughts, triggered by what you have read or experienced
- Write clear, even oversized quotation marks when you are quoting a passage directly. Make them stand out so that you can't miss them later.
- Consult your instructor if you're unsure about any phase of the documentation process.

suggests some ways you can avoid plagiarism when you are working on the Internet.

26d What don't I have to document?

You don't have to document common knowledge or your own thinking. **Common knowledge** is information that most educated people know, although they might need to remind themselves of certain facts by looking them up in a reference book.

For example, you would not need to document that

- Newfoundland entered Confederation in 1949
- Mercury is the planet closest to the sun
- The normal human body temperature is 37°C
- All the oceans on our planet contain salt water

Guidelines for avoiding plagiarism on the Internet 37

- Never cut material from an online source and paste it directly into your paper. You can too easily lose track of which material is your own and which comes from a source.
- Keep material that you downloaded or printed from the Internet in separate files from your own writing, whether you intend to QUOTE from, SUMMARIZE, or PARAPHRASE the material. Be careful how you manage those files. When you know the exact place in your paper where you will use each passage, record that location clearly, using another colour or a much larger font. Just as important, make sure that you write down all the information you need to identify each source, according to the documentation style you need to use.
- Copy or paste downloaded or printed material into your paper only when you intend to use it as a direct quotation. Immediately place quotation marks around the material, or set off a long passage as a block quotation. Be sure to document the source at the same time as you copy or paste the quotation into your paper. If you put off documenting the passage until later, you may forget to do it or use the wrong source.
- Summarize or paraphrase materials *before* you include them in your paper. If you have printed or downloaded Internet sources to separate files, don't copy directly from those files into your paper. Summarize or paraphrase the sources in a different file, and then paste the summaries or paraphrases into your paper. Document the source of each passage at the same time as you insert it in your paper. If you put off this task until later, you may forget to do it or get it wrong.
- Use an Internet service to check a passage you are not sure about. If you are concerned that you may have plagiarized by mistake, try submitting one or two sentences that concern you to a plagiarism-detection service. To do so, you must place quotation marks around the sentences when you type them into the search window. For-profit plagiarism-detection services charge a fee for checking your work, and they keep a copy of your paper in their databases.

Your own thinking is what you have concluded by building on what you already know. It consists of your analysis and interpretation of new material as you read or observe it. These thoughts of yours help you to formulate a thesis statement and organize your research paper. For example, suppose you're drawing on an article about the connections between emotions and logic in humans. While reading the article, you come to your own personal conclusion that computers don't have emotions. You don't need to find a source that supports this thought, although such a source might strengthen your assertion.

What *should* you document? Everything that you learn from a source, including ideas as well as specific language. Expressing the ideas of others in your own words doesn't release you from the obligation to tell exactly where you got those ideas, using correct documentation. Consider the following example:

SOURCE Searle, John R. "I Married a Computer." Rev. of *The Age of Spiritual Machines* by Ray Kurzweil. *New York Review of Books* 8 Apr. 1999: 34+. [This source information is arranged in MLA documentation style.]

ORIGINAL MATERIAL We are now in the midst of a technological revolution that is full of surprises. No one thirty years ago was aware that one day household computers would become as common as dishwashers. And those of us who used the old Arpanet of twenty years ago had no idea that it would evolve into the Internet (37). [These are Searle's exact words.]

PLAGIARISM

- The current technological revolution is surprising. Thirty years ago no one expected computers to be as common today as air conditioners. What once was the Arpanet has involved into the Internet, and no one expected that. [Searle's ideas are being used without documentation.]

Note that even though the writer has changed some of Searle's wording, the ideas are virtually the same. Therefore, the writer is required to document Searle's review as the source.

CORRECT

- John Searle states that we are in a surprising technological revolution in which computers have "become as common as dishwashers" (37). Twenty years ago no one could have predicted the Arpanet would become the Internet (Searle 37). [Quotation, paraphrase, and documentation are being used correctly.]

In this revision, the writer has properly cited Searle's ideas through a combination of quotation and paraphrase. Sections 26e through 26h explain exactly how to use sources effectively and document them correctly.

26e How should I integrate sources into my writing?

Before trying to integrate sources into your writing, you need to analyze and synthesize your material (1b). ANALYSIS is the process of breaking ideas down into their component parts, so that you can think them through separately. Do this while reading and reviewing your notes. SYNTHESIS is the process of making connections among different ideas, seeking relationships that tie them together.

Your research paper can be successful only if it reflects your personal synthesis of the ideas you are dealing with. The major requirement of a research paper is to demonstrate your ability to think well. Never simply list or summarize separate ideas. Use QUOTATION (26f), PARAPHRASE (26g), and SUMMARY (26h) to present your synthesis of the material you have read.

26f How can I use quotations effectively?

A **quotation** is the exact words of a source enclosed in quotation marks (54a–54b). You face conflicting demands when you add quotations to your writing. Although quotations provide support for your contentions, you can lose control of your paper if you add too many. You want your writing to be coherent and readable, so use quotations sparingly. If more than one-quarter of your paper consists of quotations, you've probably written what some people call a "Scotch-tape special." Depending too heavily on quotations gives your readers—including your instructor—the impression that you haven't bothered to develop your own thinking and are letting other people do your talking.

GUIDELINES FOR USING QUOTATIONS

1. Use quotations from authorities on your subject to support or challenge what you have written, or to refute opposing arguments.
2. Never use a quotation to present your thesis statement or a topic sentence.

3. Select quotations that fit your message. Choose a quotation only when
   - Its language is particularly appropriate or distinctive
   - Its idea is particularly hard to paraphrase accurately
   - The source's authority is especially important to support your thesis or main point
   - The source's words are open to interpretation
4. Never compose more than one-quarter of your paper from quotations. Instead, rely on PARAPHRASE (26g) and SUMMARY (26h).
5. Quote accurately. Always check a quotation against the original source—and then recheck it.
6. Integrate quotations smoothly into your writing.
7. Avoid plagiarism (26a–26c).
8. Document quotations carefully, just as you do for a paraphrase and a summary.

Making quotations fit smoothly with your sentences

Unless you incorporate quotations in your own writing skilfully, you may end up with incoherent, choppy sentences. You can avoid this problem by making the words you quote fit smoothly with three aspects of your writing: (1) grammar, (2) style, and (3) logic. After writing a sentence that contains a quotation, read it aloud to hear whether the language flows smoothly and gracefully. If it doesn't, revise the sentence. Here are some examples of sentences that don't mesh well with quotations, followed by a revised version.

SOURCE Goleman, Daniel. *Emotional Intelligence.* New York: Bantam, 1995. 9.

ORIGINAL MATERIAL These two minds, the emotional and the rational, operate in tight harmony for the most part, intertwining their very different ways of knowing to guide us through the world. [These are Goleman's exact words.]

INCOHERENT GRAMMAR

- Goleman explains how the emotional and rational minds "intertwining their very different ways of knowing to guide us through the world" (9).

INCOHERENT STYLE—INVERTED WORD ORDER

- Goleman explains how "intertwining their very different ways of knowing to guide us through the world," the emotional and rational minds work together (9).

INCOHERENT LOGIC

- Goleman explains how the emotional and rational minds work together by "their very different ways of knowing to guide us through the world" (9).

REVISED FOR COHERENCE

- Goleman explains how the emotional and rational minds work together by "intertwining their very different ways of knowing to guide us through the world" (9).

What do you do when a quotation doesn't fit smoothly with your writing? You can add a word or two to the quotation, in BRACKETS (56c), so that it fits seamlessly with the rest of your sentence. Make sure, however, that your bracketed additions don't distort the meaning of the quotation.

Another way to fit a quotation smoothly into your sentence is to delete the part of the quotation that seems to be causing the problem by using an ELLIPSIS (56d). When you use an ellipsis to delete troublesome words, make sure that the remaining words accurately reflect the source's meaning and that your sentence still flows smoothly. For example, suppose you want to quote from the following source:

SOURCE Goleman, Daniel. *Emotional Intelligence.* New York: Bantam, 1995. 9.

ORIGINAL MATERIAL But when passions surge, the balance tips: it is the emotional mind that captures the upper hand, swamping the rational mind. [These are Goleman's exact words.]

QUOTATION USING ELLIPSIS

- Goleman contends that "when passions surge . . . the emotional mind . . . captures the upper hand" (9).

Integrating author names, source titles, and other information

Another strategy for working quotations smoothly into your paper is to integrate the author's name, the source title, or other information into your paper. You can prepare your reader for a quotation using one of these methods:

- Mention in your sentence (before or after the quotation) the name of the author you're quoting.
- Mention in your sentence the title of the work you're quoting from.
- If the author of a quotation is a noteworthy figure, refer in your sentence to his or her credentials.
- Add your own introductory analysis to the quotation, along with the name of the author, the name of the source, and/or the author's credentials.

Here are some examples of effective integration of an author's name, source title, and credentials, along with an introductory analysis.

SOURCE Binkley, Sue. *The Clockwork Sparrow: Time, Clocks, and Calendars in Biological Organisms.* Englewood Cliffs, NJ: Prentice, 1990. [This source information is arranged in MLA documentation style.]

ORIGINAL MATERIAL Artificial lighting, jet travel, and space exploration permit sudden disruptions of natural temporal sequences (4). [These are Binkley's exact words.]

AUTHOR'S NAME

- Sue Binkley explains that "artificial lighting, jet travel, and space exploration permit sudden disruptions of natural temporal sequences" (4).

AUTHOR'S NAME AND SOURCE TITLE

- Sue Binkley explains in The Clockwork Sparrow that "artificial lighting, jet travel, and space exploration permit sudden disruptions of natural temporal sequences" (4).

AUTHOR'S NAME, CREDENTIALS, AND SOURCE TITLE

- Sue Binkley, who has researched circadian rhythms for twenty years, explains in The Clockwork Sparrow that "artificial lighting, jet travel, and space exploration permit sudden disruptions of natural temporal sequences" (4).

AUTHOR'S NAME, WITH STUDENT'S INTRODUCTORY ANALYSIS

- Sue Binkley, a leading researcher in circadian rhythms who has found that modern life interferes with our biological clocks, explains that "artificial lighting, jet travel, and space exploration permit sudden disruptions of natural temporal sequences" (4).

26g How can I write good paraphrases?

A **paraphrase** precisely restates in your own words the written or spoken words of someone else. Select for paraphrase only those passages that carry ideas you need to reproduce in detail. Because paraphrasing calls for a very close approximation of a source, avoid trying to paraphrase a whole chapter—or even a whole page.

GUIDELINES FOR WRITING PARAPHRASES

- Paraphrase the words of authorities on your subject to support or counter what you write in your paper.
- Never write a paraphrase to present your thesis statement or topic sentences.
- Say what the source says, but no more.
- Reproduce the source's emphases and order of ideas.
- Use your own words, phrasing, and sentence structure to restate the material. If some technical words in the original have only awkward synonyms, you may quote the original words—but do so very sparingly. For example, you may use the term *circadian rhythms* if you're paraphrasing the original source by Sue Binkley in 26f.
- Read your sentences over to make sure they don't distort the source's meaning.
- Expect your material to be as long as, or even longer than, the original.

- Integrate your paraphrase into your writing so that it fits smoothly.
- Avoid PLAGIARISM (26a–26c).
- Document your paraphrase carefully, just as you do for QUOTATIONS (26f) and SUMMARIES (26h). Otherwise, you'll be plagiarizing.

Here is a passage that Chandra Johnson came across while researching her MLA-style research paper (30b). Read the passage and then study the two paraphrases that follow it. The first paraphrase is unacceptable because the underlined words have been plagiarized. The second paraphrase is acceptable.

SOURCE Goleman, Daniel. *Emotional Intelligence.* New York: Bantam, 1995. 9.

ORIGINAL MATERIAL These two minds, the emotional and the rational, operate in tight harmony for the most part, intertwining their very different ways of knowing to guide us through the world. Ordinarily there is a balance between emotional and rational minds, with emotion feeding into and informing the operations of the rational mind, and the rational mind refining and sometimes vetoing the inputs of the emotions. Still, the emotional and rational minds are semi-independent faculties, each, as we shall see, reflecting the operation of distinct, but interconnected circuitry of the brain.

In many of most moments, these minds are exquisitely coordinated; feelings are essential to thought, thought to feeling. But when passions surge, the balance tips: it is the emotional mind that captures the upper hand, swamping the rational mind. [These are Goleman's exact words.]

UNACCEPTABLE PARAPHRASE

- The emotional and the rational parts of our mind <u>operate in tight harmony for the most part</u> as they help us make our way through our lives. Usually the two minds are balanced, <u>with emotion feeding into and informing the operations of the rational mind, and the</u>

rational mind refining and sometimes overruling what the emotions desire. Still, the emotional and rational minds are semi-independent faculties, for as research shows, although they function separately, they are linked in the brain.

Most of the time our two minds work together, with feelings necessary for thinking and thinking necessary for feeling. Nevertheless, if strong emotions develop, it is the emotional mind that captures the upper hand, swamping the rational mind (Goleman 9). [The underlined words are plagiarized.]

ACCEPTABLE PARAPHRASE

- According to Goleman, the emotional and rational parts of our mind work together to help us make our way through our lives. Usually, the two minds have equal input. The emotional mind provides information to the logical mind, and the logical mind processes the data and sometimes overrules emotional desires. Nevertheless, while the two minds show a biological connection in the brain, each can assert some independence. Most of the time our two minds work together, with feelings necessary for thinking and thinking necessary for feeling. Still, if strong emotions develop, passions overrule logical thinking (9).

The first attempt to paraphrase is unacceptable because the writer has simply changed a few words. What remains is plagiarized: It retains most of the original language, has the same sentence structure as the original, and uses no quotation marks. The documentation is correct, but its accuracy doesn't make up for the unacceptable paraphrasing.

The second paraphrase is acceptable. It captures the meaning of the original in the student's own words.

26h How can I write good summaries?

A **summary** differs from a PARAPHRASE (26g) in one important way: While a paraphrase restates the original material completely, a summary provides only the main point of the original source. As a result, a summary is much shorter than a paraphrase. Summarizing is the technique you will probably use most frequently in writing research papers, both for taking notes and for integrating what you have learned into your own writing.

GUIDELINES FOR WRITING SUMMARIES

- Summarize the work of authorities on your subject to support or refute what you write in your paper.
- Identify the main points you want to summarize and condense them in your own words, taking care not to lose the meaning of the original source.
- Never use a summary to present your thesis statement or a topic sentence.
- Keep your summary short.
- Integrate your summary smoothly into your writing.
- Avoid plagiarism (26a–26c).
- Document your sources carefully, just as you do for QUOTATIONS (26f) and PARAPHRASES (26g). Otherwise, you'll be plagiarizing.

As you summarize a passage in a source, don't be tempted to include your personal interpretation or judgment along with the author's thoughts. Your own opinions don't belong in a summary. This doesn't mean that your opinions and ideas have no value. On the contrary: Jot them down immediately, so you can use them in a different paragraph. Always take notes in a way that distinguishes your own opinions or ideas from your summary. If you write out your notes, use a different colour of ink for your own ideas. If you take notes on a computer, use a double underline, boldface, highlighting, or a different colour or font to mark your own thoughts.

Here are two summaries of the same passage. The first one is unacceptable because it mixes the writer's words with those of the source.

SOURCE Goleman, Richard. *Wide Awake at 3:00 A.M.: By Choice or By Chance?* New York: Freeman, 1986. 69. [This source information is arranged in MLA documentation style.]

ORIGINAL MATERIAL An important variable in determining the degree of jet lag is the direction of travel, not whether the flight is outgoing or homecoming. When traveling in a westbound direction, New York to Los Angeles, for

> example, we must set our wristwatches and biological clocks back by 3 hours because our day has been extended. (If you normally keep to a bedtime of 11:00 P.M. to 7:00 A.M. and upon arrival in Los Angeles, you also stay up till 11:00 P.M. local time, you will experience a 27-hour day. Traveling eastbound, Los Angeles to New York, requires setting your watch ahead by 3 hours, or shortening the day to 21 hours.)
>
> Because our internal biological clock naturally gravitates to a 25-hour day, it makes sense that we can more easily adjust to westbound travel, which extends the day. In a series of studies of jet lag, volunteers have been flown back and forth between Europe and the United States (six time zones) to measure cognitive-motor performance, body temperature, and fatigue ratings. When performance before and after the six-time-zone flight was assessed, it was found that the travelers reached their peak performance within two to four days following westbound flight, but required nine days following eastbound travel. [These are Coleman's exact words.]

UNACCEPTABLE SUMMARY

- The degree of jet lag is related to the direction of travel, westbound travel lengthening the day, which is easier for biological clocks to adjust to, and eastbound travel shortening it, which is harder on biological clocks (Coleman 69). [The underlined words are plagiarized.]

ACCEPTABLE SUMMARY

- Eastbound travellers find it harder than westbound travellers to adjust because travelling east shortens the day unnaturally (Coleman 69).

ALERT: Never confuse SUMMARIZING with SYNTHESIZING. For a full explanation of the differences, see 4a and 4b. In writing a research paper, you want to summarize your sources' ideas and information, but your summaries are only the foundation on which to build your synthesis. A research paper that merely offers summaries doesn't demonstrate your ability to make the connections among ideas that synthesis demands.!

26i Which verbs can help me weave source material into my sentences?

To work source material into your sentences, use these verbs appropriately according to their meanings and the attitudes they imply.

Verbs useful for integrating quotations, paraphrases, and summaries 38

agrees	confirms	explains	offers	signals
analyzes	considers	finds	points out	speculates
argues	contends	grants	recom-mends	states
asks	declares	illustrates	refutes	suggests
asserts	demon-strates	implies	remarks	supposes
believes	denies	informs	reports	thinks
claims	describes	insists	reveals	wishes
comments	discusses	maintains	says	writes
complains	emphasizes	negates	sees	
concedes	estimates	notes	shows	
concludes		observes		

27 DRAFTING AND REVISING A RESEARCH PAPER

Drafting and revising a research paper is much like drafting and revising any piece of writing (see Chapters 6 and 7). Yet you need to do much more. To write a research paper, you need extra time for planning, drafting, thinking, redrafting, rethinking, and creating a final draft. This is so because in a research paper, you need to demonstrate that

- You have followed the steps of the research process presented in Chapters 22–26

- You understand the information that you have located during your research
- You have not PLAGIARIZED your material from someone else (26a–26c)
- You have used SOURCES well in your writing, by correctly employing QUOTATIONS, PARAPHRASES, and SUMMARIES (26f–26h)
- You have moved beyond SUMMARY to SYNTHESIS, so that your sources are interwoven with each other and with your own thinking, not merely listed one by one (4a–4b)
- You have used DOCUMENTATION accurately (for MLA style, see Chapters 28–30; for APA style, see Chapters 31–33; for other documentation styles, see Chapters 34–36)

Expect to write quite a few drafts of your research paper. The first draft is your first chance to discover new insights and fresh connections. Only the act of writing makes such breakthroughs possible.

27a How do I draft a research paper?

Here are some ways to write a first draft of a research paper.

- Some researchers work with their notes at hand. They organize the notes into broad categories by making a separate pile of note cards (or printouts of their notes) for each category of information. As patterns begin to emerge, these writers might move material from one category to another. Each category becomes a section of the first draft. This method not only assures researchers that their first draft will include all the material from their research, but reveals any gaps in information that call for additional research. Of course, you may discover that some of your research does not fit your topic and thesis. Just put it aside; it might be useful in a later draft.
- Some writers finish their research and then slowly review half the information they've gathered. Next, setting aside that information, they write a partial first draft by drawing on the information they remember from their reading. Then they use the same process with the second half of the information that they've gathered. Finally, with their two partial drafts and all their research notes in front of them, they write a complete first draft. Researchers who use this method say it gives them a broad overview of their material quickly and identifies any gaps in information that they need to fill in with further research.
- Some writers stop at various points during their research and use FREEWRITING to get their ideas into words. Researchers who use

this method say that it helps them to recognize when they need to adjust their research question (22c) or change the emphasis of their search. After a number of rounds of researching and freewriting, they find that they can write their complete first draft relatively easily.

- Some writers review their sources and create an outline before drafting. Some find a formal outline helpful, while others use a less formal approach.

27b How do I revise a research paper?

Before you write your second draft, read your first one with a sharp eye. Assess all the features listed in Box 39 at the end of this section, as well as in Box 11 on page 30. For best results, take a break for a few days (or at least a few hours) before beginning this process. This gives you distance from your material and a clearer vision of what you need to REVISE. For a more objective point of view, consider asking a few people you respect to read and react to your first, or perhaps your second, draft.

One key to revising any research paper is to carefully examine the **evidence** you have included. Evidence consists of facts, statistics, expert studies and opinions, examples, and stories. As a reader, you expect writers to provide solid evidence to back up their claims and conclusions. Similarly, when you write, your readers expect you to provide evidence that clearly supports your claims and conclusions. Identify each of the points you have made in your paper, including your thesis and all your subpoints. Then ask the following questions:

- **Is the evidence sufficient?** To be sufficient, evidence cannot be thin or trivial. As a rule, the more evidence you present, the more convincing your thesis will be to readers.
- **Is the evidence representative?** Representative evidence is customary and normal, not based on exceptions. When evidence is representative, it provides a view of the issue that reflects the usual circumstances rather than rare ones.
- **Is the evidence relevant?** Relevant evidence relates directly to your thesis or topic sentence. It illustrates your reasons in a straightforward way and is never unrelated to your main point. Only if your evidence is important and central to your point will readers accept your thesis.
- **Is the evidence accurate?** Accurate evidence is correct, complete, and up to date. It comes from a reliable SOURCE (24l and 25f).

Equally important, you present it honestly, without distorting or misrepresenting it.

- **Is the evidence reasonable?** Reasonable evidence is not phrased in extreme language, such as *all, never,* or *certainly*. Reasonable evidence is well thought out and free of logical fallacies (10f).

As you reread and revise, pay attention to any uneasy feelings you may develop that hint at the need to rethink or rework your material. Most students find that research papers are their most demanding assignments. They know that no amount of careful research and good writing can make up for an incorrectly presented or sloppy paper. Be sure, therefore, to allow lots of time for rewriting, REVISING, EDITING, and PROOFREADING. **Experienced student writers know that writing is really rewriting.**

For an example of a student research paper in MLA documentation style, see 30b. For an example of a student research paper in APA documentation style, see Chapter 33.

Revision checklist for a research paper **39**

If the answer to a question in this checklist is no, you need to revise. The section numbers in parentheses tell you where to find helpful information.

WRITING

✓ Have you met the basic requirements for a written thesis statement? (7b)

✓ Does your introductory paragraph lead effectively into the material? (8b)

✓ Do you stay on the topic of each paragraph? (8c)

✓ Have you discussed the topic of each paragraph fully, using RENNS? (8d)

✓ Do your ideas follow sensibly and logically within each paragraph and from one paragraph to the next? (8e)

✓ Does the concluding paragraph end your paper effectively? (8g)

RESEARCH

✓ Does your thesis statement allude to, or directly address, the research question on which you based your research? (22c)

✓ Does the content of your paper address your research question? (22c)

→

Revision checklist for a research paper ***(continued)***

- ✓ Have you integrated your source material well without plagiarizing? (26e)
- ✓ Have you written good quotations, paraphrases, and summaries? (26f–26h)
- ✓ Have you included appropriate and effective evidence? (27b)
- ✓ Have you deleted irrelevant or insignificant evidence? (27b)

FORMAT AND DOCUMENTATION

- ✓ Have you used the correct format in your parenthetical references? (28b, 31b)
- ✓ Does each of your parenthetical references tie into an item in the WORKS CITED list (MLA style) or REFERENCES list (APA style) at the end of your paper? (29b, 32b)
- ✓ Does your paper follow the assigned format? Check the margins, spacing, title, headings, page numbers, and so on. (30a, 31a, 31e)

28 MLA IN-TEXT CITATIONS

The most frequently used documentation style in the humanities has been developed by the Modern Language Association (MLA). In MLA style, you're expected to document your sources in two separate, equally important ways:

1. Within the body of the paper, use in-text citations, as described in this chapter.
2. At the end of the paper, provide a list of sources you used in your paper. Title this list Works Cited, as described in Chapter 29.

28a What are MLA in-text citations?

In-text citations are information included in the sentences or in parenthetical references within the paper. They both signal material used from outside sources and enable readers to locate the original sources.

In most in-text citations, a name or a title usually identifies a source, and page numbers usually show the exact location in that source. In general, put page number information in parentheses at the end of a quotation, paraphrase, or summary. Try to introduce names of authors and titles of sources in your own sentences, where they become part of the flow of your writing. If that isn't possible, put the information in parentheses at the end of a quotation, paraphrase, or summary.

For advice on incorporating names, titles, and other information in your sentences to establish the authority of your sources, see 26e.

CITATIONS OF PARAPHRASES

- `People from the Mediterranean prefer an elbow-to-shoulder distance from each other (Morris 131).` [name and page number cited in parentheses]
- `Desmond Morris notes that people from the Mediterranean prefer an elbow-to-shoulder distance from each other (131).` [name cited in text, page number cited in parentheses]

A parenthetical reference belongs at the end of the material it refers to, usually at the end of a sentence. If you're citing a quotation enclosed in quotation marks, place the parentheses after the closing quotation mark but before sentence-ending punctuation:

- Binkley claims that artificial light reduced SAD-related "depression in 87 percent of patients . . . within a few days; relapses followed" (203-04) when light treatment ended.
- Research shows that "the number, rate, and direction of time-zone changes are the critical factors in determining the extent and degree of jet lag symptoms" (Coleman 67).

Place a parenthetical reference for a long quotation (one you set off from your own sentences with indentation—54b) outside the punctuation ending the last sentence; for an example, see Chandra Johnson's research paper in 30b.

28b What are MLA guidelines for in-text citations?

The directory below corresponds to the numbered examples that follow the list. The examples show you how to handle various types of citations in the body of your paper. Many of these examples show parenthetical citations, but remember that you usually can—and want to—give names and titles of your sources in your own sentences.

DIRECTORY—MLA IN-TEXT CITATIONS

1. One Author—MLA
2. Two or Three Authors—MLA
3. More Than Three Authors—MLA
4. More Than One Source by an Author—MLA
5. Two or More Authors with the Same Last Name—MLA
6. Group or Corporate Author—MLA
7. Work Cited by Title—MLA
8. Multivolume Work—MLA
9. Novel, Play, or Poem—MLA
10. Work in an Anthology or Other Collection—MLA
11. Indirect Source—MLA
12. Two or More Sources in One Reference—MLA
13. An Entire Work—MLA
14. The Bible—MLA
15. An Electronic Source with a Name or Title and Page Numbers—MLA
16. An Electronic Source with Paragraph, Screen, or Section Numbers—MLA
17. An Electronic Source Without Page or Other Numbers—MLA

1. One Author—MLA

All the examples in 28a show citations of works by one author. Notice that no punctuation separates the author's name from the page number z parenthetical citations.

2. Two or Three Authors—MLA

Give authors' names (order and spelling) as they appear on the book (title page) or article. Spell out the word *and.*

- As children get older, they become more aware of standards for personal space (Worchel and Cooper 536).

3. More Than Three Authors—MLA

For a book by more than three authors, you can name all authors, or you can use the first author's name only, followed by *et al.* [note: *al.* takes a period], either in a parenthetical reference or in your sentence.

- Fisher et al. have found that personal space gets larger or smaller depending on the circumstances of the social interaction (158).
- Personal space gets larger or smaller depending on the circumstances of the social interaction (Fisher et al. 158).

4. More Than One Source by an Author—MLA

When you use two or more sources by the same author, include the relevant title in each citation. In parenthetical citations, use a shortened version of the title. For a paper using as sources Edward T. Hall's *The Hidden Dimension* and "Learning the Arabs' Silent Language," parenthetical citations would be *Hidden* and "Learning." Shorten the titles as much as you can without making them ambiguous to readers, and start with the word by which the work is alphabetized in Works Cited. Separate the name and title with a comma, but don't use punctuation between the title and page number.

- Most people are unaware that interpersonal distances exist and contribute to people's reactions to one another (Hall, Hidden 109).
- Arabs know the practicality of close conversational distances (Hall,"Learning" 41).

When you incorporate the title into your own sentences, you can omit a subtitle, but do not shorten more than that.

5. Two or More Authors with the Same Last Name—MLA

Use each author's first initial and full last name in each parenthetical citation. In your sentences, you can use either the first initial or the full first name. If both authors have the same first initial, use the full name in all instances.

- According to British zoologist Desmond Morris, conversational distances vary between people from different countries (131). If an American backs away from an Arab, the American is considered cold, the Arab pushy (C. Morris 516).[D. Morris and C. Morris are different authors.]

6. Group or Corporate Author—MLA

When a corporation or other group is named as the author of a source you want to cite, use the corporate name just as you would an individual's name.

- In a five-year study, the Canadian Institute of Child Health reported that these tests are usually unreliable (11).
- A five-year study shows that these tests are usually unreliable (Canadian Institute of Child Health 11).

7. Work Cited by Title—MLA

If no author is named, use only the title. If the title is long, shorten it. Here's an in-text citation to an article titled "Are You a Day or Night Person?"

- The "morning lark" and "night owl" connotations typically are used to categorize the human extremes ("Are You" 11).

If two or more works with no author named have the same title, use also the year of publication or other distinguishing information.

8. Multivolume Work—MLA

If you use more than one volume of a multivolume work, include the relevant volume number in each citation. Separate the volume number and page number with a colon followed by a space.

- Although Amazon forest dwellers had been exposed to these viruses by 1900 (Rand 3: 202), Borneo forest dwellers escaped them until the 1960s (Rand 1: 543).

9. Novel, Play, or Poem—MLA

Often when you cite literary works, you can give location information that is more useful than page numbers. Part, chapter, act, scene, canto, stanza, or line numbers generally don't change no matter where the work appears. Unless your instructor tells you differently, use arabic numerals for these references. Do this even if the literary work uses roman numerals (except for lower-case roman numerals used for pages of a preface or other front matter in a book). If a novel has parts and/or chapters, give these after the page numbers. Use a semicolon after the page number but a comma to separate a part from a chapter.

- Flannery O'Connor describes one character in The Violent Bear It Away as "[seeing] himself divided in two-- a violent and a rational self" (139; pt. 2, ch. 6).

For plays, give act, scene, and/or line numbers if they are used. Use periods between these numbers.

- Among the most quoted of Shakespeare's lines is Hamlet's soliloquy beginning "To be, or not to be: that is the question" (3.1.56).

For poems and songs, give canto, stanza, and/or line numbers. Use periods between these numbers.

- In "To Autumn," Keats's most melancholy image occurs in the lines "Then in a wailful choir the small gnats mourn / Among the river swallows" (3.27-28).

10. Work in an Anthology or Other Collection—MLA

You may want to cite a work you have read in a book that contains many works by various authors and that was compiled, written, or edited by someone other than the person you are citing. For example, suppose you want to cite "When in Rome" by Mari Evans, which you have read in a literature text by Pamela Annas and Robert Rosen. Use Evans's name and the title of her work in the in-text citation.

- In "When in Rome," Mari Evans uses parentheses to enclose lines expressing the houseworker's thoughts as her employer offers lunch, as in the first stanza's "(an egg / or soup / . . . there ain't no meat)" (688-89).

11. Indirect Source—MLA

When you want to quote words that you found quoted in someone else's work, put the name of the person whose words you are quoting into your own sentence. Indicate the work where you found the quotation either in your sentence or in a parenthetical citation beginning with *qtd. in.*

- Pierre Trudeau makes a notably populist statement: "The ordinary person can be appealed to through common sense. Beyond the effects of technology. My grandfather, for instance, was not especially literate but he was able to reason choices out" (qtd. in Powe 126).
- Powe quotes Pierre Trudeau as making a notably populist statement: "The ordinary person can be appealed to through common sense. Beyond the effects of technology. My grandfather, for instance, was not especially literate but he was able to reason choices out" (126).

12. Two or More Sources in One Reference—MLA

If more than one source has contributed to an idea, opinion, or fact in your paper, cite them all. In a parenthetical citation, separate each block of information with a semicolon. You can also use a footnote or an endnote to cite several sources (28c).

- Once researchers agreed that these cultural "distance zones" existed, their next step was to try to measure or define them (Hall 110-20; Henley 32-33; Fisher, Bell, and Baum 153).

13. An Entire Work—MLA

References to an entire work usually fit best into your own sentences.

- In <u>The Clockwork Sparrow</u>, Sue Binkley analyzes studies of circadian rhythms undertaken between 1967 and 1989.

14. The Bible—MLA

When citing the Bible in MLA style, you need to give the version of the Bible cited, the book (often abbreviated), chapter, and verse number. For the first Biblical citation, give the version you're using (for example, New Revised Standard Version, New International Version, etc.). In your subsequent in-text citations from the same text, you don't need to repeat the version. For example:

- Joseph's interpretation of Pharaoh's dream as meaning "Seven years of great abundance" and "seven years of famine" was a pivotal event affecting Joseph's destiny (The Holy Bible: New International Version, Gen. 41.29-30).

When using MLA style, separate Bible chapters from verses with a period. While a colon is more commonly used today for this purpose, the fifth edition of the *MLA Handbook* permits only the use of the period. You might check with your instructor to see which punctuation you need to use.

- Paul's letter to the Galatians declaring that in Christianity there is "Neither Jew nor Greek, slave nor free, male nor female" was a revolutionary statement of equality for his time (Gal. 3.28).

Biblical citations in the form shown above are valid for Old and New Testament verses. MLA does not differentiate between the two.

When citing from the Old Testament book of Psalms, each individual Psalm is referred to in the singular form. Thus, we have Psalm 121, not Psalms 121.

- One can find solace in many different ways. Some find comfort in religion, as the psalmist of the Old Testament did when he looked upon the mountains knowing that all help was a gift of the Lord (Psalm 121.1-2).

15. An Electronic Source with a Name or Title and Page Numbers—MLA

The principles that govern in-text citations of electronic sources are exactly the same as the ones that apply to books, articles, letters, interviews, or any other information source. When an electronically accessed source identifies its author, use the author's name for in-text citations. If no author is named, use the title of the source. (If several sources have the same title and no author, use also the title of the Web site or periodical.) When an electronic source has page numbers, use them exactly as you would the page numbers of a print source.

16. An Electronic Source with Paragraph, Screen, or Section Numbers—MLA

When an electronic source has numbered paragraphs, screens, or sections instead of page numbers, use them for in-text citations as you would page numbers, with these differences: (1) Use a comma followed by one space after the name (or title); (2) use the abbreviation *par.* for a reference to one paragraph (or *pars.* for a reference to more than one paragraph) followed by the paragraph number(s); (3) use *screen* (or *screens*); and (4) use *sec.* (or *secs.*) for section(s).

- Coleman worried that psychoanalysis might destroy his musical creativity (Francis, pars. 3-7).
- The renovation cost $25 million, according to Conklin (screen 5).

17. An Electronic Source Without Page or Other Numbers—MLA

Many online sources do not number pages, paragraphs, screens, or sections.

- From March to April in 2000, violations of this important environmental regulation increased 123 percent (Procope).

28c What are MLA guidelines for content or bibliographic notes?

In MLA style, footnotes or endnotes serve two specific purposes: (1) You can use them for commentary that does not fit into your paper but is still worth relating, and (2) you can use them for extensive bibliographic information that would intrude if you were to include it in your text. See 30a for advice about formatting notes.

TEXT OF PAPER

- Ronald Wright's <u>Stolen Continents</u> surprises us by telling the story of the European conquest of North and South America "through Indian eyes."[1]

COMMENTARY ENDNOTE

- [1] Wright, who was born and educated in England, brings an outsider's point of view to his adopted country, Canada. This may explain his willingness to examine the post-conquest history of the First Nations from a new and disturbing perspective.

TEXT OF PAPER

- `Barbara Randolph believes that enthusiasm is contagious (65).[1] Many psychologists have found that panic, fear, and rage spread more quickly in crowds than positive emotions do, however.`

BIBLIOGRAPHIC ENDNOTE

- `[1] Others agree with Randolph. See Thurman 21, 84, 155; Kelley 421-25; and Brookes 65-76.`

29 MLA WORKS CITED LIST

In MLA documentation, the Works Cited list includes only the sources from which you quote or paraphrase or summarize. Never include sources that you consulted but don't refer to in the paper. Box 40 gives general information about a Works Cited list. The rest of this chapter gives models of many specific kinds of Works Cited entries.

29a What are MLA guidelines for a Works Cited list?

Guidelines for an MLA-style Works Cited list — 40

TITLE

`Works Cited`

PLACEMENT OF LIST

Start a new page numbered sequentially with the rest of the paper, after the Notes pages, if any.

CONTENTS AND FORMAT

Include all sources quoted from, paraphrased, or summarized in your paper. Start each entry on a new line and at the regular left margin. If the entry uses more than one line, indent the second and all other lines five spaces (or one-half inch—about 1.25 cm) from the left margin. Double-space all lines.

→

Guidelines for an MLA-style Works Cited list *(continued)*

SPACING AFTER PUNCTUATION
Computer type fonts have influenced many users of MLA style to leave one space rather than two spaces after punctuation at the ends of sentences. The *MLA Handbook* uses one space, as does this book. Either style is acceptable, although current practice tends strongly toward one space. Use whichever style your instructor prefers. Put one space after a comma or a colon.

ARRANGEMENT OF ENTRIES
Alphabetize by author's last name. If no author is named, alphabetize by the title's first significant word (not *A, An,* or *The*).

AUTHORS' NAMES
Use first names and middle names or middle initials, if any, as given in the source. Do not reduce to initials any name that is given in full. For one author or the first-named author in multiauthor works, give the last name first. Use the word *and* with two or more authors. List multiple authors in the order given in the source. Use a comma between the first author's last and first names and after each complete author name except the last, which ends with a period. After the last author name, use a period: `Fein, Ethel Andrea, Bert Griggs, and Delaware Rogash.`

Include *Jr., Sr., II, III,* but no other titles or degrees before or after a name. For example, an entry for a work by Edward Meep, III, M.D., and Sir Feeney Bolton would start like this: `Meep, Edward, III, and Feeney Bolton.`

CAPITALIZATION OF TITLES
Capitalize all major words in titles.

SPECIAL TREATMENT OF TITLES
Use quotation marks around titles of shorter works (poems, short stories, essays, articles). The *MLA Handbook for Writers of Research Papers* (6th edition, 2003) states that although computers can create italic type, in student papers underlined roman type may be more exact. Check which style your instructor prefers.

Underline titles of longer works (books, names of newspapers or journals containing cited articles). For underlining, use an unbroken line like this (unless your software underlines only with a broken line like this).

→

MLA MLA MLA MLA MLA MLA

MLA MLA MLA MLA MLA MLA

Guidelines for an MLA-style Works Cited list *(continued)*

When a book title includes the title of another work that is usually underlined (such as a novel, play, or long poem), the preferred MLA style is not to underline the incorporated title: `Decoding Jane Eyre`. For a second style MLA accepts, see item 20, p. 204.

If the incorporated title is usually enclosed in quotation marks (such as a short story or short poem), keep the quotation marks and underline the complete title of the book (do not underline the period): `Theme and Form in "I Shall Laugh Purely."` Drop *A, An,* or *The* as the first word of a periodical title.

PLACE OF PUBLICATION
If several cities are listed for the place of publication, give only the first. If a city name alone would be ambiguous, also give the two-letter postal abbreviation for the province or U.S. state (see any standard dictionary), or an abbreviated country name, if necessary.

PUBLISHER
Use shortened names as long as they are clear: *Simon* for *Simon & Schuster.* For university presses, use the capital letters *U* and *P* (without periods): `Oxford UP; U of Chicago P.`

PUBLICATION MONTH ABBREVIATIONS
Abbreviate all publication months except *May, June,* and *July.* Use the first three letters followed by a period (see any standard dictionary: `Dec., Feb.`)

PARAGRAPH AND SCREEN NUMBERS IN ELECTRONIC SOURCES
For electronic sources that number paragraphs instead of pages, at the end of the publication information give the total number of paragraphs followed by the abbreviation *pars.:* `77 pars.` If screens are numbered, give the total number of screens as the final information in the entry. For in-text citations, use paragraph and screen numbers for reference as you use page numbers.

PAGE RANGES
Give the page range—the starting page number and the ending page number, connected by a hyphen—of any paginated electronic source and any paginated print source that is part of a longer work (for example, a chapter in a book, an article in a journal). A range indicates that the cited work is on those pages and all pages in between. If that is not the case, use the style shown next for

→

Guidelines for an MLA-style Works Cited list *(continued)*

discontinuous pages. In either case, use numerals only, without the word *page* or *pages* or the abbreviation *p.* or *pp.*

Use the full second number through 99. Above that, use only the last two digits for the second number unless it would be unclear: *103–04* is clear, but *567–602* requires full numbers.

DISCONTINUOUS PAGES
Use the starting page number followed by a plus sign (+): `32+`.

WORKS CITED ENTRIES: BOOKS
Citations for books have three main parts: author, title, and publication information (place of publication, publisher, and date of publication).

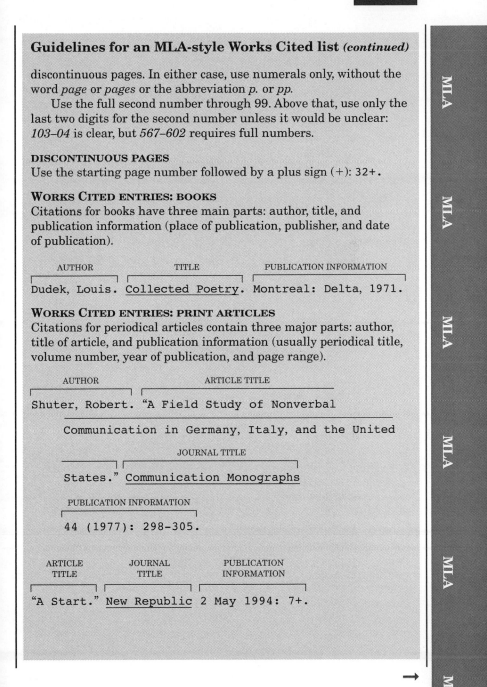

AUTHOR: Dudek, Louis. — TITLE: Collected Poetry. — PUBLICATION INFORMATION: Montreal: Delta, 1971.

```
Dudek, Louis. Collected Poetry. Montreal: Delta, 1971.
```

WORKS CITED ENTRIES: PRINT ARTICLES
Citations for periodical articles contain three major parts: author, title of article, and publication information (usually periodical title, volume number, year of publication, and page range).

AUTHOR: Shuter, Robert. — ARTICLE TITLE: "A Field Study of Nonverbal Communication in Germany, Italy, and the United States." — JOURNAL TITLE: Communication Monographs — PUBLICATION INFORMATION: 44 (1977): 298-305.

```
Shuter, Robert. "A Field Study of Nonverbal
     Communication in Germany, Italy, and the United
     States." Communication Monographs
     44 (1977): 298-305.
```

ARTICLE TITLE: "A Start." — JOURNAL TITLE: New Republic — PUBLICATION INFORMATION: 2 May 1994: 7+.

```
"A Start." New Republic 2 May 1994: 7+.
```

→

Guidelines for an MLA-style Works Cited list *(continued)*

WORKS CITED ENTRIES: ONLINE SOURCES

To document sources reached by entering a URL or Internet address (including World Wide Web, FTP, and Gopher sites), list as much of the following information as you can find: author, title, publication information about a print version if there is one, title of the Internet site or online source and its publication information, name of the organization or institution responsible for the site (if not already cited), the date you accessed the material, and the URL (electronic address). For these sources, the URL is required in the Works Cited entry, enclosed in angle brackets <like these>, after the access date and before the period at the end of the entry. Here's an entry for an article in a scientific news journal that appears only on the Web:

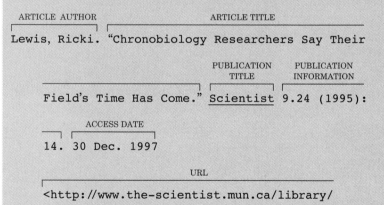

ARTICLE AUTHOR — ARTICLE TITLE

Lewis, Ricki. "Chronobiology Researchers Say Their

PUBLICATION TITLE — PUBLICATION INFORMATION

Field's Time Has Come." Scientist 9.24 (1995):

ACCESS DATE

14. 30 Dec. 1997

URL

<http://www.the-scientist.mun.ca/library/

yr1995/dec/chrono_951211.html>.

WORKS CITED ENTRIES: PORTABLE AND ONLINE SOURCES WITHOUT URLS

Citations for portable electronic sources, such as CD-ROMs, that do not have URLs contain at least these major parts: author, title, publication medium, edition or version (if relevant), and publication information (place, publisher, date). Citations for print periodicals also issued as CD-ROM databases contain these parts: author, title and publication information for the print version, title of database, publication medium, name of vendor (if relevant), and electronic publication date (see items 44 and 45, p. 210). Materials from online subscription services often lack a URL; a keyword or path can

→

Guidelines for an MLA-style Works Cited list ***(continued)***

substitute (see items 51 and 52, pp. 211–12). Here is an entry for a journal article accessed through a computer service; it also has a print version.

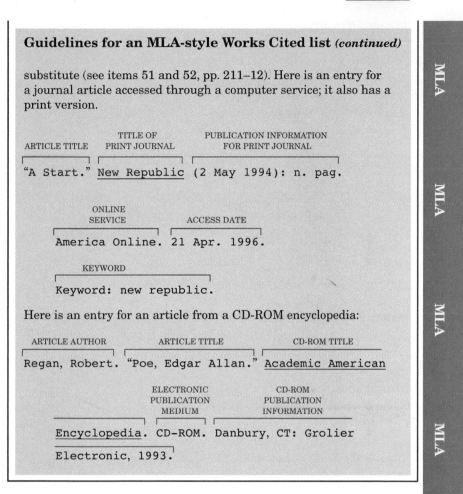

ARTICLE TITLE | TITLE OF PRINT JOURNAL | PUBLICATION INFORMATION FOR PRINT JOURNAL

"A Start." New Republic (2 May 1994): n. pag.

ONLINE SERVICE | ACCESS DATE

America Online. 21 Apr. 1996.

KEYWORD

Keyword: new republic.

Here is an entry for an article from a CD-ROM encyclopedia:

ARTICLE AUTHOR | ARTICLE TITLE | CD-ROM TITLE

Regan, Robert. "Poe, Edgar Allan." Academic American

ELECTRONIC PUBLICATION MEDIUM | CD-ROM PUBLICATION INFORMATION

Encyclopedia. CD-ROM. Danbury, CT: Grolier Electronic, 1993.

29b What are MLA guidelines for specific sources in a Works Cited list?

The directory below corresponds to the numbered examples that follow it. Not every possible documentation model is here. You may find that you have to combine features of models to document a particular source. You will also find information in the *MLA Handbook for Writers of Research Papers* (6th edition, 2003), by Joseph Gibaldi, and at <http://www.mla.org/set_stl.htm>.

Directory—MLA Style

PRINT SOURCES

1. Book by One Author—MLA
2. Book by Two or Three Authors—MLA
3. Book by More Than Three Authors—MLA
4. Two or More Works by the Same Author(s)—MLA
5. Book by Group or Corporate Author—MLA
6. Book with No Author Named—MLA
7. Book with an Author and an Editor—MLA
8. Translation—MLA
9. Work in Several Volumes or Parts—MLA
10. One Selection from an Anthology or an Edited Book—MLA
11. More Than One Selection from the Same Anthology or Edited Book—MLA
12. Signed Article in a Reference Book—MLA
13. Unsigned Article in a Reference Book—MLA
14. Second or Subsequent Edition—MLA
15. Anthology or Edited Book—MLA
16. Introduction, Preface, Foreword, or Afterword—MLA
17. Unpublished Dissertation or Essay—MLA
18. Republished Book—MLA
19. Book in a Series—MLA
20. Book with a Title Within a Title—MLA
21. The Bible—MLA
22. Government Publication—MLA
23. Published Proceedings of a Conference—MLA
24. Signed Article from a Daily Newspaper—MLA
25. Unsigned Article from a Daily Newspaper—MLA
26. Editorial, Letter to the Editor, or Review—MLA
27. Article from a Weekly or Biweekly Periodical—MLA
28. Article from a Monthly or Bimonthly Periodical—MLA
29. Article from a Collection of Reprinted Articles—MLA
30. Article from a SIRS Collection of Reprinted Articles—MLA
31. Article in a Journal with Continuous Pagination—MLA
32. Article in a Journal That Pages Each Issue Separately—MLA
33. Abstract from a Collection of Abstracts—MLA
34. Published and Unpublished Letters—MLA
35. Map or Chart—MLA

NONPRINT SOURCES

36. Interview—MLA
37. Lecture, Speech, or Address—MLA
38. Film, Videotape, or DVD—MLA
39. Musical Recording—MLA
40. Live Performance—MLA
41. Work of Art, Photograph, or Musical Composition—MLA
42. Radio or Television Program—MLA
43. Microfiche Collection of Articles—MLA

PORTABLE ELECTRONIC SOURCES

44. CD-ROM Database: Abstract with a Print Version—MLA
45. CD-ROM: Article from a Periodical with a Print Version—MLA
46. CD-ROM: Selection from a Book with a Print Version—MLA
47. CD-ROM: Material with No Print Version—MLA
48. Work in More Than One Publication Medium—MLA

ONLINE SOURCES: NO URL

49. Online Service Access: Abstract with a Print Version—MLA
50. Online Service Access: Material with No Print Version—MLA
51. Online Service Access with a Keyword: Article from a Periodical with a Print Version—MLA
52. Online Service Access Showing a Path—MLA
53. Online Service Access at a Library—MLA

URL-ACCESSED ONLINE SOURCES

54. URL Access: Book—MLA
55. URL Access: Book in a Scholarly Project—MLA
56. URL Access: Government-Published Book—MLA
57. URL Access: Articles in Online Periodicals—MLA
58. URL Access: Professional Home Page—MLA
59. URL Access: Personal Home Page—MLA
60. URL Access: Government or Institutional Web Site—MLA
61. URL Access: Poem—MLA
62. URL Access: Work of Art—MLA
63. URL Access: Interview—MLA
64. URL Access: Film or Film Clip—MLA

65. URL Access: Cartoon—MLA
66. URL Access: TV or Radio Program—MLA

OTHER ONLINE SOURCES

67. Online Posting—MLA
68. Synchronous Communication—MLA
69. E-mail Message—MLA

PRINT SOURCES

1. Book by One Author—MLA

Trudeau, Pierre E. Federalism and the French Canadians. Toronto: Macmillan, 1968.

2. Book by Two or Three Authors—MLA

Scardamalia, Marlene, Carl Bereiter, and Bryant Fillion. Writing for Results: A Sourcebook of Consequential Composing Activities. Toronto: OISE, 1981.

3. Book by More Than Three Authors—MLA

Moore, Mark H., et al. Dangerous Offenders: The Elusive Target of Justice. Cambridge: Harvard UP, 1984.

Give only the first author's name, followed by a comma and the phrase *et al.* ("and others"), or list all names in full in the order in which they appear on the title page.

4. Two or More Works by the Same Author(s)—MLA

Atwood, Margaret. The Handmaid's Tale. Toronto: McClelland, 1985.
---. Survival. Toronto: Anansi, 1972.
---. True Stories. Toronto: Oxford UP, 1981.

Give author name(s) in the first entry only. In the second and subsequent entries, use three hyphens and a period to stand for exactly the same name(s). If the person served as editor or translator, put a comma and the appropriate abbreviation (*ed.* or *trans.*) following the three hyphens. Arrange the works in alphabetical (not chronological) order according to book title, ignoring labels such as *ed.* or *trans.*

5. Book by Group or Corporate Author—MLA

Investors Group. Starting Out: Smart Strategies for Your 20s & 30s. Toronto: Stoddart, 1998.

American Psychological Association. Publication Manual of the American Psychological Association. 4th ed. Washington: APA, 1994.

Cite the full name of the corporate author first. When a corporate author is also the publisher, use a shortened form of the corporate name at the publisher position.

6. Book with No Author Named—MLA

The Chicago Manual of Style. 14th ed. Chicago: U of Chicago P, 1993.

If there is no author's name on the title page, begin the citation with the title. Alphabetize the entry according to the first significant word of the title (*Chicago,* not *The*).

7. Book with an Author and an Editor—MLA

Brontë, Emily. Wuthering Heights. Ed. David Daiches. London: Penguin, 1985.

Daiches, David, ed. Wuthering Heights. By Emily Brontë. London: Penguin, 1985.

If your paper refers to the work of the book's author, put the author's name first. If your paper refers to the work of the editor, put the editor's name first.

8. Translation—MLA

Tremblay, Michel. A Thing of Beauty. Trans. Sheila Fischman. Vancouver: Talon, 1998.

9. Work in Several Volumes or Parts—MLA

Jones, Ernest. The Last Phase. New York: Basic, 1957. Vol. 3 of The Life and Work of Sigmund Freud. 3 vols.

Randall, John Herman, Jr. The Career of Philosophy. Vol. 1. New York: Columbia UP, 1962. 2 vols.

If you are citing only one volume, put the volume number before the publication information. If you wish, you can give the total number of volumes at the end of the entry.

MLA recommends using arabic numerals, even if the source uses roman numerals (*Vol. 6* for *Vol. VI*).

10. One Selection from an Anthology or an Edited Book—MLA

Morrisseau, Norval. "The Indian That Became a Thunderbird." Canadian Short Fiction: From Myth to Modern. Ed. W. H. New. Scarborough, ON: Prentice, 1986. 26-29.

Give the author and title of the selection first and then the full title of the anthology. Information about the editor starts with *Ed.* (for "Edited by"), so do not use *Eds.* when there is more than one editor. Give the name(s) of the editor(s) in normal order rather than reversing first and last names.

11. More Than One Selection from the Same Anthology or Edited Book—MLA

Ioannou, Greg, and Lynne Missen, eds. Shivers: An Anthology of Canadian Ghost Stories. Toronto: McClelland-Bantam, 1989.

Davies, Robertson. "The Charlottetown Banquet." Ioannou and Missen. 40-52.

If you cite more than one selection from the same anthology, you can list the anthology as a separate entry with all the publication information. Then list each selection from the anthology by author and title of the selection, but give only the name of the editor(s) of the anthology and the page number(s) of the selection. Here, *ed.* stands for "editor," so use *eds.* if more than one editor is named.

12. Signed Article in a Reference Book—MLA

Burnbam, John C. "Freud, Sigmund." The Encyclopedia of Psychiatry, Psychology, and Psychoanalysis. Ed. Benjamin B. Wolman. New York: Holt, 1996.

If the articles in the book are alphabetically arranged, you don't need to give volume and page numbers. If the reference book is frequently revised, give only the edition and year of publication.

13. Unsigned Article in a Reference Book—MLA

"Ireland." Encyclopaedia Britannica. 1998 ed.

If you are citing a widely used reference work, do not give full publication information. Instead, give only the edition and year of publication.

14. Second or Subsequent Edition—MLA

Gibaldi, Joseph. MLA Handbook for Writers of Research Papers. 6th ed. New York: MLA, 2003.

If a book is not a first edition, the edition number is on the title page. Place the abbreviated information (*2nd ed., 3rd ed.,* etc.) between the title and the publication information. Give only the latest copyright date for the edition you are using.

15. Anthology or Edited Book—MLA

New, W. H., ed. Canadian Short Fiction: From Myth to Modern. Scarborough, ON: Prentice, 1986.

Here, *ed.* stands for "editor," so use *eds.* when more than one editor is named; also see items 10 and 11.

16. Introduction, Preface, Foreword, or Afterword—MLA

Allmand, Warren. Foreword. The Life and Death of Anna Mae Aquash. By Johanna Brand. Toronto: Lorimer, 1993. v-ix.

Give first the name of the writer of the part you are citing, and then the name of the cited part, capitalized but not underlined or in quotation marks. But if the introduction, preface, foreword, or afterword has a title, include that title in the citation, placing it before the name of the part. After the book title, put *By* and the book author's full name, if different from the writer of the cited material. If the book's author(s) wrote the part you are citing, after *By* repeat only the last name or names. After the publication information, give inclusive page numbers for the cited part, using roman or arabic numerals as the source does.

Fox-Genovese, Elizabeth. "Mothers and Daughters: The Ties That Bind." Foreword. Southern Mothers. Ed. Nagueyalti Warren and Sally Wolff. Baton Rouge: Louisiana State UP, 1999.

17. Unpublished Dissertation or Essay—MLA

Buckley, Joanne. "An Assessment of Kieran Egan's Theory of Educational Development." Diss. U of Western Ontario, 1991.

State the author's name first, then the title in quotation marks (not underlined), then a descriptive label (such as *Diss.* or *Unpublished essay*), then the degree-granting institution (for dissertations), and finally the date.

18. Republished Book—MLA

Lampman, Archibald. Lyrics of Earth. 1895. Ottawa: Tecumseh, 1978.

Republishing information can be found on the copyright page. Give the date of the original version before the publication information for the version you are citing.

19. Book in a Series—MLA

Courchene, Thomas J. In Praise of Renewed Federalism. The Canada Round. Toronto: C. D. Howe Institute, 1991.

20. Book with a Title Within a Title—MLA

The MLA recognizes two distinct styles for handling normally independent titles when they appear within an underlined title. In the MLA's preferred style, the embedded title should not be underlined or set within quotation marks:

Lumiansky, Robert M., and Herschel Baker, eds. Critical Approaches to Six Major English Works: Beowulf Through Paradise Lost. Philadelphia: U of Pennsylvania P, 1968.

However, the MLA now accepts a second style for handling such embedded titles. In this alternative style, the normally independent titles should be set within quotation marks, and they should be underlined:

Lumiansky, Robert M., and Herschel Baker, eds. Critical Approaches to Six Major English Works: "Beowulf" Through "Paradise Lost." Philadelphia: U of Pennsylvania P, 1968.

Use whichever style your instructor prefers.

21. The Bible—MLA

The Holy Bible: New International Version. New York: Harper, 1983.

Holy Bible: New Testament. Grand Rapids, MI: Zondervan, 2002.

22. Government Publication—MLA

Canada. Royal Commission on Bilingualism and Biculturalism. Preliminary Report. Ottawa: Queen's Printer, 1965.

Canada. Indian and Northern Affairs Canada. The Inuit. Ottawa: Supply and Services Canada, 1986.

For most government publications, use the name of the government as the first information unit (such as Canada). If no author is named, give the name of the branch of government or the government agency next (such as Department of Finance or Task Force on Program Review).

23. Published Proceedings of a Conference—MLA

Smith, Donald B., ed. Forging a New Relationship: Proceedings of the Conference on the Report of the Royal Commission on Aboriginal Peoples. 31 Jan.-2 Feb. 1997. Montreal: McGill Institute for the Study of Canada, 1997.

24. Signed Article from a Daily Newspaper—MLA

Church, Elizabeth. "Vacancy Rates Rise for First Time in Decade." Globe and Mail 27 Nov. 2002: B1+.

Omit *A* or *The* as the first word in a newspaper title. If the city of publication is not part of the title, put it in square brackets after the title, not underlined. (The city is not needed for nationally published newspapers.) Give the day, month, and year of the issue. If sections are designated, give the section letter as well as the page number. If an article runs on nonconsecutive pages, give the starting page number followed by a plus sign (for example, *23+* for an article that starts on page 23 and continues on page 42).

25. Unsigned Article from a Daily Newspaper—MLA

"Private Water May Violate Constitution." Ottawa Citizen 27 Nov. 2002: A1.

26. Editorial, Letter to the Editor, or Review—MLA

"A Black Mark on Local Government." Editorial. London Free Press 27 July 1994: B8.

Hurka, John. Letter. Calgary Sun 5 July 1994: A18.

Toews, Wendy. "Politics of the Mind." Rev. of They Say You're Crazy by Paula J. Caplan. Winnipeg Free Press 26 Aug. 1995: C3.

27. Article from a Weekly or Biweekly Periodical—MLA

Wood, Chris. "Storm Clouds over Quebec." Maclean's 6 Nov. 1989: 16-17.

As with a newspaper source, an unsigned article in a weekly or biweekly periodical has as its first item the title of the article.

28. Article from a Monthly or Bimonthly Periodical—MLA

O'Malley, Sean. "Make-It-Happen Kinda Dreamer: Theatre Director Diane Dupuy Is Nobody's Puppet." Chatelaine Aug. 1994: 36+.

An unsigned article in a monthly or bimonthly periodical has as its first item the title of the article.

29. Article from a Collection of Reprinted Articles—MLA

Brumberg, Abraham. "Russia After Perestroika." New York Review of Books 27 June 1991: 53-62. Rpt. in Russian and Soviet History. Ed. Alexander Dallin. Vol. 14 of The Gorbachev Era. New York: Garland, 1992. 300-20.

30. Article from a SIRS Collection of Reprinted Articles—MLA

Curver, Phillip C. "Lighting in the 21st Century." Futurist Jan./Feb. 1989: 29-34. Ed. Eleanor Goldstein. Vol. 4. Boca Raton: SIRS, 1990. Art. 84.

Give the citation for the original publication first, followed by the citation for the collection.

31. Article in a Journal with Continuous Pagination—MLA

Tyson, Phyllis. "The Psychology of Women." Journal of the American Psychoanalytic Association 46 (1998): 361-64.

(If the first issue of a journal with continuous pagination ends on page 228, the second issue starts with page 229.) Give only the volume number before the year. Use arabic numerals for all numbers.

32. Article in a Journal That Pages Each Issue Separately—MLA

Hogarty, Thomas F. "Gasoline: Still Powering Cars in 2050?" The Futurist 33.3 (1999): 51-55.

When each issue begins with page 1, give both the volume number (*33*) and the issue number (*3*), separated by a period.

33. Abstract from a Collection of Abstracts—MLA

To cite an abstract, first give information for the full work: the author's name, the title of the article, and publication information about the full article. If a reader could not know that the cited material is an abstract, write the word *Abstract,* not underlined, followed by a period. Give publication information about the collection of abstracts. For abstracts identified by item numbers rather than page numbers, use the word *item* before the item number.

Marcus, Hazel R., and Shinobu Kitayamo. "Culture and the Self: Implications for Cognition, Emotion, and Motivation." Psychological Review 88 (1991): 224-53. Psychological Abstracts 78 (1991): item 23878.

34. Published and Unpublished Letters—MLA

Sand, George. Letter to her mother. 31 May 1831. Letters Home: Celebrated Authors Write to Their Mothers. Ed. Reid Sherline. New York: Timkin, 1993. 17-20.

Brown, Theodore. Letter to the author. 7 Jan. 2000.

35. Map or Chart—MLA

Russia and Post-Soviet Republics. Map. Moscow: Mapping Production Association, 1992.

NONPRINT SOURCES

36. Interview—MLA

Friedman, Randi. Telephone interview. 30 June 1997.

For a face-to-face interview, use *Personal interview* in place of *Telephone interview.*

37. Lecture, Speech, or Address—MLA

Barlow, Maude. Address. League of Canadian Poets. Toronto. 25 May 1991.

38. Film, Videotape, or DVD—MLA

Shakespeare in Love. Screenplay by Marc Norman and Tom Stoppard. Dir. John Madden. Prod. David Parfitt, Donna Gigliotta, Harvey Weinstein, Edward Zwick, and Mark Norman. Perf. Gwyneth Paltrow, Joseph Fiennes, and Judi Dench. Videocassette. Miramax/Universal, 1999.

Calendar. Screenplay by Atom Egoyan. Dir. Atom Egoyan. Prod. Ego Filmarts/ZDF. Perf. Atom Egoyan and Arsinée Khanjian. 1993. DVD. Alliance Atlantis, 2001.

Give the title first, and include the director, the distributor, and the year. For older films that were subsequently released on videocassettes or DVDs, provide the original release date of the movie *before* the name of the distributor. Other information (writer, producer, major actors) is optional but helpful. Put first names first.

39. Musical Recording—MLA

Smetana, Bedrich. My Country. Cond. Karel Ancerl. Czech Philharmonic Orch. LP. Vanguard, 1975.

Springsteen, Bruce. "Local Hero." Lucky Town. Columbia, 1992.

Put first the name most relevant to what you discuss in your paper (performer, conductor, the work performed, etc.). Include the recording's title, the medium for any recording other than a CD (e.g., *LP, Audiocassette*), name of the issuer (e.g., *Vanguard*), and the year.

40. Live Performance—MLA

The Merchant of Venice. By William Shakespeare. Dir. Richard Monette. Perf. Lucy Peacock and Paul Soles. Festival Theatre, Stratford, ON. 8 May 2001.

41. Work of Art, Photograph, or Musical Composition—MLA

Pratt, Christopher. Shop in an Island. London Regional Art Gallery, London, ON.

Schubert, Franz. Symphony no. 8 in B minor.

Schubert, Franz. Unfinished Symphony.

Do not underline or put in quotation marks music identified only by form, number, and key, but do underline any work that has a title, such as an opera, a ballet, or a named symphony.

42. Radio or Television Program—MLA

"Mountie and Soul." Due South. Perf. Paul Gross and David Marciano. CTV. CFTO, Toronto. 26 Oct. 1997

Include at least the title of the program (underlined), the network, the local station and its city, and the date(s) of the broadcast. For a series, also supply the title of the specific episode (in quotation marks) before the title of the program (underlined) and the title of the series (neither underlined nor in quotation marks).

43. Microfiche Collection of Articles—MLA

Wenzell, Ron. "Businesses Prepare for a More Diverse Work Force." St. Louis Post Dispatch 3 Feb. 1990. NewsBank: Employment 27 (1990): fiche 2, grid D12.

PORTABLE ELECTRONIC SOURCES

The following basic blocks of information are used to document a portable electronic source (such as a CD-ROM or a diskette) in MLA style. A period ends each block.

1. Documentation information about the print version, if any. (Many sources accessed electronically also exist in published print versions. Others exist only in electronic form.) Follow the models in directory items 1–35 above for print sources. You may not find all the details about a print version in an electronic version, but provide as much information as you can. Information about a print version usually is given at the beginning or the end of an electronic document.
2. Author (if any) and title (underlined) of the electronic source or database. If there is no print version, start your Works Cited entry with this information.
3. Electronic medium, such as *CD-ROM, Diskette,* or *Magnetic tape.*
4. Name of the producer.
5. Publication date (preceded by place of publication unless the source is a periodical).

44. CD-ROM Database: Abstract with a Print Version—MLA

Marcus, Hazel R., and Shinobu Kitayamo. "Culture and the Self: Implications for Cognition, Emotion, and Motivation." Psychological Abstracts 78 (1991): item 23878. PsycLIT. CD-ROM. SilverPlatter. Sept. 1991.

All the information through *item 23878* is for the print version of this source. The volume number is 78, and the abstract's number is 23878. All the information from *PsycLIT* to the end of the entry is for the electronic version of the source. *PsycLIT* is the name of the CD-ROM database, and *SilverPlatter* is the name of the producer of the CD-ROM. The CD-ROM was issued in September 1991.

45. CD-ROM: Article from a Periodical with a Print Version—MLA

"The Price Is Right." Time. 20 Jan. 1992: 38. Time Man of the Year. CD-ROM. Compact. 1993.

Information for the print version ends with the article's page number, 38. The title of the CD-ROM is *Time Man of the Year,* its producer is the publisher Compact, and its copyright year is 1993. Both the title of the print publication and the title of the CD-ROM are underlined.

46. CD-ROM: Selection from a Book with a Print Version—MLA

"Prehistoric Humans: Earliest Homo sapiens." The Guinness Book of Records 1994. London: Guinness, 1994. The Guinness Multimedia Disk of Records. CD-ROM. Version 2.0. Danbury: Grolier Electronic, 1994.

Version 2.0 signals that this CD-ROM is updated periodically; the producer changes version numbers rather than giving update dates.

47. CD-ROM: Material with No Print Version—MLA

"Spanish Dance." Encarta 2000. CD-ROM. Redmond: Microsoft, 1999.

Encarta 2000 is a CD-ROM encyclopedia with no print version. "Spanish Dance" is the title of an article in *Encarta 2000.*

48. Work in More Than One Publication Medium—MLA

Clarke, David James. Novell's CNE Study Guide. Book. Network Support Encyclopedia. CD-ROM. Alameda: Sybex, 1994.

This book and CD-ROM come together. Each has its own title, but the publication information—*Alameda: Sybex, 1994*—applies to both.

ONLINE SOURCES: NO URL

Online sources fall into two categories: (1) those you access through an online service, such as America Online or at a library; and (2) those you access by entering a specific URL (Internet address). For source material reached through an online service, give the name of the service, and if you used a keyword, give it after the access date. Items 49–51 show how to document such sources.

49. Online Service Access: Abstract with a Print Version—MLA

Marcus, Hazel R., and Shinobu Kitayamo. "Culture and the Self: Implications for Cognition, Emotion, and Motivation." Psychological Abstracts 78 (1991): item 23878. PsycINFO. Dialog. 10 Oct. 1991.

This entry is for the same abstract from *Psychological Abstracts* shown in item 44, but here it is accessed from an online database (*PsycINFO*) by means of an online service (Dialog). This entry notes *PsycINFO,* the name of the online database, where item 44 notes *PsycLIT,* the name of the CD-ROM database; and it notes Dialog, the service through which *PsycINFO* was accessed, where item 44 notes the CD-ROM producer SilverPlatter. The last information unit—*10 Oct. 1991*—is the date that the abstract was accessed.

50. Online Service Access: Material with No Print Version—MLA

"Microsoft Licenses OSM Technology from Henter-Joyce." WinNews Electronic Newsletter 2:6 (1 May 1995). CompuServe. 15 May 1995.

The designation *2:6* indicates volume 2, number 6 of this electronic newsletter.

51. Online Service Access with a Keyword: Article from a Periodical with a Print Version—MLA

Kapor, Mitchell, and Jerry Berman. "A Superhighway Through the Wasteland?" New York Times 24 Nov. 1993: Op-ed page. New York Times Online. America Online. 5 May 1995. Keyword: nytimes.

MLA MLA MLA MLA MLA MLA

Information applying to the print version of this article in the *New York Times* ends with *Op-ed page,* and the information about the online version starts with the title of the database, *New York Times Online.* America Online is the service through which the database was accessed, and 5 May 1995 is the access date. The keyword *nytimes* was used to access *New York Times Online,* as noted after the access date.

52. Online Service Access Showing a Path—MLA

When you access a source by choosing a series of keywords, menus, or topics, end the entry with the "path" of words you used. Use semicolons between items in the path, and put a period at the end.

```
Futrelle, David. "A Smashing Success." Money.com 23 Dec.
     1999. America Online. 26 Dec. 1999. Path: Personal
     Finance; Business News; Business Publications;
     Money.com.
```

53. Online Service Access at a Library—MLA

For a source accessed through a library's online service, first give information about the source. Then give the name of the service, the name of the library, and the access date. Give the URL of the online service's home page, if you know it, after the access date. Use angle brackets (< >) to enclose this URL, and put a period after the closing bracket.

```
Dutton, Gail. "Greener Pigs." Popular Science 255.5 (1999):
     38-39. ProQuest Direct. Public Lib., Moncton. 7 Dec.
     1999 <http://proquest.umi.com>.
```

URL-ACCESSED ONLINE SOURCES

In this section, you will find models for online sources accessed when you enter a URL, or specific Internet address. These guidelines cover Web sites, FTP and Gopher sites, e-mail discussion lists, discussion groups, and other online sources. For such sources, provide as much of the following information as you can.

1. The author's name, if any.
2. In quotation marks, the title of a short work (poem, short story, essay, article, posted message); or underlined, the title of a book.
3. The name of an editor, translator, or compiler, if any, with an abbreviation such as *Ed., Trans.,* or *Comp.* before the name.
4. Publication information for any print version of the source.

5. The underlined title of a scholarly project or reference database. (If the site has no title, describe it: e.g., *Home page.* If available, add the name of the editor of the site.)
6. The date of electronic publication (including a version number, if any) or posting or the most recent update.
7. The name of a subscription service or sponsoring organization, if any.
8. The date you accessed the material.
9. The URL in angle brackets (< >), with a period after the closing bracket. (If the URL is very long, use the URL of the site's search page.)

54. URL Access: Book—MLA

Eaton, Arthur W. Acadian Legends and Lyrics. London and New York: White & Allen, 1889. Early Canadiana Online. 16 Feb. 2000. 25 May 2001 <http://www.canadiana.org/cgi-bin/ECO/mtq?doc=09066>.

55. URL Access: Book in a Scholarly Project—MLA

Herodotus. The History of Herodotus. Trans. George Rawlinson. The Internet Classics Archive. Ed. Daniel C. Stevenson. 11 Jan. 1998. Massachusetts Institute of Technology. 4 Dec. 1999 <http://classics.mit.edu/Herodotus/history.sum.html>.

56. URL Access: Government-Published Book—MLA

Canada. Canadian Heritage. Languages in Canada: 1996 Canadian Census. By Louise Marmen and Jean-Pierre Corbeil. New Canadian Perspectives. 6 Feb. 2001. 11 June 2001 <http://www.pch.gc.ca/offlangoff/perspectives/english/census96/census96.pdf>.

For government publications that name no author, start with the name of the government or government body, then name the government agency. For a government text, the title is followed by the writer of the publication, if available.

57. URL Access: Articles in Online Periodicals—MLA

Ignatieff, Michael. "The Man Who Was Right." Rev. of Reflections on a Ravaged Century, by Robert Conquest. New York Review of Books 23 March 2000. 5 June 2001 <http://nybooks.com/nyrev/www.archdisplay.cgi?20000323035R>.

Gold, David. "Ulysses: A Case Study in the Problems of Hypertextualization of Complex Documents." Computers, Writing, Rhetoric and Literature 3.1 (1997): 37 pars. 4 Dec. 1999 <http://www.cwrl.utexas.edu/~cwrl/v3n1/dgold/title.htm>.

Keegan, Paul. "Culture Quake." Mother Jones Nov.-Dec. 1999. 4 Dec. 1999 <http://www.mojones.com/mother_jones/ND99/quake.html>.

Lewis, Ricki. "Chronobiology Researchers Say Their Field's Time Has Come." Scientist 9.24 (1995): 14. 30 Dec. 1997 <http://www.thescientist.library.upenn.edu/yr1995/dec/chrono-951211.html>.

Pacienza, Angela. "Cities Could Become Treeless Wastelands." Winnipeg Free Press Online Edition 11 June 2001. 9 July 2001 <http://www.winnipegfreepress.com/news/canadaworld/273409436518713.html>.

When you cite online periodicals, give the following information:

1. The author's name, if any.
2. In quotation marks, the title of the article or editorial.
3. A description of the cited material as a review, an editorial, or a letter unless the title gives that information.
4. The underlined name of the periodical.
5. Volume and issue numbers, if any.
6. The date of publication.
7. The total number of pages, paragraphs, or other numbered sections, if any.
8. The date you accessed the material.
9. The URL in angle brackets (< >), with a period after the closing bracket.

58. URL Access: Professional Home Page—MLA

Mountain Culture. 2002. Banff Centre for Continuing Education. 22 Nov. 2002 <http://www.banffcentre.ca/mountainculture/>.

This is the home page of an institute based at the Banff Centre.

59. URL Access: Personal Home Page—MLA

Hunter-Kilmer, Melissa. Home page. 15 Feb. 1995. 4 Dec. 1999 <http://www.Idsonline.com/userweb/phantom/index/htm>.

For home pages, include as much of the following information as you can find:

1. If available, the name of the person who created or put up the home page. If first and last names are given, reverse the order of the first author's name.
2. The title, underlined. If there is no title, add the description *Home page,* not underlined, followed by a period. Add the date of the last update, if given.
3. For a professional home page, the name of the sponsoring organization.
4. The date you accessed the material.
5. The URL in angle brackets (< >), with a period after the closing bracket.

60. URL Access: Government or Institutional Web Site—MLA

The Banff Centre. 2002. Banff Centre for Continuing Education. 22 Nov. 2002 <http://www.banffcentre.ca/>.

This is the home page of the Banff Centre's main Web site.

61. URL Access: Poem—MLA

Nelligan, Émile. "Automne." Émile Nelligan et son oeuvre. Montreal, 1925. Canadian Poetry Archive. 2 Jan. 2002. National Library of Canada. 22 Nov. 2002 <http://www.nlc-bnc.ca/canvers-bin/entry?entry_nbr=754&l=0&page_rows=10&clctn_nbr=1>.

62. URL Access: Work of Art—MLA

Anghik, Abraham. Kittigazuit--1918. 2000. Winnipeg Art Gallery. 18 Nov. 2002 <http://www.wag.mb.ca/collection/recentacquisition.html>.

63. URL Access: Interview—MLA

Plaxco, Jim. Interview. Planetary Studies Foundation. Oct. 1992. 5 Dec. 2001 <http://www.planets.org/>.

64. URL Access: Film or Film Clip—MLA

Columbus, Chris, dir. Harry Potter and the Sorcerer's Stone. Trailer. Warner Brothers, 2001. 5 Dec. 2001 <http://www.hollywood.com>.

65. URL Access: Cartoon—MLA

Bell, Darin. "Rudy Park." Cartoon. New York Times on the Web. 5 Dec. 2001. 5 Dec. 2001 <http://wwww2.uclick.com/client/nyt/rk/>.

66. URL Access: TV or Radio Program—MLA

Walsh, Mary. "Regeneration Trilogy by Pat Barker." Open Book. CBC. 29 Sept. 2002. 15 Nov. 2002 <http://cbc.ca/openbook/episode8.html>.

OTHER ONLINE SOURCES

67. Online Posting—MLA

Woodbury, Chuck. "Free RV Campgrounds." Online posting. 4 Dec. 1999. The RV Home Page Bulletin Board. 21 Dec. 1999 <http://www.rvhome.com/wwwboard/messages/4598.html>.

Be cautious about using online postings as sources. Some postings contain cutting-edge information from experts, but some contain trash. Unfortunately, there is no way to know whether people online are who they claim to be. To cite an online message, give the author name (if any), the title of the message in quotation marks, and then *Online posting.* Give the date of the posting and the name of the bulletin board, if any. Then give the access date and, in angle brackets, the URL.

68. Synchronous Communication—MLA

Bleck, Bradley. Online discussion of "Virtual First Year Composition: Distance Education, the Internet, and the World Wide Web." 8 June 1997. DaMOO. 27 Feb. 1999 <http://DaMOO.csun.edu/CW/brad.html>.

Give the name of the speaker, a title for the event ("Virtual First Year Composition: Distance Education, the Internet, and the World Wide Web"), the forum (DaMOO), date, access date, and URL.

69. E-mail Message—MLA

```
Thompson, Jim. "Bob Martin's Address." E-mail to June Cain.
     11 Nov. 1997.
```

Start with the name of the person who wrote the e-mail message. Give the title or subject line in quotation marks. Then describe the source (*e-mail*) and identify the recipient. End with the date.

30 A STUDENT'S MLA RESEARCH PAPER

30a What are MLA format guidelines for research papers?

Check whether your instructor has special instructions for the final draft of your research paper. If there are no special instructions, you can use the MLA guidelines here. The student paper in 30b was prepared according to MLA guidelines.

General instructions—MLA

Use standard-size white paper (8 1/2 × 11 inches). Double-space throughout, whether the paper is typed or prepared on a computer. Set a 1-inch (about 2.5-cm) margin on the left, and leave at least that amount of space on the right and at the bottom. If you are using a computer, do not justify the type.

Drop down 1/2 inch (about 1.25 cm) from the top edge of the paper to the name-and-page-number line described below. Then drop down the same distance to the first line, whether that is a heading, a title, or a line of the text of your paper.

If you are typing, paragraph indents and indents in Notes and Works Cited are five characters. The indent for a set-off quotation (see p. 230) is ten characters. If you are preparing your paper on a computer, paragraph indents and indents in Notes and Works Cited are 1/2 inch (1.25 cm), and the indent for a set-off quotation is 1 inch (2.5 cm).

Order of parts—MLA

Use this order for the parts of your paper: body of the paper; endnotes, if any; Works Cited list; attachments, if any (such as questionnaires, data sheets, or any other material your instructor tells you to include). Number all pages consecutively.

Name-and-page-number line for all pages—MLA

Use a name-and-page-number line on every page of your paper. Drop down 1/2 inch (1.25 cm) from the top edge of the sheet of paper. Type your last name, then a one-character space and the page number. Align the typed line about an inch (2.5 cm) from the right edge of the paper.

First page—MLA

Use a name-and-page-number line. If your instructor does not require a cover sheet, use a four-line heading at the top of the first page. Drop down 1 inch (2.5 cm) from the top edge of the paper. Starting each line at the left margin, include the following information:

`Your name` [first line]

`Your instructor's name` [second line]

`Your course name and section` [third line]

`The date you hand in your paper` [fourth line]

For the submission date, MLA style uses day-month-year form: *26 November 2002.*

On the line below this heading, centre the title of your paper. Do not underline the title or enclose it in quotation marks. On the line below the title, start your paper.

CAPITALIZATION ALERTS: (1) Use a capital letter for the first word of your title and the first word of a subtitle, if you use one. Start every NOUN,* PRONOUN, VERB, ADVERB, ADJECTIVE, and SUBORDINATING CONJUNCTION with a capital letter. Capitalize the last word of your title, no matter what part of speech it is. In a hyphenated compound word (two or more words used together to express one idea), capitalize each word after a hyphen: Brain-Teaser. (2) Do not capitalize an article (*a, an, the*) unless one of the preceding capitalization rules applies to it. Do not capitalize any PREPOSITIONS, no matter how many letters they contain. Do not capitalize COORDINATING CONJUNCTIONS. Do not capitalize the word *to* used in an INFINITIVE.!

Set-off quotations—MLA

Set off quotations of more than four lines from your main text. Start a new line for the quoted words, indenting each line of the double-spaced

*Words printed in small capital letters (such as NOUN) are defined in the Terms Glossary on pages 497–517.

quotation ten spaces (or 1 inch—about 2.5 cm) from the left margin. Do not enclose the quoted words in quotation marks.

If you are quoting part of a paragraph or one complete paragraph, do not indent the first line of quoted words more than ten spaces. But if you quote more than one paragraph, indent the first line of each paragraph after the first an additional three spaces (thirteen spaces in all).

When the quotation is finished, leave a space after the sentence-ending punctuation, and then give the parenthetical citation. Begin a new line to resume your own words. (For examples of set-off quotations in MLA style, see 54b and Chandra Johnson's paper in 30b.)

Notes—MLA

If you use a note in your paper (28c), try to structure the sentence so that the note number falls at the end. The ideal place for a note number is after the sentence-ending punctuation. Do not leave a space before the number, but raise the number slightly above the line of words, if possible. Leave one space after the note number.

Put your notes on a separate page after the last page of the body of your paper and before the Works Cited list. Use a name-and-page-number line, then drop down 1 inch (2.5 cm) from the top edge of the paper and centre the word *Notes;* do not underline it or put it in quotation marks.

On the next line, start your first note. Indent five characters (or 1/2 inch—about 1.25 cm). Raise the note number slightly, if possible. After the number, type one space, and then start the words of your note. Do not indent any lines except the first. Use double spacing for each note and between notes.

Number the notes consecutively throughout the paper, except for notes referring to tables or figures.

Place table or figure notes below the table or illustration. Instead of note numbers, use lower-case letters (*a, b, c*).

Works Cited list—MLA

Starting a new page, type a name-and-page-number line. Then, 1 inch (2.5 cm) below the top edge of the paper, type the words Works Cited. Do not underline them or put them in quotation marks.

On the next line, start the first entry in your Works Cited list at the left margin. If an entry takes more than one line, indent each line after the first five characters (or 1/2 inch—about 1.25 cm). Use double spacing for each entry and between entries.

30b Chandra Johnson's MLA research paper

Chandra Johnson, a first-year student, wrote the following research paper in MLA documentation style for her English 101 course. Her instructor asked students to research a current topic that interested them. Chandra panicked a little at the open-endedness of the assignment, but she followed the suggestions in Chapter 22 to identify a topic. She had always been fascinated by robots in movies and television, so she decided to explore how close their depictions were to reality. Then she narrowed this broad topic to one that focused more on the role of emotions in artificial intelligence.

Chandra began her research by looking in online databases available through her school's library. She searched both popular periodicals and specialized scientific ones. Because she found so much information, she decided to focus on sources published in the past five years. References in some of those articles led her to scholarly books. After she began drafting her paper, Chandra looked at some Internet sources to find any information that was too current to be in periodicals and books.

Here is an outline of Chandra's paper, followed by the paper itself.

Outline

I. Introduction
  A. Example from the movie _A.I.: Artificial Intelligence_
  B. Thesis: An unsolved problem is whether computers need emotions for scientists to consider them intelligent.

II. Definitions of intelligence
  A. General definitions
  B. Artificial intelligence
    1. Qualities of AI
    2. Scientists' opinions of how close we are to AI
    3. Turing Test
    4. Chess room argument

III. Types of intelligence
  A. Gardner's eight intelligences
  B. Emotional intelligence
    1. Goleman's research
    2. Damasio's research

IV. Emotion and artificial intelligence
  A. Believers' and doubters' positions on emotion
  B. The role of recognizing and conveying emotions
    1. Children's learning
    2. Applying Disney's techniques to robots

V. Conclusion
  A. The remaining controversy
  B. Computers probably will not have emotions any time soon

Use 1/2-inch (1.25-cm) top margin, 1-inch (2.5-cm) bottom and side margins; double-space throughout.

Put identifying information in upper left corner; double-space.

Centre title one double space below identifying information.

Johnson 1 A

Chandra Johnson
Professor Gregor
English 101
18 November 2002

The Role of Emotions in Artificial Intelligence

The movie <u>A.I.: Artificial Intelligence</u> B
portrays a future in which distinguishing robots
from people is almost impossible. The robots look
human and can produce actions that appear to
be human. Still, one important distinction
exists: Robots lack true emotions. In the film,
released in 2001, scientists create an
experimental robotic boy who can deeply love the
woman who owns him and can believe that she is
his mother. Computer scientists, psychologists,
and philosophers today disagree over whether
creating artificial beings like this boy should
be the ultimate goal of research in artificial
intelligence. Indeed, an unsolved problem is C
whether computers need emotion for scientists to
consider them intelligent.

In MLA style, put author and page number in parentheses when author is not named in text.

Defining human intelligence is a major focus D
of cognitive science, a broad field that studies
the mind (Pfeifer and Scheier 5). Members of this E
field include psychologists, biologists,
linguists, and computer scientists. Cognitive
scientists agree that human intelligence includes
several broad abilities. These consist of the
abilities to think abstractly, to learn, to adapt

Commentary

A. Computer tip: Following MLA style. Chandra used her name and the page number as a running header throughout the paper. She used the "header" command in her word-processing program to automatically insert the proper information on each page.

B. Introductory strategy. Chandra attracts the reader's interest by referring to a recent popular movie. From that specific example she moves to introducing the topic more broadly. Because the movie *A.I.* gave her the idea for her paper topic, the introduction came fairly easily to her.

C. Thesis. The last sentence of Chandra 's introductory paragraph is her thesis statement. In it she tries to prepare readers for the main message of the paper.

D. Process note: Paragraph 2 begins to define intelligence. In an early draft, Chandra began immediately to describe attempts to create artificial intelligence in robots. Later she decided that it made more sense to talk generally about intelligence in humans and then begin the discussion of computers and robots.

E. Summarizing a source. For much of her initial definition of intelligence, Chandra drew upon a scholarly book. She decided to summarize concepts from that book rather than paraphrase or quote them. Note that she took care to include page citations.

In MLA style, header has student's last name and page number.

to new situations in life, and to profit from experiences (Pfeifer and Scheier 7). Intelligence calls for more than the ability to recall information or perform set routines. It involves using past knowledge, intuition, creativity, and experience in new, unfamiliar situations, and learning from them. It also requires using intuition and creativity (Pfeifer and Scheier 10). For example, when college student Joshua Vrana, who worked part-time in a store, was asked to develop a Web site, Vrana created it from his knowledge of Web design, the store, and its customers. In so doing, he creatively drew upon his knowledge and experience, thereby using all aspects of human intelligence. F

Cognitive scientists disagree on a definition of artificial intelligence. At one extreme are those who regard it as the ability of a machine to perform every intelligent act that a human can perform. Table 1 lists some of those acts. This is a very high standard. At the other extreme, some scientists define artificial intelligence as the ability to perform even small acts that require human intelligence. For example, the American Association for Artificial Intelligence recommends sources that argue that artificial intelligence already exists in simple machines that have been in use for years (AI Overview). This is a very low standard. G H

Put part of the Web page title (or full title, if required for clarity) in parenthetical citation when source lists no author.

Commentary

F. Example from experience. Chandra decided that the point about intuition and creativity would be clearer if she gave an example. She remembered a conversation with her friend, Joshua Varna, about a project he had completed at his job and realized it would illustrate the point effectively.

G. Elaborating a key issue from the thesis. Chandra's topic sentence in this paragraph signals to the reader that she is about to explain the disagreement between scientists over the proper measure of artificial intelligence. By starting one sentence with "At one extreme" and another sentence with "At the other extreme," she hoped to contrast and clarify the two positions. Chandra had to write several drafts to state the distinctions clearly and consisely.

H. Reference to a table. Although she did not want to interrupt her paragraph, Chandra felt that her readers would benefit from a reference to Table 1, which follows.

Johnson 3

Table number, title, and format in MLA style

Table 1 I

Some Qualities of Artificial Intelligence

Category	Examples
Problem solving	Using informed search methods to solve problems; game playing
Logical behaviour	Planning for practical action; acting appropriately for a given situation
Knowledge and reasoning	Using memory; dealing with uncertainty; reasoning using probability; making simple and complex decisions
Learning	Learning from observations and experience
Communicating, perceiving, acting	Using language with people; becoming aware of surroundings through the senses; interacting with the environment

Table source note in MLA style

Source: Adapted from Rolf Pfeifer and Christian Scheier, Understanding Intelligence. Cambridge, MA: MIT, 2000. 46

While the dream of creating robots with human intelligence has existed for almost a century, scientists disagree about how close we have come to realizing that dream. Perhaps the most famous example occurred when computer engineers developed IBM's Deep Blue computer, J

Commentary

I. Table. Chandra faced a length restriction in this paper, but she needed to present a good deal of information. She decided the most effective way to summarize much of that information would be to include a table. Developing the table also helped her to clarify the ideas it contained.

J. **Process note:** Chandra had to revise this paragraph several times because it covers several different opinions (note the number of sources she cites in a relatively short space). She included the example of Deep Blue to illustrate efforts to create intelligent computers. The quotation from one of Deep Blue's creators, she thought, was particularly effective because it takes a position opposite the one we might expect.

Johnson 4

which beat chess grandmaster Garry Kasparov in 1997 (Hayden 46). However, Murray Campbell, one of Deep Blue's creators, has conceded that the computer "did not exhibit human qualities and therefore was not 'intelligent' " (Stix 36). Some computer scientists take a much different position. For example, Hans Moravec believes that "robot computers [will] achieve human intelligence . . . around 2040" (Minerd 9). Ray Kurzweil is even more optimistic in that he believes that Moravec's prediction will come true as early as 2029 and that by the end of the 21st century, machine-based intelligences will rightfully claim to be human (Kurzweil 21).

In MLA style, put author and page number in parentheses when author is not named in text.

Square brackets show words added or changed to make a quotation flow.

The Turing Test, developed in 1950 by British mathematician Alan Turing, is one commonly accepted measure of artificial intelligence (McCarthy). A researcher sits in one room, another person in a second room, and a computer in a third room. The researcher does not know which room contains the other person and which holds the computer. Communicating only through a keyboard and screen, the researcher asks the same questions of both the person and the machine. If the computer answers so that the researcher cannot tell whether the response comes from a machine, the computer passes the test.

World Wide Web source has no page numbers.

However, some people dispute the Turing Test. Prominent philosopher John Searle argues that the appearance of proper answers does not mean the existence of intelligence. He offers "The Chess Room Argument":

Commentary

K. Key transition within a paragraph. Because she was summarizing two very different positions in this paragraph, Chandra needed a strong sentence to signal a contrast between scientists who doubt the possibility of artificial intelligence and those who think we are close to achieving it. In an early draft she had divided this material into two paragraphs, but she later decided it would work better as a single paragraph.

L. Modified quotation. To make the quotation from Moravec fit the flow of the sentence, Chandra had to add the word "will." She enclosed the word in brackets to signal that it was not part of the original quotation. (The original source was written in the hypothetical future, and simply said "computers achieve intelligence.") Chandra also omitted some words from the source and indicated the omission with an ellipsis.

M. Summary. Chandra compressed a lengthy description of the Turing Test into as brief a summary as she could.

N. Block indented quotation. After trying several times, Chandra was unable to produce a satisfactory summary or paraphrase of Searle's "Chess Room Argument." She decided instead to quote the entire passage, with some omitted words indicated by the ellipsis. Because the passage was longer than four lines, Chandra needed to indent it. She reviewed the MLA guidelines for the format of block quotations and the exact position of the parenthetical citation, explained on pages 218–19 of this book.

Johnson 5

Use 1-inch (2.5-cm) block indent for quotations longer than 4 lines.

> Imagine that a man who does not know how to play chess is locked inside a room, and there he is given a set of, to him, meaningless symbols. Unknown to him, these represent positions on a chessboard. He looks up in a book what he is supposed to do, and he passes back more meaningless symbols. We can suppose that if the rule book . . . is skillfully written, he will win chess games. People outside the room will say, "This man understands chess, and in fact he is a good chess player because he wins." They will be totally mistaken. The man understands nothing of chess, he is just a computer. (37)

Ellipsis indicates words omitted from a quotation.

In MLA style, parenthetical information goes after the period in a block quotation.

The disagreements about defining artificial intelligence result partly from how complicated the idea of human intelligence has become. Between 1980 and 1996, Howard Gardner, a well-respected researcher in psychology at Harvard University, defined seven distinctive categories of human intelligence. Those categories are linguistic, mathematical, spatial, kinesthetic, musical, interpersonal, and intrapersonal intelligence (Goleman 38). In 1996, Gardner added an eighth intelligence: naturalistic (Hoerr). He calls this eight-item list of abilities "multiple intelligences." Gardner believes that every person is born possessing a combination of all eight intelligences.

O

P

Commentary

O. Process note: In her first draft Chandra wrote two or three sentences about each of the eight types of human intelligence. Later she decided that writing that much about the topic would draw attention from the main topic of her paper, artificial intelligence. In a second draft she simply listed the eight types of intelligence, leaving extra space for emotional intelligence, the most important type for the purpose of her paper. Although she was frustrated at having to omit so much of her work from the final draft, she realized her paper was stronger as a result.

P. Expert source. When Chandra first began reading about intelligence, she came across the name Howard Gardner in several sources. When she realized that Gardner is a leading expert on multiple intelligences, she knew she could depend on the quality of his work.

Johnson 6

Daniel Goleman, another highly regarded researcher in psychology, groups the concepts of intrapersonal and interpersonal intelligence under the label "emotional intelligence." Goleman says that emotional intelligence involves more than having feelings of anger, sadness, fear, enjoyment, love, surprise, disgust, or shame (289-90). Emotional intelligence determines how well people do in life (28). A study of high school valedictorians, for example, shows that they frequently have less successful careers than classmates who excel at interpersonal or emotional skills (35). Goleman assigns five aspects to emotional intelligence: "knowing one's emotions," "managing emotions," "motivating oneself," "handling relationships," and "recognizing emotions in others" (43). The last of these is crucial in the context of artificial intelligence because it determines how people respond to other people and, in return, how the other people respond in turn. Q P

In MLA style, put only page number in parentheses when author is named in text.

Quotation marks around each phrase show that each appeared separately in the source.

Neurologist Antonio Damasio explains that scientists and philosophers historically dismissed the significance of emotions (38). Traditionally, they associated logic and reason with intelligence. Early scientists and philosophers believed emotion belonged to the body, not the mind (Damasio 39). The character of Mr. Spock in the original Star Trek television series represents this belief. Incapable of emotion, Spock is flawlessly logical. Certainly, everyone would agree that he is intelligent. S

Commentary

Q. Elaborating a key point. Since emotion is a key concept in her paper, Chandra discusses it at some length in this paragraph. Early in her search process, she had used the keywords "emotions" and "intelligence" to search her library's book catalogue. Goleman's book came up through that search; so did the book by Pfeifer and Scheier, which referred extensively to Goleman's work.

R. Example. To illustrate the point that success in life does not depend only on verbal and quantitative intelligence, the kinds of intelligence typically associated with school, Chandra gave the example of some high school valedictorians.

S. Popular example. Chandra hesitated to give Mr. Spock as an example of intelligence without emotion. The original *Star Trek* series is more than 35 years old, and she worried that the reference might be dated. However, she decided that Mr. Spock was enough a part of popular culture that even people who weren't directly familiar with the show would understand the reference. She checked with several friends just to be sure.

Johnson 7

T However, Damasio would be unconvinced by the claim that Spock is intelligent--and not just because Spock is a Vulcan. Damasio conducted numerous experiments with people who had lost various emotions through brain injuries. These people otherwise seemed to possess all their reasoning and logical abilities, but they had trouble making logical decisions. The experiments led Damasio to conclude that "emotion is integral to the process of reasoning and decision making" (41). He tells of a patient, David, who suffered a disease that destroyed parts of his brain and left him unable to learn any new fact, to recognize any new person, or to remember facts or people he had met before. Damasio and his colleagues performed an experiment in which one person treated David rudely and another person treated him well for a period of five days. Although David could not remember the facts of how these people treated him, he behaved differently in the presence of the two people. Clearly, he had learned on an emotional level, which made him respond sensibly (43-47).

Introductory phrase leads smoothly into direct quotation.

U

Paragraph summarizes several pages of source material, as parenthetical citation shows.

V The strongest believers in artificial intelligence mostly downplay the role of emotions, maintaining that only logic and reason define intelligence. Others give a qualified yes to "the provocative question whether robots will in fact need to have emotions, similar to the way humans have emotions" (Pfeifer and Scheier 642). Doubters, on the other hand, point to emotions, feelings, and intuition as the main barriers to

Commentary

T. Evaluating a source. The central issue of Chandra's paper is whether emotion is a necessary part of intelligence. In two of the sources she found early in her research, she had seen references to Antonio Damasio's work, and she wondered if it would help her to make connections between emotions and reasoning. It did, so she drew heavily on Damasio's book in this section. First, however, she checked his credentials. When she discovered that he was an award-winning researcher and head of the Neurological Sciences Department at a major medical school, she was satisfied that he was a reliable source.

U. Example. Without the example of Damasio's patient David, this paragraph was extremely thin. Chandra had to summarize several pages of the case study in just a few sentences.

V. **Process note:** In the course of her research, Chandra encountered many different opinions, both on the achievability of artificial intelligence and on the role of emotions in intelligence. She found it very difficult to synthesize all this material in a manner that read smoothly. Finally, she recognized that believers and doubters of the possibility of artificial intelligence differed in terms of the importance they assigned to emotions. The discovery gave her a way to organize this paragraph.

Johnson 8

artificial intelligence. The ability to write fiction, for example, depends on feelings that computers can never experience. One skeptic even asserts that computers have "inner lives on a par with rocks" (Bringsjord 33). Programmers design computer programs to be efficient and to sort problems into separate steps, ignoring everything that is not part of those steps. In contrast, part of being human is getting bored or angry, or wandering off the subject. John Searle believes that cognitive scientists make a terrible mistake when they imagine that the brain works the same way that computers do (Allen 30). **W**

Recognizing that the brain does not function through logic alone, some researchers are now studying how humans learn and are trying to incorporate their discoveries into computers. For example, children learn mainly by interacting with others in social situations. Emotions play a large role in those situations ("Sociable" 1). As an illustration, a baby learns that smiling causes adults to pay more attention to her, so she smiles a lot. In contrast, a two-year-old learns to recognize when someone is angry and to avoid that person. A child's growth in emotional intelligence would be hard to build into a computer. **X**

Put part of title in parenthetical citation when source lists no author.

Programming robots so that they can express emotions as well as sense is important because people's abilities to convey emotions affect the responses they get from others. To try to learn how inanimate objects suggest emotions, **Y**

Commentary

W. Colourful quotation. Bringsjord's statement that computers have "inner lives on a par with rocks" is not a particularly important or well-reasoned assertion. However, Chandra thought it added colour to her paper and helped to make her point, so she included it here.

X. Popular source. Here Chandra's information comes from a popular source, the newspaper *USA Today*. She realized that in comparison to the many scholarly sources cited in her paper, this one might seem insignificant. However, other things she had read convinced her that the position given in the article was accurate. Because she planned to include the example of Kismet, a robot described in the article, later in her paper, she decided to keep the reference to *USA Today* here. Note that no author was listed for the article, so Chanra referred instead to the first word of the title in her parenthetical citation.

Y. **Process note:** Chandra's research made clear that there are two main challenges in creating emotional intelligence in computers: getting computers to recognize emotions and getting them to convey emotions. She worked hard on the topic sentence of this paragraph to signal those challenges.

Put quotation marks around even short phrases or key terms taken directly from a source.

Johnson 9

scientists have studied some unlikely sources.
One group of reseachers analyzed how Disney Z
animators created "the illusion of life" by
seeming to give cartoon characters emotions
(Bates 122). Using Disney techniques, scientists
created computer "creatures" that seemed to
display emotions in response to simple situations
(Bates 123). Further work led to robots that
appeared more humanlike. For example, scientists
gave a robot named Kismet appealing, childlike
features. Kismet's "features, behavior, and
'emotions' " seem to allow the robot to "interact
with humans in an intuitive natural way'
("Sociable" 1). Nevertheless, creating the
appearance of emotions is much different from
creating the existence of emotions.

Do computers need emotions for scientists to AA
consider them intelligent? This question remains
unanswered. Computers can indeed do some things BB
that resemble a few kinds of intelligence that
humans possess, and that is enough to satisfy
some scientists. However, Gardner, Goleman,
Damasio, Pfeifer and Scheier, and others regard
emotions as a crucial part of human intelligence.
At present, computers lack anything like the
kinds of emotions found in human beings, and
scholars like John Searle doubt that computers
will ever have them. Clearly, robots like the CC
little boy in <u>A.I.</u> exist only in movies. The
possibility of creating real robots similar to
him remains only in the very distant future,
if at all.

Commentary

Z. Using a technical source. The article by Bates was from a scientific journal and was fairly difficult to understand. Chandra focused on the theories, findings, and implications of the article rather than on the methodologies, which were harder to follow. This is the oldest source that Johnson consulted for her paper. However, as the reference to the robot Kismet (later in the paragraph) makes clear, the Bates study is still pertinent to current research.

AA. Research question. Chandra's research question appears at the start of her last paragraph. Often, the research question doesn't directly appear at all in a paper, but Chandra thought it would be a good way to signal her conclusion.

BB. Summary of positions. Chandra summarizes both positions on the question to show that she has weighed her evidence. By choosing to summarize Searle's argument last, she shows that she agrees more with his position, that emotions are an important part of artificial intelligence, than with the others.

CC. Forceful conclusion. In her last two sentences, Chandra returned to the movie example she used at the very beginning of her paper. She thought this put a pleasing frame around the paper and made it seem complete.

Johnson 10

In MLA style, the list of sources, called Works Cited, begins a new page. Double-space throughout.

List sources in alphabetical order.

Divide a URL only after a slash.

Works Cited

AI Overview. American Association for Artificial Intelligence. 13 Sept. 2002 <http://www.aaai.org/AITopics/html/overview.html>.

Allen, Frederick E. "The Myth of Artificial Intelligence." American Heritage 52.1 (Feb.-Mar. 2001): 28-30.

Bates, Joseph. "The Role of Emotion in Believable Agents." Communications of the ACM 37.7 (July 1994): 122-25.

Bringsjord, Selmer. "Just Imagine: What Computers Can't Do." Education Digest 66.6 (Feb. 2001): 31-33.

Damasio, Antonio. The Feeling of What Happens: Body and Emotion in the Making of Consciousness. New York: Harcourt Brace, 1999.

Gardner, Howard. Frames of Mind: The Theory of Multiple Intelligences. New York: Basic, 1993.

Goleman, Daniel. Emotional Intelligence. New York: Bantam, 1995.

Hayden, Thomas. "The Age of Robots." U.S. News and World Report 130.16 (23 Apr. 2001): 44-50.

Hoerr, Thomas. "The Naturalistic Intelligence." The Building Tool Room. 20 Sept. 2002 <http://www.newhorizons.org/trm_hoermi.html>.

Commentary

DD. Search strategy. Chandra developed a working bibliography that was nearly three times as long as the list of sources she finally used. Initially, she went online to see what sources she could find on the Internet. However, she was overwhelmed by the number of references to "artificial intelligence." After some effort, she identified a few key sources. Library resources were more useful. The library's book catalogue contained many useful volumes, and the databases she searched turned up both scholarly and popular sources. PsychINFO and Computer Database were the two most useful databases.

EE. Credible Internet source. Chandra checked that this professional organization of scientists and professors would be a reliable source of information.

FF. **Computer tip:** Including a long and complicated URL in a Works Cited page is often tricky. Copying the URL from the browser window and pasting it directly into the Works Cited page reduces the chance of error. Be sure to divide a URL only after a slash, the rule in MLA style.

Johnson 11

Kurzweil, Ray. "Spiritual Machines: The Merging of Man and Machines." The Futurist 33.9 (Nov. 1999): 16-21.

McCarthy, John. What Is Artificial Intelligence? 20 July 2002. 16 Sept. 2002 <http://www-formal.stanford.edu/jmc/whatisai.html>.

Minerd, Jeff. "Robots: Our Evolutionary Heirs." Futurist 33.2 (Feb. 1999): 8-9.

Pfeifer, Rolf, and Christian Scheier. Understanding Intelligence. Cambridge, MA: MIT P, 2000.

Single quotation marks inside double quotation marks indicate words that were in quotation marks in the source.

" 'Sociable Machine' Interacts with Humans." USA Today 129.2673 (June 2001): 1-2. WilsonSelectPlus. FirstSearch. Bishop's University Library. 8 Sept. 2002 <http://www.oclc.org/firstsearch/databases/>.

Stix, Gary. "2001: A Scorecard." Scientific American 284.1 (Jan. 2001): 36.

Commentary

GG. Full text online. Although this source initially appeared in the newspaper *USA Today,* Chandra found a complete copy of the article online, through a database in the library. Because she used the online version, she cited its source.

HH. Proofreading the Works Cited page. In proofreading her paper, Chandra made sure this list contained all the works she cited in her paper—and only those works.

31 APA IN-TEXT CITATIONS

The American Psychological Association (APA) has developed a documentation style used often in the social sciences and in other disciplines. APA in-text citations, described in this chapter, alert readers to material used from outside sources.

31a What should I know about APA style?

In-text citations identify a source by a name (usually an author's name) and a year (for print sources, usually the copyright year). You can often incorporate the relevant name, and sometimes the year, into your sentence. Otherwise, put this information in parentheses, placing the parenthetical reference close by so that a reader knows exactly what it refers to. The APA *Publication Manual* (5th edition, 2001) recommends that if you refer to a work more than once in a paragraph, you give the author's name and the date at the first mention and then give only the name after that. (Exception: If you're citing two or more works by the same author or if two or more of your sources have the same name, each citation must include the date so that a reader knows which work is being cited.)

APA style requires page numbers for direct quotations and recommends them for paraphrases and summaries. Many instructors, however, require page references for all citations to a source. Find out your instructor's preference.

Put page numbers in parentheses, using the abbreviation *p.* before a single page number and *pp.* before two or more pages. For a direct quotation from an electronic source that numbers paragraphs, give a paragraph number (or numbers). Handle paragraph numbers as you do page numbers, but omit *p.* or *pp.*

CITATIONS FOR PARAPHRASES

- `People from the Mediterranean prefer an elbow-to-shoulder distance from each other (Morris, 1977).` [name and date cited in parentheses]
- `Desmond Morris (1977) notes that people from the Mediterranean prefer an elbow-to-shoulder distance from each other (p. 131).` [name cited in text, date and page cited in parentheses]

CITATIONS FOR QUOTATIONS

- A recent report of reductions in SAD-related "depression in 87 percent of patients" (Binkley, 1990, p. 203) reverses the findings of earlier studies. [name, date, and page reference in parentheses immediately following the quotation]
- Binkley reports reductions in SAD-related "depression in 87 percent of patients" (1990, p. 203). [name incorporated into the words introducing the quotation, and date and page number in parentheses immediately following the quotation]

Formatting quotations

Incorporate a direct quotation of fewer than forty words into your own sentence(s) and enclose it in quotation marks. Place the parenthetical citation after the closing quotation mark and, if the quotation falls at the end of the sentence, before the sentence-ending punctuation.

When you use a quotation of forty words or longer, set it off from your words. Start it on a new line and indent each line of the quotation five spaces (1/2 inch—about 1.25 cm) from the left margin. Don't enclose it in quotation marks, and double-space throughout. Place the parenthetical citation one space after the end punctuation of the last sentence. Start a new line for your own words following the quotation.

DISPLAYED QUOTATION

Jet lag, with its characteristic fatigue and irregular sleep patterns, is a common problem among those who travel great distances by jet airplane to different time zones:

> Jet lag syndrome is the inability of the internal body rhythm to rapidly resynchronize after sudden shifts in the timing. For a variety of reasons, the system attempts to maintain stability and resist temporal change. Consequently, complete adjustment can often be delayed for several days--sometimes for a week--after arrival at one's destination. (Bonner, 1991, p. 72)

Interestingly, this research shows that the number of flying hours is not the cause of jet lag.

31b What are APA guidelines for in-text citations?

The directory below corresponds to the numbered examples that follow it. The examples show how to cite various kinds of sources in the body of your paper. Remember, you can often introduce source names, including titles when necessary, and sometimes even publication years, in your own sentences rather than in the parenthetical citations.

DIRECTORY—APA IN-TEXT CITATIONS

1. One Author—APA
2. Two or More Authors—APA
3. Author(s) with Two or More Works in the Same Year—APA
4. Two or More Authors with the Same Last Name—APA
5. Group or Corporate Author—APA
6. Works Cited by Title—APA
7. The Bible—APA
8. Reference to More Than One Source—APA
9. Reference to an Entire Online Source—APA
10. Other References to Retrievable Online Sources—APA
11. References to Nonretrievable Online Sources—APA
12. Source Lines for Graphics and Table Data—APA

1. One Author—APA

All the examples in 31a show citations of works by one author. Notice that in a parenthetical reference, a comma and a space separate a name from a year and a year from a page reference.

2. Two or More Authors—APA

If a work has two authors, give both names in each citation.

- `One report describes 2123 occurrences (Worchel & Cooper, 1994).`
- `The results Worchel and Cooper (1994) report would not support the conclusions Davis and Shebilske draw in their review of the literature (1992).`

For three, four, or five authors, use all the authors' last names in the first reference; in all subsequent references, use only the first author's last name followed by *et al.* (not italicized).

FIRST REFERENCE

- `In one anthology, 35 percent of the selections had not been anthologized before (Elliott, Kerber, Litz, & Martin, 1992).`

SUBSEQUENT REFERENCE

- `Elliott et al. (1992) include 17 authors whose work has never been anthologized.`

For six or more authors, use the name of the first author followed by *et al.* for all references, including the first. (See Box 41, p. 256, for the format for six or more authors in the References list.)

For any work by more than one author, use an ampersand (&) between the last two names in a parenthetical citation. If you work the information into your own sentence, use the word *and* instead.

3. Author(s) with Two or More Works in the Same Year—APA

If you use more than one source written in the same year by the same author(s), alphabetize the works by their titles for the References list, and assign letters in alphabetical order to the years: *(1996a), (1996b), (1996c).* Use this year-letter combination in in-text citations. Note that if two or more of such works are listed in the same citation, the years appear in alphabetical order: *1996a, 1996b.*

- `Most recently, Jones (1996c) draws new conclusions from the results of 17 sets of experiments (1996a, 1996b).`

4. Two or More Authors with the Same Last Name—APA

Use first- and middle-name initials for every in-text citation of authors who share a last name.

- `R. A. Smith (1997) and C. Smith (1989) both confirm these results.`
- `These results have been confirmed independently (C. Smith, 1989; R. A. Smith, 1997).`

5. Group or Corporate Author—APA

For a source in which the "author" is a corporation, agency, or group, an in-text citation gives that body's name as author. Use the full name in each citation unless an abbreviated version of the name is likely to be familiar to your audience. In that case, use the full name and give its abbreviation at the first citation; then use the abbreviation for subsequent citations.

FIRST CITATION

- After 1949 the federal government took over responsibility for most public housing projects (Canada Mortgage and Housing Corporation [CMHC], 1990).

SECOND CITATION

- The cost of retrofitting older designs was substantial (CMHC, 1990).

6. Works Cited by Title—APA

If no author is named, use a shortened form of the title in citations. Ignoring *A, An,* or *The,* alphabetize by the first word in the References list. The following citation is to an article fully titled "Are You a Day or Night Person?"

- The morning lark and night owl connotations typically are used to categorize the human extremes ("Are You," 1989).

7. The Bible—APA

To cite the Bible, follow the guidelines for in-text citations of any major classical work (including ancient Greek and Roman works). You need to state the books, chapters, verses, and lines, rather than the page numbers for the words you're quoting or paraphrasing. For the first Biblical citation, give the version you're using (for example, New Revised Standard Version, New International Version, etc.). In your subsequent in-text citations from the same text, you don't need to repeat the version. In addition, APA doesn't require that citations of major classical works appear in your References list. The in-text citations suffice.

When citing from the Old Testament book of Psalms, each individual Psalm is referred to in the singular form. Thus, we have Psalm 121, not Psalms 121.

- In this time of global strife and political confusion, one can find solace in many different ways. Some find comfort in religion, as the psalmist of the Old Testament did when he looked upon the mountains knowing that all help was a gift of the Lord (Psalm 121:1–2, New International Version).

- Paul's letter to the Galatians declaring that in Christianity there is "neither Jew nor Greek, slave nor free, male nor female" was a revolutionary statement of equality for his time (Galatians 3:32).

Biblical citations in the form shown above are valid for Old and New Testament verses. APA does not differentiate between the two.

8. Reference to More Than One Source—APA

If more than one source has contributed to an idea or opinion in your paper, cite the sources alphabetically in a single reference; separate each block of information with a semicolon.

- Conceptions of personal space vary among cultures (Morris, 1977; Worchel & Cooper, 1983).

9. Reference to an Entire Online Source—APA

For a brief reference to an entire online source, just give the URL (Internet address) in parentheses. Do not include the source in your References list.

- A different approach to regional ecology can be found on the Banff Centre's Mountain Culture home page (http://www.banffcentre.ca/mountainculture/).

10. Other References to Retrievable Online Sources—APA

When you quote, paraphrase, or summarize an online source that is available to others, include the work in your References list, and cite the author (if any) or title and the date as you would for a print source.

11. References to Nonretrievable Online Sources—APA

When you quote, paraphrase, or summarize an online source not available to others, treat it as a personal communication. Do not include the work in your References list, and in your paper include the parenthetical description *personal communication* and the date. Cite an e-mail message sent to you, for example, like this:

- John LeBlanc (personal communication, June 6, 2000) expects the experiment to run for 18 months to 2 years.

12. Source Lines for Graphics and Table Data—APA

If you use a graphic from another source or create a table using data from another source, give a note in the text at the bottom of the table or graphic crediting the original author and the copyright holder. Here are examples of two source lines, one for a graphic from an article, the other for a graphic from a book.

GRAPHIC FROM AN ARTICLE—APA

- *Note*. From "Bridge over troubled waters? Connecting research and pedagogy in composition and business/ technical communication," by J. Allen, 1992, *Technical Communication Quarterly*, *1*(4), p. 9. Copyright 1992 by the Association of Teachers of Technical Writing.

GRAPHIC FROM A BOOK—APA

- *Note*. From *Additive alert: A guide to food additives for the Canadian consumer* (p. 28), by Linda R. Pim, 1979, Toronto: Doubleday. Copyright 1979 by Pollution Probe Foundation.

31c How do I write an abstract for an APA paper?

You may be asked to include an abstract at the start of a paper you prepare in APA style. As the APA *Publication Manual* explains, "an abstract is a brief, comprehensive summary" (p. 12) of a longer piece of writing. Make a summary accurate, objective, and exact. You may be familiar with effective abstracts, for many disciplines have online abstracts of longer sources. (See 31e for guidelines on formatting the Abstract page.) Here's an abstract prepared for a paper on biological clocks:

- Circadian rhythms, which greatly affect human lives, often suffer disruptions in technological societies, resulting in such disorders as jet lag syndrome and seasonal affective disorder (SAD). With growing scientific awareness of both natural circadian cycles and the effects of disturbances of these cycles, individuals are learning how to control some negative effects.

31d What are APA guidelines for content notes?

Content notes can be used in APA-style papers for additional relevant information that cannot be worked effectively into a text discussion.

Use consecutive arabic numerals for note numbers, both within your paper and on a separate page following the last text page of your paper. See 31e for instructions on formatting the Notes page.

31e What are APA format guidelines for research papers?

Ask whether your instructor has instructions for preparing a final draft. If not, you can use the APA guidelines here.

General instructions—APA

Use standard-size white bond paper (8 1/2 × 11 inches). Double-space throughout, whether the paper is typed or prepared on a computer (the APA *Publication Manual* recommends double-spacing a final manuscript like a research paper but suggests that headings, titles, captions, and quotations longer than forty words may be easier to read if they are single-spaced). Set at least a 1-inch (2.5-cm) margin on the left (1 1/2 inches—about 3.75 cm—if you submit your paper in a binder) and leave no less than 1 inch (2.5 cm) on the right and at the bottom.

Drop down 1/2 inch (about 1.25 cm) from the top edge of the paper to the title-and-page-number line, described below. Then drop down 1 inch (1.25 to 2.5 cm) from the top edge of the paper to the next line on the page, whether that is a heading (like "Abstract" or "Notes") or a line of your paper.

If you are typing, use five- to seven-character indents wherever indents are called for (see below). If you are preparing your paper on a computer, use 1/2-inch (1.25-cm) indents. Indent the first line of paragraphs five to seven characters (1/2 inch—about 1.25 cm) except in an abstract, the first line of which is flush to the left margin. Do not justify the right margin.

Order of parts—APA

Use this order for the parts of your paper: title page; abstract (if required); body of the paper; References; Notes, if any; attachments, if any (such as questionnaires, data sheets, or other material your instructor tells you to include). Number all pages consecutively.

Title-and-page-number line for all pages—APA

Use a title-and-page-number line on all pages of your paper. Drop down 1/2 inch (1.25 cm) from the top edge of the paper. Type the title (use a shortened version if necessary), leave a five-character space, and then type the page number. End the title-and-page-number line 1 inch

(2.5 cm) from the right edge of the paper. Ask whether your instructor wants you to include your last name in this title-and-page-number line.

Title page—APA

Use a separate title page. On it, begin with the title-and-page-number line described above, using the numeral 1 for this first page. Then centre the complete title vertically and horizontally on the page. Use two or more double-spaced lines if the title is long. Do not underline the title or enclose it in quotation marks. On the next line, centre your name, and below that, centre the course title and section.

CAPITALIZATION ALERTS: (1) Use the guidelines here for capitalizing the title of your own paper as well as for capitalizing titles you mention in the body of your paper. But see Box 41 (p. 256) for capitalizing titles in a References list, where different rules apply. (2) Use a capital letter for the first word of your title and the first word of a subtitle, if any. Start every NOUN, PRONOUN, VERB, ADVERB, and ADJECTIVE with a capital letter. Capitalize all major words in a hyphenated COMPOUND WORD (two or more words used together to express one idea): *Brain-Teaser.* Capitalize the word after a colon or a dash. (3) Do not capitalize articles (*a, an, the*) unless one of the preceding capitalization rules applies to it. Do not capitalize PREPOSITIONS and CONJUNCTIONS unless they are four or more letters long. Do not capitalize the word *to* used in an INFINITIVE. !

Abstract—APA

See 31c for advice about what to include in an abstract of your paper. Type the abstract on a separate page, using the numeral 2 in the title-and-page-number line. Drop down 1 inch (2.5 cm) from the top of the paper and centre the word *Abstract.* Double-space once below this title, then start your abstract, double-spacing it. Do not indent the first line, and do not exceed 120 words.

Set-off quotations—APA

Set off quotations of forty words or more from your words. Start a new line for the quoted words, indenting each line of the (double-spaced) quotation five spaces from the left margin. Do not enclose the quoted words in quotation marks.

If you are quoting part of a paragraph or one complete paragraph, do not indent the first line more than five spaces. But if you quote two or more paragraphs, indent the first line of the second and subsequent paragraphs ten spaces.

When the quotation is finished, leave a space after the sentence-ending punctuation, and then give the parenthetical citation. Begin a new line to resume your own words.

References list—APA

Start a new page for your References list immediately after the end of the body of your paper. Use a title-and-page-number line. Drop down 1 inch (2.5 cm) from the top of the paper and centre the word *References.* Do not underline it or put it in quotation marks. Double-space below it. The first line of each entry in your References list is flush to the left margin. If an entry takes more than one line, indent the second and subsequent lines five character spaces (or 1/2 inch—about 1.25 cm). This is called the "hanging indent" style. Double-space within each entry and between entries.

Notes—APA

Whenever you use a content note in your paper (31d), try to arrange your sentence so that the note number falls at the end. The ideal place for a note number is after the sentence-ending punctuation. Use a numeral raised slightly above the line of words and immediately after the sentence-ending punctuation mark.

Put your notes on a separate page after the last page of your References list. Use a title-and-page-number line. Then, drop down 1 inch (2.5 cm) from the top of the paper and centre the word *Notes.* Do not underline it or put it in quotation marks.

On the next line, start your first note, indenting five character spaces (or 1/2 inch—about 1.25 cm) from the left margin. Raise the note number slightly, and then start the words of your note. Do not leave a space between the numeral and the content note, as is done in MLA style. If the note uses more than one typed line, do not indent any lines except the first. Double-space throughout.

32 APA REFERENCES LIST

The References list provides information for readers who may want to access the sources you cite in your paper.

32a What are APA general guidelines for a References list?

Include in References all the sources you quote from (26f), paraphrase (26g), or summarize (26h) in your paper so that any other person could find these sources with reasonable effort. Do not include any source not generally available to others; see, for example, item 34 (p. 267) about personal interviews.

Guidelines for an APA-style References list 41

TITLE
References

PLACEMENT OF LIST
Start a new page numbered sequentially with the rest of the paper, immediately after the end of the text.

CONTENTS AND FORMAT
Include all quoted, paraphrased, or summarized sources in your paper that are not personal communications, unless your instructor tells you to include all the references you have consulted, not just those you have referred to. Start each entry on a new line, and double-space all lines.

In the 2001 *Publication Manual* (5th edition) and at its Web site <http://www.apa.style.org/elecref.html> the APA establishes the "hanging indent" style as standard: first line of each entry full width, other lines indented. This "hanging indent" style makes source names and dates prominent. Type the first line of each entry full width, and indent subsequent lines five spaces, 1/2 inch (about 1.25 cm) or one tab.

Shuter, R. (1977). A field study of nonverbal
     communication in Germany, Italy, and the United
     States. *Communication Monographs, 44*, 298-305.

SPACING AFTER PUNCTUATION
The 2001 APA manual calls for one space after most punctuation marks.

ARRANGEMENT OF ENTRIES
Alphabetize by the author's last name. If no author is named, alphabetize by the first significant word (not *A, An,* or *The*) in the title of the work.

AUTHORS' NAMES
Use last names, first initials, and middle initials, if any. Reverse the order for all authors' names, and use an ampersand (&) between the second-to-last and last authors: `Mills, J. F., & Holahan, R. H.`

Give names in the order in which they appear in the work (on the title page of a book, usually under the title of an article or other printed work). Put a comma between the first author's last name

→

Guidelines for an APA-style References list *(continued)*

and first initial and after each complete name except the last. After the last author's name, use a period. Name the first six authors of a source; substitute *et al.* (not italicized) for the rest.

DATES

Put date information after name information, enclosing it in parentheses and using a period followed by one space after the closing parenthesis.

For books, articles in journals that have volume numbers, and many other print and nonprint sources, the year of publication or production is the date to use. For articles from most magazines and newspapers, use the year followed by a comma and then the exact date appearing on the issue. Individual entries in 32b show how much information to give for various sources.

CAPITALIZATION OF TITLES

For books, capitalize the first word, the first word after a colon between a title and subtitle, and any proper nouns. For names of journals and proceedings of meetings, capitalize the first word, all major words, and any word four or more letters long.

SPECIAL TREATMENT OF TITLES

Use no special treatment for titles of shorter works (poems, short stories, essays, articles). Underline titles of longer works (books, names of newspapers or journals containing cited articles). Underlining is permitted if italic typeface is difficult to produce. When underlining, use an unbroken line if possible. Check with your instructor before using underlining in place of italic type.

Do not drop *A, An,* or *The* from the titles of periodicals (such as newspapers, magazines, and journals).

PUBLISHERS

Use the full name of the publisher, but drop *Co., Inc., Publishers,* and the like. Retain *Books* or *Press.*

PLACE OF PUBLICATION

For publishers in the United States, give the city and add the state (use the two-letter postal abbreviations listed in most dictionaries) for all U.S. cities except Baltimore, Boston, Chicago, Los Angeles,

→

APA

APA

APA

APA

APA

APA

Guidelines for an APA-style References list *(continued)*

New York, Philadelphia, and San Francisco. For other countries, give city and country. Canadian students and writers publishing in Canada normally use the two-letter postal abbreviations for Canadian provinces as well as U.S. states. If the province, state, or country is mentioned in the publisher's name, omit it after the name of the city.

PUBLICATION MONTHS
Do not abbreviate publication months.

PAGE NUMBERS
Use all digits, omitting none. *Only* for references to parts of books or material in newspapers, use *p.* and *pp.* before page numbers. List all discontinuous pages, with numbers separated by commas: `pp. 32, 44-45, 47-49, 53.`

REFERENCES ENTRIES: BOOKS
Citations for books have four main parts: author, date, title, and publication information (place of publication and publisher).

AUTHOR — DATE — TITLE

Dudek, L. (1971). *Collected poetry.*

PUBLICATION INFORMATION

Montreal: Delta.

REFERENCES ENTRIES: ARTICLES
Citations for periodical articles contain four major parts: author, date, title of article, and publication information (usually, the periodical title, volume number, and page numbers).

AUTHOR — DATE — ARTICLE TITLE

Shuter, R. (1977). A field study of nonverbal communication in Germany, Italy, and the United States. *Communication Monographs*, *44*, 298-305.

PERIODICAL TITLE — VOLUME NUMBER — PAGE NUMBERS

→

Guidelines for an APA-style References list *(continued)*

REFERENCES ENTRIES: ELECTRONIC AND ONLINE SOURCES Styles for documenting electronic and online sources have been changing and will continue to evolve. The 2001 APA *Publication Manual* (pp. 258–81) and the APA Web page <http://www3.apastyle.org/elecref.html> are the best sources of up-to-date advice on these formats. Here are two sample entries. The first is for an abstract on CD-ROM, a searchable "aggregated database" (i.e., a compilation of resources grouped for directed or simplified access). You are not required to document how you accessed the database—via portable CD-ROM, on a library server, or via a supplier Web site—but a "retrieval statement" that accurately names the source (in this case, the database) and lists the date of retrieval is required. (If you include an item or accession number, place it in parentheses.)

AUTHORS — DATE

Marcus, H. F., & Kitayamo, S. (1991).

ARTICLE TITLE

Culture and the self: Implications for cognition, emotion, and motivation.

JOURNAL TITLE AND PUBLICATION INFORMATION

Psychological Abstracts, 78.

RETRIEVAL INFORMATION

Retrieved October 2, 2001 from PsycLIT database Item 23873).

The second example is for an article in a newspaper on the World Wide Web. The "Retrieved from" statement gives the access date and the URL.

AUTHOR — DATE OF PUBLICATION ON THE WEB — TITLE OF ARTICLE

Lewis, R. (1995, December 24). Chronobiology researchers say their field's time has come.

→

APA

Guidelines for an APA-style References list *(continued)*

TITLE AND VOLUME OF ONLINE NEWSPAPER | PAGE NUMBER | RETRIEVAL INFORMATION

The Scientist, *9*, p. 14. Retrieved December 30, 1997 from http://www.the-scientist.mun.ca/library/yr1995/dec/chrono_951211.html

Notice that the only punctuation in the URL is part of the address. Do not add a period after a URL.

32b What are APA guidelines for specific sources in a References list?

The directory below lists the numbered examples that follow it. Not every possible documentation model is listed. You may find that you have to combine features of models to document a particular source. You will find more information in the *Publication Manual of the American Psychological Association* (5th edition, 2001) and at the APA Web site <http://www.apastyle.org/elecref.html>.

Directory—APA Style

PRINT SOURCES

1. Book by One Author—APA
2. Book by Two Authors—APA
3. Book by Three or More Authors—APA
4. Two or More Books by the Same Author(s)—APA
5. Book by Group or Corporate Author—APA
6. Book with No Author Named—APA
7. Book with an Author and an Editor—APA
8. Translation—APA
9. Work in Several Volumes or Parts—APA
10. One Selection from an Anthology or an Edited Book—APA
11. Two Selections from One Anthology or an Edited Book—APA
12. Signed Article in a Reference Book—APA
13. Unsigned Article in a Reference Book—APA
14. Second or Subsequent Edition—APA

NONPRINT SOURCES

ELECTRONIC AND ONLINE SOURCES

47. Synchronous Communications (MOO, MUD, IRC)—APA
48. Web Discussion Forum—APA
49. LISTSERV (Electronic Mailing List)—APA
50. Newsgroup—APA

PRINT SOURCES

1. Book by One Author—APA

Trudeau, P. E. (1968). *Federalism and the French Canadians*. Toronto: Macmillan Canada.

2. Book by Two Authors—APA

Leghorn, L., & Parker, K. (1981). *Woman's worth*. Boston: Routledge & Kegan Paul.

3. Book by Three or More Authors—APA

Scardamalia, M., Bereiter, C., & Fillion, B. (1981). *Writing for results: A sourcebook of consequential composing activities*. Toronto: OISE Press.

4. Two or More Books by the Same Author(s)—APA

Atwood, M. (1972). *Survival*. Toronto: Anansi.

Atwood, M. (1981). *True stories*. Toronto: Oxford University Press.

Atwood, M. (1985). *The handmaid's tale*. Toronto: McClelland & Stewart.

References by the same author are arranged chronologically, with the earlier date of publication listed first.

5. Book by Group or Corporate Author—APA

Investors Group. (1998). *Starting out: Smart strategies for your 20s & 30s*. Toronto: Stoddart.

American Psychological Association. (1994). *Publication manual of the American Psychological Association* (4th ed.). Washington, DC: Author.

Cite the full name of the corporate author first. If the author is also the publisher, use the word *Author* as the name of the publisher.

6. Book with No Author Named—APA

The Chicago manual of style (14th ed.). (1993). Chicago: University of Chicago Press.

7. Book with an Author and an Editor—APA

Brontë, E. (1985). *Wuthering Heights* (D. Daiches, Ed.). London: Penguin.

8. Translation—APA

Tremblay, M. (1998). *A thing of beauty* (S. Fischman, Trans.). Vancouver: Talon.

9. Work in Several Volumes or Parts—APA

Randall, J. H., Jr. (1962). *The career of philosophy* (Vols. 1-2). New York: Columbia University Press.

10. One Selection from an Anthology or an Edited Book—APA

Morrisseau, N. (1986). The Indian that became a thunderbird. In W. H. New (Ed.), *Canadian short fiction: From myth to modern* (pp. 26-29). Scarborough, ON: Prentice Hall.

Give the author of the selection first. The word *In* introduces the larger work from which the selection is taken.

11. Two Selections from One Anthology or an Edited Book—APA

Gilbert, S., & Gubar, S. (Eds.). (1985). *The Norton anthology of literature by women*. New York: Norton.

Kingston, M. H. (1985). No name woman. In S. Gilbert & S. Gubar (Eds.), *The Norton anthology of literature by women* (pp. 2337-2347). New York: Norton.

Provide full reference information for each selection cited from an anthology (or collection), using *In* to show the larger work from which the selection is taken.

12. Signed Article in a Reference Book—APA

Shadbolt, D. (1988). *Emily Carr*. In *The Canadian encyclopedia* (2nd ed.) (Vol. 1, p. 366). Edmonton: Hurtig.

Use *In* before the title of the larger work from which the selection is taken.

13. Unsigned Article in a Reference Book—APA

Ireland. (1997). In *Encyclopaedia Britannica*.

14. Second or Subsequent Edition—APA

Buckley, J., & Gates, D. (1995). *Put it in writing* (2nd ed.). Scarborough, ON: Prentice Hall.

When a book is not the first edition, the edition number appears on the title page. Place this information after the title and in parentheses. Use the year of the edition you are citing.

15. Anthology or Edited Book—APA

New, W. H. (Ed.). (1986). *Canadian short fiction: From myth to modern*. Scarborough, ON: Prentice Hall.

16. Introduction, Preface, Foreword, or Afterword—APA

Troyka, L. Q. (2001). Preface for ESL students. In *Simon & Schuster handbook for students* (3rd Canadian ed.) (pp. 786-788). Scarborough, ON: Prentice Hall.

If you are citing an introduction, preface, foreword, or afterword, give its author's name first. After the year, give the name of the part cited. If the writer of the material you are citing is not the author of the book, use the word *In* and the author's name before the book's title.

17. Unpublished Dissertation or Essay—APA

Buckley, J. (1991). *An assessment of Kieran Egan's theory of educational development*. Unpublished dissertation, University of Western Ontario, London.

18. Republished Book—APA

Lampman, A. (1978). *Lyrics of earth*. Ottawa: Tecumseh Press. (Original work published 1895)

Republishing information appears on the copyright page.

19. Book in a Series—APA

Courchene, T. J. (1991). *In praise of renewed federalism*. Toronto: C. D. Howe Institute.

Give the title of the book, but not of the whole series.

20. Book with a Title Within a Title—APA

Lumiansky, R. M., & Baker, H. (Eds.). (1968). *Critical approaches to six major English works:* Deowulf *through* Paradise Lost. Philadelphia: University of Pennsylvania Press.

Do not italicize an incorporated title even if it would be italicized by itself.

21. Government Publication—APA

Royal Commission on Bilingualism and Biculturalism. (1965). *Preliminary report*. Ottawa: Queen's Printer.

Indian and Northern Affairs Canada. (1986). *The Inuit*. Ottawa: Supply and Services Canada.

Use the complete name of a government agency as author when no specific person is named.

22. Published Proceedings of a Conference—APA

Smith, D. B. (Ed.). (1997). *Forging a new relationship: Proceedings of the conference on the Report of the Royal Commission on Aboriginal Peoples*. Montreal: McGill Institute for the Study of Canada.

23. Signed Article from a Daily Newspaper—APA

Church, E. (2002, November 27). Vacancy rates rise for the first time in decade. *The Globe and Mail,* pp. B1, B5.

24. Editorial, Letter to the Editor, or Review—APA

A black mark on local government. (1994, July 27). [Editorial]. *The London Free Press,* p. B8.

Hurka, J. (1994, July 5). [Letter to the editor]. *The Calgary Sun,* p. A18.

APA

Toews, W. (1995, August 26). Politics of the mind. [Review of the book *They say you're crazy*]. *Winnipeg Free Press*, p. C3.

25. Unsigned Article from a Daily Newspaper—APA

Private water may violate Constitution. (2002, November 27). *The Ottawa Citizen*, pp. A1, A7.

26. Article from a Weekly or Biweekly Periodical—APA

Wood, C. (1989, November 6). Storm clouds over Quebec. *Maclean's*, 16-17.

Use the abbreviation *p.* (or *pp.* for more than one page) for newspapers. Do not use this abbreviation for magazines or journals. Give year, month, and day-date for a periodical published every week or every two weeks.

27. Article from a Monthly or Bimonthly Periodical—APA

Bonner, J. T. (1999, April). The evolution of evolution. *Natural History, 108*(3), 20-21.

Give the year and month(s) for a periodical published every month or every other month.

28. Unsigned Article from a Weekly or Monthly Periodical—APA

10 ways to sleep easy. (1994, August). *Canadian Living*, 19.

29. Article from a SIRS Collection of Reprinted Articles—APA

Curver, P. C. (1990). Lighting in the 21st century. In *Social issues resources series. Energy* (Vol. 4, Article 84). Boca Raton, FL: Social Issues Resources.

When citing an article in a collection of reprinted articles, you do not have to cite the original source of publication. Cite only the reprinted publication.

30. Article in a Journal with Continuous Pagination—APA

Tyson, P. (1998). The psychology of women. *Journal of the American Psychoanalytic Association, 46*, 361-364.

Give only the volume number after the journal title and italicize the volume number.

31. Article in a Journal That Pages Each Issue Separately—APA

Zeleza, P. T. (1997). Visions of freedom and democracy in postcolonial African literature. *Women's Studies Quarterly, 25*(3-4), 10-31.

Give the volume number, italicized with the journal title. Give the issue number in parentheses; do not italicize it.

32. Published and Unpublished Letters—APA

Sand, G. (1993). Letter to her mother. In Reid Sherline (Ed.), *Letters home: Celebrated authors write to their mothers* (pp. 17-20). New York: Timkin.

In the APA system, unpublished letters are considered personal communication inaccessible to general readers, so they do not appear in the References list. Personal communications do not provide recoverable data and so are cited only in the body of the paper, as shown in item 34.

33. Map or Chart—APA

Russia and post-Soviet republics [Map]. (1992). Moscow: Mapping Production Association.

NONPRINT SOURCES

34. Interview—APA

In APA style, a personal interview is considered personal correspondence and is not included in the References list. Cite the interview in the text with a parenthetical notation that it is a personal communication.

Randi Friedman (personal communication, June 30, 1997) endorses this view.

35. Lecture, Speech, or Address—APA

Barlow, M. (1991, May 25). Address. Speech presented to the League of Canadian Poets, Toronto.

36. Film, Videotape, or DVD—APA

Ego Filmarts/ZDF (Producer), & Egoyan, A. (Director). (1993). *Calendar* [Film].

Ego Filmarts/ZDF (Producer), & Egoyan, A. (Director). (1993). *Calendar* [Videocassette].

Madden, J. (Director), Parfitt, D., Gigliotta, D., Weinstein, H., Zwick, E., & Norman, M. (Producers). (1999). *Shakespeare in Love* [DVD].

37. Musical Recording—APA

Smetana, B. (1975). *My country* [With K. Anserl conducting the Czech Philharmonic Orchestra]. [Record]. London: Vanguard Records.

Cohen, L. (Performer). (1988). Tower of song. On *I'm your man* [CD]. Toronto: Sony Music Canada.

38. Live Performance—APA

Shakespeare, W. (Author), Monette, R. (Director), Peacock, L., & Soles, P. (Performers). (2001, May 8). *The merchant of Venice* [Live performance]. Stratford, ON: Festival Theatre.

39. Work of Art, Photograph, or Musical Composition—APA

Pratt, C. *Shop on an island* [Artwork]. London, ON: London Regional Art Gallery.

Handel, G. F. *Water music* [Musical composition].

McMillan, D. (2001). *Village grave, Commemoration Day, April, 1995*. [Photograph]. Winnipeg: Winnipeg Art Gallery.

40. Radio or Television Program—APA

Offman, J. (Writer, Director, & Producer), & Cuttler, M. (Producer). (2001, October 21). *Hard times* [Television series episode]. In M. Starowicz (Producer), *Canada: A people's history*. Toronto: CBC.

41. Information Services: ERIC and NewsBank—APA

Chiang, L. H. (1993). *Beyond the language: Native Americans' nonverbal communication*. (ERIC Document Reproduction Service No. ED 368 540).

Wenzell, R. (1990). *Businesses prepare for a more diverse work force*. (NewsBank Document Reproduction Service No. EMP 27:DIZ).

ELECTRONIC AND ONLINE SOURCES

Information from online sources that your readers probably cannot retrieve for themselves—many e-mail messages and discussion list communications, for example—should be treated as personal communications. Identify the material in your paper, but do not include it in your References list.

The APA system for documenting electronic and online sources in a References list has been evolving. (Refer to the 2001 *Publication Manual* or log on to <http://apastyle.org/elecref.html> when you have a question not answered here.) In general, APA recommends giving author, title, and publication information as for a print source. This information is followed by a "retrieval statement" showing when each source was accessed and naming the source and/or giving its correct URL (online address).

42. Article from an Encyclopedia on CD-ROM—APA

Spanish dance. (2000). *Encarta 2000*. Retrieved May 20, 2001, from Encarta database.

The retrieval statement gives the full date the information was obtained and names the database. Note that the entry ends with a period.

43. Books Retrieved from Databases on the Web—APA

Eaton, A. W. (1889). *Acadian legends and lyrics*. London & New York: White & Allen. Retrieved May 25, 2001, from Early Canadiana Online database on the World Wide Web: http://www.canadiana.org/cgi-bin/ECO/mtq?doc=09066

The first information is for the printed version of *Acadian Legends and Lyrics.* The retrieval statement gives the access date, the name of the database, and the URL, with no final punctuation added.

44. Article from a Periodical on the Web—APA

Parrott, Andy C. (1999). Does cigarette smoking cause stress? *American Psychologist, 54*, 817-820. Retrieved December 7, 1999 http://www.apa.org/journals/amp/amp5410817.html

45. Personal or Professional Site on the Web—APA

Hunter-Kilmer, M. (1996, February). Retrieved December 4, 1999, from http://www.idsonline.com/userweb/phantom/index/htm

APA

46. File Transfer Protocol (FTP), Telnet, or Gopher Site—APA

After the retrieval date, supply the FTP, telnet, or gopher search path.

Taine, H. A. (2001, April). *The French Revolution* (Vol. 2). Retrieved 21 October, 2002, from ftp://ibiblio.org/pub/docs/books/gutenberg

APA

47. Synchronous Communications (MOO, MUD, IRC)—APA

Give the name of the speaker, a title for the event, the event or posting date, access date, and URL.

Bleck, B. (1997, June 8). Online discussion of Virtual first year composition: Distance education, the Internet and the World Wide Web. Retrieved February 27, 1999, from http://DaMoo.csun.edu/CW/brad.html

APA

48. Web Discussion Forum—APA

Higa, S. (2002, June 29). A potential bookmark [Msg 463]. Message posted to: http://groups.yahoo.com/group/Modern_Era/messages/489

APA

49. LISTSERV (Electronic Mailing List)—APA

Caruso, T. (2002, June 30). CFP: Flannery O'Connor and feminism. Message posted to Call for Papers electronic mailing list, archived at http://www.english.upenn.edu/CFP/

50. Newsgroup—APA

Boyle, F. (2002, October 11). Psyche: Cemi field theory: The hard problem made easy [Msg 1]. Message posted to news://sci.psychology.consciousness

33 A STUDENT'S APA RESEARCH PAPER

Carlos Velez wrote the research paper beginning on the next page in response to an assignment calling for a research paper about an unconscious process in humans.

Biological Clocks 1

APA STYLE: Use 1″ (2.5-cm) margins; double-space throughout.

Biological Clocks:

The Body's Internal Timepieces

Life in modern technological societies is built around timepieces. People set clocks on radios, microwave ovens, VCRs, and much more. Students respond to bells that start and end the school day from kindergarten to the end of high school. While carefully managing the minutes and hours each day, individuals are often forced by styles of family and work life to violate another kind of time: their body's time. Biological clocks, also known as circadian cycles, are a significant feature of human design that greatly affect people personally and professionally.

INTRODUCTION: Gets reader's attention.

See 31e for format of cover page and abstract.

THESIS STATEMENT: Gives paper's focus.

The Body's Natural Cycles

FIRST HEADING

The term *circadian*, which is Latin for "about a day," describes the rhythms of people's internal biological clocks. Circadian cycles are in tune with external time cycles such as the 24-hour period of the earth's daily rotation as signalled by the rising and setting of the sun. In fact, according to William Schwartz, professor of neurobiology and a researcher in the field of chronobiology (the study of circadian rhythm), " 'All such biological clocks are adaptations to life on a rotating world' " (Lewis, 1995, p. 14). Usually, humans set their biological clocks by seeing these cycles of daylight and darkness. Studies conducted in caves or similar

PARAGRAPH 2: First body paragraph gives background information.

Single quotation marks inside double quotation marks indicate statement by Schwartz is in article by Lewis.

In APA style, header has shortened title and page number.

environments that allow researchers to control light and darkness have shown that most people not exposed to natural cycles of day and night create cycles of slightly over 24 hours (Czeisler et al., 1999; Recer, 1999). Human perception of the external day-night cycle affects the production and release of a brain hormone, melatonin, which is important in initiating and regulating the sleep-wake cycle, as Alfred Lewy and other scientists at the National Institutes of Health in Bethesda, Maryland, have found (Winfree, 1987).

In APA style, summary of two sources separated by semicolon.

No page numbers for paraphrases and summaries.

PARAGRAPH 3: Defines *larks* and *owls*.

Each individual's lifestyle reflects that person's own circadian cycle. Scientists group people as "larks" or "owls" on the basis of whether individuals are more efficient in the morning or at night. The idea behind the labels is that "in nature certain animals are diurnal, active during the light period; others are nocturnal, active at night. The 'morning lark' and the 'night owl' connotations typically are used to categorize the human extremes" ("Are You," 1989, p. 11).

Partial title used because source does not give an author.

SECOND HEADING

Disruptions of Natural Cycles

PARAGRAPH 4: Applies terms to jet lag.

"Larks" who must stay up late at night and "owls" who must awaken early in the morning experience mild versions of "jet lag," the disturbances that time-zone travellers often suffer from. Jet lag, which is characterized by

→

fatigue and irregular sleep patterns, results from disruption of circadian rhythms in most people who fly in jets to different time zones:

> Jet lag syndrome is the inability of the internal body rhythm to rapidly resynchronize after sudden shifts in the timing. For a variety of reasons, the system attempts to maintain stability and resist temporal change. Consequently, complete adjustment can often be delayed for several days--sometimes for a week--after arrival at one's destination. (Bonner, 1991, p. 72)

According to Richard Coleman (1986), "the number, rate, and direction of time-zone changes are the critical factors in determining the extent and degree of jet lag symptoms" (p. 67). In general, eastbound travellers find it harder than westbound travellers to adjust.

Proof of this theory can be found in professional baseball. Three researchers analyzed win-loss records to discover whether jet lag affected baseball players' performance (Recht, Lew, & Schwartz, 1995). The study focused on the records of eastern- and western-based teams over a period of three years. If a visiting team did not have to travel through any time zones, it lost 54% of the time. If the visiting team had travelled from east to west, it lost 56.2% of

In APA style, block-indented paragraph for quotations over 40 words

Quotations require page number with *p.,* or *pp.* for more than one page.

PARAGRAPH 5: Additional specific support for previous paragraph

Statistics illustrate example.

→

Biological Clocks 4

the time. But if they had travelled from west to east, the visitors lost only 37.1% of the time.

PARAGRAPH 6: New example describes problem as it affects another group, shift workers.

Another group that suffers greatly from biological-clock disruptions consists of people whose livelihoods depend on erratic schedules. This situation affects 20 to 30 million U.S. workers whose work schedules differ from the usual morning starting time and afternoon or early evening ending time (Weiss, 1989). Sue Binkley (1990) reports that Charles Czeisler, director of the Center for Circadian and Sleep Disorders at Brigham and Women's Hospital in Boston, found that 27% of the U.S. workforce does shift work. Shift work can mean, for example, working from 7:00 a.m. to 3:00 p.m. for six weeks, from 3:00 p.m. to 11:00 p.m. for six weeks, and from 11:00 p.m. to 7 a.m. for six weeks. Many shift workers endure stomach and intestinal-tract disorders, and, on average, they have three times as much risk of heart disease as non-shift workers (Bingham, 1989). In a 1989 report to the American Association for the Advancement of Science, Czeisler states that "'police officers, [medical] interns, and many others who work nights perform poorly and are involved in more on-the-job accidents than their daytime counterparts'" (Binkley, 1990, p. 26).

Specific details to illustrate example

PARAGRAPH 7: Additional specific support

Other researchers confirm that safety is at risk during late-shift hours. In a study of 28

→

medical interns observed during late-night shifts over a one-year period, 25% admitted to falling asleep while talking on the phone, and 34% had had at least one accident or near-accident during that period (Weiss, 1989). Investigations into the *Challenger* space shuttle explosion and the nuclear-reactor disasters at Three Mile Island and Chernobyl reveal critical errors made by people undergoing the combined stresses of lack of sleep and unusual work schedules (Toufexis, 1989).

Emergency room physicians experience these two stresses all the time. Their professional group, the American College of Emergency Physicians (ACEP), after investigating circadian rhythms and shift work, drafted a formal policy statement, approved by ACEP's board of directors in 1994. The policy calls for "shifts . . . consistent with circadian principles" to prevent burnout and keep emergency physicians from changing their medical specialty. Also, such a policy would provide the best care for patients (Thomas, 1996).

PARAGRAPH 8: One group's response to information on biological clocks

Ellipsis indicates words have been omitted within a direct quotation.

If jet lag and circadian disruptions caused by shift work are obvious ways to upset a biological clock, a less obvious disruption is increasingly recognized as a medical problem: the disorder known as seasonal affective disorder (SAD). Table 1 lists some of the major symptoms of SAD.

PARAGRAPH 9: Applies problem to a medical condition.

→

Table 1

Table title

Common Symptoms of Seasonal Affective Disorder (SAD)

Table lists items efficiently, making them easy to read.

Sadness	Later waking
Anxiety	Increased sleep time
Decreased physical activity	Interrupted, unrefreshing sleep
Irritability	Daytime drowsiness
Increased appetite	Decreased sexual drive
Craving for carbohydrates	Menstrual problems
Weight gain	Work problems
Earlier onset of sleep	Interpersonal problems

Note below table provides source.

Note. From *The Clockwork Sparrow* (p. 204), by S. Binkley, 1990, Englewood Cliffs, NJ: Prentice Hall. Copyright 1990 by Prentice Hall.

THIRD HEADING

Ways to Help People Affected by Cycle Disruptions

PARAGRAPH 10: Solutions to problem

SAD appears to be related to the short daylight (photoperiod) of winter in the temperate zones of the northern and southern hemispheres. Michael Terman, a clinical psychologist at a leading psychiatric institute in the northeastern United States, has studied SAD patients for many years. He has observed their inability to function at home or at work from fall to spring (Caldwell, 1999). The phenomenon of SAD not only

Author's name and year in parentheses when not included in text

→

illustrates the important role of circadian rhythms but also dramatically proves that an understanding of circadian principles can help scientists improve the lives of people who experience disruptions of their biological clocks. Binkley (1990) claims that exposure to bright light for periods of up to two hours a day during the short-photoperiod days of winter reduces SAD-related "depression in 87 percent of patients . . . within a few days; relapses followed" (pp. 203-204) when light treatment ended.

Specific method for reducing SAD

Lengthening a person's exposure to bright light can also help combat the effects of jet lag and shift work. Specific suggestions for using light to help reset a jet traveller's biological clock include "a late-afternoon golf game or early-morning walk" or, for night-shift workers, staying in the dark during the day and during the night being in artificial light that mimics daylight (Mayo Clinic, 1997).

PARAGRAPH 11: Applies solution in previous paragraph.

Establishing work schedules more sensitive to biological clocks can increase a sense of well-being and reduce certain safety hazards. A group of police officers in Philadelphia were studied while on modified shift schedules (Locitzer, 1989; Toufexis, 1989). The officers were changed between day shifts and night shifts less frequently than they had been on former

PARAGRAPH 12: Specific system to reduce time-shift problems

→

shift schedules. Also, they rotated forward rather than backward in time, and they worked four rather than six consecutive days. The officers reported 40% fewer patrol car accidents and decreased use of drugs or alcohol to get to sleep. Overall, the police officers preferred the modified shift schedules. Charles Czeisler, who conducted the study, summarizes the importance of these results: " 'When schedules are introduced that take into account the properties of the human circadian system, subjective estimates of work schedule satisfaction and health improve, personnel turnover decreases, and work productivity increases' " (Locitzer, 1989, p. 66).

CONCLUSION

Conclusion

Scientists like Charles Czeisler are guiding individuals to live harmoniously with their biological clocks. The growing awareness of the negative effects of shift work and travel across time zones has led to significant advances in reducing problems caused by disruptions of people's natural cycles. The use of light to manipulate the body's sense of time has also helped. As more of us realize how circadian rhythms can affect our lifestyles, we might learn to control our biological clocks instead of our biological clocks controlling us.

→

Biological Clocks 9

References

Are you a day or night person? (1989, March 4). *USA Today,* p. 11.

Bingham, R. (Writer & Director). (1989, June 10). *The time of our lives* [Television production]. Los Angeles: KBTC Public Television of Seattle, PBS.

Binkley, S. (1990). *The clockwork sparrow.* Englewood Cliffs, NJ: Prentice Hall.

Bonner, P. (1991, July). Travel rhythms. *Sky Magazine,* 72-73, 76-77.

Caldwell, M. (1999, July). Mind over time. *Discover, 20,* 52. Retrieved October 2, 2002, from General Reference Gold database (Article A55030836).

Coleman, R. (1986). *Wide awake at 3:00 a.m.: By choice or by chance?* New York: Freeman.

Czeisler, C., et al., (1999, June 25). Stability, precision, and near-24-hour period of the human circadian pacemaker. *Science,* 2177–2181.

Lewis, R. (1995, December 24). Chronobiology researchers say their field's time has come. *The Scientist, 9,* p. 14. Retrieved September 6, 2002, from http://www.the-scientist.mun.ca/library/yr1995/dec/chrono_951211.html

Locitzer, K. (1989, July/August). Are you out of sync with each other? *Psychology Today,* 66.

Begin References on new page.

Double-space throughout.

List References in alphabetical order.

See pages 256–270 for advice about formatting an APA-style References list in "flush left" or "hanging indent" style.

In APA style, italicized (underlined) text includes end punctuation.

→

Biological Clocks 10

Example of source by a corporate author

Source is a letter appearing in *Nature* publication

Mayo Clinic. (1997, December 30). Tricks to try when you're out of sync. *Mayo Health Oasis* [On-line newsletter]. (Original work published in *Mayo Clinic Health Letter,* March 1995). Retrieved October 16, 2002, from http://www.mayohealth.org/mayo/9503/htm/sync_sb.htm

Recer, P. (June 25, 1999). Study gives a new reason for insomnia among elderly. *Philadelphia Inquirer*. Retrieved October 3, 2002, from SIRS Researcher database, Item 101619.

Recht, L., Lew, R., & Schwartz, W. (1995, October 19). Baseball teams beaten by jet lag [Letter]. *Nature, 377,* 583.

Thomas H. A. (1996). Circadian rhythms and shift work. ACEP Online. Retrieved August 28, 2002, from http://www.acep.org/POLICY/PR004166.HTM

Toufexis, A. (1989, June 5). The times of your life. *Time,* 66-67.

Weiss, R. (1989, January 21). Safety gets short shrift on long night shift. *Science News,* 37.

Winfree, A. (1987). *The timing of biological clocks*. New York: Freeman.

34 CM-STYLE DOCUMENTATION

The University of Chicago Press endorses two styles of documentation. One is a name-date style similar to the MLA and APA systems of in-text information; it directs readers to a bibliographic list. The other, described in this chapter, is a note system often used in the disciplines of English, history, and general humanities.

34a What should I know about CM documentation with bibliographic notes?

The CM (for *Chicago Manual*) note system gives complete bibliographic information within a footnote or endnote the first time a source is cited. If the source is cited again, the note gives less information. A separate bibliography is unnecessary because each first-citation note contains all the information a reader needs to identify the source. (As *The Chicago Manual of Style* points out, a separate bibliography is a convenience for readers of long works citing many sources.)

In CM style, the notes are either at the end of a paper (endnotes) or at the foot of the page on which a citation falls (footnotes).

TEXT `Welty also makes this point.`[3]

NOTE `3. Eudora Welty,` <u>`One Writer's Beginnings`</u> `(Cambridge: Harvard University Press, 1984), 17.`

Endnotes may be easier for you to format than footnotes, especially if you are hand-writing or typing your paper. Most word-processing programs facilitate either system.

Guidelines for CM-style bibliographic notes 42

TITLE

For endnotes, use the title `Notes` on a new page numbered sequentially with the rest of the paper, after the last text page of the paper. (Footnotes appear at the bottom of the page where the relevant citation appears.)

CONTENTS AND FORMAT

Include a note every time you use a source. Place endnotes after the text of your paper, on a separate page titled *Notes*. Centre the word

→

Guidelines for CM-style bibliographic notes *(continued)*

Notes, neither italicized (underlined) nor in quotation marks, about an inch (2.5 cm) from the top of the page, and double-space after it. Single-space the notes themselves. Indent each note's first line three characters (or one tab space in your word-processing program), but do not indent the note's subsequent lines.

In the body of your paper, use raised (superscript) arabic numerals for the note numbers. Position note numbers after any punctuation marks except the dash, preferably at the end of a sentence. On the Notes page, make note numbers the same type size as the notes, and position them on, not above, the line, followed by a period. (Not all word-processing programs allow you to observe these guidelines. Adapt these guidelines if necessary, using a consistent style throughout your paper.)

SPACING AFTER PUNCTUATION

No specific requirements. (It is now usual to single-space.)

ARRANGEMENT

Use sequential numerical order throughout the paper. Even if you use footnotes, do not start with 1 on each page.

AUTHORS' NAMES

Give the name in standard order (first name first), with names and initials as given in the original source. Use the word *and* before the last author's name.

CAPITALIZATION OF TITLES

Capitalize the first word and all major words.

SPECIAL TREATMENT OF TITLES

Underline or italicize (ask your instructor's preference) the titles of long works, and use quotation marks around the titles of shorter works.

Omit *A, An,* and *The* from the titles of newspapers and periodicals. In parentheses, give the city (and province or state, if the city is not well known) for an unfamiliar newspaper title: *(Prince George, B.C.) Citizen,* for example. Note that CM style uses province and state name abbreviations, which can be found in dictionaries, and which are different from the two-letter postal abbreviations.

→

Guidelines for CM-style bibliographic notes *(continued)*

PUBLICATION INFORMATION

Enclose in parentheses. Use a colon and one space after the city of publication. Give complete publishers' names or abbreviate them according to standard abbreviations in *Books in Print.* Omit *Co., Inc.,* and the like. You can use *Univ.* for *University;* spell out *Press.* Do not abbreviate publication months.

PAGE NUMBERS

In inclusive page numbers, give the full second number for 2 through 99. For 100 and beyond, give the full second number only if a shortened version is ambiguous: *243–47, 202–6, 300–304.*

List all discontinuous page numbers; see the model at "First Citation: Book," below.

Use a comma to separate parenthetical publication information from the page numbers that follow it. Use the abbreviations *p.* and *pp.* with page numbers only for material from newspapers or from journals that do not use volume numbers and to avoid ambiguity.

CONTENT NOTES

Try to avoid using content notes. If you must use them, make them footnotes, and use symbols rather than numbers: an asterisk (*) for the first note on a page and a dagger (†) for a second note on that page.

FIRST CITATION: BOOK

Citations for books include the author, title, publication information, and page numbers if applicable.

1. Eudora Welty, One Writer's Beginnings (Cambridge: Harvard University Press, 1984), 25-26, 30, 43-51, 208.

FIRST CITATION: ARTICLE

Citations for articles include the author, article title, journal title, volume number, year, and page numbers.

35. D. D. Cochran, W. Daniel Hale, and Christine P. Hissam, "Personal Space Requirements in Indoor versus Outdoor Locations," Journal of Psychology 117 (1984): 132-33.

34b What are CM-style guidelines for specific sources in bibliographic notes?

The directory below corresponds to the sample bibliographic note forms that follow it. Not every possible documentation model is here. *The Chicago Manual of Style,* 14th edition, gives note and reference-list forms for every imaginable source. If you cannot find the information you need in this section, consult the *Chicago Manual.*

DIRECTORY—CM STYLE

29. Article from a Collection of Reprinted Articles—CM
30. Article in a Journal with Continuous Pagination—CM
31. Article in a Journal That Pages Each Issue Separately—CM
32. Personal Interview—CM
33. Published and Unpublished Letters—CM
34. Film, Videotape, or DVD—CM
35. Musical Recording—CM
36. Computer Software—CM
37. ERIC Information Service—CM
38. Electronic Documents—CM
39. Secondary Source—CM

1. Book by One Author—CM

1. Pierre E. Trudeau, Federalism and the French Canadians (Toronto: Macmillan Canada, 1968), 25.

CM style can combine notes with a bibliography (34a). Here is the bibliographic entry for note 1:

Trudeau, Pierre E. Federalism and the French Canadians. Toronto: Macmillan Canada, 1968.

2. Book by Two or Three Authors—CM

2. Lisa Leghorn and Katherine Parker, Woman's Worth (Boston: Routledge, 1981).

3. Marlene Scardamalia, Carl Bereiter, and Bryant Fillion, Writing for Results: A Sourcebook of Consequential Composing Activities (Toronto: OISE Press, 1981), 73.

If you are using a bibliography as well as notes, invert only the first name listed.

Scardamalia, Marlene, Carl Bereiter, and Bryant Fillion. Writing for Results: A Sourcebook of Consequential Composing Activities. Toronto: OISE Press, 1981.

3. Book by More Than Three Authors—CM

4. Mark H. Moore et al., Dangerous Offenders: The Elusive Target of Justice (Cambridge: Harvard University Press, 1984), 104.

Give the name of the author listed first on the title page, and follow it with either *et al.* or *and others,* using no punctuation after the author's name.

4. Multiple Citations of a Single Source—CM

For subsequent references to a work you have already cited, give the last name of the author followed by a comma and the page number. Note 5 shows the form for a subsequent reference to the work fully described in note 1.

```
5. Trudeau, 25.
```

If you cite more than one work by the same author, give the title between the name and the page number. If the title is long, you may shorten it.

```
6. Trudeau, Federalism, 25.
```

If you cite two or more authors with the same last name, include first names or initials in each note.

```
7. Pierre E. Trudeau, 25.
```

If you cite the same source as the source immediately preceding, you may use *Ibid.* (not italicized) followed by a comma and the page number rather than repeating the author's name.

```
8. Ibid., 25.
```

5. Book by a Group or Corporate Author—CM

```
9. Investors Group, Starting Out: Smart Strategies
for Your 20s and 30s. (Toronto: Stoddart Publishing, 1998),
94.
10. American Psychological Association, Publication Manual
of the American Psychological Association, 4th ed.
(Washington, D.C.: American Psychological Association,
1994).
```

If a work issued by an organization has no author listed on the title page, cite the name of the organization as the author of the work. The organization may also be the publisher of the work.

6. Book with No Author Named—CM

```
11. The Chicago Manual of Style, 14th ed. (Chicago:
University of Chicago Press, 1993).
```

Begin the citation with the name of the book.

7. Book with an Author and an Editor—CM

12. Emily Brontë, Wuthering Heights, ed. David Daiches (London: Penguin, 1985).

In this position, the abbreviation *ed.* stands for "edited by," not "editor." Therefore, *ed.* is correct whether a work has one or more than one editor. (Also see items 10 and 15.)

8. Translation—CM

13. Michel Tremblay, A Thing of Beauty, trans. Sheila Fischman (Vancouver: Talon Books, 1998).

The abbreviation *trans.* stands for "translated by," not "translator."

9. Work in Several Volumes or Parts—CM

The two notes numbered 14 show ways to give bibliographic information for a specific place in *one* volume of a multivolume work. Use whichever you prefer, being consistent throughout a paper. If you are writing about the volume as a whole (as opposed to citing specific pages), end the note with the publication information.

14. Ernest Jones, The Last Phase, vol. 3 of The Life and Work of Sigmund Freud (New York: Basic Books, 1957), 97.

14. Ernest Jones, The Life and Works of Sigmund Freud, vol. 3, The Last Phase (New York: Basic Books, 1957), 97.

If you are citing an entire work in two or more volumes, use the form shown in note 15.

15. John Herman Randall, Jr., The Career of Philosophy, 2 vols. (New York: Columbia University Press, 1962).

10. One Selection from an Anthology or an Edited Book—CM

16. Norval Morrisseau, "The Indian That Became a Thunderbird," in Canadian Short Fiction: From Myth to Modern, ed. W. H. New (Scarborough, Ont.: Prentice Hall, 1986), 26-29.

Give page numbers for the cited work.

11. Two Selections from an Anthology or an Edited Book—CM

If you cite selections from an anthology or edited book, give complete bibliographical information in each citation.

12. Signed Article in a Reference Book—CM

17. Doris Shadbolt, "Emily Carr," in The Canadian Encyclopedia, 2nd ed.

13. Unsigned Article in a Reference Book—CM

18. Encyclopaedia Britannica, 15th ed., s.v. "Ireland."

The abbreviation *s.v.* stands for *sub verbo,* meaning "under the word." Capitalize the heading of the entry only if it is a proper noun. Omit publication information except for the edition number.

14. Edition—CM

19. Joanne Buckley and David Gates, Put It in Writing, 2nd ed. (Scarborough, Ont.: Prentice Hall, 1995).

Here the abbreviation *ed.* stands for "edition," not "edited by" (see item 7). Give the copyright date for the edition you are citing.

15. Anthology or Edited Book—CM

20. W. H. New, ed., Canadian Short Fiction: From Myth to Modern (Scarborough, Ont.: Prentice Hall, 1986).

16. Introduction, Preface, Foreword, or Afterword—CM

21. Warren Allmand, foreword to The Life and Death of Anna Mae Aquash, by Johanna Brand (Toronto: Lorimer, 1993).

If the author of the book is different from the author of the cited part, give the name of the book's author after the title of the book.

17. Unpublished Dissertation or Essay—CM

22. Joanne Buckley, "An Assessment of Kieran Egan's Theory of Educational Development" (Ph.D. diss., University of Western Ontario, 1991), 42-55.

List the author's name first, then the title in quotation marks (not underlined or italicized), a descriptive label (such as *Ph.D. diss.* or *master's thesis*), the degree-granting institution, the date, and finally the page numbers.

23. Kimberli M. Stafford, "Trapped in Death and Enchantment: The Liminal Space of Women in Three Classical Ballets" (paper presented at the annual meeting of the American Comparative Literature Association Graduate Student Conference, Riverside, Calif., April 1993).

To cite a paper read at a meeting, give the name of the meeting in parentheses, along with the location and the date.

18. Reprint of an Older Book—CM

24. Archibald Lampman, Lyrics of Earth (1895; reprint, Ottawa: Tecumseh Press, 1978).

Republishing information is located on the copyright page. List the original date of publication first, followed by the publication information for the reprint.

19. Book in a Series—CM

25. Thomas J. Courchene, In Praise of Renewed Federalism, The Canada Round (Toronto: C. D. Howe Institute, 1991).

If the series numbers its volumes and the volume number is not part of the title, include the volume number after the series title. Separate the volume number from the title with a comma.

20. Book with a Title Within a Title—CM

26. Aljean Harmetz, The Making of "The Wizard of Oz" (New York: Hyperion, 1998).

If the name of a work that is usually underlined appears in a title, add quotation marks around it. If the name of a work that is usually in quotation marks appears in a title, keep it in quotation marks and italicize or underline it.

21. Government Publication—CM

27. Indian and Northern Affairs Canada, The Inuit (Ottawa: Supply and Services Canada, 1986), 46.

If a government department, bureau, agency, or committee produces a document, cite that group as the author.

22. Published Proceedings of a Conference—CM

28. Ovide Mercredi, "The Future Is Our Collective Rights as Distinct Peoples," in Forging a New Relationship: Proceedings of the Conference on the Report of the Royal Commission on Aboriginal Peoples, ed. Donald B. Smith (Montreal: McGill Institute for the Study of Canada, 1997), 23-26.

Treat published conference proceedings as you would a chapter in a book.

23. Article from a Daily Newspaper—CM

29. James Christie, "Award Bittersweet for Hockey Women," Globe and Mail, 26 March 1998, sec. D, p. 1.

If a large paper prints more than one edition a day (such as a morning edition and a final edition), identify the specific edition; make this the last information in the entry, preceded by a comma. For a paper that specifies sections, use *sec.* before the page number, and for a paper that gives column numbers, use *col.* after the page number. Separate all items with commas.

24. Editorial, Letter to the Editor, or Review—CM

30. "A Black Mark on Local Government," editorial, London Free Press, 27 July 1994, sec. B, p. 8.

31. John Hurka, letter, Calgary Sun, 5 July 1994, sec. A, p. 18.

32. Wendy Toews, "Politics of the Mind," review of They Say You're Crazy, by Paula J. Caplan, Winnipeg Free Press, 26 August 1995, sec. C, p. 3.

Before page numbers, use a comma for popular magazines and a colon for journals.

25. Unsigned Article from a Daily Newspaper—CM

33. "Private Water May Violate Constitution," Ottawa Citizen, 27 November 2002, sec. A, p. 1.

26. Article from a Weekly or Biweekly Magazine or Newspaper—CM

34. Chris Wood, "Storm Clouds over Quebec," Maclean's, 6 November 1989, 16-17.

For general-readership weekly or biweekly magazines or newspapers, give the day-date, month, and year of publication. Separate page numbers from the year with a comma.

27. Article from a Monthly or Bimonthly Periodical—CM

35. John Tyler Bonner, "The Evolution of Evolution," Natural History, April 1999, 20-21.

For general-readership monthly or bimonthly magazines, give the month and year of publication. Separate page numbers from the year with a comma.

28. Unsigned Article from a Weekly or Monthly Periodical—CM

36. "10 Ways to Sleep Easy," Canadian Living, August 1994, 19-21, 34-35.

If the article is printed on discontinuous pages, give all pages in the note.

29. Article from a Collection of Reprinted Articles—CM

37. Phillip C. Curver, "Lighting in the 21st Century," *Energy,* Social Issues Resources Series, vol. 4 (Boca Raton, Fla.: Social Issues Resources, 1990).

Cite only the publication actually consulted, not the original source. If you use a bibliography, in it cite both the reprinted publication you consulted and the publication where the article first appeared.

30. Article in a Journal with Continuous Pagination—CM

38. Phyllis Tyson, "The Psychology of Women," Journal of the American Psychoanalytic Association 46 (1997): 361-64.

31. Article in a Journal That Pages Each Issue Separately—CM

39. Thomas F. Hogarty, "Gasoline: Still Powering Cars in 2050?" The Futurist 33, no. 3 (1999): 51-55.

The issue number of a journal is required only if each issue of the journal starts with page 1. In this example, the volume number is 33 and the issue number, abbreviated as *no.*, is 3.

32. Personal Interview—CM

40. Randi Friedman, interview by author, Winnipeg, Manitoba, 30 June 1997.

For an unpublished interview, give the name of the interviewee and the interviewer, the location of the interview, and the date of the interview.

33. Published and Unpublished Letters—CM

41. George Sand to her mother, 31 May 1831, Letters Home: Celebrated Authors Write to Their Mothers, ed. Reid Sherline (New York: Timkin Publishers, 1993), 17-20.

42. Theodore Brown, letter to author, 7 December 1999.

For an unpublished letter, give the name of the author, the name of the recipient, and the date the letter was written.

34. Film, Videotape, or DVD—CM

43. Marc Norman, <u>Shakespeare in Love</u> (New York: Miramax Films/Universal Pictures, 1999).

44. Atom Egoyan, <u>Calendar</u> (Canada/Armenia/Germany: Ego Filmarts/ZDF, 1993), videocassette.

45. Atom Egoyan, <u>Calendar</u> (Canada/Armenia/Germany, 1993; Alliance Atlantis, 2001), DVD.

35. Musical Recording—CM

46. Bedrich Smetana, <u>My Country</u>, Czech Philharmonic, Karel Anserl, Vanguard SV-9/10.

Bedrich Smetana is the composer and Karel Anserl is the conductor.

47. Leonard Cohen, "Tower of Song," on <u>I'm Your Man</u>, Sony CK 44191.

36. Computer Software—CM

48. Microsoft Word Ver. 8.0, Microsoft, Seattle, Wash.

Place the version or release number, abbreviated *Ver.* or *Rel.,* directly after the name of the software. Then list the company that owns the rights to the software, followed by that company's location.

37. ERIC Information Service—CM

49. Hunter M. Breland, <u>Assessing Writing Skills</u> (New York: College Entrance Examination Board, 1987), ERIC, ED 286920.

ERIC stands for Educational Resources Information Center.

38. Electronic Documents—CM

The Chicago Manual of Style (14th edition, 1993) describes electronic sources as an "exceedingly complex, fluid, and rapidly expanding field of source material" (634). The *Chicago Manual* shows several samples of acceptable documentation of electronic sources. The note below shows CM style for documenting a newsgroup posting. CM style for electronic sources is based on the International Standards Organization (ISO) documentation system. If you are using CM style and do not find enough information in this book to help you document your electronic sources, consult the ISO guidelines. Your college or university library should have a copy of ISO recommendations.

50. Dan S. Wallach, "FAQ: Typing Injuries (2/5): General Info.," in typing-injury-faq/general.Z [electronic bulletin

board], 1993- [cited 14 November 1993]; available from mail-server@rtfm.mit.edu; INTERNET.

39. Secondary Source—CM

51. Mary Wollstonecraft, A Vindication of the Rights of Woman (1792), 90, quoted in Caroline Shrodes, Harry Finestone, and Michael Shugrue, The Conscious Reader, 4th ed. (New York: Macmillan Publishing, 1988), 282.

When you quote one person's words, having found them in another person's work, give information as fully as you can about both sources. Note 51 shows the form when the point of your citation is Mary Wollstonecraft's words. If your point is what Shrodes, Finestone, and Shugrue have to say about Wollstonecraft's words, handle the information as in note 52.

52. Caroline Shrodes, Harry Finestone, and Michael Shugrue, The Conscious Reader, 4th ed. (New York: Macmillan Publishing, 1988), 282, quoting Mary Wollstonecraft, A Vindication of the Rights of Woman (1792), 90.

Using and Citing Graphics—CM

Place the credit line for a table or illustration from another source next to the reproduced material. (If you intend to publish your paper, you must receive permission to reprint copyrighted material from a source.) Spell out the terms *map, plate,* and *table,* but abbreviate *figure* as *fig.*

Reprinted, by permission, from Linda R. Pim, Additive Alert: A Guide to Food Additives for the Canadian Consumer (Toronto: Doubleday, 1979), 28, fig. 2. Copyright 1979 by Pollution Probe Foundation.

CM CM CM

35 CSE-STYLE DOCUMENTATION

In its 1994 style manual, *Scientific Style and Format* (6th edition),* the Council of Biology Editors (now called the Council of Science Editors—CSE) endorses two documentation systems widely used in mathematics and the physical and life sciences.

35a What should I know about CSE documentation?

The first system endorsed by CSE uses name-year parenthetical citations in the text of a paper, together with an alphabetically arranged

*Revisions for a 7th edition were underway when this book went to press: for information, visit the CSE Web site at <www.councilscienceeditors.org/>.

References list that gives full bibliographic information for each source. The second system uses numbers to mark citations in the text of a paper that correlate with a numerically arranged References list. This chapter focuses on this numbered reference system. Here is the way it works:

1. The first time you cite each source in your paper, assign it a number in sequence, starting with 1.
2. Mark each subsequent reference to that source with the assigned number.
3. For your References list, number each entry in the order of its appearance in your paper, starting with 1. Do not list sources alphabetically.

CSE recommends using superscript numbers for source citations in your paper, although numbers in parentheses are also acceptable.

IN-TEXT CITATIONS Sybesma[1] insists that this behaviour occurs periodically, but Crowder[2] claims never to have observed it.

REFERENCES LIST

1. Sybesma C. An introduction to biophysics. New York: Academic Press; 1977. 648 p.
2. Crowder W. Seashore life between the tides. New York: Dodd, Mead; 1931. New York: Dover Reprint; 1975. 372 p.

Thereafter, each citation of Sybesma's *Introduction to Biophysics* would be followed by a superscript 1, and each citation of Crowder's *Seashore Life* by a superscript 2.

Guidelines for a CSE-style list of references 43

TITLE

References or Cited References

PLACEMENT OF LIST

Start a new page numbered sequentially with the rest of the paper.

CONTENTS AND FORMAT

Include all sources quoted from, paraphrased, or summarized in your paper. Centre the title about an inch (2.5 cm) from the top of the page. Start each entry on a new line. Put the number, followed by a period and a space, at the left margin. If an entry takes more than

→

Guidelines for a CSE-style list of references *(continued)*

one line, use a "hanging indent" for all other lines. Double-space each entry and between entries.

SPACING AFTER PUNCTUATION
Follow the spacing in the models.

ARRANGEMENT OF ENTRIES
Arrange the entries in the sequence in which each is first cited in the text.

AUTHORS' NAMES
Invert all authors' names, giving the last name first. You can give first names or use only initials of first and middle names. If you use initials, do not put a period or a space between first and middle initials, and separate the names of multiple authors with a comma. If you use full first names, separate the names of multiple authors with a semicolon. With multiple authors, do not use & or *and.* Place a period after the last author's name.

TREATMENT OF TITLES
Capitalize a newspaper title's major words, dropping *A, An,* or *The* as the first word. Capitalize the titles of academic journals. If a journal title is one word, give it in full; otherwise, abbreviate it according to *American National Standard for Abbreviations of Titles of Periodicals* recommendations. Do not underline or italicize titles or enclose them in quotation marks.

PLACE OF PUBLICATION
Use a colon after the city of publication. Add a provincial or state postal abbreviation, in parentheses, or a country name to a city whose name by itself might be ambiguous or unfamiliar (see the example in item 8 on page 298).

PUBLISHERS
Give publishers' names, omitting *Co., Press, Ltd.,* and so on. Place a semicolon after the publisher's name.

PUBLICATION MONTHS
Abbreviate publication months to their first three letters. Do not use a period at the end.

INCLUSIVE PAGE NUMBERS
Shorten the second number as much as possible while keeping the number unambiguous (*233–4* for *233 to 234, 233–44* for *233 to 244,*

→

Guidelines for a CSE-style list of references *(continued)*

233–304). Where *p* is used, do not follow it with a period unless it is the last item in the entry. Follow the guidelines in the models.

DISCONTINOUS PAGE NUMBERS
List all discontinous pages, shortening inclusive page numbers.

TOTAL PAGE NUMBERS
When citing an entire book, for the last information unit give the total number of pages followed by the abbreviation *p* and a period to end the information unit.

REFERENCES ENTRY: BOOK
Citations for books usually have four main parts: author(s), title, publication information, and pages (either total pages for citing an entire book or inclusive pages for citing part of a book). A period ends each information unit.

```
1. Stacy RW, Williams DT, Worden RE, McMorris RO.
   Essentials of biological and medical sciences. New
   York: McGraw-Hill; 1955. 747 p.
```

REFERENCES ENTRY: ARTICLE
Citations for articles usually have four main parts: author(s), article title, journal name, and publication information. The first two sections end with a period. In the example below, *Sci Am* is the abbreviated form of *Scientific American.* Note that there is no space between elements after the year. The volume number is 269, and the issue number is 3.

```
1. Weissmann IL, Cooper MD. How the immune system
   develops. Sci Am 1993;269(3):65-71.
```

35b What are CSE guidelines for specific sources in a list of references?

The directory below corresponds to the sample references that follow it. Not every possible documentation model is here. For guidance in citing other sources, consult CSE's *Scientific Style and Format* (6th edition, 1994), the CSE Web site at <www.councilscienceeditors.org/> (for changes proposed for the 7th edition), or a journal in the discipline in which you are writing.

DIRECTORY—CSE STYLE

1. Book by One Author—CSE

```
1. Hawking SW. Black holes and baby universes and other
   essays. New York: Bantam Books; 1993. 320 p.
```

Use one space but no punctuation between an author's last name and the initial of the first name. Do not put punctuation or a space between a first and middle initial. Do, however, keep the hyphen in a hyphenated first and middle name. See model 2, where *Gille J-C* represents *Jean-Claude Gille.*

2. Book by More Than One Author—CSE

```
1. Wegzyn S, Gille J-C, Vidal P. Developmental systems:
   at the crossroads of system theory, computer science, and
   genetic engineering. New York: Springer; 1990. 595 p.
```

CSE CSE CSE CSE CSE CSE

3. Book by Group or Corporate Author—CSE

1. Canadian Institute of Child Health. Family-centred maternity and newborn care. Ottawa: CICH; 1980. 178 p.

4. Anthology or Edited Book—CSE

1. Heerman B, Hummel S, editors. Ancient DNA: recovery and analysis of genetic material from paleontological, archeological, museum, medical, and forensic specimens. New York: Springer; 1994. 1020 p.

5. One Selection or Chapter from an Anthology or Edited Book—CSE

1. Basov NG, Feoktistov LP, Senatsky YV. Laser driver for inertial confinement fusion. In: Bureckner KA, editor. Research trends in physics: inertial confinement fusion. New York: American Institute of Physics; 1992. p 24-37.

6. Translation—CSE

1. Magris C. A different sea. Spurr MS, translator. London: Harvill; 1993. 194 p. Translation of: Un mare differente.

7. Reprint of an Older Book—CSE

1. Carson R. The sea around us. New York: Oxford University; 1951. New York: Limited Editions Club Reprint; 1980. 220 p.

8. All Volumes of a Multivolume Work—CSE

1. Crane FL, Moore DJ, Low HE, editors. Oxidoreduction at the plasma membrane: relation to growth and transport. Boca Raton (FL): Chemical Rubber Company; 1991. 2 vol.

9. Unpublished Dissertation or Thesis—CSE

1. Baykul MC. Using ballistic electron emission microscopy to investigate the metal-vacuum interface [dissertation]. Orem (UT): Polytechnic University; 1993. 111 p.

10. Published Article from Conference Proceedings—CSE

1. Tsang CP, Bellgard MI. Sequence generation using a network of Boltzmann machines. In: Tsang CP, editor. Proceedings of the 4th Australian Joint Conference on Artificial Intelligence; 1990 Nov 8-11; Perth, Australia. Singapore: World Scientific; 1990. p 224-33.

11. Signed Newspaper Article—CSE

1. Hoke F. Gene therapy: clinical gains yield a wealth of research opportunities. Scientist 1993 Oct 4;Sect A: 1, 5, 7.

Sect stands for *Section.*

12. Unsigned Newspaper Article—CSE

1. [Anonymous]. Arctic drilling study. Globe and Mail 1995 Sep 2;Sect D:8.

13. Article in a Journal with Continuous Pagination—CSE

1. Lomas J, Woods J, Veenstra G. Devolving authority for health care in Canada's provinces: 1. an introduction to the issues. CMAJ 1997;156:371-7.

Give only the volume number, not an issue number, before the page numbers.

14. Article in a Journal That Pages Each Issue Separately—CSE

1. Driver D. Doctor turnout high in Saskatchewan health board vote. Med Post 1995;31(40):53.

Give both the volume number and the issue number (here, *31* is the volume number and *40* is the issue number).

15. Journal Article on Discontinuous Pages—CSE

1. Richards FM. The protein folding problem. Sci Am 1991 Nov;246(1):54-7, 60-6.

16. Article with Author Affiliation—CSE

1. DeMoll E, Auffenberg T (Dept. of Microbiology, Univ. of Kentucky). Purine metabolism in Methanococcus vannielii. J Bacteriol 1993;175:5754-61.

17. Entire Issue of a Journal—CSE

1. Whales in a modern world: a symposium held in London, November 1988. Mamm Rev 1990 Jan;20(9).

November 1988, the date of the symposium, is part of the title of this issue.

18. Article with No Identifiable Author—CSE

1. [Anonymous]. Cruelty to animals linked to murders of humans. AWI Q 1993 Aug;42(3):16.

19. Map—CSE

1. Russia and Post-Soviet Republics [political map]. Moscow: Mapping Production Association; 1992. Conical equidistant projection; 100 × 120 cm; colour, scale 1:8 000 000.

20. Unpublished Letter—CSE

1. Darwin C. [Letter to Mr. Clerke, 1861]. Located at: University of Iowa Library, Iowa City, IA.

21. Filmstrip—CSE

1. Volcano: the eruption and healing of Mount St. Helens [filmstrip]. Westminster (MD): Random House; 1988. 114 frames: colour; 35 mm. Accompanied by: cassette tape; 22 min.

After the title and description of the filmstrip, give the author, producer, and year. Then give other descriptive information.

22. Videorecording—CSE

1. The discovery of the pulsar: the ultimate ignorance [videocassette]. London: BBC; 1983. 1 cassette: 48 min, sound, colour.

23. Slide Set—CSE

```
1. Human parasitology [slides]. Chicago (IL): American
   Society of Clinical Pathologists; 1990. Colour.
   Accompanied by: 1 guide.
```

24. Electronic Sources—CSE

In general, the CSE manual advises that you cite electronic sources by starting with a statement of the type of document, and then giving the information you would give for a print version. Next, give information that would help a reader to locate the electronic source. End with a date: your access date for online sources or the date of the update you used for CD-ROM databases that are updated periodically.

36 COS DOCUMENTATION

For electronic publications, *The Columbia Guide to Online Style* (COS or CO style) by Janice R. Walker and Todd Taylor (Columbia UP, 1998) provides an alternative to other documentation styles.

36a What should I know about COS documentation?

COS uses many of the same citation elements present in predominantly print documentation styles such as MLA and APA. However, COS includes some new format elements unique to electronic publications. COS for the humanities is similar to MLA style, while COS for the sciences shares elements of APA style. Be sure to find out from your instructor which style to use.

Citing sources in the body of a paper in COS

In print publications, in-text or PARENTHETICAL REFERENCES* include elements such as the author's last name and the page number of the reference. Many electronic sources lack such elements, so the documentation style needs to allow for these differences. If the author's name is unknown, refer to the source by its title. Since pages in most electronic sources are not numbered, page references may be irrelevant. Commonly, COS parenthetical citations use only the author's name for humanities style and the author's name and date of publication for scientific style.

*Words printed in small capital letters (such as PARENTHETICAL REFERENCES) are defined in the Terms Glossary on pages 497–517.

COS CITATION ALERT: If page numbers, sections, or other navigational aids are available, include them at the end of the parenthetical citation.!

HUMANITIES STYLE

```
According to the survey, over 80% of the students on
campus waited until the night before an exam to begin
studying (Jani).
```

COS CITATION ALERT: When the author's name is included in the sentence, the in-text citation is unnecessary. If you cite more than one work by the same author, refer to each by its title.!

SCIENTIFIC STYLE

```
The research proved conclusively that individuals deprived
of sleep were as dangerous as those driving under the
influence of drugs or alcohol (Rezik, 2000).
```

COS CITATION ALERT: If the publication is unavailable, use the date of access (in day-month-year format).!

Creating COS bibliographic citations

Box 44 gives guidelines for a COS Works Cited List. The labelled screen on page 305 identifies elements mentioned in that box.

Guidelines for a COS Works Cited list 44

TITLE
Works Cited should be centred, 1 inch (about 2.5 cm) below the top of the bibliography page. The title should not be enclosed in quotation marks or be boldfaced, italicized, or underlined.

PLACEMENT OF LIST
If you are producing a print document, number the Works Cited page sequentially with the rest of the paper and begin on a separate page. If your document is a hypertext publication, you may use a separate file and a link to this page in the table of contents.

→

Guidelines for a COS Works Cited list *(continued)*

CONTENT AND FORMAT
See MLA guidelines in Box 40.

ARRANGEMENT OF ENTRIES
See MLA guidelines in Box 40.

AUTHORS' NAMES
Finding the author of a source may not be simple. Often, online writers use an alias or go by their login/user name. List a source by these alternative names if they are the only ones you find. If no author name or alias can be identified, cite the source by its title.

In the humanities style, give the author's full first, middle (if available), and last names; in the scientific style, give the author's full last name and first and middle initials (if applicable). List any second author by first name (humanities) or first initial (scientific), followed by the full last name.

CAPITALIZATION AND SPECIAL TREATMENT OF TITLES
Use italics rather than underlining for the titles of complete works. Since hypertext links are underlined online, an underlined title may confuse your readers. Also italicize online sites and the names of information services.

In the humanities style, enclose titles of articles or excerpts in quotation marks and capitalize all major words. In the scientific style, do not distinguish titles of articles or excerpts in any way, and capitalize only the first word of the title and proper nouns. (If a title is not available, use the file name.)

PLACE OF PUBLICATION, PUBLISHER, AND ELECTRONIC ADDRESS
With electronic sources available in fixed formats, such as software and certain electronic publications, a publisher and city are usually listed and should be cited.

In online publishing, the city of publication and publisher often are not relevant to the Web site and other electronic sources that are not in fixed formats. In those cases, provide the Uniform Resource Locator (URL), which is a source's entire electronic address. For addresses that exceed a line in length, follow MLA style: Break only after slashes and do not insert your own hyphens.

→

Guidelines for a COS Works Cited list *(continued)*

VERSION OR FILE NUMBER
When applicable, provide the specific file number or version of a program.

DOCUMENT DATE OR DATE OF LAST REVISION
Include a Web page's publication date or date of last revision unless it is identical to the access date. For humanities style, abbreviate month names to their first three letters.

DATE OF ACCESS
With the constant updates of online content, readers may have a difficult time finding the content that you cite. Always provide the date of access for an online source because it specifies the version of the page you have cited. For humanities style, abbreviate month names to their first three letters.

NAVIGATION POINTS
On the World Wide Web, a given site is usually one page, regardless of its length. List any helpful navigational aids, such as page references, paragraph numbers, or parts, when they are available. Keep in mind that these aids are often not available.

BIBLIOGRAPHIC ENTRIES: HUMANITIES
Follow this form as closely as possible in your citations:

Author's Last Name, First Name. "Title of Document." *Title of Complete Work* [if applicable]. Version or file number [if applicable]. Document date or date of last version [if different from access date]. Protocol and address, access path or directories (date of access).

BIBLIOGRAPHIC ENTRIES: SCIENCES
Follow this form as closely as possible in your citations:

Author's Last Name, Initial(s). (Date of document) [if different from date accessed]). Title of document. *Title of complete work* [if applicable]. Version or file number [if applicable]. (Edition or revision [if applicable]). Protocol and address path, or directories (date of access).

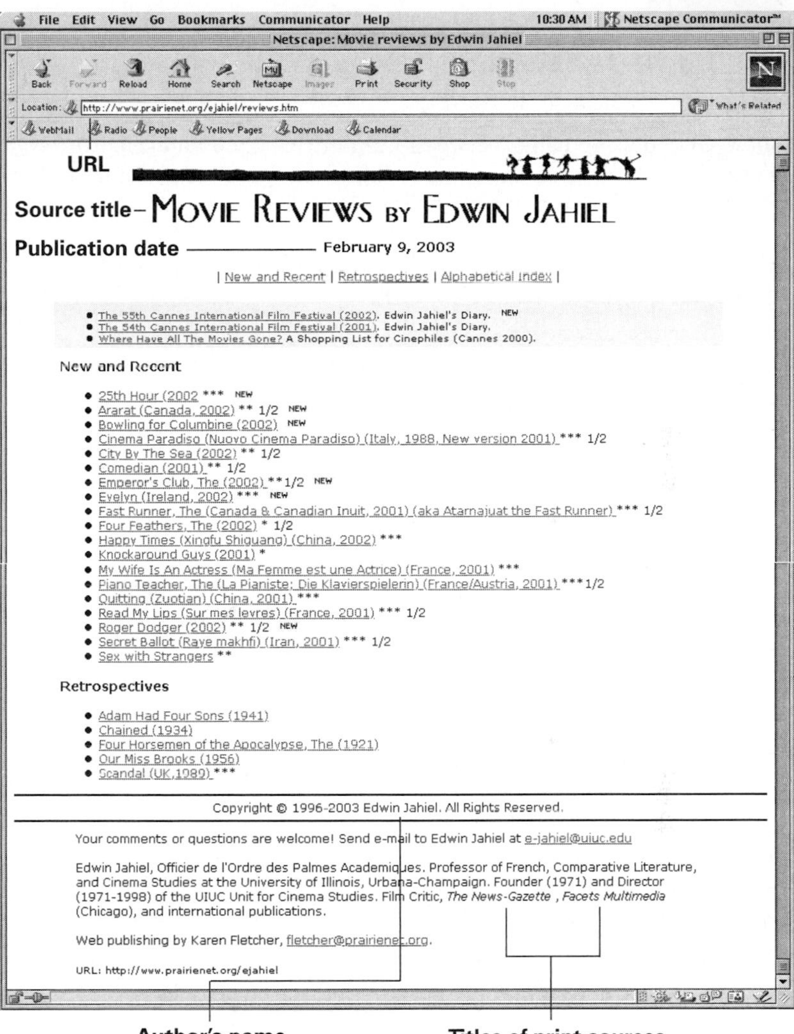

Web page with links to author's movie reviews

36b What are COS guidelines for specific sources in a Works Cited list?

The directory below corresponds to the sample bibliographic forms that follow. COS distinguishes between humanities style and scientific style in creating a bibliography, so you will find models first given in humanities style and then repeated in scientific style.

DIRECTORY—COS GUIDELINES

1. Site on the World Wide Web—COS
2. Modified or Revised Site—COS
3. Maintained or Compiled Site—COS
4. Article from a Periodical—COS
5. Article from an Online Journal—COS
6. Work by a Group or Organization—COS
7. Corporate Home Pages and Information—COS
8. Government Information and Sites—COS
9. Book Accessed Online—COS
10. Graphic, Video, or Audio File on the Page—COS
11. Personal Electronic Mail (E-mail)—COS
12. Posting to a Discussion List—COS
13. Posting to a Newsgroup or Forum—COS
14. Archived Posting—COS
15. Online Reference Source—COS
16. Computer Information Services and Online Databases—COS
17. Gopher Site—COS
18. FTP Site—COS
19. Telnet Site—COS
20. Synchronous Communication—COS
21. Software—COS

Humanities Style

1. Site on the World Wide Web—COS Humanities

Blackmon, Samantha. *Cows in the Classroom?: MOOs and MUDs and MUSHes ... Oh My!!!* 24 Aug. 2000. http://www.sla.purdue.edu/people/engl/blackmon/moo/index.html (11 Mar. 2001).

2. Modified or Revised Site—COS Humanities

Sheppard, James E., and Arthur Young. *The Canadian 19th Century: A Chronology*. Mod. spring 2000. http://www.ablu.ca/histproj/1800.html (22 Nov. 2000).

For a revised site, use the abbreviation *Rev.* instead of *Mod.*

3. Maintained or Compiled Site—COS Humanities

E-Zine-List. Maint. John Labovitz. 8 Mar. 2000. http://www.meer.net/~johnl/e-zine-list (15 Sep. 2000).

If it is a compiled site, use the abbreviation *Comp.* instead of *Maint.*

4. Article from a Periodical—COS Humanities

Cheadle, Bruce. "Lab Workers Infected with Mysterious Monkey Virus." *Winnipeg Free Press*. 30 Jun. 2001. http://www.winnipegfreepress.com/news/canadaworld/275385538938334.html (9 Oct. 2001).

5. Article from an Online Journal—COS Humanities

Winickoff, Jonathan P., et al. "Verve and Jolt: Deadly New Internet Drugs." *Pediatrics* 106.4 (Oct. 2000). http://www.pediatrics.org/cgi/content/abstract/106/4/829 (10 May 2000).

6. Works by a Group or Organization—COS Humanities

SIL International. *Ethnomusicology: Studying Music from the Outside In and from the Inside Out*. 7 May 1999. http://www.sil.org/anthro/ethnomusicology.htm (20 Feb. 2000).

7. Corporate Home Pages and Information—COS Humanities

Pearson Canada. 2002. Pearson Canada Inc. http://www.pearsoned.ca (22 Apr. 2002).

8. Government Information and Sites—COS Humanities

Citizenship and Immigration Canada. "Staying the Course: 1997 Annual Immigration Plan." 29 Oct. 1996. *Annual Immigration Plans*. http://cicnet.ci.gc.ca/english/pub/index.html (5 Mar. 2001).

9. Book Accessed Online—COS Humanities

BOOK PUBLISHED FIRST IN PRINT VERSION

Eaton, Arthur W. *Acadian Legends and Lyrics*. London and New York: White & Allen, 1889. 16 Feb. 2000. *Early Canadiana Online*. http://www.canadiana.org/cgi-bin/ECO/mtq?doc=09066 (25 May 2001).

BOOK PUBLISHED ONLINE

Shires, Bob. *CPR (Cardiopulmonary Resuscitation) Guide*. 17 Jan. 2000. http://www.memoware.com/Category=Medicine_ResultSet=1.htm (17 Apr. 2000).

10. Graphic, Video, or Audio File on the Page—COS Humanities

owl.gif. 2000. "Original free clipart." *Clipart.com*. http://www.free-clip-art.net/index4.shtml (27 Oct. 2000).

11. Personal Electronic Mail (E-mail)—COS Humanities

Torres, Nadia. "Re: Online Translation Programs." Personal e-mail (11 Sep. 2000).

12. Posting to a Discussion List—COS Humanities

Sheldon, Amy. "Re: Request for Help on Sexism Inscription." 2 Jan. 2000. *FLING List for Feminists in Linguistics*. http://listserv.linguistlist.org (14 Nov. 2000).

13. Posting to a Newsgroup or Forum—COS Humanities

Markowitz, Al. "The Changing Face of Work: A Look at the Way We Work." 28 Sep. 2000. http://www.yourturn.npr.org/cgi-bin/WebX?50@121.HjNGardZdaj^0@.ee7a9aa (8 Jan. 2001).

14. Archived Posting—COS Humanities

Radev, Dragomir R. "Natural Language Processing FAQ." 16 Sep. 1999. *Institute of Information and Computing Sciences*. http://www.cs.ruu.nl/wais/html/na-dir/natural-lang-processing-faq.html (27 Jan. 1999).

15. Online Reference Source—COS Humanities

Reference sources such as online encyclopedias, dictionaries, thesauruses, style manuals, bibliographies, and other forms of factual material can be cited using this model.

Nordenberg, Tamar. 2000. "Make No Mistake! Medical Errors Can Be Deadly Serious." *Britannica.com*. Ebsco Publishing. http://britannica.com/bcom/original/article/0,5744,12430,00.html (18 Oct. 2000).

16. Computer Information Services and Online Databases—COS Humanities

Raintree Nutrition, Inc. "Pata de Vaca." Jun. 2000. *Raintree Tropical Plant Database*. http://www.rain-tree.com/patadevaca.htm (9 Sep. 2000).

17. Gopher Site—COS Humanities

"Elections." May 1996. gopher://israel-info.gov.il/00/facts/state/st4 (27 Dec. 2000).

18. FTP Site—COS Humanities

Project Gutenberg. 2000. *Ibiblio.org*. ftp://metalab.unc.edu/pub/docs/books/gutenberg/ (12 Aug. 2000).

19. Telnet Site—COS Humanities

Schweller, Kenneth G. "How to Design a Bot." *Collegetown MOO*. 28 May 1999. telnet://galaxy.bvu.edu:7777 (16 Nov. 2000).

20. Synchronous Communication—COS Humanities

Dominguez, Jose. "Interchange." *Daedalus Online*. http://daedalus.pearsoned.com (11 Mar. 2001).

21. Software—COS Humanities

Wresch, William. *Writer's Helper*. Vers. 4.0. Upper Saddle River: Prentice Hall, 1998.

Scientific Style

1. Site on the World Wide Web—COS Scientific

Blackmon, S. (2000, August 24). *Cows in the Classroom?: MOOs and MUDs and MUSHes ... Oh My!!!* http://www.sla.purdue.ed/people/engl/blackmon/moo/index.html (11 Mar. 2001).

2. Modified or Revised Site—COS Scientific

Sheppard, J. E., & Young, A. (2000). *The Canadian 19th century: A chronology*. (Mod. spring 2000). http://www.ablu.ca/histproj/1800.html (22 Nov. 2000).

For a revised site, use the abbreviation *Rev.* instead of *Mod.*

3. Maintained or Compiled Site—COS Scientific

E-zine-list. (2000, March 8). (John Labovitz, Maint.). http://www.meer.net/~johnl/e-zine-list (15 Sep. 2000).

If the site has been compiled, use the abbreviation *Comp.* instead of *Maint.*

4. Article from a Periodical—COS Scientific

Cheadle B. (2001, June 30). Lab workers infected with mysterious monkey virus. *Winnipeg Free Press*. http://www.winnipegfreepress.com/news/canadaworld/275385538938334.html (9 Oct. 2001).

5. Article from an Online Journal—COS Scientific

Winickoff, J. P., et al. (2000, October). Verve and jolt: Deadly new Internet drugs. *Pediatrics, 106*(4). http://www.pediatrics.org/cgi/content/abstract/106/4/829 (10 May 2000).

6. Work by a Group or Organization—COS Scientific

SIL International. (1999, May 7). *Ethnomusicology: Studying music from the outside in and from the inside out*. http://www.sil.org/anthro/ethnomusicology.htm (20 Feb. 2000).

7. Corporate Home Pages and Information—COS Scientific

Pearson Canada. (2002). Pearson Canada Inc. http://www.pearsoned.ca (22 Apr. 2002).

8. Government Information and Sites—COS Scientific

Citizenship and Immigration Canada. (1996, October 29). Staying the course: 1997 annual immigration plan. *Annual immigration plans*. http://cicnet.ci.gc.ca/english/pub/index.html (5 Mar. 2001).

9. Book Accessed Online—COS Scientific

BOOK PUBLISHED FIRST IN PRINT VERSION

Eaton, A. W. (1889). *Acadian legends and lyrics*. London & New York: White & Allen. (2000, February 16). *Early Canadiana Online*. http://www.canadiana.org/cgi-bin/ECO/mtq?doc=09066 (25 May 2001).

BOOK PUBLISHED ONLINE

Shires, B. (2000, January 17). *CPR (cardiopulmonary resuscitation) guide*. http://www.memoware.com/Category=Medicine_ResultSet=1.htm (17 Apr. 2000).

10. Graphic, Video, or Audio File on the Page—COS Scientific

owl.gif. [Graphic file] (2000). Original free clipart. *Clipart.com*. http://www.free-clip-art.net/index4.shtml (27 Oct. 2000).

11. Personal Electronic Mail (E-mail)—COS Scientific

Torres, N. Re: Online translation programs. [Personal e-mail]. (11 Sep. 2000).

12. Posting to a Discussion List—COS Scientific

Sheldon, A. (2000, January 2). Re: Request for help on sexism inscription. *FLING List for Feminists in Linguistics*. http://listserv.linguistlist.org (14 Nov. 2000).

13. Posting to a Newsgroup or Forum—COS Scientific

Markowitz, A. (2000, September 28). The changing face of work: A look at the way we work. http://www.yourturn.npr.org/cgi-bin/WebX?50@121.HjNGardZdaj^0@.ee7a9aa (8 Jan. 2001).

14. Archived Posting—COS Scientific

Radev, D. R. (1999, September 16). Natural language processing FAQ. *Institute of Information and Computing Sciences*. http://www.cs.ruu.nl/wais/html/na-dir/natural-lang-processing-faq.html (27 Jan. 1999).

15. Online Reference Sources—COS Scientific

Reference sources such as online encyclopaedias, dictionaries, thesauruses, style manuals, bibliographies, and other forms of factual material can be cited using this model.

Nordenberg, T. (2000). Make no mistake! Medical errors can be deadly serious. *Britannica.com*. Ebsco Publishing. http://britannica.com/bcom/original/article/0,5744,12430,00.html (18 Oct. 2000).

16. Computer Information Services and Online Databases—COS Scientific

Raintree Nutrition, Inc. (2000, June). Pata de vaca. *Raintree Tropical Plant Database*. http:////www.rain-tree.com/patadevaca.htm (9 Sep. 2000).

17. Gopher Site—COS Scientific

Elections. (1996, May). gopher://israel-info.gov.il/00/facts/state/st4 (27 Dec. 2000).

18. FTP Site—COS Scientific

Project Gutenberg. (2000, March 26). *Ibiblio.org*. ftp://metalab.unc.edu/pub/docs/books/gutenberg/ (12 Aug. 2000).

19. Telnet Site—COS Scientific

Schweller, K. G. (1999, May 28). How to design a bot. *Collegetown MOO*. telnet://galaxy.bvu.edu:7777 (16 Nov. 2000).

20. Synchronous Communication—COS Scientific

Dominguez, J. Interchange. *Daedalus Online*. http://daedalus.pearsoned.com (11 Mar. 2001).

21. Software—COS Scientific

Wresch, W. (1998). *Writer's helper*. Ver. 4.0. Upper Saddle River: Prentice Hall.

37 DOCUMENT DESIGN

37a What is document design?

Document design refers to the **layout,** also called *format,* of print and any accompanying GRAPHICS* on each page of your essays, papers, and Web pages. First impressions count. When readers see your document, they immediately form opinions about you and your information. A well-designed document influences readers positively because it reflects your respect for the assignment and the effort you made to master the required format.

Today, few instructors accept handwritten essays and research papers, so check before you submit your work. If you don't own a computer, use one at your college or university computer lab. Always find out whether you need to sign up in advance or can use the computers on a "first come, first served" basis. Give yourself sufficient time to get there, wait your turn, and return to the lab repeatedly as needed. Use your computer time efficiently by taking your final handwritten draft with you.

37b What is the document design process?

The process of designing documents involves the same steps as the WRITING PROCESS (Chapters 5–7), with a few added considerations.

Plan ahead by finding out the specific page layout and other features your instructor requires, so you can avoid last-minute confusion. If you're going to use GRAPHICS, plan their form, content, and size from the beginning of your project.

As you revise, integrate the layout and other design features as you go along. One decision you need to make is whether to put all your graphics in an appendix (recommended in MLA STYLE) or insert them where you discuss them in the text (fitting them exactly where you want them can be difficult). Check whether your instructor has a preference. As you revise, check that the content of your graphics matches what you say about them in the revised text of your paper. You might need to revise a graphic to match your text, or your wording to match a graphic.

*Words printed in small capital letters (such as GRAPHICS) are defined in the Terms Glossary on pages 497–517.

37c What are some general guidelines for designing documents?

If your instructor gives you specific layout or format instructions, use them. Otherwise, follow these guidelines:

- **Margins:** Margins are the blank areas on each side of a page and at the top and bottom. In academic writing, always leave a margin measuring no less than 2.5 centimetres on all sides.
- **Spacing of lines:** For college and university essays and research papers, double spacing is standard. The extra space gives you, your peers, and your instructors room to write comments in response to your writing. In contrast, business writing usually calls for single-spaced lines in BLOCK STYLE, with double spaces between paragraphs (for more details, see Chapter 63).
- **Font:** A font is the typeface you use. Select a standard font such as Times Roman, Bookman Old Style, or New Century Schoolbook. Avoid sans-serif fonts such as Helvetica, Arial, Gothic, and Univers, as well as fancy fonts such as MS Comic Sans and handwriting typefaces. When your content requires, use ITALICS (or underlining) and boldface type in the same font as the rest of the document. For size, select the standard 12-point (easiest to read) and 10-point fonts.
- **Paragraph style:** Academic essays and research papers call for paragraphs with indented first lines and double spacing throughout the paper. No extra space is left between paragraphs. Business writing calls for unindented first lines, single spacing of paragraphs, and double spacing between paragraphs, a format called block style. (Check for your instructor's preferences.) Never mix these two paragraph styles.
- **Title:** Never underline the title or enclose it in quotation marks. For academic essays and research papers, place the title at the top of the first page of a document—unless your instructor tells you to create a **title page** containing only the title, your name, and the course name and number. (For examples of how titles appear in research papers, see Chapters 30 and 33.)

37d How do I format each type of document?

Throughout this book, you can find examples of specific formats for many types of documents, including the following:

- essays to inform and to argue (Chapters 5–10)
- MLA-style research papers (Chapters 22–27 and 28–30)
- APA-style research papers (Chapters 31–33)
- Web pages (Chapter 38)
- essays about literature (Chapter 62)
- business letters and memos (Chapter 63)
- résumés and job-application letters (Chapter 63)

Most word-processing software doesn't provide the standard formats for academic essays or research papers, so you need to follow your instructor's guidelines or the guidelines in this book. However, most word-processing programs do provide page layouts for letters, envelopes, and memos in the form of **templates** ("fill-in-the-blank" forms) or **wizards** (advice and instructions in question-and-answer format).

37e How do I use headings in my writing?

Headings, like newspaper and magazine headlines, guide your reader through your document. Write headings that are brief and informative so that your readers can scan them easily. Always use PARALLELISM in their wording, capitalization, and typeface. Headings, like outlines, are organized in levels: first level, second level, and so on. Undergraduate essays and research papers rarely call for more than two heading levels. Be consistent in the form you use for each level of heading. For example, if you capitalize or boldface one heading, do the same with other headings at the same level. Here are some common types of headings with examples:

NOUN PHRASES, FOR A VARIETY OF SUBTOPICS

- Federal Government Responsibilities
- Provincial Government Responsibilities
- Municipal Government Responsibilities

QUESTIONS, FOR EVOKING INTEREST

- Can the Federal Government Overrule Provincial Legislation?
- Who Mediates Between Ottawa and the Provinces?
- What Is the "Notwithstanding Clause"?

***-ING* PHRASES, FOR EXPLAINING INSTRUCTIONS OR SOLVING PROBLEMS**

- Submitting the Federal Budget
- Debating the Federal Budget
- Approving the Federal Budget

IMPERATIVE SENTENCES, FOR ADVICE OR DIRECTIONS

- Identify Problem
- Consult Interest Groups
- Draft Bill
- Introduce Bill in Parliament

37f When are graphics appropriate in my writing?

Graphics include tables, bar graphs, line graphs, pie charts, timelines, and diagrams that you create or import from the Internet. You can also import photographs, clip art, and drawings. Be sure to check whether you need official permission to use imported items—and ask for it according to the instructions on each Web site. Usually, a student who is writing for a college or university course can use such material for free "one time only." Equally important, be sure to DOCUMENT your source.

Graphics convey information that lends itself to visual presentation. Sometimes, a graphic can condense, compare, and display information more effectively than words can. Most word-processing programs offer standard conversion methods to change words into tables. The programs also provide **templates** for some types of graphs and charts. If you have access to a colour printer, some of your graphics can look quite dramatic. Never be tempted, however, to present all your information in graphics. Strive instead for a balance between text and graphics; let the graphics enhance your writing, not replace it. Here is an excellent URL to consult about using graphics:

http://www.io.com/~hcextres/tcm1603/acchtml/graphics.html

- **Tables** present lists of data or words, as in the MLA-style research paper (Chapter 30) and the APA-style research paper (Chapter 33). The following table presents a list of selected local and mid-sized Canadian film festivals.

Table 1-1 Canadian Local and Mid-Sized Film Festivals, 2001 and 2002

Short Films	Themed Films	General/ Unrestricted Program
Dawson City International Short Film Festival	Antimatter Festival of Underground Short Film & Video (Victoria)	Banff Mountain Film Festival
Antimatter Festival of Underground Short Film & Video (Victoria)	St. John's International Women's Film & Video Festival	Festival du Cinéma International en Abitibi-Témiscamingue
	Festival Macabre (Montreal)	Sudbury Cinefest
		Festival du Nouveau Cinéma (Montreal)

- **Bar graphs** compare values, such as the numbers of students following different programs at a college, as shown in the following graph.

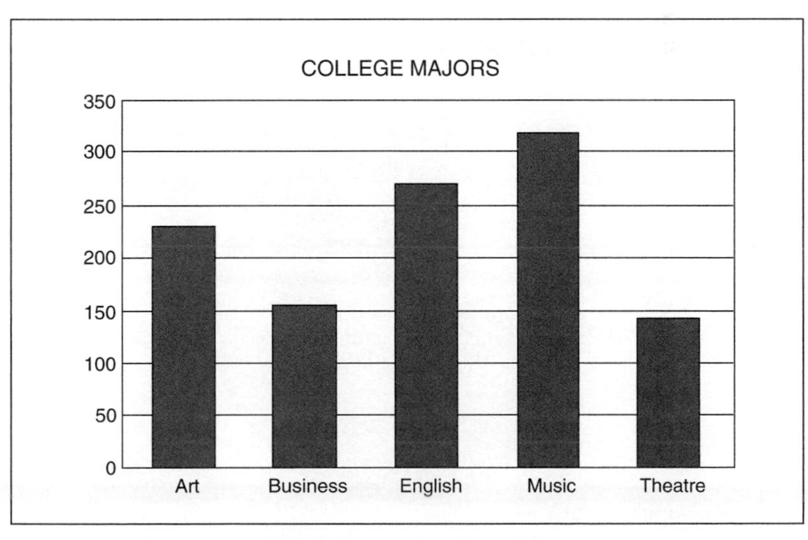

- **Line graphs** indicate changes over time. For example, the following graph shows advertising revenue over an eight-month period.

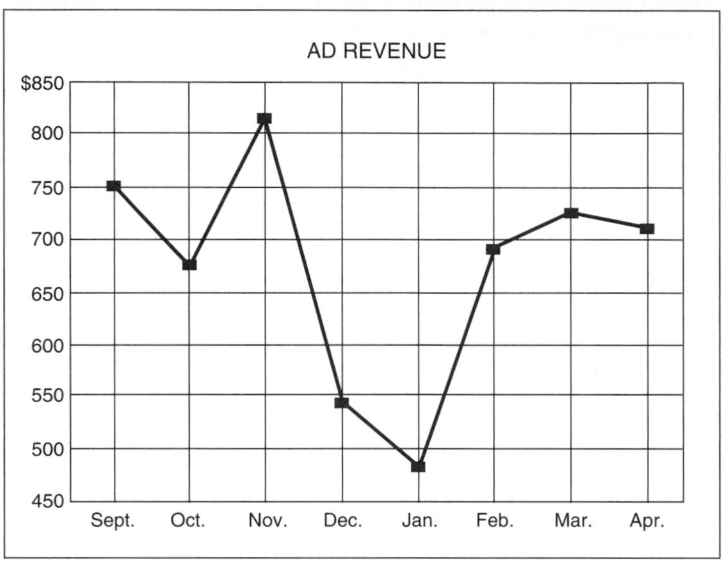

- **Pie charts** show the relationship of each part to a whole, such as a typical budget for an undergraduate student, shown in the following chart.

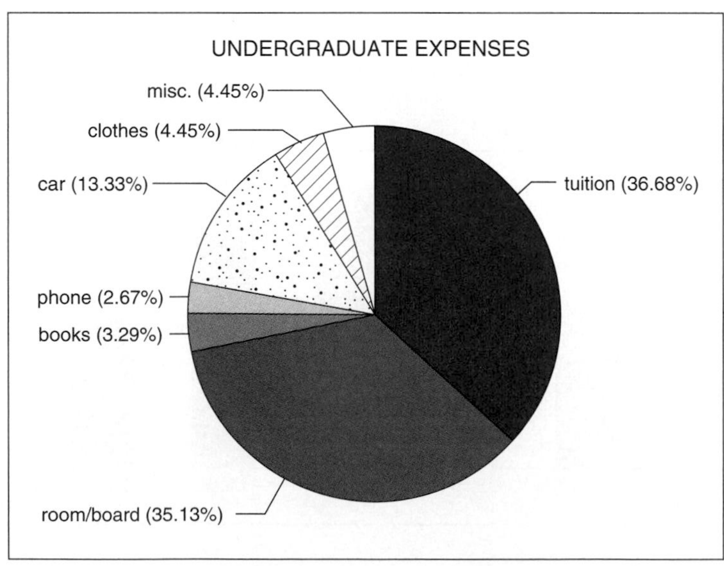

- **Timelines** display events over time, such as the progress of historical events or a manufacturing process.

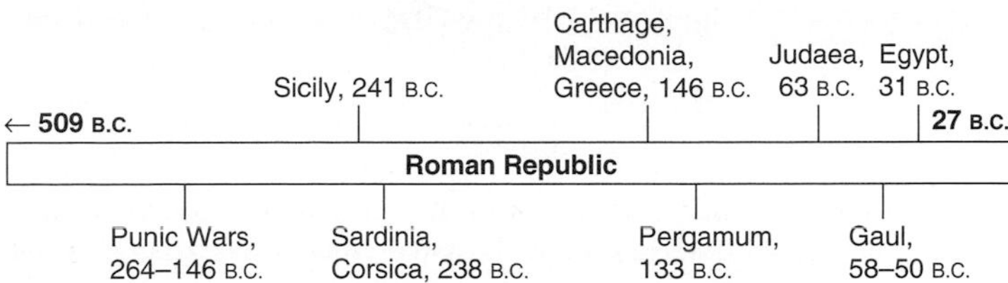

- **Diagrams** show the parts of a whole, as in this diagram of the human brain.

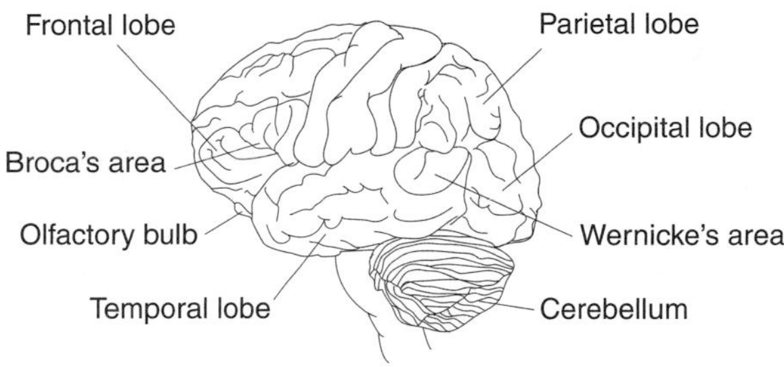

38 WRITING FOR THE WEB

38a What is the Web-writing process?

The **Web-writing process** is visual as well as verbal. This process, which has four parts, starts with writing the content; moves to making decisions about the structure of the content; continues with planning the layout of the material on the computer screen; and ends with checking whether the Web material is usable. Box 45 outlines the Web-writing process.

The four parts of the Web-writing process are interconnected. Therefore, the decisions you make for one part affect those you make for the other three. As with the WRITING PROCESS for any essay or paper (see Chapters 5–7), the parts of the Web-writing process loop back and forth, leading you to revise one or more of them until you achieve a unified

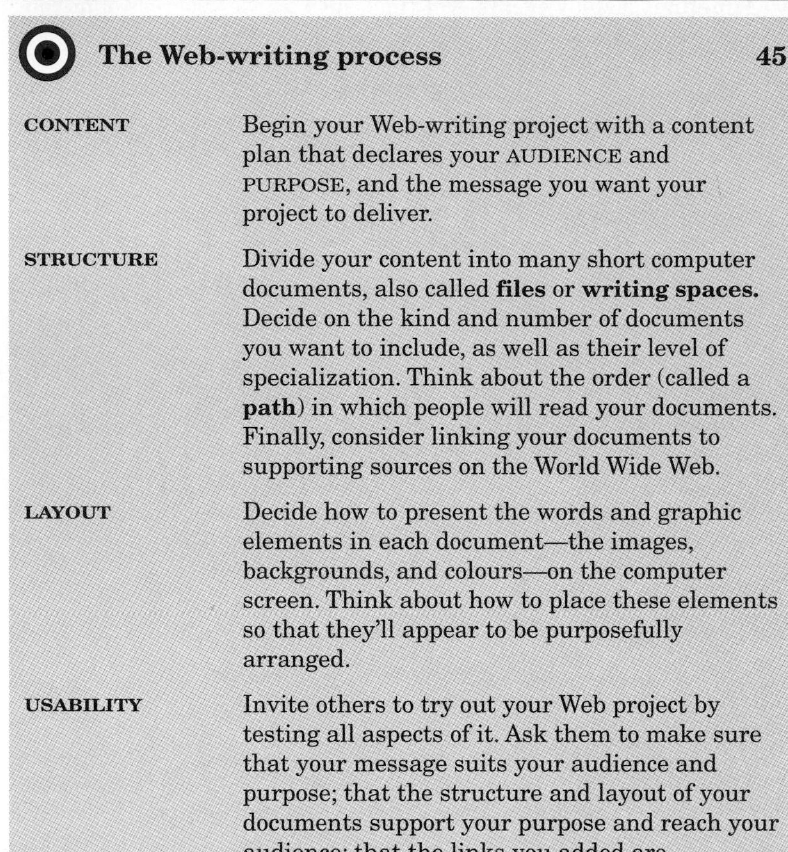

The Web-writing process **45**

CONTENT	Begin your Web-writing project with a content plan that declares your AUDIENCE and PURPOSE, and the message you want your project to deliver.
STRUCTURE	Divide your content into many short computer documents, also called **files** or **writing spaces.** Decide on the kind and number of documents you want to include, as well as their level of specialization. Think about the order (called a **path**) in which people will read your documents. Finally, consider linking your documents to supporting sources on the World Wide Web.
LAYOUT	Decide how to present the words and graphic elements in each document—the images, backgrounds, and colours—on the computer screen. Think about how to place these elements so that they'll appear to be purposefully arranged.
USABILITY	Invite others to try out your Web project by testing all aspects of it. Ask them to make sure that your message suits your audience and purpose; that the structure and layout of your documents support your purpose and reach your audience; that the links you added are appropriate and function well; and that the entire project works effectively as a unit.

whole. For example, suppose that you have decided on your site's *content* and purpose, and that its audience is the general reading public. However, if you find that when you work on the *structure,* it becomes specialized and technical, and the *layout* becomes too busy, loop back to your thinking about your purpose and audience in relation to the content. Then adjust the structure and layout accordingly.

The details of your Web-writing assignment and the amount of time assigned for its completion influence your decisions for each of the four parts of the Web-writing process. In some cases, your instructor may assign a specific kind or number of documents or may give you other writing requirements. Knowing this information, you can plan your time and organize your ideas to reach your goal.

38b How do I plan content for my Web site?

Planning logically

To start planning logically, you first need to choose a TOPIC suitable for a Web-writing project. You can do this by using the strategies suggested in Chapter 5, but with your eye on the unique medium of the Web. The Web differs from other media in distinct ways that affect your writing:

- Web writing calls for smaller sections than print writing.
- Web writing highlights the connections or links between related Web sites.
- Web writing emphasizes visual elements such as colour and pictures.

Your next step is to plan your writing PURPOSE, choose your AUDIENCE, and analyze your WRITING SITUATION. Ask yourself these questions and act on your answers:

- What is my overall purpose in writing for the Web? Will I aim to create a site that seeks to INFORM, or to PERSUADE, or to combine these purposes? Your purpose is the most important part of your plan because it informs every level of your Web project.
- What is the size of my Web-writing project? Web projects function as collections of computer documents (individual files ending in "htm," "html," "asp," and the like) that are linked together and displayed as pages on a computer screen. You will need to determine the number of documents you want and the amount of content to include in each. Keep in mind that readers scan Web pages quickly and prefer not to scroll down long sections of information.
- How many links to other Web and Internet sites should I include? Choose links that directly support your Web project's message by going to an illustration, explanation, reference, or other material that can expand a reader's thinking. You can choose links to **internal Web sites** (ones available on the intranet at your university or college), which can be especially useful when other class members are working on the same or a related topic. You can also choose links to **external Web sites** to give readers an even wider perspective.
- Who will my readers be? Can I assume that they're comfortable with computers and know how to navigate from one document to another?

Readers need to be able to move around without getting lost, which is why many Web writers include a table of contents or site map on the opening document, called the **home page.**

Collaborating effectively

Collaborative writing means sharing and distributing tasks among members of a group. It is especially suitable for Web-writing projects. By involving others or working as part of a team, you can improve each part of the plan for your Web-writing project, especially at the *usability* stage. Little is as stimulating as soliciting ideas and reactions from others as you work. After all, your Web writing needs to reach and hold the interest of an audience. What you thought was clever or absorbing might fall flat when others look at it. The more people who preview your work, the better are your chances for success. Even if you don't complete each part of your Web-writing project in collaboration with others, ask one or more of your peers or others who can play the role of your audience to assess the logic and appeal of your material.

38c How do I create a structure for my Web site?

Web structure is the organization of the content and documents included in a Web project. Often this process begins with the opening or home page document, which includes links to all the documents included in the Web project. Many Web writers draw a map of their Web structure so that they can keep track of all their documents and links.

Forming structures

Use a structure that fits your purpose and audience. Just as writers use paragraphing strategies to organize their essays (see Chapter 8), so you can use Web structures to organize your Web writing. When you start writing for the Web, you may want to choose only one structure, so that your Web readers are less likely to get lost as they navigate among your Web documents. As you gain more experience writing and using Web sites, you might want to try complex Web projects that include more than one structure. Here are the most common single structures for Web writing:

LINEAR STRUCTURE A series of documents linked in a sequence that establishes expectations of what will come next (for example, using consecutive numbering)

OUTLINE STRUCTURE A series of documents arranged from general to specific or specific to general

CLUSTER STRUCTURE Groups of documents that are related to your overall message

MEANDERING STRUCTURE No apparent structure

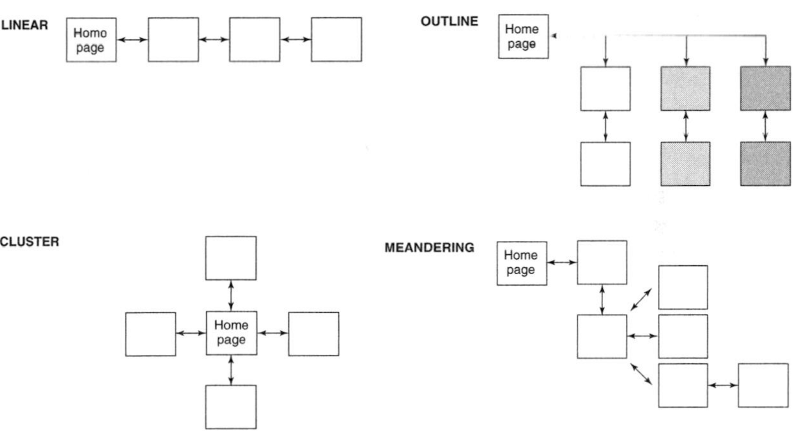

Some common Web structures

To connect your documents into one of these structures, use **hyperlinks,** direct electronic connections between documents. Combinations of hyperlinks hold Web documents together and make them interactive by allowing readers to select what they want to see next from among your hyperlink choices.

At a minimum, each of your Web documents should include at least two links, though more are better: a **home link** to take people looking at other pages on your Web site right back to where they started—that is, to your home page; and at least one additional link to an internal Web site or external Web site. With your structure in mind, choose the types of hyperlinks you need. Here are the major types of hyperlinks:

HOME LINK Moves back to the opening document, or home page, on which you might want to include a table of contents and/or a comprehensive list of hyperlinks.

SEQUENTIAL LINK Moves to the next document in an outline or hierarchical progression.

ASSOCIATIVE LINK Moves to a related document with content that supports your Web site's central controlling idea (also called a *related link*).

CONTRASTIVE LINK Moves to a document with content that challeges your Web site's central controlling idea (also called a *refutation link*).

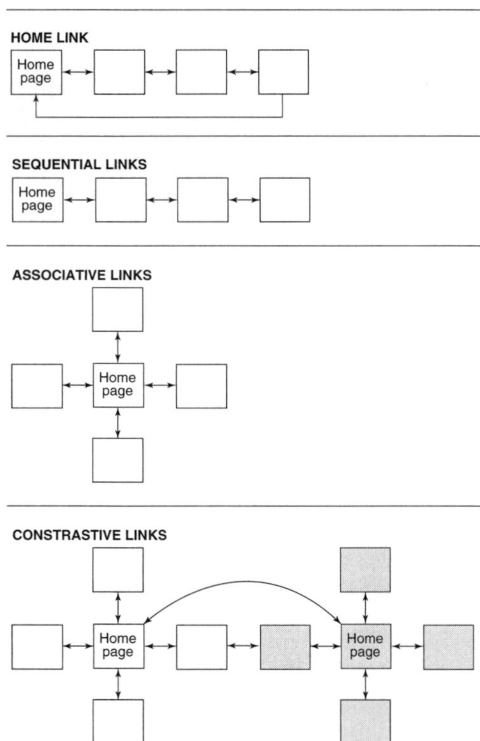

How hyperlinks work

Providing departure and arrival information

Departure and arrival information tells readers where they are in your Web project and where they can go next if they follow a hyperlink. Letting readers know about the document they have just arrived at or the document they are about to visit keeps them from getting lost in your Web project and helps clarify your message:

- Name your documents so that people can identify their content based on the names.
- Start each document in your Web project with a brief heading and perhaps a short description. This gives readers a rationale for spending time with the document.
- Name your hyperlinks so that people can identify their content based on the names. If a hyperlink connects to a written document, name it so that readers will know what to expect. If a hyperlink connects to a graphic or other type of visual, name it accordingly, so that readers can choose intelligently where to go next in your Web project.
- Maintain PARALLELISM as you name your documents and hyperlinks, so that your Web project conveys a sense of unity and consistency.

38d How do I compose a layout for my Web site?

Web layout is the process of arranging and presenting the elements of your Web project on the screen—typestyles, headings, lines, colours, graphics, animated images, or video, if any. In laying out your Web writing, try to find the right balance among these elements, so that they complement your overall message and communicate it directly. Don't try to pack too much into a single screen or writing space.

Using Web-writing software

One early layout decision to make is which kind of software you'll use to compose your documents. Web programs such as Netscape Composer, HoTMetal Pro, Miscrosoft FrontPage, and Dreamweaver allow you to construct Web documents in much the same way as you compose word-processing documents. Use of these programs does not require learning **HTML code,** the programming language used on the Web. Web-writing software also allows you to organize your document files in folders and edit them at the same time. Many provide ready-made templates from which you can select prepared layout choices, including background colours, heading styles, placement of graphic elements, and text styles (font, size, colour).

Some word-processing programs can convert and save word-processed documents as Web documents. These programs—for example, Microsoft Word, AppleWorks, WordPerfect—allow you to change the file type, margins, and general layout so that they're compatible with the World Wide Web, thus saving you the effort of keying the material a second time. These are the most common file types used in Web writing:

WORD PROCESSED	.doc, .wps, .rtf (the most common), .txt
WEB	.html (the standard), .htm, .dhtml, .asp
VISUAL	.jpeg (the quickest to download), .eps, .tiff, .bmp

Using the most common and quickest file types helps your readers because they don't have to convert your document files or wait a long time for them to download.

Your layout plan includes choices for how the text and visual elements will appear on screen. To create the impression of a unified and thoughtful project, build a layout plan that establishes a consistent style. To do this, use the same or similar typefaces, graphics, and colour styles throughout your entire Web project.

Choosing typefaces

A **typeface,** also called a *font,* is the style of the individual letters that make up your Web writing. You may think that the typeface is not a visual element, but it is. Your choice of typeface greatly affects the appearance of your documents. As you lay out your material, consider the size and style you want to use. Generally, you want a typeface that's easy to read on screen. Most Web writers rely on 12-point Arial, which is the font built into most Web-writing software. You can change to another font if you wish.

Selecting the right graphics

Graphics are the visual means of communication that accompany your text. Graphics can increase the effectiveness of your Web writing if you choose them cautiously. To select appropriate graphics, ask yourself the following questions:

- What graphics should I include? (Text content is the most important part of your Web project, which means that you may decide to use only one or two graphic elements.)
- What does each graphic that I choose contribute to the overall message I'm trying to communicate?
- How do I know whether I need legal permission from the graphic's creator to use a graphic on my Web site? Examine the graphic, its surrounding material, and the site's home page carefully for any statement that the material on the site may be reproduced without permission (watch for any restrictions on such use). If no such statement is present, you must get permission to use the graphic. The

site usually includes an e-mail address to which you can send a brief note explaining exactly what material you want to use, why you want to use it, and, most importantly, whether you intend to make money from your Web project. (You may be given free permission if you are writing for a class project or other educational purpose, but if you're writing a for-profit Web project, you will definitely be expected to pay a fee.)

- How do I DOCUMENT a graphic appropriately to show its source? You need to do this whether or not you must pay a permission fee for using the graphic. The graphic can come from a print or online source. For the correct format for documenting your graphic sources, whether in print or online, see Chapters 28 and 29 for MLA style; Chapters 31 and 32 for APA style; Chapter 34 for CM style; Chapter 35 for CSE style; and Chapter 36 for Columbia online style.

Using colour

Computer screens can reproduce millions of colour combinations, allowing Web writers to choose from a rich array of hues for their layouts. For consistency in appearance, use the same colour combinations in all your documents for a particular Web project.

Not all colours work well together. In addition, too many colours in the same Web project may distract readers. Here's the best rule of thumb: Successful colour combinations include no more than two or three colours. For examples of effective use of colour, browse professional Web pages, study Microsoft PowerPoint's suggested colour groupings, or use the colour templates that accompany many software programs.

Arranging text and graphics on the screen

Use the following general principles to arrange your text and graphics on the screen:

CONSISTENCY Keep the overall appearance of your Web documents about the same in terms of typefaces, graphics, and colour.

CONTINUITY Place repeated elements in about the same location in each of your Web documents, so that readers always know where to find them. These elements include the home page link, other hyperlinks, your e-mail address, a signature graphic image, and so on.

COHERENCE Choose graphics that match your text, and text that matches and clarifies your graphics.

SIMPLICITY Keep it simple. Computer screens are small (usually 400 × 600 pixels), and most readers move quickly through the Web.

38e How do I make sure my Web writing is usable?

Usability refers to the tests your Web project must meet if it is to suit your audience and purpose. Working collaboratively with your peers and instructor is the best way to test your Web project's effectiveness. When you collaborate with others or work individually, consider the following questions:

- Is my Web project trouble free? Make sure that all the hyperlinks work and that the documents upload correctly.
- Is my Web project user friendly? This test is more subjective. Look for (or ask your readers to report on) any sections in which information is difficult to find.
- Does my project's message come through? Is any material distracting? This question is also subjective. Ask for feedback on what your readers remember about your message.
- Is everything consistent and correct? Do I need to edit my content (using the content plan that I developed during my planning process) or my layout and design?

38f How can I publish my Web project?

When you have finished your Web project, the final step is publishing it on the Internet. If you wrote your Web project for a class, your instructor most likely has arranged to provide you with access to the Internet, either through your school's Web site (though many universities and colleges restrict use of their official Web sites) or through an intranet Web site that operates privately. If your Web project is unrelated to your class work—for example, if it is a project for a student organization or club—you will need to locate a **Web host.** To find a company that provides Web sites on which you can publish your project, begin by contacting an **Internet service provider (ISP)** such as Sympatico, Rogers@Home, Cybersurf, or a smaller provider that operates in your local area.

39 PARTS OF SPEECH AND PARTS OF SENTENCES

PARTS OF SPEECH

Knowing the parts of speech gives you a basic vocabulary for identifying words and understanding how language works. No part of speech exists in a vacuum. To identify a word's part of speech correctly, you need to see how the word functions in the sentence you are analyzing. Often, the same word functions differently in different sentences.

- We ate **fish.** [*Fish* is a NOUN.* It represents a thing.]
- We **fish** on weekends. [*Fish* is a VERB. It represents an action.]

39a What is a noun?

A **noun** represents a person, place, thing, or idea: *student, college, textbook, education.*

Types of nouns 46

PROPER	names of specific people, places, or things (first letter is always capitalized)	*Céline Dion, Paris, Buick*
COMMON	general groups, places, people, or things	*singer, city, automobile*
CONCRETE	things experienced through the senses: sight, hearing, taste, smell, and touch	*landscape, pizza, thunder*
ABSTRACT	things not knowable through the senses	*freedom, shyness*
COLLECTIVE	groups	*family, team*
NONCOUNT	"uncountable" things	*beef, dirt*
COUNT	countable items (singular or plural)	*lake (lakes), minute (minutes)*

Some nouns fit into more than one category. For example, *family* is both a common noun and a collective noun.

* Words printed in small capital letters (such as NOUN) are defined in the Terms Glossary on pages 497–517.

ESL NOTES: (1) Nouns often appear with words that tell how much, how many, whose, which one, and similar information. These words include ARTICLES (*a, an, the*), ADJECTIVES, and other DETERMINERS. (2) Words with these SUFFIXES (word endings) are usually nouns: *-ance, -ence, -ment, -ness,* and *-ty.*!

39b What is a pronoun?

A **pronoun** takes the place of a NOUN. The word or words a pronoun replaces is called its **antecedent.** (Also see Chapter 42.)

- **David** is an accountant. [noun]
- **He** is an accountant. [pronoun]
- The budget committee needs to consult **him.** [The pronoun *him* refers to its antecedent, *David.*]

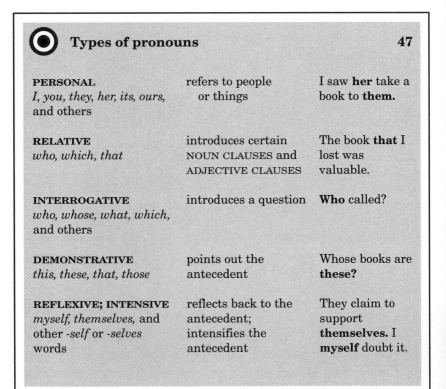

Types of pronouns 47

PERSONAL *I, you, they, her, its, ours,* and others	refers to people or things	I saw **her** take a book to **them.**
RELATIVE *who, which, that*	introduces certain NOUN CLAUSES and ADJECTIVE CLAUSES	The book **that** I lost was valuable.
INTERROGATIVE *who, whose, what, which,* and others	introduces a question	**Who** called?
DEMONSTRATIVE *this, these, that, those*	points out the antecedent	Whose books are **these?**
REFLEXIVE; INTENSIVE *myself, themselves,* and other *-self* or *-selves* words	reflects back to the antecedent; intensifies the antecedent	They claim to support **themselves.** I **myself** doubt it.

→

Types of pronouns ***(continued)***

RECIPROCAL *each other, one another*	refers to individual parts of a plural antecedent	We respect **each other.**
INDEFINITE *all, anyone, each,* and others	refers to nonspecific persons or things	**Everyone** is welcome here.

39c What is a verb?

Main verbs express action, occurrence, or state of being.

- I **dance.** [action]
- The audience **became** silent. [occurrence]
- Your dancing **was** excellent. [state of being]

(For more about verbs, see Ch. 40; for MODAL AUXILIARY VERBS, see Ch. 49.)

ALERT: When you are not sure if a word is a verb, try putting it into a different TENSE. If the sentence still makes sense, the word is a verb. (For help with verb tense, see 40e.)

NO He is a **changed** person. He is a **will change** person. [The sentence does not make sense when the verb *will change* is substituted, so *changed* is not functioning as a verb.]

YES The store **changed** owners. The store **will change** owners. [Because the sentence still makes sense when the verb *will change* is substituted, *changed* is functioning as a verb.]!

39d What is a verbal?

Verbals are verb parts functioning as NOUNS, ADJECTIVES, or ADVERBS.

ESL NOTE: The word *to* has several functions.

He has nothing **to eat.**

Here, *to* is part of the INFINITIVE *to eat,* which modifies the PRONOUN *nothing,* one of the few structures in which a MODIFIER follows a noun or pronoun.

He **has to eat** something.

Here, *to* is part of the modal auxiliary *have to,* meaning "must" (49b).

He is **accustomed to eating** at noon.

Here, *to* is a preposition that requires a noun, pronoun, or gerund OBJECT—*eating* (48a).!

Types of verbals 48

INFINITIVE *to* + SIMPLE FORM of verb	1. Noun: represents an action, state, or condition 2. Adjective or adverb: describes or modifies	**To eat** soon is our goal. Still, we have nothing **to eat.**
PAST PARTICIPLE *-ed* form of REGULAR VERB or equivalent in IRREGULAR VERB	Adjective: describes or modifies	**Boiled, filtered** water is usually safe to drink.
PRESENT PARTICIPLE *-ing* form of verb	1. adjective: describes or modifies 2. noun:* represents an action, state, or condition	**Running** water may not be safe. **Drinking** contaminated water is dangerous.

* A present participle functioning as a noun is called a **gerund.**

39e What is an adjective?

Adjectives modify—that is, they describe or limit—NOUNS, PRONOUNS, and word groups that function as nouns.

- I saw a **green** and **leafy** tree. [*Green* and *leafy* modify the noun *tree.*]

Descriptive adjectives, such as *green* and *leafy,* can show levels of intensity: *green, greener, greenest; leafy, more leafy, most leafy* (43e). **Proper adjectives** are formed from proper nouns: *Canadian, Victorian.* Words with these SUFFIXES (word endings) are usually adjectives: *-ful, -ish, -less,* and *-like* (21b).

Determiners are sometimes called *limiting adjectives* because they "limit" nouns. The limitations tell whether a noun is general (*a tree*) or specific (*the tree*). Determiners also tell which one (*this tree*), how many (*twelve trees*), whose (*our tree*), and similar information. (Also see Chapters 44–45.)

Types of determiners 49

ARTICLES *a, an, the*	**A** reporter working on **an** assignment is using **the** telephone.
DEMONSTRATIVE *this, these, that, those*	**Those** students rent **that** house.
INDEFINITE *any, each, few, other, some,* and others	**Few** films today have complex plots.
INTERROGATIVE *what, which, whose*	**What** answer did you give?
NUMERICAL *one, first, two, second,* and others	The **fifth** question was tricky.
POSSESSIVE *my, your, their,* and others	**My** dog is older than **your** cat.
RELATIVE *what, which, whose, whatever,* and others	He is the instructor **whose** course I enjoyed.

39f What is an adverb?

An **adverb** modifies—that is, it describes or limits—VERBS, ADJECTIVES, other adverbs, and CLAUSES.

- Chefs plan meals **carefully.** [*Carefully* modifies the verb *plan.*]
- Vegetables provide **very** important vitamins. [*Very* modifies the adjective *important.*]

- Those potato chips are **too** heavily salted. [*Too* modifies the adverb *heavily*.]
- **Fortunately,** people realize that salt can do harm. [*Fortunately* modifies the entire sentence.]

Descriptive adverbs show levels of intensity, usually by adding *more* (or *less*) and *most* (or *least*): *more happily, least clearly.* Many descriptive adverbs are formed by adding *-ly* to adjectives: *sadly, loudly, normally.* Some adjectives look like adverbs but are not: *brotherly, lovely.* Also, many adverbs do not end in *-ly: very, always, not, yesterday,* and *well* are a few. (Also see Chapter 43.)

When words such as *where, why,* and *when* are used to introduce ADJECTIVE CLAUSES, they are called **relative adverbs.**

Conjunctive adverbs modify by creating logical connections in meaning to express relationships.

Conjunctive adverbs and the relationships they express 50

RELATIONSHIP	WORDS
ADDITION	*also, furthermore, moreover, besides*
CONTRAST	*however, still, nevertheless, conversely, nonetheless, instead, otherwise*
COMPARISON	*similarly, likewise*
RESULT OR SUMMARY	*therefore, thus, consequently, accordingly, hence, then*
TIME	*next, then, meanwhile, finally, subsequently*
EMPHASIS	*indeed, certainly*

39g What is a preposition?

Prepositions include common words such as *in, under, by, after, to, on, over,* and *since.* Prepositions function with other words in PREPOSITIONAL PHRASES. These phrases often set out relationships in time or space: *in April, under the orange umbrella.* (Also see Chapter 47.)

- **In** the fall, we will hear a concert **by** our favourite tenor.
- **After** the concert, he will fly **to** Paris.

39h What is a conjunction?

A **conjunction** connects words, PHRASES, or CLAUSES. **Coordinating conjunctions,** which express relationships, join two or more grammatically equivalent structures.

Coordinating conjunctions and the relationships they express 51

RELATIONSHIP	WORDS
ADDITION	*and*
CONTRAST	*but, yet*
RESULT OR EFFECT	*so*
REASON OR CAUSE	*for*
CHOICE	*or*
NEGATIVE CHOICE	*nor*

- We hike **and** camp every summer. [*And* joins two words.]
- I love the outdoors, **but** my family does not. [*But* joins two independent clauses.]

Correlative conjunctions function in pairs to join equivalent grammatical structures. They include *both . . . and, either . . . or, neither . . . nor, not only . . . but (also), whether . . . or,* and *not . . . so much as.*

- **Not only** students **but also** businesspeople should study a second language.

Subordinating conjunctions introduce DEPENDENT CLAUSES. Subordinating conjunctions express relationships that show that dependent clauses are grammatically less important than any independent clause within the same sentence.

- Many people were happy **after** they heard the news.
- **Because** it snowed, school was cancelled.

Subordinating conjunctions and the relationships they express 52

RELATIONSHIP	WORDS
TIME	*after, before, once, since, until, when, whenever, while*
REASON OR CAUSE	*as, because, since*
RESULT OR EFFECT	*in order that, so, so that, that*
CONDITION	*if, even if, provided that, unless*
CONTRAST	*although, even though, though, whereas*
LOCATION	*where, wherever*
CHOICE	*rather than, than, whether*

39i What is an interjection?

An **interjection** is a word or words of surprise or strong emotion. Alone, punctuate an interjection with an exclamation point: *Hooray!* As part of a sentence, set off an interjection with a comma or commas: *Hooray, you got the promotion.* Use interjections sparingly, if at all, in academic writing.

PARTS OF SENTENCES

When you know how sentences are formed, you have one tool for understanding the art of writing.

39j What are subjects and predicates?

A sentence consists of two basic parts: a subject and a predicate.

A **simple subject** is the word, or words, that acts, is described, or is acted upon: *The* ***telephone*** *rang.* A **complete subject** is the subject and all its MODIFIERS: ***The red telephone*** *rang.*

The **predicate** contains the VERB: *The telephone* ***rang.*** The **complete predicate** is the verb and all its modifiers: *The telephone* ***rang loudly.***

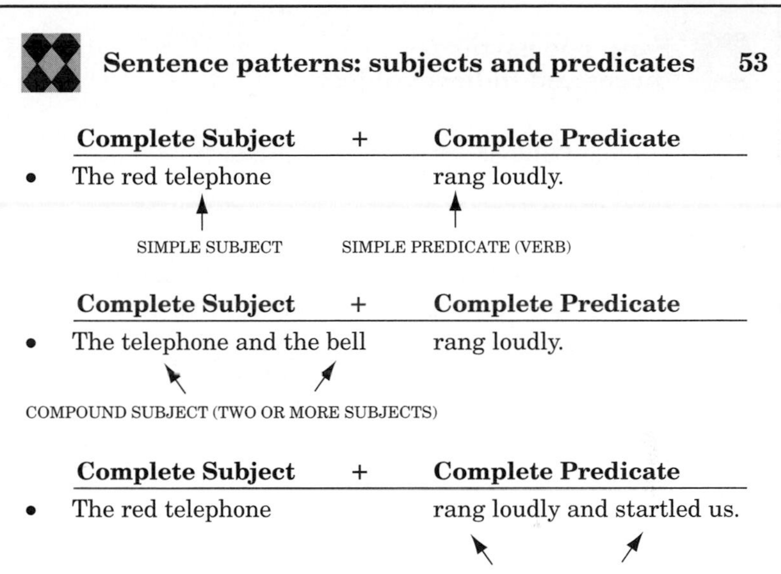

Sentence patterns: subjects and predicates 53
Complete Subject + Complete Predicate
The red telephone rang loudly.
SIMPLE SUBJECT
SIMPLE PREDICATE (VERB)
Complete Subject + Complete Predicate
The telephone and the bell rang loudly.
COMPOUND SUBJECT (TWO OR MORE SUBJECTS)
Complete Subject + Complete Predicate
The red telephone rang loudly and startled us.
COMPOUND PREDICATE (TWO OR MORE VERBS)

ESL NOTE: Avoid repeating a subject with a personal pronoun in the same clause.

NO **My grandfather he** lived to be eighty-seven.

YES **My grandfather** lived to be eighty-seven. **!**

39k What are direct and indirect objects?

A **direct object** completes the meaning of VERBS that are TRANSITIVE. To find a direct object, ask *whom?* or *what?* about the verb: *Keisha bought* [what?] ***a sweater.*** To find an **indirect object,** ask *to whom? for whom? to what?* or *for what?* about the verb: *Keisha bought* [for whom?] ***me*** *a sweater.*

ESL NOTES: (1) In sentences with indirect objects that follow the word *to* or *for,* always put the direct object before the indirect object.

NO Will you please give **to John** this letter?

YES Will you please give this letter **to John**?

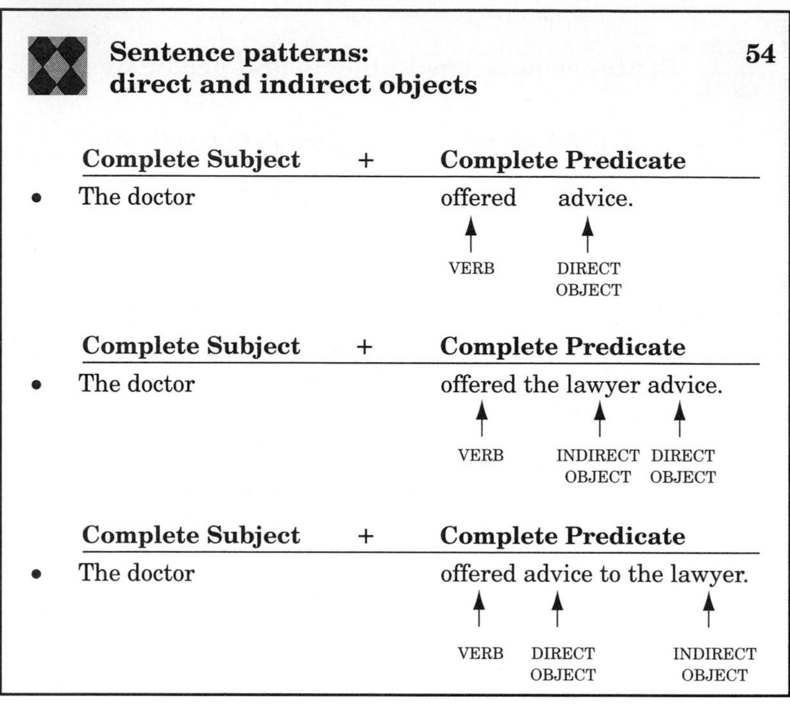

(2) When a PRONOUN is used as an indirect object, some verbs require *to* or *for* before the pronoun, and others do not.

NO Please explain **me** the rule. [*Explain* requires *to* before an indirect object.]

YES Please explain the rule **to me.**

YES Please give **me** that book. Please give that book **to me.** [*Give* uses both patterns.]

(3) When both the direct object and indirect object are pronouns, put the direct object first and use *to* with the indirect object.

NO He gave **me it.**

YES He gave **it to me.**

YES Please give **me the letter.** [*Give* does not require *to* before an indirect object.]

(4) Even if a verb does not require *to* before an indirect object, you may use *to* if you prefer. Just be sure if you do use *to,* that you put the direct object before the indirect object.

YES Please give the letter **to me.**!

39l What are complements, modifiers, and appositives?

Recognizing complements

A **complement** renames or describes a SUBJECT or an OBJECT. It appears in the PREDICATE of a sentence.

A **subject complement** is a NOUN, PRONOUN, or ADJECTIVE that follows a LINKING VERB. An **object complement** is a noun or an adjective that follows a DIRECT OBJECT.

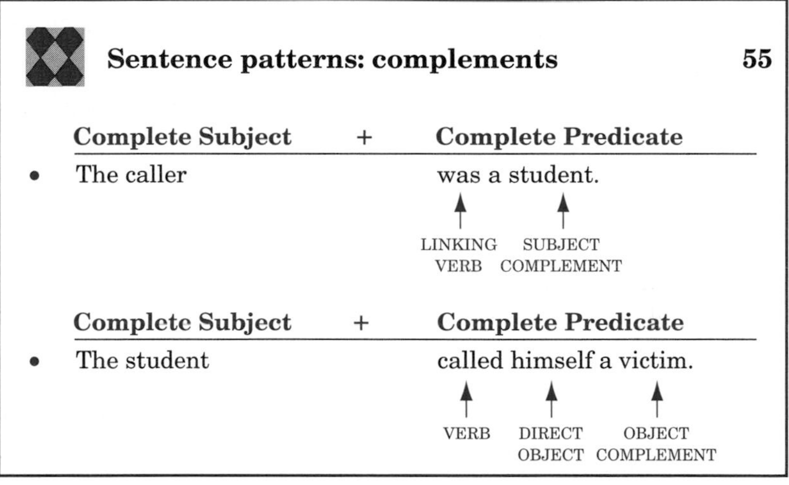

Sentence patterns: complements
55
Complete Subject + Complete Predicate
The caller
was a student.
LINKING VERB
SUBJECT COMPLEMENT
Complete Subject + Complete Predicate
The student
called himself a victim.
VERB
DIRECT OBJECT
OBJECT COMPLEMENT

Recognizing modifiers

A **modifier** is a word or words that function as an adjective or ADVERB. Modifiers can appear anywhere in a sentence.

- The **large red** telephone rang. [The adjectives *large* and *red* modify the noun *telephone*.]
- The lawyer answered **quickly.** [The adverb *quickly* modifies the verb *answered*.]

- The person **on the telephone** was **extremely** upset. [The PREPOSITIONAL PHRASE *on the telephone* modifies the noun *person;* the adverb *extremely* modifies the adjective *upset*.]
- **Therefore,** the lawyer spoke gently. [The adverb *therefore* modifies the INDEPENDENT CLAUSE *the lawyer spoke gently*.]
- **Because the lawyer's voice was calm,** the caller felt reassured. [*Because the lawyer's voice was calm* is called an ADVERB CLAUSE; it modifies the independent clause *the caller felt reassured*.]

Recognizing appositives

An **appositive** is a word or group of words that renames the noun or pronoun preceding it.

- The student's story, **a tale of broken promises,** was complicated. [*A tale of broken promises* is an appositive that renames the noun *story*.]
- The lawyer consulted an expert, **her law professor.** [*Her law professor* is an appositive that renames the noun *expert*.]

ALERT: When an appositive is not essential for identifying the noun or pronoun it renames (that is, when an appositive is NONRESTRICTIVE), use a comma or commas to set the appositive off from whatever it renames and from any words following it (50f).

39m What is a phrase?

A **phrase** is a group of related words that may contain a SUBJECT or a PREDICATE but not both. A phrase cannot stand alone as an independent unit.

A **noun phrase** functions as a NOUN: ***The modern population census*** *started in the seventeenth century.*

A **verb phrase** functions as a VERB: *The Romans* ***had been conducting*** *a census every five years.*

A **prepositional phrase,** which starts with a PREPOSITION and contains a noun or PRONOUN, functions as a MODIFIER: ***After the collapse of Rome,*** *censuses were discontinued* ***until modern times.*** (*After the collapse, of Rome,* and *until modern times* are all prepositional phrases.)

An **absolute phrase** is a word group that contains a noun or pronoun and a PARTICIPLE. It modifies the entire sentence: ***Censuses being the fashion,*** *Quebec and Nova Scotia took sixteen counts between 1665 and 1754.*

A **verbal phrase** is a word group that contains a VERBAL (Box 48).

- In 1814, the Red River Colony began **to count** its settlers in a census. [infinitive phrase = direct object]
- **Going from door to door,** census takers interview millions of people. [participial phrase = adjective modifying *census takers*]
- **Amazed by some people's answers,** the census takers always listen carefully. [participial phrase = adjective modifying *census takers*]

The key to telling the difference between a gerund phrase and a present-tense participial phrase is to determine how the verbal phrase is functioning. Although both use the *-ing* form, a **gerund phrase** functions only as a noun, and a **participial phrase** functions only as a modifier.

- **Including each person** in the census was important. [gerund phrase = noun used as the subject]
- **Including each person in the census,** Abby spent many hours on the crowded city block. [participial phrase = modifier used as adjective describing *Abby*]

39n What is a clause?

A **clause** is a group of words that contains both a SUBJECT and a PREDICATE. *Independent clauses* are also known as *main clauses. Dependent clauses* are also known as *subordinate clauses.*

Recognizing independent clauses

An **independent clause** can stand alone as a sentence.

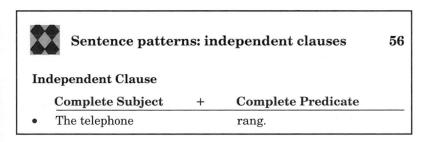

Sentence patterns: independent clauses **56**

Independent Clause

	Complete Subject	+	Complete Predicate
•	The telephone		rang.

Recognizing dependent clauses

A **dependent clause** contains a subject and a predicate, but it cannot stand alone as a sentence. Therefore, a dependent clause must be joined to an independent clause.

Some dependent clauses start with SUBORDINATING CONJUNCTIONS (Box 52). These clauses are called **adverb clauses.** They function as ADVERBS, usually answering a question about the independent clause: *how? why? when? under what circumstances?*

- **If the vote passes,** the city will install sewers. [The adverb clause modifies the verb *install,* explaining under what circumstances.]
- They are drawing up plans **as quickly as they can.** [The adverb clause modifies the verb *drawing up,* explaining how.]
- The homeowners feel happier **because they know the flooding will soon be better controlled.** [The adverb clause modifies the entire independent clause, explaining why.]

ALERT: When an adverb clause comes before its independent clause, the clauses are usually separated by a comma (50b).**!**

Adjective clauses are also dependent clauses and are sometimes called **relative clauses.** These clauses start with RELATIVE PRONOUNS (*who, whom, which, whose,* and *that*) or occasionally with RELATIVE ADVERBS such as *when* or *where.*

- The car **that Jack bought** is practical. [The adjective clause *that Jack bought* describes the noun *car*.]
- The day **when I can buy my own car** is getting closer. [The adjective clause *when I can buy my own car* modifies the noun *day*.]

Noun clauses often begin with *that, who,* or *which,* but they can also start with *whoever, whichever, when, where, whether, why,* or *how.*

- **Promises** are not always dependable. [noun]
- **What politicians promise** is not always dependable. [noun clause]
- Often, voters do not know **the truth.** [noun]
- Often, voters do not know **that the truth is being manipulated.** [noun clause]

Because they start with similar words, noun clauses and adjective clauses are sometimes confused with each other. A noun clause *is* a

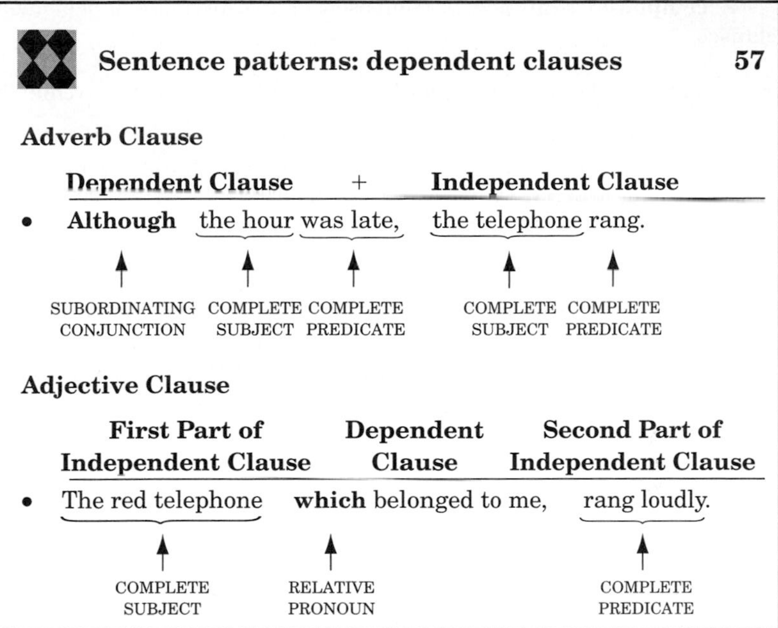

SUBJECT, an OBJECT, or a COMPLEMENT; an adjective clause *modifies* a subject, an object, or a complement.

- Politicians understand **whom they must please.** [The noun clause *whom they must please* is an object.]
- Politicians **who make promises** sometimes fail to keep them. [The adjective clause *who make promises* modifies the noun *politicians*.]

ALERT: Use a singular verb to agree with a noun clause functioning as a subject: *What most politicians try to do* ***is*** [not *are*] *serve the public. What most politicians need* ***is*** [not *are*] *new careers.*

39o What are sentence types?

A sentence can be simple, compound, complex, or compound-complex.

A **simple sentence** is composed of a single INDEPENDENT CLAUSE with no DEPENDENT CLAUSES.

- Charlie Chaplin was born in London on April 16, 1889.
- As a mime, he was famous for his character the Little Tramp.

A **compound sentence** is composed of two or more independent clauses.

- Chaplin's father died early, **and** his mother spent time in psychiatric hospitals.
- Many people enjoy Chaplin's films**;** they laugh at his characters.

A **complex sentence** consists of one independent clause and one or more dependent clauses.

- When Chaplin was performing with a troupe that was touring the United States, he was hired by Mack Sennett, who owned the Keystone Comedies. [dependent clause starting *When;* dependent clause starting *that;* independent clause starting *he;* dependent clause starting *who*]

A **compound-complex sentence** joins a compound sentence with a complex sentence.

- Once studios could no longer afford him, Chaplin co-founded United Artists, and then he was able to produce and distribute his own films. [dependent clause starting *Once;* independent clause starting *Chaplin;* independent clause starting *then he was able*]

40 VERBS

40a How do verbs function?

A **verb** expresses an action (*Many people **overeat***), an occurrence (*Thanksgiving **falls** on a Monday*), or a state of being (*Thanksgiving **is** a national holiday*). Verbs also convey other information. Verbs vary in type (Box 59).

40b What are the forms of main verbs?

- The simple form represents an action, occurrence, or state of being that takes place in the present (*I laugh*). With an AUXILIARY VERB, the simple form makes the future tense (*I will laugh*).
- The past-tense form represents an action, occurrence, or state completed in the past (*I laughed*). Regular verbs add *-ed* or *-d* to the simple form. Irregular verbs vary as shown in Box 60 on pages 349–351.

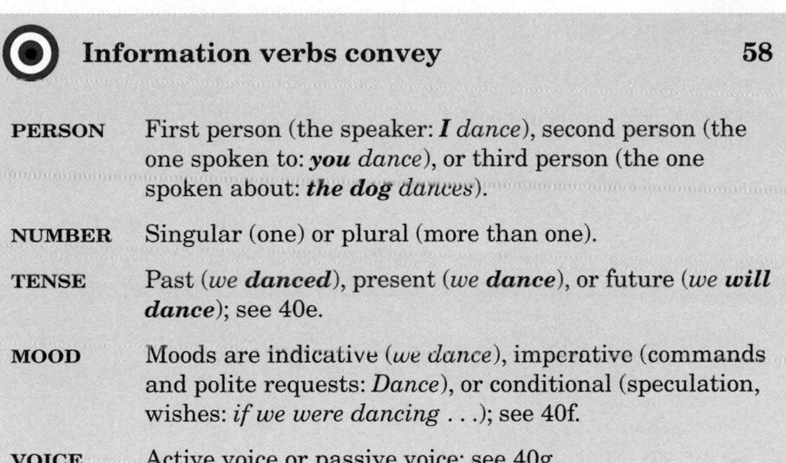

Information verbs convey 58

PERSON	First person (the speaker: ***I*** *dance*), second person (the one spoken to: ***you*** *dance*), or third person (the one spoken about: ***the dog*** *dances*).
NUMBER	Singular (one) or plural (more than one).
TENSE	Past (*we* ***danced***), present (*we* ***dance***), or future (*we* ***will dance***); see 40e.
MOOD	Moods are indicative (*we dance*), imperative (commands and polite requests: *Dance*), or conditional (speculation, wishes: *if we were dancing . . .*); see 40f.
VOICE	Active voice or passive voice; see 40g.

Types of verbs 59

MAIN VERB	The word in a PREDICATE that says something about the SUBJECT: *She* ***danced*** for the group.
AUXILIARY VERB	A verb that combines with a main verb to convey information about TENSE, MOOD, or VOICE (40c). The verbs *be, do,* and *have* can be auxiliary verbs or main verbs. The verbs *can, could, may, might, should, would, must,* and others are MODAL AUXILIARY VERBS. They add shades of meaning such as ability or possibility to verbs: *She* ***might dance*** *again.*
LINKING VERB	The verb that links a subject to a **complement,** a word or words that rename or describe the subject: *She* ***was*** *happy dancing. Be* is the most common linking verb; sometimes sense verbs (*smell, taste*) or verbs of perception (*seem, feel*) function as linking verbs. (For a sentence pattern with linking verbs, see Box 55, page 341.)

→

Types of verbs ***(continued)***

TRANSITIVE VERB	The verb followed by a DIRECT OBJECT that completes the verb's message: *They* ***sent*** *her a fan letter.* (For sentence patterns with objects, see Box 54, page 340.)
INTRANSITIVE VERB	A verb that does not require a direct object: *Yesterday she* ***danced.***

- The past participle form uses the same form as the past tense for regular verbs. Irregular verbs vary; see Box 60. To function as a verb, a past participle must combine with one or more auxiliary verbs: *I have laughed.* Used alone, past participles function as ADJECTIVES: *crumbled cookies.*
- The present participle is formed by adding *-ing* to the simple form (*laughing*). To function as a verb, a present participle must combine with one or more auxiliary verbs (*I was laughing*). Used alone, present participles function as NOUNS (*laughing is healthy*) or as adjectives (*my laughing friends*).
- The infinitive uses the simple form, usually but not always following *to* (*I started to laugh*). The infinitive functions as a noun or an adjective, not as a verb.

Using the *-s* form

The *-s* form of a verb functions only in the third-person singular of the present tense. The *-s* ending attaches to the verb's simple form (*laugh, laughs*).

ALERT: Only the verbs *be* and *have* have irregular forms for third-person singular of the present tense: *is* and *has.* They are the standard third-person singular forms to use in edited Canadian English.

NO Jasper **be** studying hard, so he **have** a chance to win a scholarship.

YES Jasper **is** studying hard, so he **has** a chance to win a scholarship. !

Using regular verbs

Most verbs in English are regular. **Regular verbs** form the past tense and past participle by adding *-ed* or *-d* to the simple form: *enter, entered, entered; smile, smiled, smiled.*

ALERT: Speakers sometimes skip over or swallow the *-ed* sound in the past tense. If you do not pronounce this sound, you may forget to add it when you write.

- The birthday cake was **supposed** [*not* suppose] to be ready.

Using irregular verbs

More than two hundred verbs in English are irregular. You can look in a dictionary for the principal parts of any verb, but memorizing the most common ones saves time.

Common irregular verbs 60

SIMPLE FORM	PAST TENSE	PAST PARTICIPLE
awake	awoke *or* awaked	awoken *or* awaked
be	was, were	been
become	became	become
begin	began	begun
blow	blew	blown
break	broke	broken
bring	brought	brought
build	built	built
buy	bought	bought
catch	caught	caught
choose	chose	chosen
come	came	come
cost	cost	cost
deal	dealt	dealt
dive	dived *or* dove	dived
do	did	done
drink	drank	drunk
drive	drove	driven
eat	ate	eaten
fall	fell	fallen
fight	fought	fought
find	found	found
fly	flew	flown

→

Common irregular verbs ***(continued)***

SIMPLE FORM	PAST TENSE	PAST PARTICIPLE
freeze	froze	frozen
get	got	got *or* gotten
give	gave	given
go	went	gone
grow	grew	grown
have	had	had
hear	heard	heard
hide	hid	hidden
hurt	hurt	hurt
keep	kept	kept
know	knew	known
lay	laid	laid
lead	led	led
lend	lent	lent
lie	lay	lain
lose	lost	lost
make	made	made
read	read	read
ring	rang	rung
rise	rose	risen
run	ran	run
say	said	said
see	saw	seen
send	sent	sent
shake	shook	shaken
shoot	shot	shot
sing	sang	sung
sink	sank	sunk
sit	sat	sat
sleep	slept	slept
speak	spoke	spoken
stand	stood	stood
steal	stole	stolen

→

Common irregular verbs ***(continued)***

SIMPLE FORM	PAST TENSE	PAST PARTICIPLE
strike	struck	struck
swear	swore	sworn
swim	swam	swum
take	took	taken
teach	taught	taught
throw	threw	thrown
wear	wore	worn
write	wrote	written

40c What are auxiliary verbs?

Auxiliary verbs, also called *helping verbs,* combine with MAIN VERBS to make verb phrases.

- Clothing prices **have** [auxiliary verb] **soared** [main verb] recently. [*have soared* = verb phrase]
- Leather shoes **can** [auxiliary verb] **be** [main verb] expensive. [*can be* = verb phrase]

Three frequently used verbs are *be, do, have.* They vary in form more than most irregular verbs.

FORMS OF *BE, DO,* AND *HAVE*

	be	**do**	**have**
SIMPLE FORM	be	do	have
PAST TENSE	was, were	did	had
PAST PARTICIPLE	been	done	had
***-S* FORM**	is	does	has
PRESENT PARTICIPLE	being	doing	having

ALERTS: (1) Academic writing requires standard uses of the forms of *be.*

- The gym **is** [*not* be] a busy place.
- The gym **is** [*not* be] filling with eager athletes.

(2) If you use an auxiliary verb with a main verb, the auxiliary may change to an *-s* form to agree with a third-PERSON singular subject, but the main verb does not change: ***Does*** *the gym* **close** [not *closes*] *at midnight?*!

The verbs *can, could, may, might, must, shall, should, will, would,* and others are **modal auxiliary verbs** (Chapter 49). Modals communicate meanings of ability, permission, obligation, advisability, necessity, or possibility.

40d Should I use *lie* or *lay*?

Use the irregular verbs *lie* ("to recline") and *lay* ("to place something down") with care. *Lie* is intransitive, so it cannot be followed by a DIRECT OBJECT. *Lay* is transitive, so it must be followed by a direct object. Confusion arises because *lay* is both the SIMPLE FORM of *lay* and the PAST-TENSE FORM of *lie.*

FORMS OF *LIE* AND *LAY*

	lie	**lay**
SIMPLE FORM	lie	lay
PAST TENSE	lay	laid
PAST PARTICIPLE	lain	laid
***-S* FORM**	lies	lays
PRESENT PARTICIPLE	lying	laying

- The hikers are ~~laying~~ lying down to rest.
- The hikers ~~laid~~ lay down to rest.
- The hikers took off their gear and ~~lay~~ laid it on the rocks.

40e What are verb tenses?

Verb tenses express time. MAIN VERBS change form and combine with AUXILIARY VERBS to do this. PROGRESSIVE FORMS show ongoing actions or conditions.

SUMMARY OF TENSES

SIMPLE TENSES

		Progressive Forms
PRESENT	I talk.	I am talking.
PAST	I talked.	I was talking.
FUTURE	I will talk.	I will be talking.

PERFECT TENSES

		Progressive Forms
PRESENT PERFECT	I have talked.	I have been talking.
PAST PERFECT	I had talked.	I had been talking.
FUTURE PERFECT	I will have talked.	I will have been talking.

Using the simple present tense

The simple present tense describes what is happening now, what is true at the moment, and what is generally or consistently true. It is also used to express that an event will take place at a fixed time in the future.

- The tourists **are** on vacation. [happening now]
- They **enjoy** the sunshine. [true at the moment]
- Ocean voyages **make** them seasick. [consistently true]
- A cruise **is** an expensive vacation. [generally true]
- Their ship **departs** at midnight. [fixed-time future event]

ALERT: Use the present tense to discuss action in a work of literature.

- In *Romeo and Juliet,* Juliet's father wants her to marry Paris.
- Shakespeare's play depicts the tragedy of ill-fated love.!

Using accurate tense sequences

Accurate sequences of verb tenses in each sentence communicate time relationships correctly. Such sequences become an issue only when your sentence contains both an INDEPENDENT CLAUSE and a DEPENDENT CLAUSE. The sequence of verb tenses concerning actions, occurrences, or conditions in each sentence communicates when something is happening, happened, or will happen.

Sequence of tenses with independent and dependent clauses 61

- If your independent clause contains a simple-present-tense verb, then in your dependent-clause verb you can
  - Use the PRESENT TENSE to show same-time action:

    I **avoid** shellfish because I **am** allergic to it.

  - Use the PAST TENSE to show earlier action:

    I **am** sure that I **deposited** the cheque.

  - Use the PRESENT PERFECT TENSE to show (1) a period of time extending from some point in the past to the present or (2) an indefinite past time:

    I **believe** that I **have seen** that movie before.

    They **claim** that they **have visited** the planet Venus.

  - Use the FUTURE TENSE for action to come:

    The book **is** open because I **will be reading** it later.

- If your independent clause contains a past-tense verb, then in your dependent-clause verb you can
  - Use the past tense to show another completed past action:

    I **closed** the door because you **told** me to.

  - Use the PAST PERFECT TENSE to show earlier action:

    The sprinter **knew** that she **had broken** the record.

  - Use the present tense to state a general truth:

    Christopher Columbus **determined** that the world **is** round.

- If your independent clause contains a present-perfect or past-perfect-tense verb, then in your dependent-clause verb you can
  - Use the past tense:

    The agar plate **has become** mouldy since I **poured** it.

    Sugar prices **had** already **declined** when artificial sweeteners first **appeared.**

→

Sequence of tenses with independent and dependent clauses ***(continued)***

- If your independent clause contains a future-tense verb, then in your dependent-clause verb you can
  - Use the present tense to show action happenig at the same time:

    You **will be** rich if you **win** the prize.
  - Use the past tense to show earlier action:

    You **will** surely **win** the prize if you **remembered** to mail the entry form.
  - Use the present perfect tense to show future action earlier than the action of the independent-clause verb:

    The river **will flood** again next year unless we **have built** a better dam by then.
- If your independent clause contains a future-perfect-tense verb, then in your dependent-clause verb you can
  - Use either the present tense or the present perfect tense:

    Dr. Chang **will have delivered** 5000 babies by the time she **retires.**

    Dr. Chang **will have delivered** 5000 babies by the time she **has retired.**

40f What are indicative, imperative, and subjunctive moods?

The **indicative mood** expresses statements about real things (*The door **opened***) or highly likely ones (*She **seemed** lost*) or questions about fact (***Do** you **need** help?*).

The **imperative mood** expresses commands and direct requests: *Please **shut** the door. **Watch out!*** When the SUBJECT is omitted in an imperative sentence, assume it to be *you*.

The **subjunctive mood** expresses conditions about wishes, recommendations, demands, indirect requests, and speculations: *If I **were** you, I would ask for directions.*

Using the subjunctive with *if, as if, as though,* and *unless* clauses

Not all CLAUSES introduced by *if, as if, as though,* and *unless* require the subjunctive. Use the subjunctive only when such clauses describe a speculation or condition contrary to fact.

INDICATIVE If she **leaves** late, I will drive her to the track meet. [fact, not speculation]

SUBJUNCTIVE If she **were** [*not* was] **going to leave** late, I would drive her to the track meet. [speculation]

SUBJUNCTIVE If it **were** [*not* was] raining, fewer people would attend. [condition contrary to fact—it is not raining]

ALERT: When you use *would, could,* or *should* to express speculation or conditions contrary to fact, make sure they appear in the independent clause only.

- If he **had** [*not* would have] trained, he **would have won** the race. **!**

Using the subjunctive in *that* clauses

When *that* clauses express wishes, indirect requests, recommendations, and demands, use the subjunctive.

- I wish that this race **were** [*not* was] over.
- It is important that the doctor **be** [*not* is] present because someone is insisting that she **examine** [*not* examines] the runners.

40g What is *voice* in verbs?

Voice indicates how the subject relates to the action of the verb. In the **active voice,** the subject performs the action. In the **passive voice,** the subject is acted upon.

ACTIVE **Svetlana considers** clams a delicacy. [The subject, *Svetlana,* performs the action: she *considers.*]

PASSIVE **Clams are considered** a delicacy by Svetlana. [The subject, *clams,* is acted upon—they *are considered*—by Svetlana.]

The active voice—which is usually more direct, concise, and dramatic than the passive—emphasizes the doer of an action. The passive voice may be appropriate when who or what did something is unknown or unimportant.

- The lock **was broken** sometime last night.

Also, the passive voice delivers appropriate emphasis when the action is more important than who did it.

- Oxygen **was discovered** in 1774 by Joseph Priestley.

Do not use the passive voice to make writing seem "lofty" or to hide who has done an action.

NO An experiment was conducted by me to demonstrate the existence of carbon.

YES I conducted an experiment to demonstrate the existence of carbon.

41 SUBJECT–VERB AGREEMENT

41a What is subject–verb agreement?

Subject–verb agreement means that SUBJECTS and VERBS must match in NUMBER (singular or plural). Singular subjects require singular verbs. Plural subjects require plural verbs. Subjects and verbs must also match in PERSON: *I like you. He likes you.*

Problems can arise with the letter *s* at the end of words. Box 62 on page 358 gives a memory device to show how the *-s* works in most cases of agreement. The *-s* or *-es* can take only one path at a time, going either to a noun subject at the top or to a verb at the bottom.

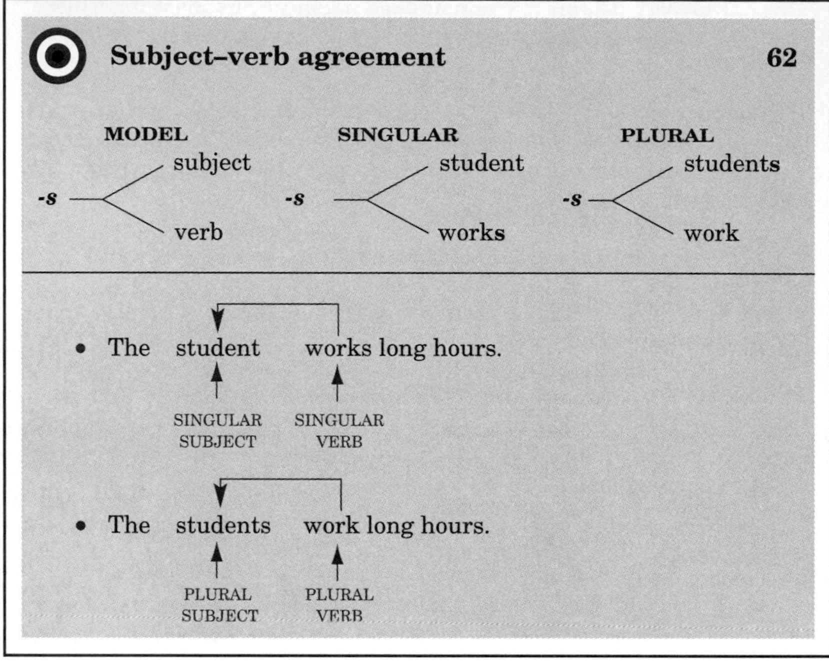

41b Can I ignore words between a subject and verb?

You can ignore words between a SUBJECT and VERB. Such words do not influence subject–verb agreement.

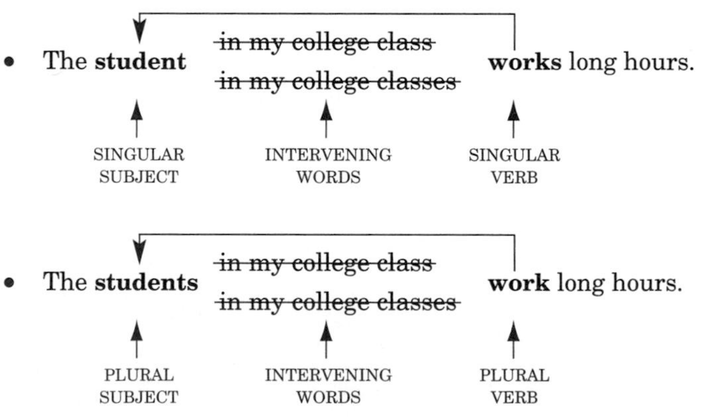

NO The **winners** in the provincial competition **goes** to the national finals. [*Winners* is the subject, so the verb must agree with it; *in the provincial competition* is an intervening PREPOSITIONAL PHRASE that does not alter basic subject–verb agreement.]

YES The **winners** in the provincial competition **go** to the national finals.

To locate the subject of a sentence, eliminate PHRASES that start with PREPOSITIONS or with the words *including, together with, along with, accompanied by, in addition to,* and *as well as.*

NO The **moon,** as well as Venus, **are** visible in the night sky. [*Moon* is the subject, so the verb must agree with it; ignore *as well as Venus.*]

YES The **moon,** as well as Venus, **is** visible in the night sky.

Using *one of the*

A construction that starts with the words *one of the* takes a singular verb to agree with the word *one.* (For *one of the . . . who,* see 41g.)

41c How do verbs work when subjects are connected by *and*?

Two or more SUBJECTS joined by *and* become plural as a group. The group requires a plural verb.

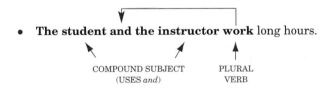

- **The student and the instructor work** long hours.

- **The Cascade Diner and the Wayside Diner have** [*not* has] fried catfish today.

An exception occurs when subjects are joined by *and* and combine to form a single thing or person. In such cases, use a singular verb.

- **Spaghetti and meatballs has** [*not* have] a place on many menus.

Using *each* and *every*

Each and *every* are singular PRONOUNS and require singular verbs. Even when *each* or *every* comes before subjects joined by *and,* use a singular verb.

- **Each** human hand and foot **leaves** a distinctive print.

41d How do verbs work when subjects are connected by *or*?

When SUBJECTS are joined with *or, nor, either . . . or, neither . . . nor,* or *not only . . . but (also),* the verb agrees with the subject nearest it. Ignore everything before the final subject.

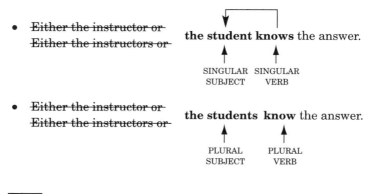

- ~~Either the instructor or~~
~~Either the instructors or~~

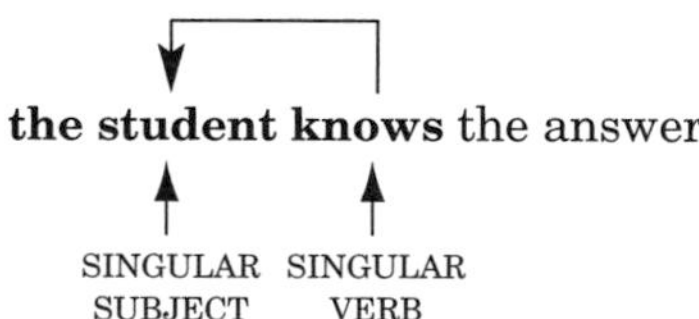
the student knows the answer.
SINGULAR SUBJECT
SINGULAR VERB

- ~~Either the instructor or~~
~~Either the instructors or~~ **the students know** the answer.

PLURAL SUBJECT PLURAL VERB

41e How should verbs agree with indefinite pronouns?

Indefinite pronouns refer to nonspecific people or things. They are usually singular, so they usually take singular verbs.

INDEFINITE PRONOUNS (MOST COMMONLY USED)

another	each	everything	nothing
anybody	either	neither	somebody
anyone	every	nobody	someone
anything	everyone	no one	something

- Whenever **anyone says** anything, **nothing is** done.
- **Everything** about these roads **is** [*not* are] dangerous.
- **Each** of the roads **has** [*not* have] to be resurfaced.

A few indefinite pronouns—*none, some, more, most, any,* and *all*—can be either singular or plural, depending on the meaning of the sentence.

- **Some** of our streams **are** polluted; **some** pollution **is** reversible, but **all** pollution **is** a threat to the balance of nature. [The first *some* refers to the plural *streams* and requires the plural verb; the second *some* and *all* refer to the singular word *pollution* and require the singular verbs.]

41f How do verbs work with *who, which,* and *that*?

When *who, which,* or *that* starts a CLAUSE, the verb agrees with the noun or pronoun to which *who, which,* or *that* refers (its ANTECEDENT).

- The scientist will share the income from her new patent with the graduate students **who work** with her. [*Who* refers to the plural *students,* and *work* is a plural verb.]
- George Jones is the student **who works** in the science lab. [*Who* refers to the singular *student,* and *works* is a singular verb.]

41g Using *one of the . . . who*

In *one of the . . . who* (*which, that*) phrases, the verb agrees with what precedes *who*—which is always a plural word. Therefore, the verb is always plural.

- Tracy is one of the **students who talk** [*not* talks] in class. [*Who* refers to plural *students* and requires the plural verb *talk.*]

If the phrase is *the only one of the . . . who,* the ANTECEDENT of *who* is the singular word *one*. Therefore, the verb is always singular.

- Tracy is **the** only **one** of the students **who talks** [*not* talk] in class. [*Who* refers to the singular *one* and requires the singular verb *talks.*]

41h How do verbs work in other complicated cases of subject–verb agreement?

Finding the subject in inverted word order

Inverted word order changes the usual order in a sentence: *In walked the mayor* instead of *The mayor walked in.* Most questions use inverted word order: *Is the mayor here?* In inverted word order, you want the verb to agree with the SUBJECT, which *follows* its verb.

- Across the street **stand** [*not* stands] the protesters.

Finding the subject with an expletive construction

Expletive constructions, such as *there is, it is,* and *there were,* put a sentence's verb before the subject. Therefore, you want the verb to agree with the subject, which *follows* it.

- There **are** nine **planets** in our solar system. [For agreement purposes, think of this sentence as *Nine planets are in our solar system.*]

Agreeing with the subject, not the subject complement

LINKING VERBS connect the subject to a SUBJECT COMPLEMENT—a word that renames or describes the subject. You want the verb to agree with the subject, not the subject complement.

NO The worst **part** of owning a car **are** the bills. [The subject is the singular noun *part,* which requires the singular verb *is; bills* is a subject complement and should be ignored.]

YES The worst **part** of owning a car **is** the bills.

YES **Bills are** the worst **part** of owning a car. [The plural noun *bills* is now the subject and requires the plural verb *are.*]

Making verbs agree with collective nouns

A **collective noun** names a group of people or things, such as *family, group, audience, class, number.* When you want to convey that the group is acting as one unit, use a singular verb. When you want to convey that the members of the group are acting individually, use a plural verb.

- The graduating **class has** 793 people in it. [*Class* is meant as one unit, so the singular verb *has* agrees with it.]
- The graduating **class were fitted** for their graduation robes today. [The people in the class are meant as individual members within the group, so the plural verb *were fitted* agrees with it.]

Making verbs agree with subjects that specify amounts

Use a singular verb with a subject that specifies an amount of money, time, weight, or distance considered as one unit.

- **Ninety cents is** the current bus fare.
- **Five kilometres passes** quickly for a serious jogger.

In contrast, when a subject refers to units of measurement considered individually rather than as one amount, use a plural verb.

- **Fifteen centimetres are** marked off on that ruler.
- **Fifty percent** of these peaches **are** bruised.

Making verbs agree with singular subjects in plural form

Some words that end in *-s* or *-ics* are singular in meaning. They need singular verbs, despite their plural appearance. These words include *news, ethics, athletics,* and *measles,* as well as *economics, mathematics, physics,* and *statistics* when they refer to a course of study.

- **Statistics is** a requirement for science majors. [*Statistics* refers to a course of study, so the singular verb agrees with it.]
- **Statistics show** that a recession is coming. [*Statistics* refers to items of data, so the plural verb agrees with it.]

Series and *means* have the same form in singular and plural. Context determines whether the verb is singular or plural.

- Six new television **series are** beginning this week.
- A **series** of disasters **is** delaying our production.

Using singular verbs with titles and terms

The title of a work or a word referred to as a term is a single thing. Therefore, use a singular verb even when the title or term contains plural words.

- ***Cats*** **was** a popular musical.
- **"Protective reaction strikes" is** a euphemism for bombing.

Using names containing the word *States*

The word *states* is always plural, but names such as *the United States* or the *Organization of American States* refer to singular things—a country and an organization—so they require singular verbs: ***The United States has*** [not *have*] *a large television industry.*

42 PRONOUNS: AGREEMENT, REFERENCE, CASE

PRONOUN–ANTECEDENT AGREEMENT

42a What is pronoun–antecedent agreement?

Pronoun–antecedent agreement means that a PRONOUN must match the grammatical form of the word or words it refers to (its **antecedent**). For example, if the antecedent is third-person singular, the pronoun must be third-person singular too.

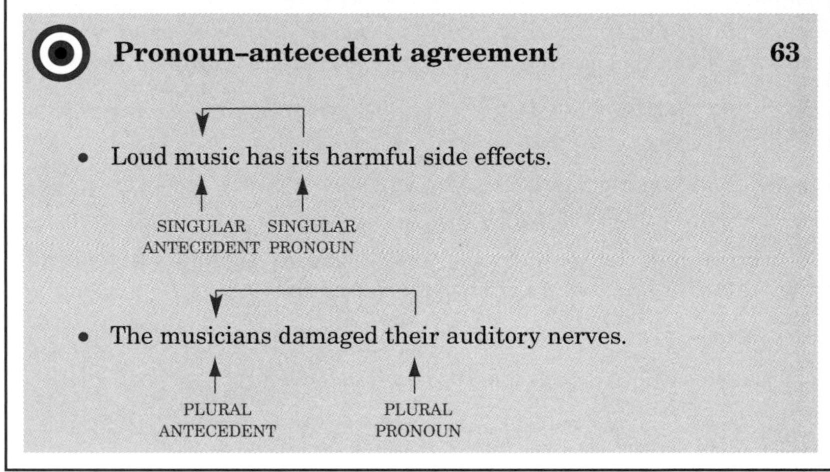

Pronoun–antecedent agreement
63
Loud music has its harmful side effects.
SINGULAR ANTECEDENT
SINGULAR PRONOUN
The musicians damaged their auditory nerves.
PLURAL ANTECEDENT
PLURAL PRONOUN

42b How do pronouns work when *and* connects antecedents?

Two or more antecedents joined by *and* require a plural pronoun, even if each antecedent is singular.

- **The United States and Canada** maintain **their** border as the world's longest open frontier.
- **The Cascade Diner and the Wayside Diner** closed for New Year's Eve to give **their** employees the night off.

An exception occurs when *each* or *every* precedes singular nouns joined by *and*. In such cases, a singular pronoun is correct.

- **Every car and truck** that comes through the border station has **its** [*not* their] contents inspected.

Another exception occurs when singular nouns joined by *and* refer to a single person or thing. In such cases, a singular pronoun is correct.

- Our **guide and translator** told us to watch out for traffic as **she** helped us off the tour bus. [The guide is the same person as the translator.]

42c How do pronouns work when *or* connects antecedents?

Antecedents joined by *or, nor,* or CORRELATIVE CONJUNCTIONS such as *either . . . or* and *not only . . . but (also)* can mix the masculine and feminine as well as singular and plural. For the purposes of agreement, however, ignore everything before the final antecedent.

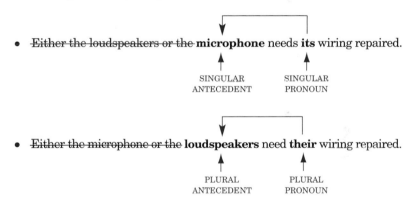

- ~~Either the loudspeakers or the~~ **microphone** needs **its** wiring repaired.

- ~~Either the microphone or the~~ **loudspeakers** need **their** wiring repaired.

42d How do pronouns work when antecedents are indefinite pronouns?

Indefinite pronouns are pronouns that do not refer to any particular person, thing, or idea. They take on definite meanings only in context with other words.

Indefinite pronouns are usually singular: ***Anyone*** *who knows the answer should raise* ***his or her*** *hand.* (For advice about using gender-neutral indefinite pronouns, see Chapter 20.)

ALERT: *He or she* always functions as a singular pronoun. **!**

Some indefinite pronouns can be either singular or plural (*none, some, more, most, any, all*) depending on the meaning of the sentence.

- **None** fear that **they** will fail. [All the people in the group expect to succeed; using a plural pronoun reflects this meaning.]
- **None** fears that **he or she** will fail. [No individual expects to fail; using a singular pronoun reflects this meaning.]

The indefinite pronouns *each* and *every* are singular, no matter what words follow.

- Each of the students handed in ~~their~~ his or her final term paper.
- Every student in my classes is studying ~~their~~ his or her hardest.

Be especially careful about agreement when you use the words *this* (singular) and *these* (plural): ***This*** *kind of hard work has* ***its*** *advantages.* ***These*** *kinds of difficult jobs have* ***their*** *advantages.*

42e How do pronouns work when antecedents are collective nouns?

A **collective noun** names a group of people or things, such as *family, group, audience, class, number.* When the group acts as one unit, use a singular PRONOUN to refer to it. When the members of the group act individually, use a plural pronoun.

- The **audience** cheered as **it** rose to applaud. [The singular pronoun *it* conveys that the audience is acting as one unit.]
- The **audience** put on **their** coats and walked to the exits. [The plural pronoun *their* conveys that the audience is acting as many individuals.]

PRONOUN REFERENCE

The word (or group of words) a pronoun replaces is called its **antecedent.** In order for your writing to communicate its message clearly, each pronoun must relate precisely to an antecedent.

42f How can I avoid unclear pronoun reference?

In sentences that contain more than one logical antecedent, meaning can become unclear.

UNCLEAR PRONOUN REFERENCE In 1911, Roald Amundsen reached the South Pole just thirty-five days before Robert F. Scott arrived. He [Who, Amundsen or Scott?] had told people that he was going to sail north to the Arctic, but then he turned south for the Antarctic. On the journey home, he [Who, Amundsen or Scott?] and his party froze to death just a few kilometres from safety.

REVISED In 1911, Roald Amundsen discovered the South Pole just thirty-five days before Robert F. Scott arrived. Amundsen had told people that he was going to sail north to the Arctic, but then he turned south for the Antarctic. On the journey home, Scott and his party froze to death just a few kilometres from safety.

Further, if too much material comes between a pronoun and its antecedent, readers can lose track of the meaning.

- Alfred Wegener, a German meteorologist and professor of geophysics at the University of Graz, was the first to suggest that all the continents on earth were originally part of one large land mass. According to this theory, the supercontinent broke up long ago and the fragments drifted apart. ~~He~~ *Wegener* named this supercontinent Pangaea.

[*He* can refer to only Wegener, but material about Wegener's theory intervenes, so using *Wegener* again instead of *he* jogs the reader's memory and makes reading easier.]

42g Can I use a pronoun to refer to an adjective?

A pronoun can refer to a NOUN or other pronoun. Therefore, because an ADJECTIVE never serves as a noun, a pronoun can't refer to an adjective.

NO Dan likes to study **geological** records. **That** is his major. [*Geological* is an adjective, so it is imprecise to use the pronoun *That* to refer to it.]

YES Dan likes to study **geological** records. **Geology** is his major.

42h How do pronouns work with *it, that, this,* and *which*?

When you use *it, that, this,* and *which,* be sure that your readers can easily understand what each word refers to.

NO Comets usually fly by the earth at 160 000 km/h, whereas asteroids sometimes collide with the earth. **This** interests scientists. [*This* could refer to the speed of comets, comets flying by the earth, or asteroids colliding with the earth.]

YES Comets usually fly by the earth at 160 000 km/h, whereas asteroids sometimes collide with the earth. **This difference** interests scientists.

In speech, statements sometimes begin with "It said on the news . . ." or "On Parliament Hill they say. . . ." Avoid such inexact and wordy expressions in academic writing.

NO In Alberta **they say** that Eastern politicians have never understood the West.

YES **Many Albertans say** that Eastern politicians have never understood the West.

42i When should I use *you* for direct address?

Reserve *you* for **direct address,** writing that addresses the reader directly. *You* is not a suitable substitute for specific words that refer to people, situations, or occurrences.

NO Prison uprisings often happen **when you allow** overcrowding. [The reader, *you,* did not allow the overcrowding.]

YES Prison uprisings often happen **when prisons are** overcrowded.

42j When should I use *who, which,* and *that*?

Who refers to people and to animals mentioned by name.

- **John Polanyi, who** was awarded the Nobel Prize in chemistry, speaks passionately in favour of nuclear disarmament.
- **Lassie, who** was known for her intelligence and courage, was actually played by a series of male collies.

Which and *that* refer to animals, things, and sometimes anonymous or collective groups of people. Box 64 shows how to choose between *that* and *which*. For information about the role of commas with *that* and *which*, see 50f.

Choosing between *that* and *which* **64**

Choice: Some instructors and style guides use either *that* or *which* to introduce a RESTRICTIVE CLAUSE (a DEPENDENT CLAUSE that is essential to the meaning of the sentence or part of the sentence). Others may expect you to use only *that* so that your writing distinguishes clearly between restrictive and NONRESTRICTIVE CLAUSES. Whichever style you use, be consistent in each piece of writing.

- The zoos ***that*** [*or* ***which***] **most children like** display newborn and baby animals. [The point in this sentence concerns children's preferences. Therefore, the words *most children like* are essential for delivering the meaning and make up a restrictive clause.]

No choice: You are required to use *which* to introduce a nonrestrictive clause (a dependent clause that isn't essential to the meaning of the sentence or part of the sentence).

- Zoos, **which most children like,** attract more visitors if they display newborn and baby animals. [The point in this sentence concerns attracting more visitors to zoos. Therefore, the words *most children like* are not essential to the meaning of the sentence and make up a nonrestrictive clause.]

PRONOUN CASE

42k What is pronoun case?

Case applies in different ways to PRONOUNS and to NOUNS. For pronouns, case refers to three pronoun forms: **subjective** (pronoun SUBJECTS), **objective** (pronoun OBJECTS), and **possessive** (pronouns that are POSSESSIVE). For nouns, case refers to only one noun form: possessive. (For help in using apostrophes in the possessive case, see Chapter 53.)

42l What are personal pronouns?

Personal pronouns refer to persons or things. Box 65 shows the case forms of personal pronouns (subjective, objective, and possessive), in both the SINGULAR and the PLURAL.

Many of the most difficult questions about pronoun case concern *who/whom* and *whoever/whomever*. For a full discussion, see 42q.

Case forms of personal pronouns **65**

	SUBJECTIVE	OBJECTIVE	POSSESSIVE
SINGULAR	I, you, he, she, it	me, you, him, her, it	mine, yours, his, hers, its
PLURAL	we, you, they	us, you, them	ours, yours, theirs

42m How can I select the correct case?

Whenever you're unsure whether to use the subjective or the objective case, you can use the "Troyka test." In this three-step test, you simply drop some of the words from your sentence so that you can tell which case sounds correct. Box 66 shows how the test works.

42n Which case is correct when *and* connects pronouns?

When *and* connects more than one noun and/or pronoun, it forms a compound subject or a compound object. Compounding doesn't affect pronoun case: Use the same case for all pronouns.

COMPOUND PRONOUN SUBJECT	**He and I** saw the solar eclipse.
COMPOUND PRONOUN OBJECT	The eclipse astonished **him and me.**

Whenever you're unsure of whether to use pronouns in the subjective or objective case, use the "Troyka test" (Box 66) to get the answer.

Testing for case **66**

This test for case asks you to choose what "sounds right." In other words, it invites you to rely on your intuition (another way of saying "your own good judgment") about English grammar. After you've used this test to choose the correct case for the pronouns in your sentence, you can compare your result with Box 65 in section 42l to see the grammatical rule that you were following.

STEP 1 Write the sentence twice, once using the subjective case and once using the objective case. Then cross out enough words to isolate the element you are questioning.

- ~~Janet and~~ **me** / ~~Janet and~~ **I** > learned about the moon.

STEP 2 Omit the crossed-out words and read both sentences aloud to see which one sounds right.

- Me learned about the moon. [No, this doesn't sound right. Look at 42l to remind yourself why.]
- I learned about the moon. [This sounds right.]

STEP 3 Select the correct version and restore the words you crossed out.

- Janet and I learned about the moon.

You can find the grammatical points that lie behind the "Troyka test"—and confirm your grammatical intuition—by referring to 42l and 42n through 42q.

- **She and I** [*not* Her and me, She and me, *or* Her and I] learned about the moon.
- The instructor taught **her and me** [*not* she and I, her and I, *or* she and me] about the moon.

ALERT: In PREPOSITIONAL PHRASES, pronouns are always in the objective case.

NO Ms. Panich gave an assignment to **Sam and I.** [The prepositional phrase starts with *to,* so the subjective case *I* is wrong.]

YES Ms. Panich gave an assignment to **Sam and me.** [The prepositional phrase starts with *to,* so the subjective case *me* is correct.]

Be especially careful when a pronoun object follows the preposition *between*.

NO Ms. Panich divided the work between **he and I.** [The prepositional phrase starts with *between,* so the subjective case *I* is wrong.]

YES Ms. Panich divided the work between **him and me.** [The prepositional phrase starts with *between,* so the objective case *me* is correct.]!

42o How can I match case in appositives?

The words that make up APPOSITIVES match in their function within a sentence. They also match in their case. You can match case in appositives by putting pronouns and nouns in the same case. Whenever you're unsure whether to use the subjective or objective case, use the "Troyka test" (Box 66) to get the answer.

- We [*not* us] tennis players practise hard. [*We* is the subject of the sentence and is in the subjective case. *Tennis players* renames the pronoun *we*.]
- The winners, **she and I** [*not* her and me], advanced to the finals. [Because the pronouns rename the noun *winners,* which is the subject, the pronouns are in the subjective case.]
- The coach tells **us** [*not* we] tennis players to practise hard. [*Us* is the object of the sentence and is in the objective case. *Tennis players* renames the pronoun *us*.]
- The crowd cheered the winners, **her and me** [*not* she and I]. [Because the pronouns rename the noun *winners,* which is the object, the pronouns are in the objective case.]

42p How does the subjective case work after linking verbs?

A pronoun coming after any LINKING VERB either renames the SUBJECT or shows possession by the subject. Always use a pronoun in the subjective case.

- The contest winner was **I.** [*I* renames *contest winner,* the subject, so the subjective case is correct.]
- The prize was **mine.** [*Mine* shows possession, so the possessive case is correct.]

42q When should I use *who, whoever, whom,* and *whomever*?

The pronouns *who* and *whoever* are in the SUBJECTIVE CASE. The pronouns *whom* and *whomever* are in the OBJECTIVE CASE.

Informal spoken English tends to blur distinctions between *who* and *whom,* so with these words some people can't rely entirely on what "sounds right." Whenever you're unsure of whether to use the subjective case *who* and *whoever* or the objective case *whom* and *whomever,* use a variation of the "Troyka test" (Box 66). For *who* and *whoever,* substitute *he, she,* or *they*. For *whom* and *whomever,* substitute *him, her,* or *them*. Doing so, you get the following results:

- Enumerators located **whoever/whomever** was eligible to vote.
- **He/~~him~~** was eligible to vote. [By temporarily substituting the subjective case *he* and the objective case *him* for *whoever/whomever,* you see that *he* is correct. Therefore, the subjective case *whoever* is correct.]
- Enumerators located **whoever** was eligible to vote.

Sometimes you need to invert the word order to make the test work:

- Babies **who/whom** mothers cuddle grow faster and are happier.
- Mothers cuddle **~~they~~/them**. [By inverting the word order of the phrase *whom mothers cuddle* (*mothers cuddle whom*) and substituting *they/them* for *who/whom,* you can see that *them* is correct. Therefore, the objective case *whom* is correct.]
- Babies **whom** mothers cuddle grow faster and are happier.

At the beginning of questions, use *who* if the question is about the subject and *whom* if the question is about the object. To determine case, recast the question into a statement, temporarily substituting *he* or *him* (or *she* or *her*).

- **Who** watched the space shuttle liftoff? [*He* (not *Him*) *watched the space shuttle liftoff* uses the subjective case, so *Who* is correct.]
- Ted admires **whom?** [*Ted admires him* (not *he*) uses the objective case, so *whom* is correct.]
- **Whom** does Ted admire? [*Ted admires him* (not *he*) uses the objective case, so *whom* is correct.]
- To **whom** does Ted speak about becoming an astronaut? [*Ted speaks to them* (not *they*) uses the objective case, so *whom* is correct.]

42r What case should I use after *than* and *as*?

When a pronoun follows *than* or *as,* choose the pronoun case according to the meaning you want to deliver. For example, these two sentences convey very different messages simply because of the choice between the words *me* and *I* after *than.*

1. My sister loved that dog more than me.
2. My sister loved that dog more than I.

Because the pronoun *me* is in the objective case, sentence 1 means "My sister loved that dog more than she loved me." Because the pronoun *I* is in the subjective case, sentence 2 means "My sister loved that dog more than I loved it."

To make sure that your sentences of comparison deliver the message you intend, mentally fill in the implied words.

42s What case should I use with infinitives and gerunds?

Pronouns in the objective case act as both SUBJECTS and OBJECTS of INFINITIVES.

- Our tennis coach expects **him** to beat **me.** [The word *him* is the subject of the infinitive *to beat,* and *me* is the object of the infinitive; both are in the objective case.]

The possessive case communicates important information with *-ing* words (GERUNDS and PRESENT PARTICIPLES; see 39d). For example, these two sentences convey two different messages because of the possessive.

1. The detective noticed the **man** staggering. [object of the verb and present participle]
2. The detective noticed the **man's** staggering. [possessive case and gerund]

Sentence 1 means that the detective noticed the *man;* sentence 2 means that the detective noticed the *staggering.*

The same distinction applies to pronouns:

1. The detective noticed **him** staggering. [objective case and present participle]
2. The detective noticed **his** staggering. [possessive case and gerund]

42t What case should I use for *-self* pronouns?

Reflexive pronouns reflect back on the SUBJECT when the subject is restated as the OBJECT or as the SUBJECT COMPLEMENT: *The detective disguised **himself*** [object of verb *disguised;* reflects back on subject *detective*]. *The distraught victim was not **himself** for several days* [subject complement of LINKING VERB *was;* reflects back on subject *victim*].

Intensive pronouns provide emphasis by making another word more intense in meaning: *The detective felt that his career **itself** was at risk.*

Do not use a reflexive pronoun to replace a personal pronoun as a subject, and do not use a reflexive pronoun as an object unless the object restates the subject.

NO The detective and **myself** had a long talk. He wanted my partner and **myself** to help him.

YES The detective and **I** had a long talk. He wanted my partner and **me** to help him.

43 ADJECTIVES AND ADVERBS

43a What are the differences between adjectives and adverbs?

Both **adjectives** and **adverbs** are MODIFIERS. Modifiers describe other words. The key to distinguishing between adjectives and adverbs is understanding that they modify different grammatical categories of words.

WHAT ADJECTIVES MODIFY

NOUNS	The ***busy*** **lawyer** rested.
PRONOUNS	**She** felt ***tired.***

WHAT ADVERBS MODIFY

VERBS	The lawyer **spoke** ***quickly.***
ADVERBS	The lawyer spoke ***very*** **quickly.**
ADJECTIVES	The lawyer was ***extremely*** **busy.**
INDEPENDENT CLAUSES	***Undoubtedly,*** **the lawyer needed a rest.**

Many adverbs end in *-ly* (*run* ***swiftly***), but some do not (*run* ***often***). Also, some adjectives end in *-ly* (***friendly*** *dog*), so do not depend on an *-ly* ending to identify an adverb.

43b When should I use adverbs—not adjectives—as modifiers?

NO The candidate made promises **careless.** [An adjective, *careless,* cannot modify a verb, *made.*]

YES The candidate made promises **carelessly.**

NO The candidate felt **unusual** energetic today. [An adjective, *unusual,* cannot modify another adjective, *energetic.*]

YES The candidate felt **unusually** energetic today.

NO The candidate spoke **exceptional** forcefully today. [An adjective, *exceptional,* cannot modify an adverb, *forcefully.*]

YES The candidate spoke **exceptionally** forcefully today.

43c What is wrong with double negatives?

A **double negative** is nonstandard form. Use only one negative (for example, *no, not, never, none, nothing,* and *hardly*) in a sentence.

NO The union members did **not** have **no** money in the reserve fund.

YES The union members did **not** have **any** money in the reserve fund.

YES The union members had **no** money in the reserve fund.

43d Do adjectives or adverbs come after linking verbs?

LINKING VERBS use adjectives as COMPLEMENTS. In contrast, ACTION VERBS are modified by adverbs.

- Anne **looks happy.** [*Looks* functions as a linking verb; *happy* is an adjective.]
- Anne **looks happily** at the sunset. [*Looks* functions as an action verb; *happily* is an adverb.]

Using *bad* and *badly*

Do not mix up *bad* (adjective) and *badly* (adverb). They are often misused with linking verbs such as *feel, grow, smell, sound,* and *taste.*

NO The student felt **badly.**

YES The student felt **bad.**

Using *good* and *well*

Good is always an adjective. *Well* is an adjective only when it is referring to health; otherwise, *well* is an adverb.

- You look **well.** [This means "You look in fine health"; *well* functions as an adjective.]
- You write **well.** [This means "You write skilfully"; *well* functions as an adverb.]

43e What are correct comparative and superlative forms?

When comparisons use adjectives and adverbs, the forms of the adjectives and adverbs may be either regular or irregular.

Regular forms

Regular adjectives and adverbs show comparisons in two ways. Either they add an *-er* ending or the words *more* or *less* (**comparative**), or they add an *-est* ending and the words *most* or *least* (**superlative**).

POSITIVE [1]	COMPARATIVE [2]	SUPERLATIVE [3+]
green	greener	greenest
happy	happier	happiest
selfish	less selfish	least selfish
beautiful	more beautiful	most beautiful

[1] That tree is **green.**

[2] That tree is **greener** than this tree.

[3+] That tree is the **greenest** tree on the block.

The number of syllables in the adjective or adverb usually determines whether you use *-er* or *more* and *-est* or *most*. Use *-er* and *-est* endings with most common one-syllable words: *large, larger, largest* (adjective); *far, farther, farthest* (adverb). With adverbs of two or more syllables, use *more* and *most: easily, more easily, most easily.* For two-syllable adjectives, check the dictionary because the forms vary. For adjectives of three or more syllables, use *more* and *most.*

ALERT: Never use *more* or *most* together with the *-er* or *-est* ending: not *more louder* and not *most happiest.*

Irregular forms

A few common adjectives and adverbs have irregular forms in the comparative and superlative.

POSITIVE [1]	COMPARATIVE [2]	SUPERLATIVE [3+]
good [adjective]	better	best
well [adverb]	better	best
well [adjective]		

POSITIVE [1]	COMPARATIVE [2]	SUPERLATIVE [3+]
bad [adjective]	worse	worst
badly [adverb]	worse	worst
many	more	most
much	more	most
some	more	most
little	less	least

[1] The Millers had **little** trouble finding jobs.

[2] The Millers had **less** trouble finding jobs than the Smiths did.

[3+] The Millers had the **least** trouble finding jobs of everyone.

ALERT: Never use *less* and *fewer* interchangeably. Use *less* with uncountable items and *fewer* with numbers or other countable things: *They consumed **fewer calories.** The sugar substitute had **less aftertaste.***!

43f Why should I avoid too many nouns as modifiers?

Sometimes NOUNS function as MODIFIERS of other nouns: *truck driver, train track, security system.* The problem arises when modifying nouns pile up. A reader does not know which nouns are being modified and which nouns are doing the modifying. You can use any of several routes to revise a long string of nouns.

SENTENCE REWRITTEN

NO I asked my adviser to write **two college recommendation** letters for me.

YES I asked my adviser to write **letters of recommendation** to **two colleges** for me.

ONE NOUN CHANGED TO POSSESSIVE CASE AND ANOTHER TO ADJECTIVE FORM

NO Advanced students may use the **university psychology lab facilities** for **cognition research projects.**

YES Advanced students may use the **university's psychology lab facilities** for **cognitive research projects.**

NOUN CHANGED TO PREPOSITIONAL PHRASE

NO Our **student adviser training program** has won awards for excellence.

YES Our training program **for student advisers** has won awards for excellence. [Notice that this change requires the plural *advisers*.]

MESSAGE FROM LYNN TROYKA TO MULTILINGUAL WRITERS

If you ever worry about your English writing, you have much in common with me and with many college and university students. Still, I recognize that because you are a multilingual writer, you face special challenges. In becoming a skilled writer in English, you need to consider almost every word, phrase, sentence, and paragraph in ways native speakers of English do not.

The good news is that errors you make demonstrate the reliable truth that you are moving normally through the unavoidable, necessary stages of second-language development. Unfortunately, there are no shortcuts. As with your progress in speaking, listening, and reading in a new language, development of writing skills takes time. The process is like learning to play a musical instrument. Few people learn to play fluently without making many errors.

What can you do to progress as quickly as possible from one writing stage to another? I recommend that you start by bringing to mind what school writing is like in your first language. Specifically, recall how ideas are presented in your written native language, especially when information is explained or a topic requires a logical argument.

Most college and university writing in Canada is very direct in tone and straightforward in structure. In a typical essay or research paper, the reader expects to find a THESIS STATEMENT* that clearly states the central message of the entire piece of writing. Usually, the thesis statement falls in the first paragraph, or in a longer piece, perhaps in the second paragraph. Then, each paragraph that follows relates in content directly to the essay's thesis statement. Also, each paragraph begins with a TOPIC SENTENCE that contains the main point of the paragraph, and the rest of the paragraph supports the point made in the topic sentence. This support consists of RENNS (8d) that provide specific details. The final paragraph brings the piece of writing to a logical conclusion that grows out of the rest of the essay.

Writing structures typical of your first language most likely differ from those in this country. Always honour your culture's writing traditions and structures, for they reflect the richness of your heritage. At the same time, try to adapt to and practise the academic writing style characteristic of English-speaking Canada. Later, some instructors might encourage you to practise other, more subtle English writing styles that allow greater liberty in organization and expression.

Distinctive variations in school writing styles among people of different cultures and language groups have interested researchers for

* Words printed in small capital letters (such as THESIS STATEMENT) are defined in the Terms Glossary on pages 497–517.

the past twenty years. Such research is ongoing, so scholars hesitate to generalize. Even so, interesting differences have been observed. Many Spanish-speaking students feel that English-language school writing in North America lacks grace because writers do not include any wide-ranging background material: in fact, writing teachers here usually say such broad introductory material is wordy or not really relevant to the central message. Japanese school writing customarily begins with references to nature. In some African nations, a ceremonial, formal opening is expected to start school writing as an expression of respect for the reader. As a person, I greatly enjoy discovering the rich variations in the writing traditions of the many cultures of the world. As a college teacher, however, my responsibility is to explain the expectations in this culture.

If you were in my class, I would say "Welcome!" and then ask you to teach me about writing in your first language. Using that knowledge, I would respectfully teach you the approach to writing that is used here so that I can do my best to help you succeed in a North American academic program.

L.Q.T.

44 SINGULARS AND PLURALS

44a What are count and noncount nouns?

Count nouns represent items that can be counted: *radio, fingernail, street, idea.* **Noncount nouns** represent things that cannot be counted: *knowledge, rain, traffic.*

Count nouns can be SINGULAR (*radio, street*) or PLURAL (*radios, streets*), and so they may use singular or plural VERBS. Noncount nouns are used in singular form only, and so they use only singular verbs.

ALERT: If you are not sure whether a noun is count or noncount, look it up in a dictionary that distinguishes the two types. !

Some nouns can be countable or uncountable depending on their meaning in a sentence. Most of these nouns represent things that can be meant either individually or as "wholes" made up of individual parts.

COUNT Two hairs were on his collar. [individual, countable hairs]

NONCOUNT His hair was cut very short. [all the hairs on his head considered together]

Uncountable items 67

- Groups of similar items making up "wholes": *clothing, equipment, furniture, luggage, mail, money*
- Abstractions: *equality, fun, health, ignorance, knowledge, peace, respect*
- Liquids: *blood, coffee, gasoline, water*
- Gases: *air, helium, oxygen, smog, smoke, steam*
- Materials: *aluminum, cloth, cotton, ice, wood*
- Food: *beef, bread, butter, macaroni, meat, cheese*
- Collections of particles or grains: *dirt, dust, hair, rice, salt, wheat*
- Sports, games, activities: *chess, reading, sailing, soccer*
- Languages: *Arabic, Chinese, Japanese, Spanish*
- Fields of study: *biology, computer science, history, physics, literature, math*
- Natural phenomena: *electricity, heat, moonlight, sunshine, thunder*

When you are EDITING your writing, be sure that you have not added a plural *s* to any noncount nouns, which are always singular in form.

ALERT: Be sure to use a singular verb with any noncount noun that functions as a SUBJECT in a CLAUSE. !

44b Which determiners should I use with singular and plural nouns?

Determiners, including expressions of quantity, are used to tell *which, how much,* or *how many* about NOUNS. Choosing the right determiner with a noun can depend on whether the noun is NONCOUNT or COUNT. For count nouns, you must also decide whether the noun is SINGULAR or PLURAL.

ALERTS: (1) *Many, most,* and *some* require *of the* for a noun that is specific, but not when the noun is a generalization.

- **Most** supervisors are well qualified. [general]
- Most **of the** supervisors **here** are well qualified. [specific]

(2) The phrases *a few* and *a little* convey the meaning "some": *I have* ***a few*** *rare books* means "I have some rare books." *They are worth* ***a little*** *money* means "They are worth some money." Without the word *a*, the meaning of *few* and *little* is "almost none": *I have* ***few*** [or *very few*] *books* means "I have almost no books." *They are worth* (***very***) ***little*** *money* means "They are worth almost no money." (3) A phrase with *one of the* always has a plural noun as the OBJECT of the PREPOSITION *of.* The verb agrees with *one,* not with the plural noun, so it is always singular: *One of the most important inventions of the twentieth century is* [not *are*] *television.* (Chapter 41).!

Using determiners with count and noncount nouns 68

GROUP 1: DETERMINERS FOR SINGULAR COUNT NOUNS

With every singular count noun, always use one of the determiners listed in Group 1.

- We live in **an** apartment in **that** large white house.

■ *a, an, the*

- **a** house (**an** egg) • **the** egg • **the** house

■ *one, any, some, every, each, either, neither, another, the other*

- **any** book • **each** person • **another** year

■ *my, our, your, his, her, its, their,* nouns with *'s* or *s'*

- **your** father • **its** cover • **Connie's** car

■ *this, that*

- **this** week • **that** desk

■ *one, no, the first, the second,* etc.

- **one** example • **no** reason • **the fifth** chair

GROUP 2: DETERMINERS FOR PLURAL COUNT NOUNS

All the determiners listed in Group 2 can be used with plural count nouns. Plural count nouns can also be used without determiners (45b).

- ~~The~~ Tomatoes are tasty in salad. Be sure that all **the** tomatoes you select are ripe.

→

Using determiners with count and noncount nouns *(continued)*

- *the*
  - **the** bicycles
  - **the** rooms
  - **the** ideas
- *some, any, both, many, more, most, few, fewer, the fewest, a number of, other, several, all, all the, a lot of*
  - **some** people
  - **many** jobs
  - **all** managers
- *my, our, your, his, her, its, their,* nouns with *'s* or *s'*
  - **our** coats
  - **her** books
  - **students'** grades
- these, those
  - **these** days
  - **those** computers
- *no, two, three, four,* etc., *the first, the second, the third,* etc.
  - **no** exceptions
  - **four** students
  - **the first** months

GROUP 3: DETERMINERS FOR NONCOUNT NOUNS
All the determiners listed in Group 3 can be used with noncount nouns (always singular). Noncount nouns can also be used without determiners (45b).

- **The** homework in this course is heavy.
- We have **some** work to do. Do you have **work** to do?

- *the*
  - **the** rice
- *some, any, much, more, most, other, the other, little, less, the least, enough, all, all the, a lot of*
  - **enough** snow
  - **a lot of** equipment
  - **more** food
- *my, our, your, his, her, its, their,* nouns with *'s* or *s'*
  - **their** training
  - **India's** heat
  - **your** leadership
- *this, that*
  - **this** staff
  - **that** expertise
- *no, the first, the second, the best,* etc.
  - **no** smoking
  - **the first** rainfall
  - **the best** vocabulary

44c What forms are correct for nouns used as adjectives?

Some words that function as NOUNS can also function as ADJECTIVES. Adjectives in English do not have plural forms. If you use a noun as an adjective, do not add *s* or *es* to the adjective even when the noun or PRONOUN it modifies is PLURAL.

- Many Canadian~~s~~ students are basketball fans.

- My nephew likes to look at picture~~s~~ books.

EXCEPTION a sports car

45 ARTICLES

The words *a, an,* and *the* are **articles.** Articles are one type of DETERMINER. They signal that a NOUN will follow and that any MODIFIERS between the article and the noun refer to that noun.

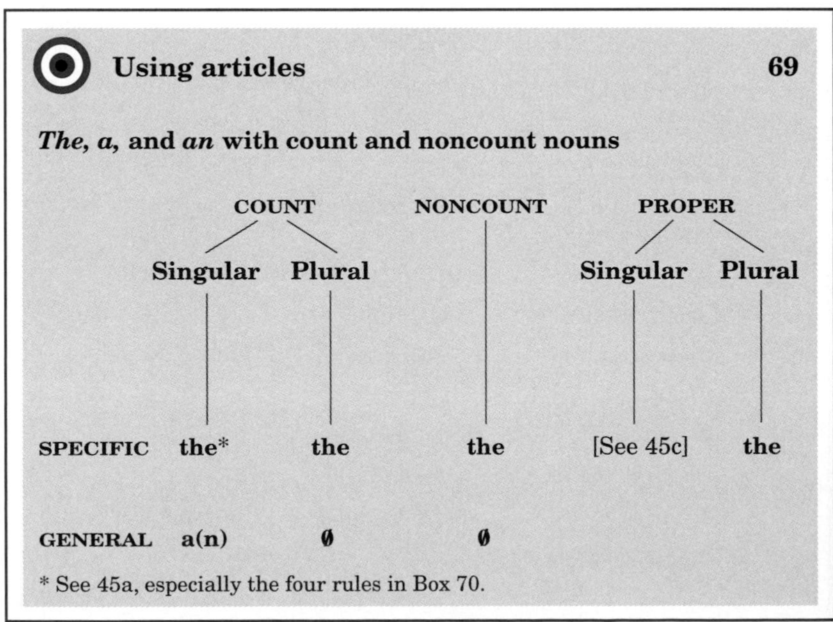

- **a** chair
- **a** cold metal chair
- **the** computer
- **the** lightning-fast computer

45a How should I use articles with singular count nouns?

When you use a singular COUNT NOUN (Box 70), the noun requires a DETERMINER; for a list, see Group 1 in Box 68 (pp. 384–385). If you have to choose between *a* or *an* and *the,* decide whether the noun is specific or nonspecific. A noun is considered specific when a reader can understand from the context exactly and specifically what the noun is referring to.

Using *the* with singular count nouns 70

RULE 1

A noun is specific and requires *the* when it names something either unique or commonly known.

- **The** sun has risen above **the** horizon. [Because only one *sun* and one *horizon* exist, they are specific nouns.]

RULE 2

A noun is specific and requires *the* when it names something used in a representative or abstract sense.

- I would like to know who chose **the** unicorn to be **the** symbolic animal on Canada's coat of arms. [Because *unicorn* and *symbolic animal* are representative references rather than references to a particular unicorn or animal, they are specific nouns in this context.]

RULE 3

A noun is specific and requires *the* when it names something that is defined elsewhere in the same sentence or in an earlier sentence.

- **The** ship *St. Roch* was the first vessel to navigate the Northwest Passage in both directions. [*St. Roch* names a specific ship.]
- **The** carpet in my bedroom is new. [*In my bedroom* defines exactly which carpet is meant, so *carpet* is a specific noun in this context.]

→

Using *the* with singular count nouns *(continued)*

- I have a computer and a fax machine in my office. **The** computer is often broken. [*Computer* is introduced in the first sentence, so it uses *a*. *Computer* has been made specific by the first sentence, so the second sentence uses *the* to refer back to the same noun.]

RULE 4
A noun is specific and requires *the* when it represents something that can be inferred from the context.

- I need an expert to fix **the** problem. [If you read this sentence after the example about a computer in Rule 3, above, you understand that *problem* refers to the broken computer; *problem* is specific in this context. Here the word *the* is similar to the word *this*.]

For nonspecific singular count nouns, use *a* or *an*. When the singular noun is specific, use *the* or some other determiner. Box 70 can help you decide when a singular count noun is specific and therefore requires *the*.

ALERT: *An* is used before words that begin with a vowel sound; *a* is used before words that begin with a consonant sound. Sound, not spelling, is the key. Words that begin with *h* or *u* can have either a vowel or a consonant sound; check your dictionary. Choose *a* or *an* based on the sound of the first word after the article, even if that word is not the noun.

- **an** idea
- **an** honour
- **a** useless umbrella
- **an** umbrella
- **a** good idea
- **a** history book **!**

ALERT: One common exception affects Rule 3 in Box 70. A noun may still require *a* or *an* after the first use if one or more descriptive adjectives come between the article and the noun: *I bought a sweater today. It was a* [not *the*] ***red*** *sweater*.**!**

45b How should I use articles with plural count nouns and with noncount nouns?

Like singular count nouns, PLURAL COUNT NOUNS and NONCOUNT NOUNS that are *specific* usually use *the* according to the rules in Box 70. When a noun has a *general* meaning, it usually does not use *the*.

Plural count nouns

- Geraldo planted tulips and roses this year. **The** tulips will bloom in April.

The plural count noun *tulips* is used in a general sense in the first sentence, without *the.* Because the first sentence identifies *tulips,* the second sentence refers specifically to ***the*** *tulips.* This example is related to Rule 3 in Box 70.

Noncount nouns

- Kalinda served rice and chicken to us. She flavoured **the** rice with curry.

Rice is a noncount noun. By the second sentence, *rice* has become specific, so *the* is used. This example is related to Rule 3 in Box 70.

Generalizations with plural or noncount nouns

Omit *the* in generalizations using plural or noncount nouns.

- ~~The~~ ~~t~~Tulips are ~~the~~ flowers that grow from ~~the~~ bulbs.

Compare this to a generalization with a singular count noun.

- **A** tulip is **a** flower that grows from **a** bulb.

45c How should I use *the* with proper nouns?

Proper nouns represent specific people, places, or things. Most proper nouns do not require ARTICLES: *We visited Lake Louise* [not *the Lake Louise*] *with Asha and Larry.* However, certain types of proper nouns do require *the.*

- Nouns with the pattern *the . . . of . . .: the Dominion of Canada, the president of Mexico*
- Plural proper nouns: *the Johnsons, the Vancouver Canucks, the United Arab Emirates*
- Collective proper nouns (nouns that name a group): *the Society of Friends, the CLC*
- Some, but not all, geographical features: *the Amazon, the Gobi Desert, the Indian Ocean*

46 WORD ORDER

46a What are standard and inverted word orders?

Standard word order is the most common pattern for DECLARATIVE SENTENCES in English. The SUBJECT comes before the VERB: *That book* [subject] *was* [verb] *heavy.*

Inverted word order, with a verb coming before the subject, is common for direct questions in English: *Was* [verb] *that book* [subject] *heavy? Were* [verb] *you* [subject] *close to it when it fell?*

A very common way to form questions with MAIN VERBS other than *be* is to use inverted order with a form of the verb *do* as an AUXILIARY VERB before the subject and the SIMPLE FORM of the main verb after the subject: ***Do you want*** *me to put the book away?* ***Do you have*** *my pencil?*

Also, use inverted order when a question begins with a question-forming word such as *what, why, when, where,* or *how:* ***Where does*** *the* ***book*** *belong?*

When a question has more than one auxiliary verb, put the subject after the first auxiliary verb: ***Would you*** *have replaced the book?*

ALERT: Do not use inverted word order with indirect questions: *She asked where I saw the book* [not *She asked where did I see the book*]. **!**

Verb–subject word order is also required by certain ADVERBS at the beginning of a sentence.

- Only once **did she** ask my advice.
- Never **have I** seen such a mess!

Verb–subject word order rules also apply to emphatic exclamations: ***Was*** *that* ***book*** *heavy!* ***Did she*** *enjoy that book!* (For advice about inverted word order to create emphasis in declarative sentences, see 46c.)

46b Where should I place adjectives?

In English, an ADJECTIVE ordinarily comes directly before the NOUN it modifies. Box 71 shows the most common order for positioning several adjectives that modify the same noun.

Word order for adjectives 71

1 Determiner, if any: *a, an, the, my, your, Jan's, these,* etc.

2 Expressions of order, including ordinal numbers, if any: *first, second, next, last, final,* etc.

3 Expressions of quantity, including cardinal numbers, if any: *one, two, few, each, every, some,* etc.

4 Adjectives of judgment or opinion, if any: *smart, happy, interesting, sad, boring,* etc.

5 Adjectives of size and/or shape, if any: *big, small, short, round, rectangular,* etc.

6 Adjectives of age and/or condition, if any: *new, young, broken, dirty, shiny,* etc.

7 Adjectives of colour, if any: *red, green, beige, turquoise,* etc.

8 Adjectives that can also be used as nouns, if any: *German, metal, Protestant, cotton,* etc.

9 The noun

1	2	3	4	5	6	7	8	9
A		few		tiny		red		ants
The	last	six					Thai	drums
My			fine		old		oak	table

46c Where should I place adverbs?

Adverbs and adverbial PHRASES modify VERBS, ADJECTIVES, other adverbs, or whole sentences. They can go in three different places in a CLAUSE: first, middle, or last. ("Middle" means after the subject and usually just after the auxiliary verb, if any.)

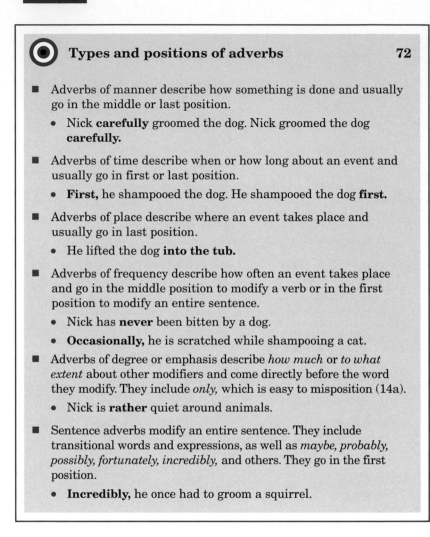

Types and positions of adverbs 72

- Adverbs of manner describe how something is done and usually go in the middle or last position.
  - Nick **carefully** groomed the dog. Nick groomed the dog **carefully.**
- Adverbs of time describe when or how long about an event and usually go in first or last position.
  - **First,** he shampooed the dog. He shampooed the dog **first.**
- Adverbs of place describe where an event takes place and usually go in last position.
  - He lifted the dog **into the tub.**
- Adverbs of frequency describe how often an event takes place and go in the middle position to modify a verb or in the first position to modify an entire sentence.
  - Nick has **never** been bitten by a dog.
  - **Occasionally,** he is scratched while shampooing a cat.
- Adverbs of degree or emphasis describe *how much* or *to what extent* about other modifiers and come directly before the word they modify. They include *only,* which is easy to misposition (14a).
  - Nick is **rather** quiet around animals.
- Sentence adverbs modify an entire sentence. They include transitional words and expressions, as well as *maybe, probably, possibly, fortunately, incredibly,* and others. They go in the first position.
  - **Incredibly,** he once had to groom a squirrel.

ALERT: If a sentence begins with a negative adverb of frequency (*never, rarely, only once, seldom,* etc.), the subject–verb word order must be inverted. This creates emphasis (41h).

- **Never *has Nick*** been bitten by a dog. **!**

47 PREPOSITIONS

Prepositions, along with their OBJECTS, form prepositional PHRASES, which often describe relationships in time or space. Prepositions, when combined with certain verbs, sometimes have idiomatic meanings in English. A dictionary such as the *Longman Dictionary of Contemporary English* or the *Oxford Advanced Learner's Dictionary* can be especially helpful when you need to find the correct preposition for these idiomatic uses.

47a How should I use *in, at,* and *on* to show time and place?

TIME

- ***in*** a year or a month (*during* is also correct but less common): ***in*** *1999,* ***in*** *May*
- ***in*** a period of time: ***in*** *a few months* (*seconds, days, years*)
- ***in*** a period of a day: ***in*** *the morning* (*afternoon, evening*), ***in*** *the daytime* (*morning, evening*), but ***at*** *night*
- ***on*** a **specific** day: ***on*** *Friday,* ***on*** *my birthday,* ***on*** May 12
- ***at*** a **specific** time or periods of time: ***at*** *noon,* ***at*** *2:00,* ***at*** *dawn,* ***at*** *nightfall,* ***at*** *takeoff* [the time a plane leaves], ***at*** *breakfast* [the time a specific meal takes place]

PLACE

- ***in*** a location surrounded by something else: ***in*** *Alberta,* ***in*** *Utah,* ***in*** *downtown New Delhi,* ***in*** *the kitchen,* ***in*** *my apartment,* ***in*** *the tub*
- ***at*** a specific location: ***at*** *your house,* ***at*** *the bank,* ***at*** *the corner of Maple Avenue and King Street,* ***at*** *376 Oak Street,* ***at*** *home*
- ***on*** a street: ***on*** *Oak Street,* ***on*** *Maple Avenue,* ***on*** *the road*

47b How should I use prepositions in phrasal verbs?

Phrasal verbs are verbs that combine with PREPOSITIONS to deliver their meaning. The meaning of many phrasal verbs is idiomatic, not literal; *pick on,* for example, means "annoy" or "tease" rather than anything associated with either *pick* or *on.* Also, many phrasal verbs are informal and more appropriate for conversation than for academic writing. For a research paper, for example, *propose* or *suggest* would usually be better choices than *come up with.*

In some phrasal verbs, the verb and the preposition should not be separated by other words: ***Look at*** *the moon* [not ***Look*** *the moon* ***at***].

In other phrasal verbs, called *separable phrasal verbs,* words can separate the verb and the preposition without interfering with meaning: *I* ***threw*** *my homework* ***away*** [or *I* ***threw away*** *my homework.*] When a separable phrasal verb has a PRONOUN OBJECT, that object should be positioned between the verb and the preposition: *I* ***threw*** *it* ***away*** [not *I* ***threw away*** *it*]. Object PHRASES or CLAUSES with more than four or five words should usually be positioned after the preposition: *I threw away* ***the homework that was assigned last week.***

Here is a list of some common phrasal verbs. The ones that cannot be separated are marked with an asterisk (*).

SELECTED PHRASAL VERBS

ask out	find out	look into*
break down	get along with*	look out for*
bring about	get back	look over
call back	get off*	make up
call off	go over*	run across*
call up	hand in	speak to*
drop off	keep up with*	speak with*
figure out	leave out	throw away
fill out	look after*	throw out
fill up	look around*	turn down

47c How should I use prepositions with past participles?

PAST PARTICIPLES are verb forms that function as ADJECTIVES (39d, 40b). Past participles end in either *-ed* or *-d,* or in an equivalent irregular form (40b). When past participles follow the LINKING VERB *be,* it is easy to confuse them with PASSIVE verbs (40g), which have the same endings. Passive verbs express actions. Past participles, because they act as adjectives, modify NOUNS and PRONOUNS and often describe situations and conditions. Passive verbs follow the pattern *be* + past participle + *by: The child* ***was frightened by*** *a snake*. An expression containing a past participle, however, can use either *be* or another linking verb, and can be followed by either *by* or a different preposition.

- The child **seemed frightened by** snakes.
- The child **is frightened of** all snakes.

Here is a list of some expressions containing past participles and the prepositions that often follow them. Look in a dictionary for others. (See 48a on using GERUNDS after some of these expressions, and 47d on using prepositions with other adjectives.)

SELECTED PAST PARTICIPLE PHRASES + PREPOSITIONS

be accustomed to	be interested in
be acquainted with	be known for
be composed of	be located in
be concerned/worried about	be made of (*or* from)
be disappointed with (*or* in someone)	be married to
be discriminated against	be pleased/satisfied with
be divorced from	be prepared for
be excited about	be tired of (*or* from)
be finished/done with	

47d How should I use prepositions in expressions?

In many common expressions, different PREPOSITIONS convey great differences in meaning. For example, check a dictionary to see that four prepositions can be used with the VERB *agree* to create different meanings: *agree to, agree about, agree on,* and *agree with.*

Many ADJECTIVES also require certain prepositions: *afraid of, familiar with, famous for, friendly toward* (or *with*), *guilty of, patient with, proud of.*

You can find entire books listing English expressions containing prepositions, and comprehensive dictionaries often give meanings for verb–preposition combinations as part of the entry for the verb.

48 GERUNDS AND INFINITIVES

GERUNDS and INFINITIVES are types of verbals. **Verbals** are VERB forms that function as NOUNS or MODIFIERS. Like all nouns, gerunds and infinitives can be DIRECT OBJECTS. Some verbs are followed by gerunds as objects, and other verbs must be followed by infinitive objects. Still other verbs can be followed by either gerund or infinitive objects. A few verbs change meaning depending on whether a gerund object or an infinitive object is used.

48a What verbs use a gerund, not an infinitive, object?

Certain VERBS cannot be followed by INFINITIVES as DIRECT OBJECTS; they require GERUNDS: *Yuri considered* ***calling*** [not *to call*] *the mayor.*

VERBS THAT USE GERUND OBJECTS

acknowledge	discuss	mind
admit	dislike	object to
advise	dream about	postpone
anticipate	enjoy	practise
appreciate	escape	put off
avoid	evade	quit
cannot help	favour	recall
complain about	finish	recommend
consider	give up	resent
consist of	have trouble	resist
contemplate	imagine	risk
deter from	include	suggest
delay	insist on	talk about
deny	keep (on)	tolerate
detest	mention	understand

Using a gerund after *go*

Although *go* is usually followed by an infinitive object (*We can* ***go to see*** [not *go to seeing*] *a movie*), *go* is followed by a gerund in such phrases as *go swimming, go fishing, go shopping,* and *go driving: I will* ***go swimming*** [not *go to swim*] *tomorrow.*

Using gerunds after *be* + complement + preposition

A COMPLEMENT often follows a form of *be.* Some complements require certain prepositions (47c).

SELECTED *BE* + COMPLEMENT + PREPOSITION EXPRESSIONS

be (get) accustomed to	be interested in
be angry about	be prepared for
be bored with	be responsible for
be capable of	be tired of (*or* from)
be committed to	be (get) used to
be concerned about	be worried about
be excited about	

- We are excited about **voting** [*not* to vote] in the election.
- They were interested in **hearing** [*not* to hear] the candidates' debate.

ALERT: Always use a gerund, not an infinitive, as the object of a preposition. Be especially careful when the word *to* is functioning as a preposition in a phrasal verb (47b): *We are committed to **saving** the elephants* [not *committed to save*].

48b What verbs use an infinitive, not a gerund, object?

Certain VERBS cannot be followed by GERUNDS as DIRECT OBJECTS; they use INFINITIVES: *Three people decided **to question*** [not *decided questioning*] *the speaker.*

VERBS THAT USE INFINITIVE OBJECTS

afford	claim	intend	refuse
agree	consent	know how	seem
aim	decide	learn	struggle
appear	decline	like*	tend
arrange	demand	manage	threaten
ask	deserve	mean	try*
attempt*	expect	offer	volunteer
be able (unable)	fail	plan	wait
be left*	give permission	prepare	want
beg	hesitate	pretend	would like
care (not care)	hope	promise	

*These verbs may be followed by either an infinitive or a gerund object, depending on context and meaning.

Using infinitives after *be* + some complements

- We are eager **to go** [*not* going] to the mountains.
- I am ready **to sleep** [*not* sleeping] in a tent.

Using unmarked infinitive objects

An **unmarked infinitive** uses a verb's SIMPLE FORM but not the word *to.*

Some common verbs followed by unmarked infinitive objects are *feel, have, hear, let, listen to, look at, make* (meaning "compel"), *notice, see,* and *watch.*

- Please **let** me **take** [not *to take*] you to lunch. [*Take* is an unmarked infinitive used after *let.*]
- I want **to take** you to lunch. [*To take* is a marked infinitive used after *want.*]

The verb *help* can be followed by either a marked or an unmarked infinitive: *Help me put* [or *Help me to put*] *these groceries away.*

ALERT: Be careful about parallel structure when you use two or more verbals as objects after one verb. Put the verbals into the same form.

- We went sailing and ~~to~~ scuba ~~dive~~ diving.
- We heard the wind blow and the waves crash~~ing~~.

But if you are using verbal objects in a COMPOUND PREDICATE, be sure to use the kind of verbal that each verb requires.

- We enjoyed scuba diving but do not want ~~sailing~~ to sail again.

[*Enjoyed* requires a gerund object and *want* requires an infinitive object.] !

48c How does meaning change if an infinitive object or a gerund follows *stop, remember,* or *forget*?

Followed by a GERUND, *stop* means "finish, quit": *We stopped eating* means "We finished our meal." Followed by an INFINITIVE, *stop* means "stop or interrupt one activity to begin another": *We stopped to eat* means "We stopped doing something [such as driving or painting the house] to eat."

Followed by a gerund, *remember* means "recall a memory": *I remember talking to you last night.* Followed by an infinitive, *remember* means "not to forget to do something": *I must remember to talk with Isa.*

Followed by a gerund, *forget* means "to do something and not recall it": *I forget having put my keys in the refrigerator.* Followed by an infinitive, *forget* means "to not do something": *If you forget to put a stamp on that letter, it will be returned.*

48d Do sense verbs change meaning with a gerund or an infinitive object?

Sense VERBS such as *see, notice, hear, observe, watch, feel, listen to,* and *look at* usually do not change meaning whether a GERUND or an INFINITIVE is used as an OBJECT. *I saw the water rising* and *I saw the water rise* (unmarked infinitive—see 48b) both deliver the same message.

48e How should I choose between *-ing* and *-ed* forms of adjectives?

Deciding whether to use the *-ing* form (PRESENT PARTICIPLE) or the *-ed* form (PAST PARTICIPLE of a REGULAR VERB) as an ADJECTIVE in a specific sentence can be difficult. For example, *I am amused* and *I am amusing* are both correct in English, but their meanings are very different.

- **I am amused** by something. [I experience amusement.]
- **I am amusing** to other people. [I cause their amusement.]

To make the right choice, decide whether the modified NOUN or PRONOUN is causing or experiencing what the participle describes.

Use a present participle (*-ing*) to modify a noun or pronoun that is the agent or the cause of the action. This meaning is ACTIVE.

- Mica explained your interesting plan. [The noun *plan* caused interest, so *interesting* is correct.]
- I find your plan exciting. [The noun *plan* causes excitement, so *exciting* is correct.]

Use a past participle (*-ed* in regular verbs) to modify a noun or pronoun that experiences or receives whatever the modifier describes. This meaning is PASSIVE.

- An interested committee wants to hear your plan. [The noun *committee* experiences interest, so *interested* is correct.]
- Excited by your plan, I called a board meeting. [The noun *I* experiences excitement, so *excited* is correct.]

Here is a list of some frequently used participles that require your close attention when you use them as adjectives. To choose the right form, decide whether the noun or pronoun *experiences* or *causes* what the participle describes.

amused, amusing	appalled, appalling
annoyed, annoying	bored, boring
confused, confusing	offended, offending
depressed, depressing	overwhelmed, overwhelming
disgusted, disgusting	pleased, pleasing
fascinated, fascinating	reassured, reassuring
frightened, frightening	satisfied, satisfying
insulted, insulting	shocked, shocking

49 MODAL AUXILIARY VERBS

Modal auxiliary verbs include *can, could, may, might, should, had better, must, will, would,* and others. Like the auxiliary verbs *be, do,* and *have,* modal auxiliary verbs help main verbs convey more information. Modal auxiliary verbs convey meaning about ability, necessity, advice, possibility, and other conditions.

49a How do modal auxiliary verbs differ from *be, do,* and *have*?

Modal auxiliary verbs are always followed by the SIMPLE FORM of a main verb: *I might go tomorrow.*

One-word modal auxiliary verbs usually do not have an *-s* ending in third-person singular: *She* ***could*** *go with me, you* ***could*** *go with me,* and *they* ***could*** *go with me.* Exceptions include modals such as *have to* and *need to,* which make the third-person singular changes that *have* and *need* ordinarily do (for example, *I* ***have*** *to stay, she* ***has*** *to stay; you* ***need*** *to smile, he* ***needs*** *to smile*).

ALERT: *Ought to* does not add *-s* in third-PERSON singular. *Be supposed to* makes all the usual changes to the verb *be* (See 49c). **!**

49b Which modal auxiliary verbs express ability, necessity, advisability, or probability?

Expressing ability

Can means "ability in the present." *Could* sometimes means "ability in the past." These words deliver the meaning of "able to."

- You **can work** late tonight.
- I **could play** the piano when I was younger.

Could often expresses some condition that must be fulfilled.

- If you **could** come early, then we can start on time.
- I **could** have gone to bed at 10:00 if I had finished my homework.

Adding *not* between a MODAL AUXILIARY VERB and the MAIN VERB makes the sentence negative: *I could **not** work late last night.*

ALERT: Negative forms of modal auxiliary verbs are often turned into contractions: *can't, couldn't, won't, wouldn't,* and so on. Because contractions can be considered informal usage, you will never be wrong to avoid them in academic writing. !

Expressing necessity

Must, have to, and *need to* express a requirement to do something. *Must* implies future action. *Have to* and *need to* are used in all verb tenses.

- You **must leave** before midnight. She **has to leave** when I leave. We **needed to be** with you last night. You **will need to be** here before dark.

ALERT: *Must* has no past tense form when it expresses necessity. Use *had to.* !

Expressing advice or the notion of a good idea

Should and *ought to* mean that doing the action of the main verb in the present or future is a good idea. The PAST-TENSE forms are *should have* and *ought to have;* they are followed by the PAST PARTICIPLE.

- You **should call** your sister tonight. I **ought to have *gone*** to the dentist last week.

The modal *had better* expresses the meaning of good advice or warning or threat.

- You **had better see** a doctor before your cough gets worse.

Expressing probability

May, might, could, and *must* usually express probability, possibility, or likelihood.

- We **might** see a tiger in the zoo. We **could** go this afternoon.

The past-tense forms for *may, might, could,* and *must* add *have* and the main verb's past participle to the modals.

- I'm hungry; I **must have neglected** to eat breakfast.

49c Which modal auxiliary verbs express preference, plan, or past habit?

Expressing preferences

Would rather (present tense) and *would rather have* (past tense) express a preference. In the past tense, the modal is also followed by a past participle.

- We **would rather see** a comedy than a mystery. We **would rather *have seen*** a movie last night.

Expressing a plan or obligation

A form of *be* followed by *supposed to* and the SIMPLE FORM of a MAIN VERB, in both present and past tense, delivers a meaning of something planned or an obligation.

- I **was supposed to meet** them at the bus stop.

The word *supposed* may be omitted with no change in meaning.

- I **was to meet** them at the bus stop.

Expressing past habit

Used to and *would* mean that something happened repeatedly in a time that has passed.

- I **used to hate** getting a flu shot. I **would dread** the injection for weeks beforehand.

ALERT: Both *used to* and *would* can be used for repeated actions in the past, but *would* cannot be used for a situation that lasted for a period of time in the past.

- I ~~would~~ used to live in New Brunswick. **!**

50 COMMAS

The comma separates sentence parts for greater clarity. You can avoid most comma errors with these two bits of advice: (1) As you write or reread what you've written, don't insert a comma simply because you happen to pause to think or take a breath before moving on. (2) If you are unsure about a comma, insert it and circle the spot. Then, when you are editing, look in this book for the rule you need to review.

50a When do I use commas?

To see basic patterns for using commas, look over Box 73. For quick answers to most comma questions, use this box. The cross-references tell you where you can find fuller explanations.

When to use commas **73**

COMMAS AFTER INTRODUCTORY ELEMENTS (50b)

- **Although most postcards cost only a dime,** one recently sold for thousands of dollars. [clause]
- **On postcard racks,** several designs are usually available. [phrase]
- **For example,** animals are timeless favourites. [transitional expression]
- **However,** most cards show local landmarks. [transitional word]

COMMAS WITH COORDINATING CONJUNCTIONS LINKING INDEPENDENT CLAUSES (50c)

- Postcards are ideal for brief greetings**, and** they can also be miniature works of art.

COMMAS WITH ITEMS IN SERIES (50d)

- **Places, paintings, and people** appear on postcards. [*and* between last two items]
- **Places, paintings, people, animals** occupy dozens of display racks. [no *and* between last two items]

COMMAS WITH COORDINATE ADJECTIVES (50e)

- Some postcards feature **appealing, dramatic** scenes.

→

When to use commas *(continued)*

NO COMMAS WITH CUMULATIVE ADJECTIVES (50e)

- Other postcards feature **famous historical** scenes.

COMMAS WITH NONRESTRICTIVE ELEMENTS (50f)

- **A few years after the first postcard appeared,** some governments began to issue stamped postcards. [nonrestrictive element introduces independent clause]
- The Golden Age of postcards**, which lasted from about 1900 to 1929,** yielded many especially valuable cards. [nonrestrictive element interrupts independent clause]
- Collectors attend postcard shows**, which are similar to baseball-card shows.** [nonrestrictive element ends independent clause]

NO COMMAS WITH RESTRICTIVE ELEMENTS (50f)

- Collectors **who attend these shows** may specialize in a particular kind of postcard. [restrictive clause]

COMMAS WITH QUOTED WORDS (50g)

- One collector told me**,** "Attending a show is like digging for buried treasure." [quoted words at end of sentence]
- "I always expect to find a priceless postcard**,**" he said. [quoted words at start of sentence]
- "Everyone there**,**" he joked**,** "believes a million-dollar card is hidden in the next stack." [quoted words interrupted mid-sentence]

50b How do I use a comma to set off introductory words?

When a DEPENDENT CLAUSE,* PHRASE, expression, or word comes before an INDEPENDENT CLAUSE, place a comma after the introductory material.

- **When the topic is dieting,** many people say sugar craving is their worst problem. [introductory DEPENDENT CLAUSE]

*Words printed in small capital letters (such as DEPENDENT CLAUSE) are defined in the Terms Glossary on pages 497–517.

- **Between 1850 and 1910,** sugar refineries appeared in several Canadian cities. [introductory PREPOSITIONAL PHRASE]
- **Beginning in infancy,** we develop lifelong tastes for sweet and salty foods. [introductory PARTICIPIAL PHRASE]
- **Sweets being a temptation for many adults,** parents need to know that most commercial baby foods contain sugar. [introductory ABSOLUTE PHRASE]
- **For example,** fructose comes from fruit, but it is still sugar. [TRANSITIONAL EXPRESSION]
- **Nevertheless,** many people think fructose is not harmful. [CONJUNCTIVE ADVERB]

50c How do I use a comma before a coordinating conjunction?

When you link INDEPENDENT CLAUSES, place a comma before a COORDINATING CONJUNCTION (*and, but, for, or, nor, so, yet*).

- The sky turned black**, and** the wind blew fiercely.
- The sky began to brighten**, but** the wind continued blowing strongly.

In one particular situation, you need to use a SEMICOLON instead of a comma and coordinating conjunction to link independent clauses. When commas are already part of one or both independent clauses, the semicolon clearly shows exactly where the link between independent clauses occurs.

- With temperatures below freezing, the snow did not melt**; and** people wondered, gazing at the white landscape, when they would see grass again.

ALERTS: (1) Do not put a comma *after* a coordinating conjunction that joins independent clauses.

NO A house is renovated in two weeks **but,** an apartment takes a week.

YES A house is renovated in two weeks**, but** an apartment takes a week.

(2) When a coordinating conjunction links only two words, PHRASES, or DEPENDENT CLAUSES, do not use a comma.

NO Habitat for Humanity depends on volunteer **labour, and donations** for its construction projects. [TWO WORDS, SO COMMA SHOULD NOT BE USED.]

YES Habitat for Humanity depends on volunteer **labour and donations** for its construction projects.

(3) To avoid the error of a COMMA SPLICE, do not use a comma between independent clauses unless they are linked by a coordinating conjunction (12c).

NO Ten centimetres of snow fell in two hours**,** driving was hazardous.

YES Ten centimetres of snow fell in two hours**, and** driving was hazardous. **!**

50d How do I use commas with a series?

A **series,** which always calls for commas, consists of three or more elements with the same grammatical form. The elements in a series can be words, PHRASES, or CLAUSES.

WORDS The earliest clothing fabrics were made from natural fibres such as **cotton, silk, linen,** and **wool.**

PHRASES Fabric today is made **from natural fibres, from synthetic fibres,** and **from natural and synthetic fibre blends.**

CLAUSES Natural fibres are durable and absorbent**,** synthetic fibres resist wrinkling and retain dyes well**,** and blends offer the advantages of both.

Although some very good writers omit the comma before a final COORDINATING CONJUNCTION used in a series, this handbook recommends using that comma. The comma helps readers understand the sentence.

- Ivan wears only natural fibres, nylon and Thinsulate. [This appears to say that nylon and Thinsulate are natural fibres.]
- Ivan wears only natural fibres**,** nylon**,** and Thinsulate. [This says Ivan wears three items: natural fibres and nylon and Thinsulate.]

Numbered or lettered lists within a sentence are items in a series. Use commas (or semicolons if the items are long) to separate three or more items.

- Three synthetic fibres predominate in clothing manufacture: (1) rayon**,** (2) polyester**,** and (3) acrylic.

When some or all items in a series contain commas or other punctuation, or when the items are complex, separate them with semicolons instead of commas (50c).

ALERTS: (1) Do not use a comma before the first item or after the last item in a series, unless another rule makes it necessary.

NO This October Ivan wore**, galoshes, sneakers,** and **sandals** to class.

NO This October Ivan wore **galoshes, sneakers,** and **sandals,** to class.

YES This October Ivan wore **galoshes, sneakers,** and **sandals** to class.

(2) Never use a comma when only two items are linked by a COORDINATING CONJUNCTION.

NO October brought both a **blizzard,** and **an Indian summer.**

YES October brought both a **blizzard** and **an Indian summer.**

50e When do I use a comma between adjectives?

Coordinate adjectives are two or more ADJECTIVES that carry equal weight in modifying a NOUN. Use a comma between them unless a COORDINATING CONJUNCTION (such as *and* or *but*) links them. In contrast, do not use a comma between **cumulative adjectives,** which do not carry equal weight in modifying a noun. Instead, cumulative adjectives build up meaning from word to word as they move toward the noun.

To determine whether adjectives are carrying equal weight in a sentence, use the test in Box 74.

Test for coordinate and cumulative adjectives 74

- Can the order of the adjectives be interchanged without changing the meaning or creating nonsense? If the answer is yes, the adjectives are coordinate and need commas.
  - The **restless, large, noisy** crowd wanted the concert to start. [The order of adjectives can be changed (*noisy, restless,* and *large*), so they are coordinate adjectives and need commas.]
  - The concert featured **several familiar backup** singers. [*Several familiar backup* cannot be changed to *backup familiar several,* so they are cumulative adjectives and do not need commas.]
- Can *and* be inserted between the adjectives without changing the meaning or creating nonsense? If the answer is yes, the adjectives are coordinate and need commas.
  - The **large and noisy and restless** crowd wanted the concert to start. [Inserting *and* does not change meaning. The adjectives are coordinate and need commas.]
  - The concert featured **several and familiar and backup** singers. [Inserting *and* creates nonsense. The adjectives are cumulative and do not need commas.]

50f How do commas work with nonrestrictive and restrictive elements?

A **nonrestrictive element** (also called a **nonessential element**) adds information without changing the general meaning of the sentence. Nonrestrictive elements can be clauses, phrases, or appositives. Always use commas to set off nonrestrictive elements. In contrast, a **restrictive element** (also called an **essential element**) limits and creates the specific meaning of the sentence. Restrictive elements are not set off with commas because the elements are needed to provide information.

Punctuating nonrestrictive and restrictive clauses

Set off nonrestrictive ADJECTIVE CLAUSES with commas. Most adjective clauses begin with *who, which,* or *that.* Never put commas around restrictive clauses.

NONRESTRICTIVE CLAUSE Farming**, which is our major source of food production,** is relentlessly affected by the weather. [Here, the focus is on the fact that farming is relentlessly affected by the weather. Therefore, *which is our major source of food production* is not essential information, so the clause is nonrestrictive and needs commas.]

RESTRICTIVE CLAUSE Much food **that consumers buy canned or frozen** is processed. [Here, the focus is on *food that consumers buy canned or frozen*. Therefore, *that consumers buy canned or frozen* is essential information, so the clause is restrictive and does not need commas.]

Punctuating nonrestrictive and restrictive phrases

NONRESTRICTIVE PHRASE Farmers**, trying to enhance crop growth,** use pesticides and fertilizers. [Here, the focus is on the fact that farmers use pesticides and fertilizers. Therefore, *trying to enhance crop growth* is not essential information, so the clause is nonrestrictive and needs commas.]

RESTRICTIVE PHRASE Farmers **trying to enhance crop growth** use pesticides and fertilizers. [Here, lack of commas indicates that *farmers* depends on *trying to enhance crop growth* for its complete meaning, so the phrase is restrictive and does not need commas.]

Punctuating nonrestrictive and restrictive appositives

An **appositive** renames the noun preceding it. Most appositives are nonrestrictive. But occasionally, depending on context, appositives can be restrictive. Set off nonrestrictive appositives, but not restrictive appositives, with commas.

NONRESTRICTIVE APPOSITIVE Agricultural scientists**, a new breed of farmer,** control the farming environment. [Here, the focus is on the fact that agricultural scientists control the farming environment. Therefore, the appositive *a new breed of farmer* is not essential information, so the appositive is nonrestrictive and needs commas.]

RESTRICTIVE APPOSITIVE The agricultural scientist **Wendy Singh** has helped develop a crop rotation system. [Here, the lack of commas indicates that the meaning of *The agricultural scientist* depends upon the name *Wendy Singh* for its complete meaning. Therefore, the appositive is restrictive and does not need commas.]

50g How do I use commas with quoted words?

Use a comma to set off quoted words from explanations anywhere in the same sentence.

- The poet William Blake wrote**,** "Love seeketh not itself to please." [explanatory words before quoted words]
- "I love you**,**" Mary told John**,** "but I cannot marry you." [explanatory words interrupt quoted words]
- "My love is a fever**,**" declared William Shakespeare. [explanatory words after quoted words]

However, when you use *that* before or after a quotation, whether or not the quotation is direct or indirect, do not use a comma before or after *that.*

NO Mary claims, that "our passion is strong, but we have nothing else in common."

NO Mary claims that, "our passion is strong, but we have nothing else in common."

YES Mary claims that "our passion is strong, but we have nothing else in common."

50h What other word groups do I set off with commas?

All the following are set off with commas from the rest of a sentence: TRANSITIONAL EXPRESSIONS, CONJUNCTIVE ADVERBS, asides, contrasts, words addressed directly to a reader or listener, and tag questions. This rule applies whether these elements start, interrupt, or end a sentence.

TRANSITIONAL EXPRESSIONS

- **For example,** Saskatchewan is Canada's breadbasket.
- Saskatchewan**, for example,** is Canada's breadbasket.
- Saskatchewan is Canada's breadbasket**, for example.**

CONJUNCTIVE ADVERBS

- **However,** Quebec is Canada's largest dairy producer.
- Quebec**, however,** is Canada's largest dairy producer.
- Quebec is Canada's largest dairy producer**, however.**

ASIDES

- Most large growers**, I imagine,** hope to export food.
- Most large growers hope to export food**, I imagine.**

CONTRASTS

- Quebec**, not Ontario,** is Canada's largest dairy producer.

WORDS ADDRESSED DIRECTLY TO READER OR LISTENER

- **All you computer majors,** perhaps the future lies in soybeans rather than software.
- Perhaps the future**, all you computer majors,** lies in soybeans rather than software.
- Perhaps the future lies in soybeans rather than software**, all you computer majors.**

TAG QUESTIONS

- You know**, don't you,** what tag questions are?
- You know what tag questions are**, don't you?**

50i How do I use commas in dates, names, addresses, letter format, and numbers?

Punctuating dates

Use a comma between the day and the month; also, use a comma between a day of the week and the month.

- July 20, 1969 • Sunday, July 20, 1969

Within a sentence, use commas after the day and the year in a month-day-year date.

- Everyone watched television on July 20, 1969, to see Neil Armstrong walk on the moon.

When you use day-month-year order, never use commas.

- Everyone watched television on 20 July 1969 to see Neil Armstrong walk on the moon.

Do not use a comma between only a month and year, only a month and day, or only a season and year.

- The major news story in July 1969 was the moon landing; news coverage was especially heavy on July 21. Many older people will always remember summer 1969.

Punctuating names, places, and addresses

When an abbreviated title (*Jr., M.D., Ph.D.*) comes after a name, use a comma between the name and the title. When a sentence continues after a name and title, also use a comma after the title.

- Rosa Gonzales, M.D., was the principal witness for the defence.

Use a comma in an inverted name between last and first names.

- Troyka, David

Use a comma between a city and province. When a sentence continues after a city and province, also use a comma after the province.

- Winnipeg, Manitoba, is home to the Royal Winnipeg Ballet.

When a sentence includes a complete address, separate all the items except the postal code with commas. The postal code follows the province after a space and is not followed by a comma.

- I wrote to Mr. U Lern, 10-01 Rule Road, Mississauga, ON L5A 2Z2 for the instruction manual.

Punctuating letter openings and closings

Use a comma after the opening of an informal letter. (Use a colon after the opening in a formal letter.)

- Dear Betty,

After the closing of a formal or informal letter, use a comma.

- Sincerely yours,
- Love,

Punctuating numbers

The SI—the international system of metric measurements used in Canada—does not use commas in numbers; it uses spaces to separate sets of three digits. Nevertheless, many people still use commas. This section explains both number systems.

RULES FOR NUMBERS IN SI

Counting from the right, put a space after every three digits in numbers with more than four digits.

- 72 867
- 150 567 066

In four-digit numbers, a space is optional for money, distance, amounts, and most other measurements. Be consistent in each piece of writing in using or omitting it.

- $1867
- $1 867
- 1867 km
- 1 867 km
- 1867 potatoes
- 1 867 potatoes

Always use a space in four-digit numbers when they are aligned in columns in a table or a chart.

RULES FOR NUMBERS IN SYSTEMS USING COMMAS

Counting from the right, put a comma after every three digits in numbers over four digits.

- 72,867
- 150,567,066

In a four-digit number, a comma is optional for money, distance, amounts, and most other measurements. Be consistent in each piece of writing.

- $1867
- 1867 miles
- 1867 potatoes
- **$1,867**
- **1,867 miles**
- **1,867 potatoes**

Use a comma to separate related Imperial measurements written in words.

- five feet**,** four inches

Use a comma to separate act and scene numbers in references to plays. Also, use a comma to separate a page reference from a line reference.

- act ii**,** scene iv [*or* act 2**,** scene 4]
- page 120**,** line 6

50j How can a comma prevent a misreading?

Use a comma to clarify the meaning of a sentence, even if no other rule calls for one.

NO Those who can practise many hours a day.

YES Those who can**,** practise many hours a day.

NO George dressed and performed for a sellout crowd.

YES George dressed**,** and performed for a sellout crowd.

50k When are commas wrong?

In explaining comma rules in this chapter so far, I've covered the errors associated with those rules. The list below sumarizes what I've already discussed; see the sections in parentheses for a full explanation.

- Commas with introductory words, phrases, clauses (50b)
- Commas with coordinating conjunctions to link independent clauses (50c)

- Commas with items in a series (50d)
- Commas with coordinate adjectives (50e)
- Commas with nonrestrictive elements (50f)
- Commas with quoted words (50g)
- Commas with other material—transitional expressions, conjunctive adverbs, asides, contrasts, directly addressed words, and tag questions (50h)
- Commas in dates, names, places, addresses, letter format, and numbers (50i)
- Commas to prevent misreadings (50j)

THE OVERRIDING RULE FOR USING COMMAS

If advice in this handbook against using a comma clashes with a rule requiring it, *use the comma.*

- Banff**,** Alberta**,** attracts thousands of tourists each year. [Although the comma after *Alberta* could be wrong because it separates the subject and verb, the comma here is correct because it is required to set off a city–province combination from the rest of the sentence.]

ADDITIONAL TYPES OF COMMA ERRORS

(1) Never put a comma in any number of an address or in page numbers.

- 11263 Dean Drive
- see page 1338

(2) Never put a comma in years expressed in four figures. If the year is expressed in five or more figures, use a space or a comma.

- 1995, 1998, and 2002
- 25 000 B.C.E. *or* 25**,**000 B.C.E.

(3) Never put a comma after *such as.*

NO Canada has developed many small airplanes**, such as,** the de Havilland Otter and Dash 7.

YES Canada has developed many small airplanes**, such as** the de Havilland Otter and Dash 7.

(4) Never put a comma before *than* in a comparison.

NO The Twin Otter did more to open up the Arctic**, than** any other aircraft.

YES The Twin Otter did more to open up the Arctic **than** any other aircraft.

(5) Never put a comma before an opening parenthesis. When a comma is required, put it *after* the closing parenthesis.

NO Because aviation enthralls many of us**, (especially children)** enthusiasts from all over Canada visit the National Aviation Museum.

YES Because aviation enthralls many of us **(especially children),** enthusiasts from all over Canada visit the National Aviation Museum.

(6) Never put a comma after a PREPOSITION.

NO People expected more damage **from,** the high winds.

YES People expected more damage **from** the high winds.

(7) Never put a comma after a SUBORDINATING CONJUNCTION.

NO **Although,** winds exceeded eighty kilometres an hour, little damage occurred.

YES **Although** winds exceeded eighty kilometres an hour, little damage occurred.

(8) Never put a comma between a SUBJECT and its VERB.

NO **Orville and Wilbur Wright, made** their first successful airplane flights in 1903.

YES **Orville and Wilbur Wright made** their first successful airplane flights in 1903.

(9) Never put a comma between a verb and its OBJECT.

NO These inventors enthusiastically **tackled, the problems** of powered flight.

YES These inventors enthusiastically **tackled the problems** of powered flight.

(10) Never put a comma between a verb and its COMPLEMENT.

NO Flying has **become, an important industry** and a popular hobby.

YES Flying has **become an important industry** and a popular hobby.

51 SEMICOLONS

Use a semicolon in only two situations. (1) A semicolon can replace a period between sentences that are closely related in meaning. (2) Use a semicolon to replace a comma when a COORDINATING CONJUNCTION links INDEPENDENT CLAUSES that already contain commas.

51a When can I use a semicolon instead of a period between independent clauses?

You can choose whether to use a semicolon to replace a period between two INDEPENDENT CLAUSES that are closely related in meaning.

- British Columbia has some of the wettest territory in Canad**a;** it also has some of the driest.

ALERT: Do not use a semicolon between a DEPENDENT CLAUSE and an independent clause.

NO **Although summers are hot in the Okanagan Valley;** visitors can ski down surrounding mountain glaciers all year long.

YES **Although summers are hot in the Okanagan Valley,** visitors can ski down surrounding mountain glaciers all year long. !

Also, you can choose to use a semicolon to replace a period between closely related sentences when the second sentence starts with a CONJUNCTIVE ADVERB or a TRANSITIONAL EXPRESSION.

CONJUNCTIVE ADVERB

- The average annual rainfall in the Okanagan Valley is less than 40 cm**; nevertheless,** it lies in the shadow of the rainy Cascade Mountains.

TRANSITIONAL EXPRESSION

- Irrigation came to the semidesert valley in the 1930s**; as a result,** it now produces much of Canada's fruit and wine.

51b When do I need to use a semicolon to replace a comma?

A semicolon needs to replace a comma when you use a COORDINATING CONJUNCTION to link INDEPENDENT CLAUSES that already contain commas.

- A tour operator in British Columbia's interior offers a package that includes skiing, either downhill or cross-country, in the morning**; but** afternoon activities, in contrast, are soccer, tennis, canoeing, and other warm-weather sports.

Also, items in a series can contain commas. In such cases, use a semicolon to separate the comma-containing items so that your reader can more easily understand how you have grouped your material.

- Alexander Mackenzie's overland voyage to the Pacific in 1793 took him through grassy uplands, steep canyons, and tangled swamp**;** into the habitats of the grizzly bear, bald eagle, and sea otter**;** and down rivers that required running rapids, portaging, and even towing his canoe.

ALERT: Do not use a semicolon to introduce a list of items. Use a colon instead (52a).

NO The Mackenzie expedition hunted and traded for fresh food**; venison, trout, and, especially, salmon.**

YES The Mackenzie expedition hunted and traded for fresh food**: venison, trout, and, especially, salmon.**

52 COLONS

52a How do I use a colon with a list, an appositive, or a quotation?

When you introduce a list, an appositive, or a quotation with an INDEPENDENT CLAUSE, use a colon. This rule applies when the words *the following* and *as follows* end an independent clause. In contrast, when the words you use to introduce a list, an appositive, or a quotation form an incomplete sentence, never use a colon. This rule applies after the words *such as, like*, and *including.*

LISTED ITEMS **The students demanded the following:** an expanded menu in the cafeteria, improved janitorial services, and more up-to-date textbooks.

APPOSITIVE **The UBC Museum of Anthropology has one outstanding exhibit:** its collection of Northwest Coast Indian artifacts. [*Collection of . . . artifacts* renames *outstanding exhibit*.]

QUOTATION **The little boy in *E.T.* did say something neat:** "How do you explain school to a higher intelligence?"

—George F. Will, "Well, I Don't Love You, E.T."

ALERT: If an incomplete sentence introduces a direct quotation, use a comma, not a colon (50g). **!**

52b When should I use a colon between sentences?

When a sentence serves as an introduction to a second sentence, you can choose to use a colon between them.

- We will never forget the first time we made dinner at home together: He got food poisoning and was too sick to work for four days.

ALERTS: (1) Never use a colon when a DIRECT OBJECT consists of a series or list of items.

NO We bought: eggs, milk, cheese, and bread.

YES We bought eggs, milk, cheese, and bread.

(2) Never separate a DEPENDENT CLAUSE from an INDEPENDENT CLAUSE with a colon. Use a comma instead.

NO After the drought ended**:** water restrictions were dropped.

YES After the drought ended**,** water restrictions were dropped.

(3) You can choose whether to capitalize the first word of an independent clause following a colon. Be consistent in each piece of writing.!

52c What conventional formats call for colons?

BETWEEN TITLE AND SUBTITLE

- *Literature***:** *An Introduction to Critical Reading*

BETWEEN HOURS AND MINUTES AND MINUTES AND SECONDS

- The runner passed the halfway point at 1**:**23**:**02.

BETWEEN NUMBERS IN RATIOS

- a proportion of 7**:**1
- a 3**:**5 ratio

AFTER WORDS IN MEMO HEADINGS

- To**:** Dean Kristen Joy

  From**:** Professor Daniel Black

  About**:** Student work-study program

AFTER FORMAL LETTER OPENINGS

- Dear Ms. Carter**:**

BETWEEN BIBLE CHAPTERS AND VERSES (APA STYLE ONLY)

- Jeremiah 23**:**1–3

ALERT: In MLA STYLE, as presented in the sixth edition of the *MLA Handbook*, a period takes the place of the colon.!

53 APOSTROPHES

53a How do I use an apostrophe to show that a noun is possessive?

The **possessive case** communicates ownership (*the writer's pen*) or other similar relationships (*the writer's parent*). To indicate possession in NOUNS, you can choose to use *-'s* (*the instructor's comment*), which calls for an apostrophe, or a PHRASE beginning with *of* (*a comment of the instructor*).

Here are some applications of this general rule:

1. Add *-'s* to nouns not ending in *-s*.
   - She felt a **parent's** joy. [*Parent* is a singular noun not ending in *-s*.]
   - They care about their **children's** education. [*Children* is a plural noun not ending in -s.]
2. Add *-'s* to singular nouns ending in *-s*.
   - The **business's** system for handling complaints is inefficient.
   - Lee **Jones's** car insurance is expensive.
3. Add only an apostrophe to plural nouns ending in *-s*.
   - The **boys'** statements were printed in the newspaper.
   - Three **months'** maternity leave is in the **workers'** contract.
4. Add *-'s* to the last word in compound words and phrases.
   - His **mother-in-law's** company makes scuba gear.
5. Add *-'s* to each noun in individual possession.
   - **Olga's and Joanne's** houses are next to each other. [Olga and Joanne each own a house; they do not own the houses jointly.]
6. Add *-'s* to only the last noun in joint or group possession.
   - **Brina and Avram's** house has a screened porch. [Brina and Avram own one house.]

ALERTS: (1) Never use an apostrophe at the end of a nonpossessive noun ending in *-s*.

NO A medical **crisis'** often involves a heart attack.

YES A medical **crisis** often involves a heart attack.

(2) Never use an apostrophe with a nonpossessive plural noun.

NO **Team's** of doctors are researching the effects of cholesterol.

YES **Teams** of doctors are researching the effects of cholesterol.

53b How do I use an apostrophe to show that an indefinite pronoun is possessive?

INDEFINITE PRONOUNS refer to general or nonspecific persons or things: *somebody, anything, no one* (41e). To indicate possession, use *-'s*.

- I would appreciate **someone's** help in studying for the test.
- Are everyone **else's** notes more complete than mine?

53c Do I ever use an apostrophe with *hers, his, its, ours, yours,* and *theirs*?

Do not use an apostrophe with possessive pronouns: *hers, his, its, ours, yours, theirs.* Possessive pronouns already carry possessive meaning.

NO Because cholesterol has been widely publicized, it's role in heart disease is well known.

YES Because cholesterol has been widely publicized, **its** role in heart disease is well known.

ALERT: Never confuse *its,* the possessive pronoun, with the contraction *it's,* which stands for *it is* or *it has*. A similar confusion arises between *you're* and *your; who's* and *whose;* and *they're* and *their*.

53d Do I ever add an apostrophe to a verb that ends in *-s*?

Never add an apostrophe to a VERB that ends in *-s*.

NO Cholesterol **play's** a key role in longevity.

YES Cholesterol **plays** a key role in longevity.

53e How do I use apostrophes in contractions?

In **contractions,** an apostrophe indicates that one or more letters have been omitted: *can't, don't, I'm, isn't, let's, they're, wasn't, weren't, we've, who's, won't,* and *you're*.

- **It's** still snowing. [contraction for *it is*]

In choosing whether to use a contraction or a full form, consider that many instructors and other readers think that common contractions aren't appropriate in academic writing. Check with your instructor before using contractions in your academic writing.

53f Do I use an apostrophe with plurals of letters, numerals, symbols, and terms?

Some writers use *-'s* to form plurals of letters, numerals, symbols, and words used as terms. Others use *s* alone. Either style is acceptable as long as one style is used consistently throughout a piece of writing.

Here are some examples using *-'s*. Note that the **'s** is not italicized.

LETTER PLURALS	Printing ***w*'s** is hard for Billie.
NUMERALS	The address includes six **2's.**
SYMBOLS	A line of **&'s** onscreen may mean the keyboard is jammed.
WORDS USED AS TERMS	All the ***for*'s** were misspelled *four*.

ALERT: When you use letters as letters or words as words, you can choose to underline them, put them in italics, or enclose them in quotation marks (54e). Be consistent in each piece of writing. **!**

54 QUOTATION MARKS

54a How do I use quotation marks with short direct quotations?

Direct quotations are exact words of prose or poetry copied from a written SOURCE, either print or electronic, or transcribed exactly from an audio medium or from life. In MLA STYLE, a **short quotation** of prose runs four or fewer lines in your handwriting or on your word processor. In APA STYLE, a short quotation contains no more than forty words of prose or three lines of poetry. Whenever you write a short quotation, enclose it in quotation marks and run it in with the rest of your sentence.

ALERT: At the end of a short quotation, place the page number or the author's name and the page number in parentheses (if you haven't already mentioned the author's name in the sentence that leads into the quotation). Put the period that ends the sentence *after the parentheses,* not before them. **!**

A **long quotation** needs to be *set off* or *displayed* as a whole block of words; see 54b.

ALERT: Never use quotation marks to enclose INDIRECT QUOTATIONS (54f) or PARAPHRASES (26g).

- The mayor said that she wants to call a meeting. [This indirect quotation needs no quotation marks. As a direct quotation, this sentence would read *The mayor said, "I want to call a meeting."*] **!**

Using double quotation marks (" ")

Double quotation marks are standard. Single quotation marks are used only for quotation marks within quotation marks. (In materials published in Great Britain, this convention is reversed.) Use double quotation marks to enclose a short quotation.

- Edward T. Hall explains the practicality of close conversational distances: **"**If you are interested in something, your pupils dilate: if I say something you don't like, they tend to contract**"** (47). Some cultures prefer arm's length for all but the most intimate conversations.
- As W. H. Auden wittily defined personal space, **"**Some thirty inches from my nose / The frontier of my person goes**"** (539).

ALERTS: (1) When quoting short passages of poetry, use a slash with a space on either side to signal the end of one line and the start of another. (2) Capitalize and punctuate quotations of poetry exactly as in the original. **!**

Using single quotation marks (' ')

If quotation marks occur in short quotations, replace any double quotation marks in the original source with single quotation marks.

ORIGINAL SOURCE

- He has also said that he does not wish to be the arbiter for what is or is not an **"**official**"** intelligence.

—Thomas Hoerr, "The Naturalistic Intelligence"

EXAMPLE FROM A RESEARCH PAPER

- As Thomas Hoerr reports, Gardner "does not wish to be the arbiter for what is or is not an 'official' intelligence."

54b How do I use quotation marks with long direct quotations?

In MLA STYLE, a **long quotation** of prose runs five or more lines in your handwriting or on your word processor. In APA STYLE, a long quotation contains more than forty words of prose or more than three lines of poetry. A long quotation needs to start on a new line and should be indented, or *displayed* as a whole block of words, 2.5 cm/1 inch (one tab) from the left margin (MLA style) or 1.25 cm/0.5 inch from the left margin (APA style).

COMPUTER TIP: To indent the left margin of a long quotation, go to FORMAT> PARAGRAPH> and, in the space for LEFT MARGIN, enter the appropriate width of the indentation. Click OK. At the end of the long quotation, return to the standard margin by following the same route, but entering 0 cm/0″.

Never use quotation marks to enclose indented blocks of prose or poetry. The block indentation signals that the material is a quotation. Of course, if within a long quotation some words in the original are in quotation marks, use them exactly as in the original. In the example below, the words *wrist distance* are in double quotation marks in the original source; they are therefore shown in double quotation marks in the long quotation as well.

- As Desmond Morris explains, personal space varies among cultures:

> When you are talking to someone in the street or in any open space, reach out with your arm and see where the nearest point on his body comes. If you hail from western Europe, you will find that he is at roughly fingertip distance from you. In other words, as you reach out, your fingertips will just about make contact with his shoulder. If you come from eastern Europe you will find you are standing at "wrist distance." If you come from the

```
Mediterranean region you will find that you are
much closer to your companion. (23)
```

ALERT: At the end of a long quotation, place the page number or the author's name and the page number in parentheses (if you haven't already mentioned the author's name in the sentence that leads into the quotation). Put the period that ends the sentence *before the parentheses,* not after them. !

54c How do I use quotation marks to indicate spoken words?

When you quote spoken words (DIRECT DISCOURSE) or want to write dialogue, use quotation marks to enclose the speaker's words. Start a new paragraph—that is, indent the first line—each time the speaker changes.

- "I don't know how you can see to drive," she said.
- "Maybe you should put on your glasses."
- "Putting on my glasses would help you to see?"
- "Not me; you," Macon said. "You're focused on the windshield instead of the road."

—Anne Tyler, *The Accidental Tourist*

When a speaker's words continue for more than one paragraph, use quotation marks at the start of each paragraph but at the end of only the last paragraph of the speech.

ALERT: Do not enclose INDIRECT DISCOURSE in quotation marks.

- The mayor said that he was tired. [In contrast, the direct-discourse version is *The mayor said, "I am tired."*] !

54d How do I use quotation marks with titles?

Use quotation marks around the titles of short published works: poems, short stories, essays, articles from periodicals, pamphlets, brochures, song titles, and individual episodes of a television or radio series. In contrast, use italics (or underlining) for longer works. Box 80 (pages 449–451) shows when to use quotation marks, italics or underlining, or neither.

54e How do I use quotation marks to indicate terms, words in another language, translated words, and irony?

You can choose to use either quotation marks or italics (or underlining) to indicate words that are technical terms, words used as words, words in another language, translated words, and words meant ironically. Be consistent in each piece of writing.

TECHNICAL TERM "Plagiarism"—the unacknowledged use of another person's words or ideas—is a serious offence. Plagiarism by students can result in expulsion. [Once the term has been introduced and (usually) defined, it needs no further quotation marks.]

WORDS USED AS TERMS Many people confuse "affect" and "effect."

TRANSLATED WORDS My grandfather usually ended arguments with *de gustibus non disputandum est,* "there is no arguing about tastes." [If you italicize or underline the words being translated and enclose the translation in quotation marks, your reader's job is easier.]

IRONIC WORD The proposed "reform" is actually a tax increase.

54f When are quotation marks wrong?

Never use quotation marks around CLICHÉS, SLANG, or other language that is inappropriate in academic writing. Revise for accurate, appropriate, fresh wording.

NO They "eat like birds" in public and "stuff their faces" in private.

YES They nibble in public and gorge themselves in private.

Never enclose a word or phrase in quotation marks merely to call attention to it.

NO Remember, the "customer" matters to your business.

YES Remember, the customer matters to your business.

Never enclose indirect quotations or paraphrases in quotation marks.

NO The College Code of Conduct points out that "plagiarism can result in expulsion." [The original words in the Code of Conduct are "Grounds for expulsion include plagiarism."]

YES The College Code of Conduct points out that plagiarism can result in expulsion.

Never use quotation marks around the title of your own paper, whether at the top of the page or on a title page, or if you mention it in the body of your paper. There is one exception: If the title of your paper includes another title, use quotation marks or italics (or underlining), as appropriate, around the other title (Box 80, pages 449–451).

NO "The Elderly in Nursing Homes: A Case Study"

YES The Elderly in Nursing Homes: A Case Study

NO Character Development in Shirley Jackson's The Lottery

YES Character Development in Shirley Jackson's "The Lottery"

54g How do I use quotation marks with other punctuation?

1. Put commas and periods *inside* closing quotation marks.
   - Having enjoyed Katherine Govier's "After the Fire," we were eager to read her longer works.
   - Edward T. Hall coined the word "proxemics."
2. Put colons and semicolons *outside* closing quotation marks.
   - We try to discover "how close is too close": We do not want to invade others' personal space.
   - Anne Agnastos claims that the current job market "offers opportunities that never existed before"; others disagree.
3. Put question marks, exclamation points, and dashes inside or outside closing quotation marks, depending on their function. If a question mark, exclamation point, or dash punctuates the words enclosed in quotation marks, put it inside the closing quotation mark.
   - "Did I Hear You Call My Name?" was the winning song.
   - They shouted, "We won the lottery!"

If a question mark, exclamation point, or dash punctuates words that are not enclosed in quotation marks, put it outside the closing quotation marks.

- Have you read Irving Layton's poem "The Birth of Tragedy"?
- Edward T. Hall's coined word "proxemics"—a term that refers to proximity—can now be found in the dictionary.

55 PERIODS, QUESTION MARKS, AND EXCLAMATION POINTS

55a When should I use a period?

A period is correct after a statement, a mild command, or an **indirect question,** which reports a question that someone has asked. An indirect question never uses quotation marks. (For punctuation of a direct question, see 55b. For periods in abbreviations, see Chapter 60.)

STATEMENT	Mountain climbers enjoy the outdoors**.**
MILD COMMAND	Pack warm clothes for the climb**.**
INDIRECT QUESTION	I asked whether they wanted to climb Mt. Everest**.**

55b When should I use a question mark?

A question mark is correct after a **direct question** (which asks a question outright), a directly quoted question, a series of questions, or a polite request. A **directly quoted question** calls for quotation marks and ends with a question mark *inside* the quotation marks. (For help in punctuating an indirect question, see 55a.) Questions in a series can be either complete or incomplete sentences. Whichever type of sentence the questions in the series are, use a question mark after each.

ALERT: When questions in a series are incomplete sentences, you can choose whether to capitalize the first letter of each. Whatever your choice, be consistent in each piece of writing. **!**

DIRECT QUESTION	Have you ever wanted to climb Mt. Everest**?**
DIRECTLY QUOTED QUESTION	I asked, "Do you want to climb Mt. Everest**?"**
SERIES OF QUESTIONS WITH CAPITALS	The mountain climbers debated what to do: **T**urn back**? M**ove on**? R**est**?**
SERIES OF QUESTIONS LOWER CASE	The mountain climbers debated what to do: **t**urn back**? m**ove on**? r**est**?**

To end a **polite request,** you can choose between a question mark and a period.

- Would you please send me the report**?** [This version emphasizes the request more than the politeness.]
- Would you please send the report**.** [This version emphasizes the politeness more than the request.]

To communicate irony or sarcasm, use words, not a question mark in parentheses.

NO Having altitude sickness is a pleasant **(?)** experience.

YES Having altitude sickness is as pleasant as having a terrible case of the flu.

55c When should I use an exclamation point?

An exclamation point is correct after a strong command (*Look out!*); an emphatic declaration (*Those cars are going to crash!*); or an **interjection,** a word that conveys surprise or other emotion (*Oh! You're afraid of heights.*). Avoid overusing exclamation points in your academic writing. Reserve them for dialogue. Otherwise, use words that have enough impact to communicate a strong message.

NO Each day in Nepal, we tried to see Mt. Everest. Each day we failed**!** The summit remained shrouded**!** Clouds defeated us**!**

YES Each day in Nepal, we tried to see Mt. Everest. Each day we failed**.** The summit remained shrouded**.** Clouds defeated us**!**

To communicate amazement or sarcasm, use words, not an exclamation point in parentheses.

NO At 8882 metres (!), Mt. Everest is the world's highest mountain.

YES At a staggering 8882 metres, Mt. Everest is the world's highest mountain.

56 OTHER PUNCTUATION MARKS

56a When should I use a dash?

Dashes let you interrupt a sentence's structure to add information. They can also add a little suspense if the meaning calls for it. Use dashes sparingly so that you do not dilute their effect by overexposure.

COMPUTER TIP: You create a dash on a computer by typing two hyphens with no space before, between, or after them. In some word-processing software, the two hyphens automatically turn into one unbroken line to form a dash, but only when you type a word after the hyphens and hit the space bar on your keyboard.

You can use a dash to add information such as examples, definitions, APPOSITIVES, contrasts, and asides. Sometimes parentheses (56b) serve the same purposes, but while dashes tend to emphasize material, parentheses typically speak in a quieter voice.

- Two of the strongest animals in the jungle are vegetarians—the elephant and the gorilla. [examples]

  —Dick Gregory, *The Shadow That Scares Me*

- Although the emphasis at the school was mainly language—speaking, reading, writing—the lessons always began with an exercise in politeness. [definition]

  —Elizabeth Wong, *Fifth Chinese Daughter*

- And what of our national heroine—Laura Secord—our Paul Revere in drag? [appositive]

  —Barry Callaghan, *Canadian Wry*

- Tampering with time brought most of the house tumbling down, and it was this that made Einstein's work so important—and controversial. [contrast]

—Banesh Hoffmann, "My Friend, Albert Einstein"

- As I observed all this and felt its effects on my daily life—and received wounds from my struggle to be a part of it—another part of me itched to make a record of what I was seeing. [aside]

—Sharon Butala, *Rural Saskatchewan: Creating the Garden*

ALERTS: (1) If the words within a pair of dashes are a complete sentence and call for a question mark or an exclamation point, place that punctuation *before* the second dash: *A first love—do you remember?—stays in the memory forever.* (2) Do not use commas, semicolons, or periods next to dashes. Revise to avoid such double punctuation. !

56b When should I use parentheses?

Like dashes (56a), **parentheses** let you interrupt a sentence's structure to add information. Parentheses tend to de-emphasize whatever they enclose; dashes tend to call attention to whatever they set off.

Using parentheses to add information

Parentheses can enclose the same kind of material that dashes can, such as explanations, definitions, examples, contrasts, and asides.

- In division (also known as partition) a subject commonly thought of as a single unit is reduced to its separate parts.

—David Skwire, *Writing with a Thesis*

- Though other cities (Dresden, for instance) had been utterly destroyed in World War II, never before had a single weapon been responsible for such destruction.

—Lawrence Behrens and Leonard J. Rosen, *Writing and Reading Across the Curriculum*

- The sheer decibel level of the noise around us is not enough to make us cranky, irritable, or aggressive. (It can, however, affect our mental and physical health, which is another matter.)

—Carol Tavris, *Anger: The Misunderstood Emotion*

Using parentheses to enclose numbers or letters

Conventional uses of parentheses include enclosing numbers or letters of listed items: *The topics to be discussed are (1) membership, (2) fund-raising, (3) networking, and (4) special events.* Another conventional use occurs in business writing, when parentheses sometimes enclose a numeric version of a spelled-out number: *The order of fifteen (15) cartons was shipped yesterday.*

Using parentheses with other punctuation

Never put a comma *before* an opening parenthesis, even if what precedes the parenthetical material requires a comma; put the comma *after* the closing parenthesis.

NO Although different from the first film we watched**, (***The Wizard of Oz***)** *Kamouraska* is also worth studying.

YES Although different from the first film we watched **(***The Wizard of Oz***),** *Kamouraska* is also worth studying.

A parenthetical sentence meant to stand alone starts with a capital and ends with a period (or question mark or exclamation point) inside the closing parenthesis.

When a complete sentence in parentheses occurs within another sentence, do not use a period to signal the end of the parenthetical sentence. Do, however, use a question mark or exclamation point if either is called for. (Capitalize the first word only if it is a PROPER NOUN.)

NO Searching for his car keys **(He** had left them in the kitchen**.)** wasted an hour.

YES Searching for his car keys **(he** had left them in the kitchen**)** wasted an hour.

YES Searching for his keys **(why** can't he learn to put them in the same place all the time**?)** wasted an hour.

YES Searching for his car keys wasted an hour. **(He** had left them in the kitchen**.)**

56c When should I use brackets?

Brackets enclose words that a writer inserts into quotations. As a writer, you use such brackets

- to fit the wording of the quotation into the structure of your own sentence

- to enclose explanatory words within quoted material to help your reader understand the quotation

ORIGINAL SOURCE

- Ordinarily there is a balance between emotional and rational minds, with emotion feeding into and informing the operations of the rational mind.

—Daniel Goleman, *Emotional Intelligence,* p. 9

QUOTATION

- Goleman asserts that "emotion [feeds] into and [informs] the operations of the rational mind" (9).

Use brackets to enclose explanatory words within quoted material to help your reader understand the quotation.

ORIGINAL SOURCE

- For a variety of reasons, the system attempts to maintain stability and resist temporal change.

—Peter Bonner, "Travel Rhythms," *Sky Magazine,* p. 72

SOURCE IN A QUOTATION

- In "Travel Rhythms," Bonner explains that "**maintain[ing]** stability and **resist[ing]** temporal change" are natural goals for human beings. [Brackets are used to fit the quotation's wording into the rest of the sentence structure.]

SOURCE IN A QUOTATION

- Bonner says that a "system [undergoing large and sudden time shifts] attempts to maintain stability and resist temporal change" (72). [Brackets are used for explanatory words added by the writer, not the original author.]

ALERT: The bracketed term [*sic*] means you have found a mistake in something you want to quote—a wrong date, perhaps, or an error of fact. You cannot change the wording in the original source; adding [*sic*] says to a reader, "It is this way in the original." In MLA STYLE, use regular (roman) type, not italics or underlining, for the term. In APA STYLE, underline or italicize the word *sic* but not the brackets. !

56d When should I use ellipses?

An **ellipsis** is a set of three spaced periods. Its most important function is to show that a quotation omits some of the original writer's words. This rule applies only when you're quoting more than an isolated word or short phrase from the original source; quoted words and phrases are simply enclosed in quotation marks.

Using ellipses in prose quotations

MLA STYLE (as of the sixth edition [2003] of the *MLA Handbook for Writers of Research Papers*)—in most instances—and APA STYLE use three spaced periods *without brackets* for an ellipsis. The fifth edition of the APA *Publication Manual* makes the following recommendations, which match the recommendations of MLA style:

1. Use an ellipsis to replace words you omit from the middle of a sentence of quoted material.
2. Never use an ellipsis to signal words you have omitted from the start or the end of a sentence unless you need to call attention to the fact that the quoted words come from the middle of a sentence.
3. Add a fourth period to the ellipsis in two cases: (a) to stand for sentence-ending punctuation, and (b) to indicate the omission of one or more sentences from the quotation.

ORIGINAL For over a century twins have been used to study how genes make people what they are. Because they share precisely the same genes but live in different surroundings under different influences, identical twins reared apart are helping science sort out which qualities of body and mind are shaped by our genes and which by upbringing. Researchers needn't worry about running out of subjects: according to the Twins Foundation, there are approximately 4.5 million twin individuals in the United States alone, and about 70,000 more are born each year.

—Sharon Begley, "Twins," p. 84

ELLIPSES WITHOUT SQUARE BRACKETS

- Begley says, "Because they share precisely the same genes . . . , identical twins reared apart are helping science sort out which qualities of body and mind are shaped by our genes and which by upbringing" (p. 84). [words within quoted sentence omitted]

- Begley says, "Because they share precisely the same genes but live in different surroundings under different influences, identical twins reared apart are helping science." (p. 84). [last words of quoted sentence omitted, but no ellipsis is used]
- Begley says, "Because they share precisely the same genes but live in different surroundings under different influences, identical twins reared apart are helping science . . ." (p. 84). [last words of quoted sentence omitted; ellipsis is used to call attention to omission]
- Begley says, "For over a century twins have been used to study how genes make people what they are. . . . Researchers needn't worry about running out of subjects" (p. 84). [The sentence-ending period is followed by three spaced periods.]

MLA distinguishes between (1) an ellipsis that signals the words you omit *from* the quoted material and (2) an ellipsis that appears in the original source. If an ellipsis appears in the original source, and if you omit words from that material when you quote it, use three spaced periods in square brackets [. . .] to create your ellipsis. Leave one space before the opening bracket and after the closing bracket. Don't put an ellipsis that appears in the original source in brackets. Never split an ellipsis between the end of a line and the beginning of the next. Never put other punctuation inside the brackets.

The sixth edition of the *MLA Handbook* (2003) notes that some instructors ask for brackets around all ellipses that signal words omitted from quoted material. (This was the recommendation of the fifth edition of the *MLA Handbook*.) Ask your instructor for his or her preference.

ELLIPSES INSIDE SQUARE BRACKETS

- Begley says, "Because they share precisely the same genes but live in different surroundings under different influences, identical twins reared apart are helping science [. . .]" (84). [last words of quoted sentence omitted]
- Begley says, "For over a century twins have been used to study how genes make people what they are. [. . .] Researchers needn't worry about running out of subjects" (84). [Even if more than one sentence is omitted, use three spaced periods within square brackets.]

Using ellipsis in quotations from poetry

In MLA STYLE and APA STYLE, show omissions from short quotations of poetry—that is, quotations of three lines or less—with an ellipsis. To show an omission of one or more lines from a long quotation of poetry, use a full line of spaced periods. For an omission of less than a line, use an ellipsis. As with prose quotations, MLA style specifies that if the original source contains ellipses, you should enclose your own ellipses in brackets. Ask if your instructor prefers you to enclose every ellipsis and line of spaced periods that you insert in brackets. The sixth edition of the *MLA Handbook* permits this style as well.

ORIGINAL SOURCE

- Fear no more the heat o' the sun

  Nor the furious winter's rages;

  Though thy worldly task has done,

  Home art gone, and ta'en thy wages;

  Golden lads and girls all must,

  As chimney-sweepers, come to dust.

—William Shakespeare, from *Cymbeline*

ELLIPSES WITHOUT SQUARE BRACKETS

- Ultimately, however, as Shakespeare reminds us, "Golden lads and girls all must **. . .** come to dust. [short quotation with a few words omitted]
- Fear no more the heat o' the sun

  Nor the furious winter's rages;

  . . . .

  Golden lads and girls all must,

  . . . come to dust. [long quotation with lines and words omitted]

ELLIPSES INSIDE SQUARE BRACKETS

- Ultimately, however, as Shakespeare reminds us, "Golden lads and girls all must **[. . .]** come to dust. [short quotation with a few words omitted]

- Fear no more the heat o' the sun

  Nor the furious winter's rages;

  [...........................]

  Golden lads and girls all must,

  [. . .] come to dust. [long quotation with lines and words omitted]

56e When should I use a slash?

When quoting three or fewer lines of poetry, use a slash to divide one line from the next. Leave a space on each side of the slash.

- Consider the beginning of Anne Sexton's poem "Words": "Be careful of words, / even the miraculous ones."

To type numerical fractions that don't appear on your keyboard, use the slash to separate the numerator and denominator, leaving no space before or after the slash.

- 1/16
- 1 2/3

Avoid word combinations like *and/or* when writing in the humanities. In academic disciplines in which the use of word combinations is acceptable, separate the words with a slash, leaving no space before or after it.

57 HYPHENS

57a When can I hyphenate at the end of a line?

When you use a word-processing program, set the default to allow no hyphenation. If you write by hand, follow the rules in Box 75.

57b When should I hyphenate prefixes and suffixes?

Prefixes and **suffixes** are syllables attached to words, prefixes at the beginning and suffixes at the end. Some prefixes and suffixes are hyphenated; others are not (see Box 76).

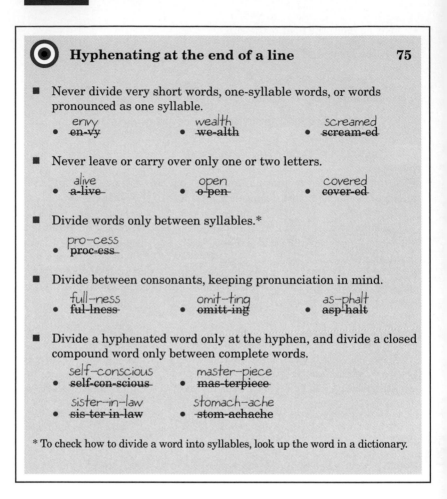

Hyphenating at the end of a line 75

- Never divide very short words, one-syllable words, or words pronounced as one syllable.
  - envy ~~en-vy~~
  - wealth ~~we-alth~~
  - screamed ~~scream-ed~~
- Never leave or carry over only one or two letters.
  - alive ~~a-live~~
  - open ~~o-pen~~
  - covered ~~cover-ed~~
- Divide words only between syllables.*
  - pro-cess ~~proc-ess~~
- Divide between consonants, keeping pronunciation in mind.
  - full-ness ~~ful-lness~~
  - omit-ting ~~omitt-ing~~
  - as-phalt ~~asp-halt~~
- Divide a hyphenated word only at the hyphen, and divide a closed compound word only between complete words.
  - self-conscious ~~self-con-scious~~
  - master-piece ~~mas-terpiece~~
  - sister-in-law ~~sis-ter-in-law~~
  - stomach-ache ~~stom-achache~~

* To check how to divide a word into syllables, look up the word in a dictionary.

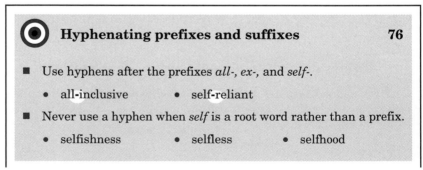

Hyphenating prefixes and suffixes 76

- Use hyphens after the prefixes *all-*, *ex-*, and *self-*.
  - all-inclusive
  - self-reliant
- Never use a hyphen when *self* is a root word rather than a prefix.
  - selfishness
  - selfless
  - selfhood

→

Hyphenating prefixes and suffixes ***(continued)***

- Use a hyphen to avoid a distracting string of repeated letters.
  - anti-intellectual
  - bell-like
- Use a hyphen between a prefix and the first word of a compound word.
  - anti-gun control
- Use a hyphen to prevent confusion in meaning or pronunciation.
  - re-dress ("dress again")
  - un-ionize ("remove the ions")
  - redress ("set right")
  - unionize ("form a union")
- Use a hyphen when two or more prefixes apply to one root word.
  - two-, three-, or four-year program
  - pre- and postwar eras
- Use a hyphen before the suffix *-elect*.
  - president-elect
- Use a hyphen when a prefix comes before a number or before a word that starts with a capital letter.
  - post-1950
  - pro-American

57c When should I hyphenate compound words?

A **compound word**—two or more words combined to express one concept—can be written in one of three ways: as separate words (*night shift*), as hyphenated words (*tractor-trailer*), or as one word (*handbook*). Follow the rules in Box 77.

57d When should I hyphenate spelled-out numbers?

For information about when to use numerals and when to spell out numbers, see Chapter 61.

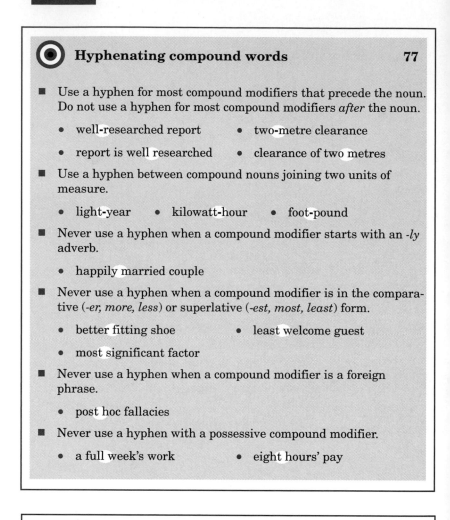

Hyphenating compound words 77

- Use a hyphen for most compound modifiers that precede the noun. Do not use a hyphen for most compound modifiers *after* the noun.
  - well-researched report
  - two-metre clearance
  - report is well researched
  - clearance of two metres
- Use a hyphen between compound nouns joining two units of measure.
  - light-year
  - kilowatt-hour
  - foot-pound
- Never use a hyphen when a compound modifier starts with an *-ly* adverb.
  - happily married couple
- Never use a hyphen when a compound modifier is in the comparative (*-er, more, less*) or superlative (*-est, most, least*) form.
  - better fitting shoe
  - least welcome guest
  - most significant factor
- Never use a hyphen when a compound modifier is a foreign phrase.
  - post hoc fallacies
- Never use a hyphen with a possessive compound modifier.
  - a full week's work
  - eight hours' pay

Hyphenating spelled-out numbers 78

- Use a hyphen between two-word numbers from twenty-one through ninety-nine.
  - thirty-five
  - two hundred thirty-five

→

Hyphenating spelled-out numbers (continued)

- Use a hyphen in a compound modifier formed from a number and a word.
  - fifty-minute class [*also* 50-minute class]
  - three-to-one odds [*also* 3-to-1 odds]
- Use a hyphen between the numerator and the denominator of a two-word fraction.
  - one-half • two-fifths • seven-tenths

ALERT: Use numerals for any fraction that requires more than two words. If you cannot avoid spelling out a fraction that has three or more words, do this: (1) Use a hyphen between all words in the numerator. (2) Use a hyphen between all words in the denominator. (3) Use a space (no hyphen!) to separate the numerator from the denominator. For example: *2/100* in words is *two one-hundredths,* and *33/10 000* is *thirty-three ten-thousandths.* **!**

58 CAPITALS

Sections 58a–c explain when to use capital as opposed to lower-case letters. For more examples, see Box 79 on pages 445–448.

58a When should I capitalize a "first" word?

1. Capitalize the first word in a sentence.
   - **T**wo metres of snow fell last winter.
2. If you wish, capitalize the first word of a complete sentence after a colon. When a complete sentence follows a colon, you can begin the first word with a capital or a lower-case letter, but be consistent in each piece of writing. When the words after a colon are not a complete sentence, do not capitalize.
   - Only one solution occurred to her**: S**he picked up the ice cream and pushed it back into the cone.
   - Only one solution occurred to her**: s**he picked up the ice cream and pushed it back into the cone.

- She bought four pints of ice cream: **v**anilla, chocolate, strawberry, and butterscotch swirl.

3. If you wish, capitalize the first word in a series of questions. When questions in a series are *not* complete sentences, you can begin the first word of each question with either a capital or a lower-case letter. Be consistent within each piece of writing.

   - What facial feature would most people like to change? **E**yes? **E**ars? **N**ose?
   - What facial feature would most people like to change? **e**yes? **e**ars? **n**ose?

4. Capitalize the first word in a list of items that are complete sentences.

   - Three problems caused the shortage: (1) **B**ad weather delayed delivery. (2) **P**oor scheduling created slowdowns. (3) **I**nadequate maintenance caused equipment breakdowns.

   Never capitalize listed items that are not complete sentences:

   - The delays resulted from (1) **b**ad weather, (2) **p**oor scheduling, and (3) **e**quipment breakdowns.

5. Capitalize the first word of a complete sentence that stands alone inside parentheses. A complete sentence enclosed in parentheses may stand alone or fall within another sentence. A sentence that stands alone starts with a capital letter and ends with a period, a question mark, or an exclamation point.

   A complete sentence in parentheses that falls within another sentence does not start with a capital letter and does not end with a period. However, if the parenthetical sentence is a question, end it with a question mark; if it is an exclamation, end it with an exclamation point.

   - You may have to line the section of river between the Mazinaw Lake Dam and Marble Lake when water levels are low. (**L**ining is guiding the canoe along from shore with ropes tied to bow and stern.) To the right, a 150-metre portage works around the worst of this shallow stretch.
   - After turning off Highway 38 onto Perth Road, north of Kingston, and picking up our vehicle permit at the park office trail centre (**b**ooking a reservation for this route is strongly recommended), we drove down bumpy Salmon Road to the designated launch site.

     —Kevin Callan, *Up the Creek*

58b How should I capitalize quotations?

Capitalize the first word in a quotation.

- Encouraging students to study in other countries, Mme Paquette says, "**Y**ou will absorb a good accent with the food."

When you interrupt quoted words, do not capitalize the continued part of the quoted words.

- "You will absorb a good accent," says Mme Paquette, "**w**ith the food."

If quoted words are part of your own sentence, never capitalize the first quoted word unless it is a PROPER NOUN. A phrase such as *writes that, thinks that,* or *says that* usually signals this kind of integrated quotation.

- Mme Paquette believes that "**y**ou will absorb a good accent with the food" if you study in another country.

If you are quoting poetry, capitalize the way the original is capitalized. (For more information on quotations, see Chapter 54.)

58c When should I capitalize nouns and adjectives?

Capitalize PROPER NOUNS (*Mexico, Arthur*) and PROPER ADJECTIVES (*a Mexican diplomat, the Arthurian legend*). Certain COMMON NOUNS are capitalized when specific names or titles are added to them: *We visit a lake every summer. This summer we went to Lake Ontario.*

ALERTS: (1) Do not capitalize DETERMINERS and other words just because they accompany proper nouns or proper adjectives: *Here is an American penny* [not *An American penny*]. (2) Be aware that some proper nouns and proper adjectives become so common they lose their capital letters: *french fries, italics, pasteurized.* **!**

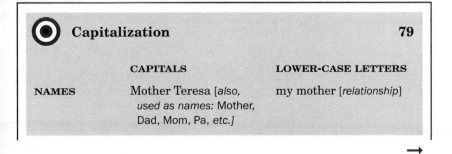

Capitalization 79

	CAPITALS	LOWER-CASE LETTERS
NAMES	Mother Teresa [*also, used as names:* Mother, Dad, Mom, Pa, *etc.]*	my mother [*relationship*]

→

Capitalization ***(continued)***

	CAPITALS	LOWER-CASE LETTERS
NAMES	Doctor Who	the doctor [*role*]
TITLES	Prime Minister Campbell	a prime minister
	the Prime Minister [*now in office*]	
	Liberal [*a party member*]	liberal [*a believer in liberal ideals*]
	Member of Parliament Sheila Copps	a member of Parliament [*also* an MP]
	The Honourable Mr. Justice John Sopinka	the judge
	Queen Elizabeth II	the queen [*also* the Queen, *referring to Canada's queen*]
GROUPS OF HUMANITY	Caucasian [*race*]	white [*also* White]
	Native Canadian [*ethnic group*]	
	Jew, Catholic, Protestant, Buddhist [*religious affiliation*]	
ORGANIZATIONS	Parliament	parliamentary
	the Supreme Court of Canada	the court [*also* the Court]
	the Progressive Conservative Party	the party
	the Canadian Broadcasting Corporation	the corporation
PLACES	Whitehorse	the city
	the West [*a region*]	turn west [*a direction*]
	King Street	the street
	Atlantic Ocean [*also* the Atlantic]	the ocean
	the Rocky Mountains	the mountains

→

Capitalization ***(continued)***

	CAPITALS	LOWER-CASE LETTERS
BUILDINGS	the House of Commons	the legislature [*but* the House, the Commons]
	Pauline Johnson High School	the high school
	China West Café	the restaurant
	St. Peter's Hospital	the hospital
SCIENTIFIC TERMS	Earth [*the planet*]	the earth [*where we live*]
	the Milky Way	the galaxy
		the moon, the sun
	Streptococcus aureus	a streptococcal infection
	Gresham's law	the theory of relativity
LANGUAGES, NATIONALITIES	Spanish	
	Chinese	
SCHOOL COURSES	Chemistry 342	a chemistry course
	Introduction to Photography	my photography class
NAMES OF THINGS	the *Calgary Herald*	the newspaper
	Canadian Living	the magazine
	Lakehead University	the university
	the Dodge Colt	the car
TIMES AND SEASONS	Friday	spring, summer, fall, autumn, winter
	August	
HOLIDAYS	New Year's Day	a new year
	Passover	a festival, a holy day, a holiday
	Ramadan	
HISTORICAL PERIODS	World War II	the war
	the Great Depression [*in the 1930s*]	the depression [*any economic depression*]
	the Reformation	an era, an age
		the eighteenth century
		fifth-century manuscripts

→

Capitalization *(continued)*

	CAPITALS		LOWER-CASE LETTERS
RELIGIOUS TERMS	God Buddhism the Torah the Koran the Bible		a god, a goddess a religion
LETTER PARTS	Dear Ms. Tauber: Sincerely, Yours truly,		
TITLES OF PUBLISHED AND RELEASED MATERIAL	"The Painted Door" *The Canadian Encyclopedia* *Under These Rocks and Stones*		[Capitalize the first letter of the first word and all other words except ARTICLES, short PREPOSITIONS, and short CONJUNCTIONS]
COMPOUND WORDS	post-Victorian Indo-European		
ACRONYMS AND INITIALISMS	NATO DNA NAFTA	NFB ACTRA CD	
COMPUTER TERMS	Microsoft Word DOS WordPerfect World Wide Web, the Web the Internet		[Capitalize software names as shown in the program documentation. Do not italicize (or underline) these names or enclose them in quotation marks.]
	Web site, Web page Netscape		a home page, a link a browser

59 ITALICS (UNDERLINING)

Most printed material is set in **roman type**. Type that slants to the right is called **italic type**. If your word-processing program does not have italic type, use the underline function. Italics and underlining mean the same thing.

HANDWRITTEN AND UNDERLINED

Great Expectations

TYPED AND UNDERLINED

Great Expectations

ITALIC TYPE

Great Expectations

59a How should I choose between italics and quotation marks?

Generally, use italics for titles of long works or works that contain subsections. Use quotation marks for titles of shorter works or for titles of subsections within a larger work.

Italics, quotation marks, or nothing 80

TITLES

ITALICIZE	DO NOT ITALICIZE
The Englishman's Boy [a novel]	your own paper's title
Farther West [a play]	
Who Do You Think You Are? [a collection of short stories]	"Royal Beatings" [one story in the collection]
Simon & Schuster Handbook for Writers [a book]	"Writing Research" [one chapter in the book]

→

Italics, quotation marks, or nothing *(continued)*

TITLES

ITALICIZE	DO NOT ITALICIZE
Active Voice: An Anthology of Canadian, American and Commonwealth Prose [a collection of essays]	"The Calgary Stampede" [one essay in the collection]
The Iliad [a long poem]	"Ark Anatomical" [a short poem]
The Lotus Eaters [a film]	
Equinox [a magazine]	"Nanook Passage" [an article in the magazine]
The Barber of Seville [title of an opera]	Concerto in B-flat Minor [identification of a musical work by form, number, and key. Use neither quotation marks nor italics (underlining).]
Symphonie Fantastique [title of a long musical work]	
The Road to Avonlea [a television series]	"After the Honeymoon" [an episode of a television series]
The Visit [a record album, tape, or CD]	"Greensleeves" [a song or a single selection on an album, a tape, or a CD]
	Lotus 1-2-3 [software program names are neither italicized nor enclosed in quotation marks]

the *Brandon Sun* [a newspaper. Note: Even if *The* is part of the title printed on a newspaper, do not use a capital letter and do not italicize (or underline) it in your writing. In MLA and CM documentation, omit the word *The*. In APA and CBE documentation, keep *The*.]

→

Italics, quotation marks, or nothing *(continued)*

OTHER WORDS

ITALICIZE	DO NOT ITALICIZE
the *Haida* [a ship; don't italicize preceding initials like U.S.S. or H.M.S.]	destroyer [a general class of ship]
Voyager 2 [names of specific aircraft, spacecraft, and satellites]	Boeing 747 [general names shared by classes of aircraft, spacecraft, and satellites]
summa cum laude [term in a language other than English]	burrito, chutzpah [widely used and commonly understood words from languages other than English]
What does *our* imply? [a word referred to as such]	
the *abc*'s; confusing *3*'s and *8*'s [letters and numbers referred to as themselves]	

59b When should I use italics for emphasis?

Use italics or underlining sparingly for emphasis. Your choice of words and sentence structure normally conveys the emphasis you want to give:

- The pain from my injury was severe.
- The pain from my injury was so severe that I could not breathe. [a more effective description]

60 ABBREVIATIONS

The guidelines in this chapter apply to general writing and writing in the humanities. If you're in doubt about a particular abbreviation, check your college dictionary for correct capitalization, spacing, and use of periods.

ALERTS: (1) When the period of an abbreviation falls at the end of a sentence, it serves also as a sentence-ending period. (2) When a question mark or exclamation point ends a sentence, place it after the abbreviation's period. !

60a What abbreviations can I use with times and amounts?

Use the abbreviations *a.m.* (or *A.M.*) and *p.m.* (or *P.M.*) with exact times. You can use capital or lower-case letters for *a.m.* and *p.m.* as long as you are consistent in each piece of writing.

- 7:15 a.m.
- 3:47 p.m.
- 7:15 A.M.
- 3:47 P.M.

Use *A.D.* before the year; its equivalent *C.E.* for "common era" and *B.C.* (or *B.C.E.* for "before the common era") follow the year.

- A.D. 934
- 1200 B.C.
- 934 C.E.
- 1200 B.C.E.

As a rule, avoid symbols in your writing for classes in the humanities. However, let common sense and a concern for clarity guide you. If you mention temperatures once or twice in a paper, spell them out: *thirty degrees, minus twenty-six degrees.* But if you mention temperatures throughout, use numbers and symbols: *30°, −26°.*

In tables, you can abbreviate amounts and measurements when they are used with exact numbers (such as *in., cm, km, lb., kg*) as well as days and months (such as *Mon., Jan., Aug.*). Many writers abbreviate SI units in almost any context, but if you spell out a number, you should write out any unit that accompanies it: *6 km* but *six kilometres*.

Use *$* with exact dollar-and-cent amounts expressed in numerals or numerals and words.

- $4.95
- $34 million

60b How should I use abbreviations with people's names?

The abbreviations *Mr., Mrs., Ms.,* and *Dr.* can be used with either full names or last names only.

- Dr. Anna Freud
- Mr. Daljit Singh
- Dr. Freud
- Mr. Singh

Most other abbreviated titles must be used with a full name; when you want to use these titles with a last name only, do not abbreviate them.

FULL NAME	**LAST NAME ONLY**
Rev. Kim Allen	Reverend Allen

Abbreviations of professional and academic degrees follow the person's name.

- Betty Sun, M.D.
- Seth Reichlin, Ph.D.
- Bruce Freund, D.D.S.

Never use both a title of address before a name and an abbreviated degree after a name: *Betty Sun,* ***M.D.*** or ***Dr.*** *Betty Sun* (not *Dr. Betty Sun, M.D.*)

Abbreviations indicating family generations, such as *Jr., Sr.,* and *III,* are considered part of the names they follow, so they can be used with other abbreviations.

- Mr. Kenneth Huizinga, Jr.
- Roy J. Modugno Sr., D.D.S.

ALERTS: (1) Use a comma between a name and most abbreviations following it. Some people omit the comma for the generation designation *II, III,* and so on (*Fred D. Fumia II*) but not for *Jr.* and *Sr.* (*Andrew Watson, Jr.*). (2) Separate abbreviations following a name with a comma: *Fred D. Fumia II, M.D.*

60c When can I abbreviate names of countries, organizations, and government agencies?

In general, do not abbreviate the names of countries. The abbreviation *U.S.* (or *US*) can be used as an ADJECTIVE form for *United States* (*the U.S. ski team*) but not as a NOUN: *The United States* [not *The U.S.*] *has many different climates.* The same rule applies with *U.K.* (or *UK*) and *United Kingdom.*

If you refer to an organization throughout your paper and want to use its abbreviation, spell out the full name when you first use it, and put the abbreviation in parentheses. Thereafter, you can use the abbreviation alone.

- Spain voted to continue as a member of the **North Atlantic Treaty Organization (NATO),** to the surprise of other **NATO** members.

60d What abbreviations can I use in addresses?

In addressing correspondence, you can use abbreviations such as *St., Ave., Blvd., Apt., NE,* and *SW*. Use the two-letter postal abbreviations for provinces and territories to address envelopes.

If you include a full address—street, city, province, and postal code—in the body of your writing, you can abbreviate the province name. Both two-letter postal abbreviations and traditional abbreviations (e.g., *Alta.*) are used in writing in Canada. Spell out any other combination of a city and a province, and spell out the name of a province by itself.

- I wrote to Mr. U. Lern, 10-01 Rule Road, **Mississauga, ON L5A 2Z2** for the instruction manual. He had moved to **Edmonton, Alberta,** before my letter arrived.

ALERT: When you use a city-province combination within a sentence, place a comma before *and* after the province:

- The town of **Midale, Saskatchewan,** recorded the highest temperature ever in Canada.

60e When can I use *etc.* and other Latin abbreviations?

The abbreviation *etc.* is from the Latin *et cetera,* which means "and the rest." Do not use *etc.* in the body of a paper you are writing in the humanities. Acceptable substitutes are *and the like, and so on,* and *and so forth.*

61 NUMBERS

61a When should I spell numbers out in words?

When writing in the humanities, if a number can be expressed in one or two words, use words. If, however, numbers occur frequently in your paper, spell out *one* through *nine* and use numerals for all others.

- Between them, the two families own 126 sheep and 493 chickens.

ALERT: When you use two-word numbers from *twenty-one* through *ninety-nine,* use a hyphen between the words that make up any one number. **!**

If a sentence starts with a number, spell it out; do not use a numeral. In practice, however, you can usually revise the sentence so that the number does not come first.

- **Three hundred seventy-five dollars** per credit is the tuition rate for nonresidents.
- The tuition rate for nonresidents is **$375** per credit.

Do not mix spelled-out numbers and numerals when they refer to the same thing. In the following example, all numbers referring to volunteers should be numerals, and *four* should be spelled out because it refers to a different quantity—days.

- In the past ~~4~~ four days, our volunteers increased from ~~five~~ 5 to ~~eight~~ 8 to ~~seventeen~~ 17 to 233. On Saturday, ~~thirty-seven~~ 37 people who usually volunteer on weekdays joined the usual Saturday staff of ~~forty-one~~ 41 volunteers.

61b How should I write dates, addresses, times, and other numbers?

Using numbers 81

DATES	August 6, 1941; 1732–1845; 34 B.C. to A.D. 230
ADDRESSES	10 Downing Street 237 North 8th Street London, ON N6A 3K7
TIMES	8:09 A.M.; 6:00 p.m.; six o'clock, *not* 6 o'clock; four in the afternoon [*or* 4 p.m.], *not* four p.m.
DECIMALS AND FRACTIONS	5.55; 98.6; 3.1416; 7/8; 12 1/4; three quarters, *not* 3 quarters; one-half

→

Using numbers *(continued)*

CHAPTERS AND PAGES	Chapter 27, page 245; p. 475; pp. 660–62
SCORES AND STATISTICS	a 6–0 score; a 5 to 3 ratio *or* a 5:3 ratio; 29 percent
IDENTIFICATION NUMBERS	94.4 on the FM dial; call 1-416-555-1234
MEASUREMENTS	2 cm *or* two centimetres [*not* two cm]; 100 kilometres per hour; 90 km/h; 1.5 L; 2 mL; 3 litres; 8 1/2″ × 11″ paper or 8 1/2 × 11-inch paper
ACT, SCENE, AND LINE NUMBERS	act 4, scene 2, lines 75–79 [*or* act iv, scene ii]
TEMPERATURES	43°F; 4°C; 7.5°C
MONEY	$1.2 billion; $3.41; 25 cents *or* 25¢

62 WRITING ABOUT LITERATURE

62a What is literature?

Literary works include **fiction** (novels and stories), **drama** (plays, scripts, and some films), **poetry** (poems and lyrics), and nonfiction with artistic qualities (certain memoirs, personal essays, and so on). Since ancient times, literature has been valued for the ways it represents human experience. Literature is designed to entertain and often to disrupt—and it always enlarges your perspective.

62b Why write about literature?

Writing about literature leads you to shape your reading experiences and insights. It helps you understand other people, ideas, times, and places. It shows you how authors use language to stir the imaginations, emotions, and intellects of their readers. Finally, writing is a way to share your own reading experiences and insights with other readers.

62c What general strategies can help me write about literature?

When you write about literature, you want to read the work closely as well as actively (see 2c). Of course, you may initially read a literary work for sheer enjoyment. During further readings, however, you want to pay careful attention to various aspects of the text. Readers are sometimes surprised to find that close, active reading actually enhances their enjoyment. Such reading includes asking what the work means, why the author made a particular choice, and why readers react to the work as they do. Box 82 on page 459 lists several questions that encourage active reading. The topics listed in Boxes 83 and 84 (pages 460 and 461) suggest other elements to think about as you read.

Sometimes instructors ask students to answer questions that deal with material on a literal level: to tell what is on the page. If a question asks what happens in the plot or what a passage means, you need to write a SUMMARY or PARAPHRASE* of part of the work. If a question asks for the historical context of a work or background information about its author, you will need to do some research and report what you find.

*Words printed in small capital letters (such as SUMMARY and PARAPHRASE) are defined in the Terms Glossary on pages 497–517.

Often, assignments call for you to make inferences (2b). **Making inferences** means reading between the lines to figure out what is implied but not stated—an essential activity when you read literature, which tends to *show* rather than *tell*. Literature depicts events, conversations, settings, and so on, but the author usually doesn't come out directly and say exactly what the work means. To figure out the meaning, you need to read closely and actively. Inferential thinking is necessary when your instructor asks you to discuss why a character does something for which the author provides no explicit reason. Alternatively, your instructor might ask you to explain the effect of images in a poem; to discuss how a work implies the author's stance on a social issue; or to analyze how the author depicts the role of women. Your instructor may ask you to describe your personal reaction to a literary work. In such papers, you analyze not only the literary text but also your own experiences and beliefs (62d).

Writing effective papers about literature involves more than summarizing the plot. It involves **critical thinking** and SYNTHESIS. In such papers, you state a **claim** (an observation or a thesis about the work of literature—see 10b) and convince your readers that the position you support is reasonable. Effective papers are thorough and well supported. For support, you make direct references to the work, by writing summaries, paraphrases, and quotations of specific passages, and by explaining precisely *why* and *how* the selected passages support your interpretation. What specifically do your readers need to understand about the passages?

62d How do I write different types of papers about literature?

When you read a literary work closely, look for details or passages that relate to your claim or thesis. Mark up the text as you read by selectively underlining passages or by writing notes, comments, or questions in the margin. Alternatively, take notes on paper or on a computer.

Writing a personal response

A **personal response paper** is an essay in which you explain your reaction to a literary work or some aspect of it. You might write about why you did or did not enjoy reading it, with reference to accepted standards of judgment and taste in literature. You might discuss whether situations in the work are similar to your personal experiences. You might explain whether you agree or disagree with the author's point of view—and *why*. You might answer a question or explore a problem that the work raised for you. For example, how do you react if a likable character breaks the law? Similarly, how do you respond to racial, gender, or class prejudice? As with all effective papers about literature, you need to explain your response through discussions of specific passages or elements from the text.

Writing an interpretation

An interpretation explains what you think the work means—that is, the message or viewpoint that you think it conveys. Most works of literature are open to more than one interpretation. Your task, then, is not to discover the single right answer. Instead, your task is to determine a possible interpretation and provide an argument that supports it. The questions in Box 82 can help you write an effective interpretation paper.

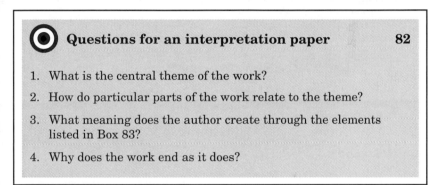

Questions for an interpretation paper **82**

1. What is the central theme of the work?
2. How do particular parts of the work relate to the theme?
3. What meaning does the author create through the elements listed in Box 83?
4. Why does the work end as it does?

Writing a formal analysis

A formal analysis explains how elements of a literary work function to create meaning or effect. Your instructor may ask you to concentrate on one of these elements (for example, "How does point of view in the story affect its meaning?") or to discuss how a writer develops a theme through several elements (for example, "How do setting, imagery, and symbolism reveal the author's viewpoint?").

To prepare to write your formal analysis, read the work thoroughly, looking for patterns and repetitions. Take notes as you go along because the act of writing helps you form insights about the patterns and repetitions you discover. For example, to analyze a character, you want to pay attention to everything that character says or does, everything that other characters say about him or her, and any descriptions of the character. Box 83 describes some of the major literary elements that you might expect to use in formal analyses.

Major elements of literary works to analyze 83

PLOT	Events and their sequence
THEME	Central idea or message
STRUCTURE	Organization and relationship of parts to each other and to the whole
CHARACTERIZATION	Traits, thoughts, and actions of the characters in the work
SETTING	Time and place of the action
POINT OF VIEW	Perspective or position from which the author (perhaps acting as a narrator or speaking through a main character) presents the material
STYLE	How words and sentence structure present the material
IMAGERY	Pictures created by the work, especially through creative use of language (see Chapter 19)
TONE	Author's attitude toward the subject of the work—and sometimes toward the reader—as expressed through choice of words, imagery, and point of view
FIGURES OF SPEECH	Unusual use or combinations of words, including METAPHORS and SIMILES, for enhanced vividness or effect
SYMBOLISM	Meanings discoverable beneath the surface of the words or images
RHYTHM	Beat, metre
RHYME	Repetition of similar sounds for their auditory effect

Writing a cultural analysis

A **cultural analysis** relates a literary work to broader historical, social, cultural, or political situations. Your instructor might ask you to explain how events or prevailing attitudes influenced the writing of a work or the way readers understand it. For example, you might be asked "How do personal identity and ethnic discrimination intersect in Joy Kogawa's novel *Obasan*?" or "How do differences between the institution of marriage in the early nineteenth century and marriage today affect readers' interpretations of *Pride and Prejudice*?" Box 84 lists some common topics appropriate for a cultural analysis.

Major topics for cultural analysis 84

GENDER	How does the work portray women or men—and define, or challenge, their roles in society?
CLASS	How does the work portray relationships among the upper, middle, and lower classes? How do characters' actions or perspectives result from their wealth and power—or from their poverty and powerlessness?
RACE AND ETHNICITY	How does the work portray the influences of race and ethnicity on the characters' actions, status, and values?
HISTORY	How does the work reflect—or challenge—past events and values in a society?
AUTOBIOGRAPHY	How did the writer's life experiences influence his or her work?
GENRE	How is the work similar to or different from other works of its type (for example, other plays, sonnets, mysteries, comic novels, memoirs)?

62e What special rules apply to writing about literature?

Using correct verb tenses

Always use the PRESENT TENSE when you describe or discuss a literary work or any of its elements.

- The various members of the narrator's family **accept** their dual identities in different ways.

In addition, always use the present tense for discussing what an author has done in a specific work.

- In *Obasan,* Joy Kogawa **assembles** fragments of memory into elements of an individual and collective identity.

Always use a PAST-TENSE VERB to discuss historical events or biographical information.

- Kogawa **was** born in Vancouver but during World War II **was** interned with her family in central British Columbia.

Using your own ideas and using secondary sources

Some assignments call only for your own ideas about the literary work. Other assignments call for you to use SECONDARY SOURCES. Secondary sources include books and articles in which experts discuss some aspect of the literary text or other material related to your topic. You might use secondary sources to support your own ideas, perhaps by citing a literary scholar who agrees with you. Alternatively, when you have a new or different interpretation, you might summarize, analyze, or critique what others have written in order to provide a framework for your own analysis. No matter what your assignment, never PLAGIARIZE (see Chapter 26 and 62f) by pretending that the ideas of others are your own. Always DOCUMENT your secondary sources. In addition, use appropriate verbs effectively so that your writing integrates QUOTATIONS, PARAPHRASES, and SUMMARIES into your paper smoothly. (For a list of useful verbs, see 26i.)

You can locate secondary sources by using the research process explained in Chapters 23 through 25. A particularly important resource for writing about literature is the *MLA International Bibliography,* which many researchers consider the most comprehensive index to literary scholarship. It is available in nearly every college and university library, both in print and online through the library's computer system or Web site.

62f How do I avoid plagiarism in writing about literature?

To avoid **plagiarism,** always DOCUMENT your sources, whether PRIMARY or SECONDARY. By documenting, you reveal to your readers exactly where to find the specific passages in the literary work from which you are quoting. Readers often want to read the source material directly, to confirm that what you have written correctly reflects the original meaning of the material. Perhaps more importantly, by documenting your sources, you're behaving as a person who never intentionally or unintentionally steals from others. Chapter 26 contains a detailed discussion of the dangers of plagiarism and how to avoid them.

The DOCUMENTATION STYLE of the Modern Language Association (MLA) (Chapters 28 and 29) is the standard reference system that most instructors require students to use in writing about literature. Some instructors, however, prefer a different documentation style (see Chapters 31 and 32, and 34–36), so always check with your instructor regarding which style to use.

Identify passages from short poems by line numbers (for example, "Song for Naomi," lines 4–5). Refer to passages from plays by act and scene (for example, *Othello* 3.4). For other types of literature, use page numbers. Document secondary sources when you write about literature, as you do when writing in the social sciences and other courses (see 23b and 26b).

62g The final draft of a student's essay about literature

Working on the assignment

Michael Choi, a first-year student in English, was assigned to write an interpretation of the images and metaphors in Yusef Komunyakaa's poem "Blackberries." When Michael first read "Blackberries," several of the images puzzled him. He wondered about their connection to an apparently simple scene of a boy picking, eating, and selling blackberries. In the process of writing his essay, Michael came to understand how those previously puzzling images and metaphors help to shape the poem's deeper meaning. His final draft is reproduced here.

Learning about the poet Yusef Komunyakaa

Yusef Komunyakaa, an African American poet, was born in 1947 and raised in Louisiana. His father was a carpenter. In 1994, Komunyakaa won the Pulitzer Prize for poetry—one of the most prestigious honours a poet can receive in the United States—for his book *Neon Vernacular*. Komunyakaa currently teaches at Princeton University.

Blackberries

by Yusef Komunyakaa

They left my hands like a printer's
Or thief's before a police blotter
& pulled me into early morning's
Terrestrial sweetness, so thick
The damp ground was consecrated
Where they fell among a garland of thorns.

Although I could smell old lime-covered
History, at ten I'd still hold out my hands
& berries fell into them. Eating from one
& filling a half gallon with the other,
I ate the mythology & dreamt
Of pies & and cobbler, almost

Needful as forgiveness. My bird dog Spot
Eyed blue jays & thrashers. The mud frogs
In rich blackness, hid from daylight.
An hour later, beside City Limits Road
I balanced a gleaming can in each hand,
Limboed between worlds, repeating *one dollar.*

The big blue car made me sweat.
Wintertime crawled out of the windows.
When I leaned closer I saw the boy
& girl my age, in the wide back seat
Smirking, & it was then I remembered my fingers
Burning with thorns among berries too ripe to touch.

A student essay about literature: the final draft

Choi 1

Michael Choi

Professor May

English 100

8 November 2002

Images, Metaphors, and Meaning in "Blackberries"

In Yusef Komunyakaa's poem "Blackberries," the poet describes himself as "limboed between worlds" (line 18). At that moment, he is a boy standing beside City Limits Road--a symbolic line between the city and the country--selling berries that he has just picked. Yet, the boy is also caught between his familiar natural world and a world of wealth and privilege. One of the poem's key issues is whether the boy is responsible for his situation. Komunyakaa uses a rich set of images and metaphors to suggest the boy's complicated position.

Some plain and direct images connect the boy to the world of nature. As he picks blackberries, the poet describes the bird dog Spot watching blue jays and thrashers, and he mentions mud frogs hiding in the dark. Readers form an impression of a rustic boy trying to earn some money from a countryside that is familiar and comfortable to him. He eats as he fills gleaming half-gallon cans and dreams of "pies & cobbler" (line 12). The day is thick with "terrestrial

→

Choi 2

sweetness," (line 4) and the atmosphere is peaceful, almost sleepy.

When the boy moves beyond the country to the City Limits Road to sell his harvest, however, his pleasant morning is shattered. After a customer drives up, the boy finds that "the big blue car made me sweat" (line 19). Partly, he sweats because the car's air conditioning makes him aware of heat that had not bothered him until that very moment. Komunyakaa uses the strong image, "wintertime crawled out of the windows," to heighten the contrast between the artificial environment of the car and the natural environment of the boy (line 20). More importantly, the boy sweats because he is suddenly self-conscious. He feels uncomfortable at the gap between himself and "the boy / & girl my age, in the wide back seat" (lines 21-22). The emphasis on the air conditioning and the width of the seat makes clear that these children come not only from the city but also from wealthier circumstances. When they smirk at him, he remembers his berry-stained fingers. Those stained hands are a metaphor for how different he is from the children in the car, both socially and economically. He feels ashamed.

Yet, should he feel this way? Several complicated images and metaphors in the poem make this question difficult to answer. For example, at the beginning, the poet says that the berries "left my hands like a printer's" (line 1). This image not only calls attention to the inky stains

→

Choi 3

on his hands but also likens berry picking to printing. Both are forms of honest manual labour. Furthermore, picking ripe berries is similar to the messy job of printing on an ink-saturated printing press. This printing metaphor suggests a subtle connection between the boy's work and the poet's. Komunyakaa immediately complicates the first image with a second that compares the boy's hands to a "thief's before a police blotter" (line 2). The common element between the two metaphors is the ink, which in the second is used for fingerprinting.

Note that the person whose fingerprints are being taken by the police is not simply a "suspect" but rather a "thief." The person is already guilty of a crime. Has the boy been stealing berries that do not belong to him, and does he feel guilty when he is caught? This possible interpretation does not completely fit the encounter with the big blue car. The smirking response of the children in the car seems snobbish. Rather than accusing him of being a thief, the children make fun of his getting dirty while picking berries, which they can buy in cool comfort. For his efforts, which even involved his "fingers / Burning with thorns" (lines 23-24), the boy receives ridicule. The reader's sympathies lie with the boy selling the berries. Even if he did steal the berries, his crime does not seem that great.

Another set of metaphors, more mythic in nature, suggests an answer to the question of

→

Choi 4

whether the boy should feel guilty. The boy reports that he "could smell old lime-covered / History" as he picks and eats (lines 7-8). While lime could refer simply to a bright shade of green or, more strangely, to the citrus fruit, another meaning seems to apply here. The chemical substance lime has two uses. Farmers use it to reduce acidity in soil, where it serves as a kind of fertilizer. Alternatively, quicklime spread over the bodies of dead animals speeds their decomposing. To cover history in lime, therefore, means either to cultivate it or to bury it. Later, the boy states that he "ate the mythology & dreamt / Of pies & cobbler . . ." (lines 11-12). Obviously, no one can literally eat mythology. This metaphor suggests that the boy is consuming the berries with little thought of any deeper significance his actions might have. There is a mythic dimension to picking blackberries, but the boy focuses on pleasant physical sensations and, eventually, the chance to make some money. Similarly, history is something to consume or ignore. If the boy is a criminal at all, maybe he is unaware that he is doing anything wrong. Furthermore, perhaps no one owns the berries, and he is merely stealing from nature.

The poem's most profound images and metaphors have religious overtones. The poet describes the ground beneath the berry bushes as "consecrated" (line 5). This powerful word choice

→

Choi 5

characterizes the ground as somehow holy. The berries do not fall simply among thorns but among "a garland of thorns" (line 6). The image of a garland suggests the crown of thorns placed upon the head of Jesus after his trial, and these images draw out the deepest meaning of the poet's being "limboed between worlds." In some religious traditions, limbo is a place where souls temporarily go before entering heaven or where innocent but unbaptized babies permanently dwell. In addition to standing between the world of wealth and status that is represented by the car and the simpler world of bird dogs and mud frogs, the boy stands outside paradise. He has left and knows that he cannot go back.

Although mythic and religious elements are present in "Blackberries," Komunyakaa's poem ultimately supports interpretations on several levels. The poet uses religious images to give depth to the boy's situation. When the boy picks the berries, he is in a peaceful, natural environment that is almost sacred, even if he does not realize it. When he sells the berries, he encounters a foreign world of wealth and privilege. Because of his background, he cannot easily join that world. Yet he cannot easily go back to his familiar ways because he now sees his actions differently. He perceives there may be something wrong with picking blackberries. Whether he <u>should</u> feel guilty, he <u>does</u> feel guilty. The poet is truly limboed between worlds.

→

Choi 6

Work Cited

Komunyakaa, Yusef. "Blackberries." Pleasure Dome: New and Collected Poems. Middletown, CT: Wesleyan UP, 2001. 280-81.

63 BUSINESS WRITING

Format and content are important in all forms of business writing. Today, **e-mail** is the most common form of business communication. E-mail exchanges take place both internally (among people working for the same company) and externally (among people working in different companies).

63a How do I format and write business e-mail?

The physical format of e-mail, which resembles some memo formats, varies slightly depending on whether you use your browser's default e-mail option or an Internet service provider (ISP). Whenever you start a new job, take the time right away to learn the company's e-mail system, including special features such as address books and electronic "filing cabinets."

Formatting business e-mail

Single-space the text of your e-mail; double-space between paragraphs and above your complimentary closing. Always fill in the exact topic of your message on the "Subject" or "Re" line of the e-mail form. Because the subject line tells your recipients and you how to sort, file, and prioritize e-mail messages, being specific about your topic shows that you're a professional who respects the importance of time management. If you need to write to the same person about more than one topic at the same time, send a separate e-mail on each topic, so that each has its specific subject line.

Use the "CC" or "Copies" space for the e-mail addresses of those who need to be informed, even if you don't necessarily expect them to respond to your message. Send copies only to those who really need the information. If you overload people with e-mail they don't need to see, you'll waste their time, and soon they will stop paying attention to all your e-mail, no matter what the topic.

Use the "BCC" space very sparingly. This feature is handy when you want to send a copy of a message to someone without the knowledge of the message's recipient. It can help when you need to be discreet (for example, you might need to send your manager a blind copy of your message to a customer). On the other hand, the "BCC" feature can reflect negatively on the sender, especially if it's used for the sake of gossip, personal opinion, put-downs, jokes, or chain letters. Never forget that recipients of a blind copy can easily forward it to others, publicly revealing what you have written. And even if recipients delete the blind copies you send them, technical experts can retrieve them years later.

Writing business e-mail

Business e-mail has PURPOSES and AUDIENCES quite different from those of the informal e-mail that you exchange with friends and family. The purpose of business e-mail is to communicate about planning, procedures, processes, purchases, and other matters that pertain to a company's business. The audience for business e-mail is other businesspeople who require information, want to exchange and discuss ideas, or need to take or request action. Because businesspeople are busy people, your writing needs to be brief, well organized, and to the point. Box 85 suggests some guidelines for writing business e-mail.

Because any e-mail you write as a business employee publicly represents your company and yourself, you want to appear professional, focused, and well informed. Remember, too, that when a business matter takes on legal importance, even your most casually written e-mail messages can become official evidence in a court case. Choose your words carefully.

Netiquette, a word coined from *etiquette,* demands that you address business recipients by their full names, including any title,

Guidelines for writing business e-mail **85**

- Always start your e-mail with a sentence that tells what your memo is about.
- If you want your recipients to take action as a result of your e-mail, alert them in your opening paragraph—though you can save the specifics of the action for the end of your message.
- Put the essence of your message in the second paragraph. Supply background information only if your recipients aren't already aware of it or might have forgotten it.
- Conclude your e-mail in the third paragraph by asking for a specific action if one is needed or by restating your reason for writing (for example, keeping someone apprised of a situation or reporting on a meeting).
- If your e-mail runs longer than three to four paragraphs, add some topic headings (in capital letters) to help your readers speed through the material.

such as *Ms., Mr.,* or *Dr.* Put the information they need to address you correctly in the closing of your e-mail. Especially when you start communicating with businesspeople you've never met or corresponded with before, use titles and last names. After you get to know your co-workers and customers well, you might decide to reduce the LEVEL OF FORMALITY. A good time to do so is after those you are writing to begin to end their messages with their first names. Wait for a few exchanges before using the first name of someone with a position considerably above yours, however.

A medium to formal level of word choice is best for your business e-mail. This level of formality calls for no slang, abbreviations, or informal words or expressions. Use standard grammar, spelling, and punctuation. Never write in all capital letters, which are difficult to read and considered the equivalent of shouting, or in all lowercase letters, which are also hard to read, suggest laziness, and show a lack of respect for your recipient. At the end of your message, before your full name and position, use a commonly accepted complimentary closing, such as *Sincerely* or *Cordially*.

Business e-mail travels quickly, so writers of e-mail usually expect a reply within one or two days. However, when the content of e-mail or your work schedule makes a speedy response impractical, always acknowledge that you've received a message. Say when you expect to be able to respond to it, and don't forget to follow up. Unless an e-mail states explicitly that the writer grants permission to forward it, never do so without first getting the writer's approval.

Finally, know your company's **e-mail policy,** or rules about computer and e-mail use. E-mail policy covers issues such as whether you can use your business e-mail address for personal purposes; the length and tone of most e-mail, whether for internal or external use; your legal responsibilities concerning your e-mail; and restrictions on visiting Web sites that are unrelated to your work. Increasingly, businesses monitor their employees' e-mail. Never forget that your manager—or perhaps an entity called the Office of Technology and Compliance—might be reading all the e-mail you send and receive at work.

63b How do I format and write business letters?

Use the following guidelines for the format and content of your business letters.

- **Paper:** Use standard-size paper (8 1/2 × 11 inches) for business writing. The most suitable colours for letters are white, slightly off-white, and light beige. Fold your business letters horizontally into thirds to fit into a standard business envelope. Never fold a page in half and then into thirds.

- **Letterhead:** Use the official letterhead stationery (name, address, and logo, if any) of the business where you are employed. If no official letterhead exists, create your own. To do this, centre your full name, the business name (if applicable), address, and phone number at the top of the page; use a larger font than for the content of your letter. Avoid fancy, distracting fonts.
- **Format:** Use single spacing within paragraphs and double spacing between paragraphs. The two most frequently used formats for business writing are block style and modified block style. **Block style** doesn't indent paragraphs or other elements, although the letterhead is centred (see the letter on page 476). **Modified block style** indents the first line of each paragraph; the letterhead sits at the left margin rather than being centred; and the complimentary closing and signature begin halfway across the page (see the letter on page 482).
- **Recipient's name:** Use the exact name of your recipient whenever possible. Take time to research the name, either through a phone call to a central switchboard or on the Internet. If you can't locate an exact name, at least use a specific category—for example, "Dear Billing Department"—and place the key word first ("Billing Department," not "Department of Billing"). Mail addressed "To Whom It May Concern" rarely reaches the people to whom you want to direct your message.
- **Content:** Write concisely, clearly, and to the point; never repeat yourself. Announce the purpose of your letter in the opening. Make sure your information is accurate and complete, and that it includes all relevant facts and dates.
- **Tone:** Remember that your writing reflects on your company and you. Choose words that achieve a medium to formal LEVEL OF FORMALITY. Try to take an evenhanded approach: Express disappointment or make a complaint without resorting to biased language. A reasonable, mature tone gets better results than an angry accusation.
- **Envelope:** Use the official envelope of the company where you work. If none exists or if you write business correspondence on your own behalf, use a standard number 10 envelope (24 × 10.5 cm or 9 1/2 × 4 inches), which fits a properly folded business letter.

On page 475, you will see the Canada Post guidelines for addressing envelopes so that they can be processed by machine.

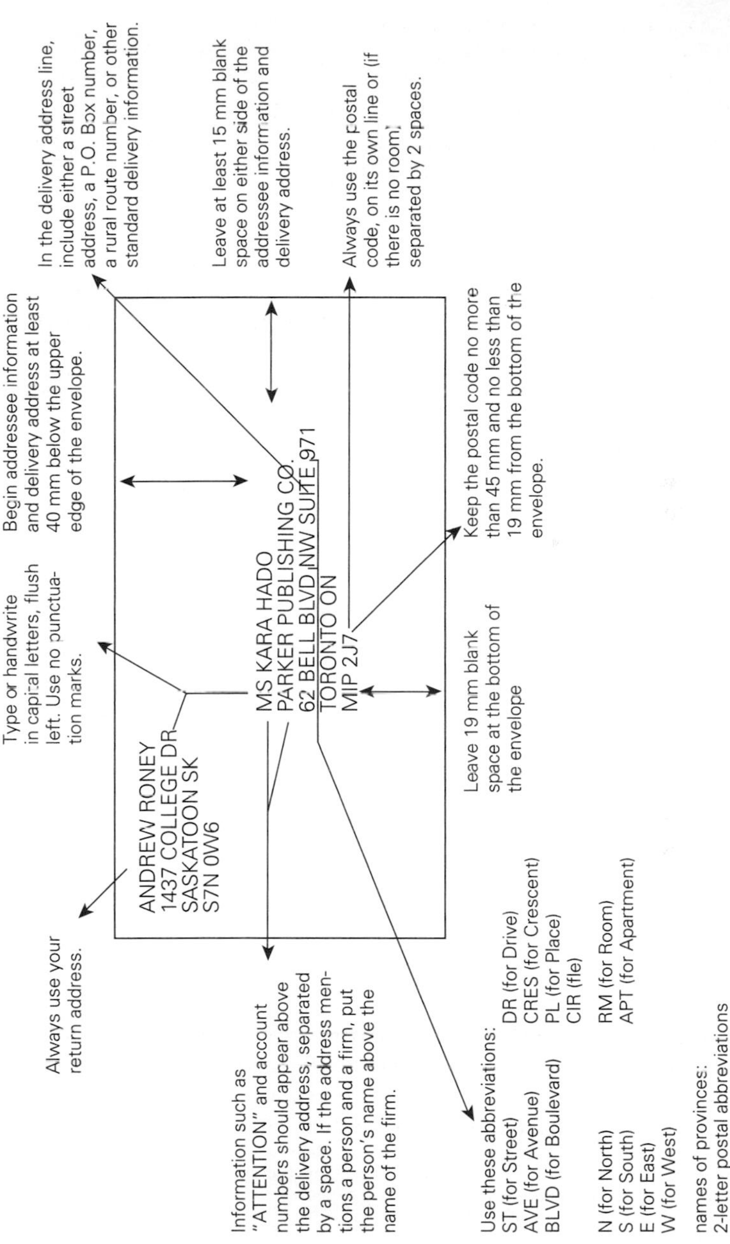

Always use your return address.
Type or handwrite in capital letters, flush left. Use no punctuation marks.
Begin addressee information and delivery address at least 40 mm below the upper edge of the envelope.
In the delivery address line, include either a street address, a P.O. Box number, a rural route number, or other standard delivery information.
ANDREW RONEY
1437 COLLEGE DR
SASKATOON SK
S7N 0W6
Leave at least 15 mm blank space on either side of the addressee information and delivery address.
Information such as "ATTENTION" and account numbers should appear above the delivery address, separated by a space. If the address mentions a person and a firm, put the person's name above the name of the firm.
MS KARA HADO
PARKER PUBLISHING CO.
62 BELL BLVD NW SUITE 971
TORONTO ON
MIP 2J7
Always use the postal code, on its own line or (if there is no room) separated by 2 spaces.
Leave 19 mm blank space at the bottom of the envelope
Keep the postal code no more than 45 mm and no less than 19 mm from the bottom of the envelope.
Use these abbreviations:
ST (for Street)
AVE (for Avenue)
BLVD (for Boulevard)
DR (for Drive)
CRES (for Crescent)
PL (for Place)
CIR (fle)
N (for North)
S (for South)
E (for East)
W (for West)
RM (for Room)
APT (for Apartment)
names of provinces:
2-letter postal abbreviations

Canada Post guidelines for business envelope format

Jan Dubitz
742 Fraser Hall Redwood College
2038 Emily Carr Blvd.
Surrey, BC V6M 2C3
(604)555-3723

September 14, 2002

4 spaces

Ms. Yolanda Harper
Abco Rental Company
1249 Logan Rd.
Vancouver, BC V6A 3D4

Dear Ms. Harper:

SALUTATION: Use an appropriate title (Mr., Ms., Dr., Professor) and the person's name. If you do not know the name, use a title (Dean of Students, Personnel Director). Add a colon at the end of the salutation.

2 spaces

I rented a refrigerator from your company on August 27. After only two weeks, the freezer compartment no longer keeps food frozen. Per the rental agreement, this is my written request for a replacement refrigerator. The agreement states that you will replace the refrigerator within five business days from the receipt of my letter.

I will call you next week to arrange the exchange. Thank you for your prompt attention.

Sincerely,

CLOSING: Capitalize only the first word (Yours truly, Sincerely yours) and follow with a comma.

4 spaces

Jan Dubitz

Jan Dubitz

SIGNATURE: If you have a title, type it underneath your name. Sign letter in space above your name.

Enc: Copy of rental agreement

OTHER: Use *Enc:* or *Enclosure:* if you include material *with* your letter. Use *cc:* to indicate that you have sent any courtesy copies.

Sample business letter in block style

63c How do I format and write memos?

Memos are communications that are exchanged within an organization or business. For communications with people who are outside your company, a business letter (63b) is more appropriate. Today, e-mail is taking the place of paper memos. The guidelines for writing e-mail (63a) also pertain to memos, which share the same PURPOSES and AUDIENCES and require the same conciseness and care in word choice. The form of communication you choose—whether a paper memo or e-mail—depends on your assessment of the situation in which you are writing.

The standard format of a memo includes two major parts: the headings and the content (see the sample memo on page 478). The headings should appear as follows:

TO: [Name your audience, a specific person or group]
FROM: [Give your name and title, if any]
DATE: [Give the date on which you write the memo]
RE: [State your subject]

Recipients of your memos need to determine the importance of your memos quickly by scanning these headings, so be as specific as possible in the "Subject" or "Re" line. The content can run for as many paragraphs as you need, as long as you don't ramble. However, if you write more than three or four paragraphs, add headings that name your subtopics.

If you need more than one or two pages, write a brief report rather than a memo. A report always includes headings for major sections (introduction, central topic, conclusion) as well as for subtopics within sections.

Follow these guidelines for your memos:

- **Introduction:** State your purpose for writing and explain why your memo is worth your readers' attention. In addition, mention whether recipients need to take action because of your memo. You can save the specifics of the action until the conclusion of your memo, if you wish.
- **Central topic:** Give the essential information on your topic, including facts the recipient needs to know and a deadline for any action that is required. (If you write more than three or four paragraphs, use headings to break down the information into subtopics.)
- **Conclusion:** End with a one- or two-sentence summary, or a specific recommendation. If your memo is short, as the sample memo on page 478 is, end it with instructions or a "thank you" line.

TO: English Teaching Assistants
FROM: Professor Thomas Nevers, Director,
First-Year Composition
DATE: December 1, 2002
SUBJECT: New Computer Programs

Several new writing programs will be installed in the English computer labs. Training sessions are scheduled during the week before classes begin next semester.

Tuesday, January 7	9:00-11:00 a.m.
Wednesday, January 8	1:00-3:00 p.m.
Thursday, January 9	8:30-10:30 a.m.
Friday, January 10	1:30-3:30 p.m.

Please stop by my office by December 12 to sign up for one of the two-hour workshops.

Sample memo

Most word-processing software provides templates, or preprogrammed formats, for memos.

63d How do I format and write a résumé?

A **résumé** details your accomplishments and employment history. The AUDIENCE for your résumé is a potential employer. Most employers scan the résumés of several applicants at a time to compare their qualifications. The impression your résumé makes on your audience determines whether you are seriously considered for employment.

To make a favourable impression, you want your résumé to be easy to read. Label its sections clearly and target the information included in it to the position you're applying for. Don't forget to proofread it carefully; even one spelling error can eliminate you from consideration. A Web site that offers a tutorial in writing résumés is <http://www.umn.edu/ohr/ecep/resume/>. Here are some additional guidelines for writing a résumé:

- Include all appropriate information.
- Put your most recent job and/or degree first.
- Adjust the emphasis of your résumé to fit your PURPOSE. For example, if you are applying for a job as a computer programmer, you want to emphasize different facts than you would emphasize if you were applying for a retail sales job.
- Try to fit all the information on one page. If you can't avoid adding a second page to give your full background, make sure the most important information is on the first page so that it catches your reader's eye right away.
- Use clear headings to separate blocks of information (see the sample résumé on page 480). Choose among the following, as appropriate: name, address, e-mail; position desired or career objective; education; experience; licences and certifications; other experience that might relate to the job you're applying for; honours or awards, if any; publications or presentations, if any; activities and interests; special abilities, skills, and knowledge; and references.
- Write telegraphically. Start with verb phrases, not with the word *I*, and omit *a, an,* and *the*. For example, write "Created new computer program to organize company's spreadsheets" instead of "*I* created *a* new computer program to organize *the* company's spreadsheets."
- Never pad your résumé with irrelevant information or wordy writing.
- Never lie on your résumé.

Margaret Lorentino
1338 Sunflower Lane
Halifax, NS B3J 3J6
(902) 555-3756
mlor94@home.ca

OBJECTIVE: Seeking a full/part-time position as a medical transcriptionist to utilize my medical, computer, and office skills

EDUCATION: Certificate of Completion, Medical Transcription
St. Francis Xavier University, Antigonish, NS, December 2002
Bachelor of Science
Dalhousie University, Halifax, NS, May 2000

EMPLOYMENT: Dalhousie University, Halifax, NS, January 2001–Present
Lab Assistant and Computer Skills Teacher
RTD Real Estate, Halifax, NS, August 1994–August 1995
Receptionist, Accounting Assistant
Atlantic Mutual Life, Dartmouth, NS May 1991–July 1992
Sales Assistant
Reliable Personnel, Summerside, PE, May 1990–May 1991
Temporary Employment Manager

SKILLS: Computer
- Experienced with Microsoft Office 2000 and WordPerfect
- Type 60 wpm
- Have experience with Lotus, Excel, and Access
- Teach WordPerfect and basic computer skills in first-year college English classes

Organizational
- Girl Scout leader, soccer coach, summer camp counsellor
- Trained employees in data entry and accounting principles
- Managed a temporary workforce of 20–30 employees

REFERENCES: Available upon request

Sample résumé

- Include references, or state that you can provide them on request (be sure to have them at hand so you can respond speedily to such a request).
- Use high-quality paper that is either white, off-white, or light beige.

ALERT: Note to multilingual writers: In applying for a job in Canada, you are not required to give personal information that could be used to discriminate against candidates for employment. Examples of such information are age, marital status, race or ancestry, place of origin, citizenship, religion, and political affiliation. **!**

63e How do I format and write a job application letter?

A job application letter needs to accompany your résumé. Avoid simply repeating what is already on the résumé. Instead, make a connection between the company's expectations and your experience by emphasizing how your background has prepared you for the position. Your job application letter, more than your résumé, reflects your personality.

Here are some guidelines for writing a job application letter:

- Use one page only.
- Think of your letter as a polite sales pitch. Don't be shy, but don't exaggerate what you can do for the company if you get the job.
- Use the same name, content, and format guidelines as you would for a business letter (63b).
- Address the letter to a specific person. If you can't discover a name, use a title such as *Personnel Director*. Avoid writing "To Whom It May Concern."
- Start your letter by identifying the position you are applying for.
- Mention your qualifications for the position, and explain how your background and skills will meet the requirements for the job.
- Let the reader know that you are familiar with the company or organization.
- End by being as specific as possible about what you can do for the company. If this is your first job, give your key attributes—but make sure they are relevant and true. For instance, you might state that you are punctual, self-disciplined, a team player, and eager to learn and work hard for the company.
- State when you are available for an interview and how the potential employer can reach you.

1338 Sunflower Lane
Halifax, NS B3J 3J6
December 1, 2002

Ms. Arlene Chang
Employment Coordinator
Rockford Medical Centre
820 Cornwallis Rd.
Halifax, NS B5A 2C2

Dear Ms. Chang:

I had a chance to talk with you last spring about your company at the Medical Professions Job Fair. I am very interested in the medical transcription position that I noticed in the *Daily News* on November 29.

I will be completing my Medical Transcription Certificate at the end of December. I have taken courses in medical transcription, medical office procedures, keyboarding, as well as numerous computer courses. I have a bachelor's degree in general science from Dalhousie University. I believe that this background would help me in this position.

The enclosed résumé will give you the details of my experience and qualifications. I think that my experience and education make a great combination for this position. I am available for an interview at your convenience. My home phone number is (902) 555-3756, and my e-mail address is mlor94@home.ca.

Sincerely yours,

Margaret Lorentino

Margaret Lorentino

Sample job application letter in modified block style

- Edit and proofread the letter carefully. Even one misspelled word can ruin your chances of employment.

The sample letter on page 482 is by Margaret Lorentino, a mother with young children.

64 ORAL PRESENTATIONS

Preparing an **oral presentation** and writing an essay involve many of the same processes. In each, you determine your PURPOSE, analyze your AUDIENCE, and work to develop a well-supported THESIS STATEMENT. Chapters 5 through 10 in this book discuss the writing process in general. This chapter explains the special demands of adapting the writing process to developing and delivering an oral presentation.

The overriding principles in an oral presentation are (1) to keep the volume of your voice high without shouting; (2) never to rush as you speak; (3) to speak slowly enough that your listeners have an extra second or two to absorb each point (listening takes more time than reading); and (4) to pronounce all your words clearly, so that your delivery enhances your message.

PREPARING AN ORAL PRESENTATION

64a How do I determine my purpose and topic?

Once your instructor assigns a TOPIC, or you have chosen a topic using the techniques suggested in Chapter 5, you need to decide whether your purpose is INFORMATIVE or PERSUASIVE. To help you focus your speech, type or write in large letters a statement of your chosen purpose. (If you want, tack the statement over your desk to help you remember your purpose while you work.) Always use one of these two lead-ins, making sure that it contains an INFINITIVE PHRASE:

- I am going **to inform** my audience that . . .
- I am going **to persuade** my audience that . . .

Other informative infinitives include *to explain why, to clarify, to show how, to report, to define, to describe,* and *to classify*. Other persuasive infinitives include *to convince, to argue, to agree with, to disagree with, to win over,* and *to influence*.

64b How do I adapt my message to my audience?

Adapting your presentation to your audience definitely doesn't mean that you need to say only what your listeners might want to hear. Rather, it means that you need to plan your presentation so that it grabs and holds your audience's interest. To start, consider your listeners' prior knowledge of your topic, their desire to learn more, and whether they agree with your point of view. You'll find that your audience falls into one of three categories: *uninformed, informed,* or *mixed*. Box 86 suggests how to adapt your message to each type of audience.

64c How do I organize my presentation?

The basic format for an oral presentation has three parts, similar to the major parts of an essay: INTRODUCTION, BODY, and CONCLUSION. Within the body, you present your major points, with two to three supports for each point. You can use the RENNS formula (8d) to help

Adapting an oral presentation to your audience — 86

UNINFORMED AUDIENCE	Start with the basics, and then move to a few new ideas. Define new terms and concepts. Use visual aids and give examples to illustrate your point. Avoid using technical terms as much as possible. As you go along, resume and repeat key ideas—but not too often.
INFORMED AUDIENCE	Never waste time with more than a very quick overview of the basics. From the beginning, say outright that you'll be covering new ground—and then do so. Devote nearly all of your talk to new ideas and concepts.
MIXED AUDIENCE	In your introduction, acknowledge the more informed audience members who are present. Explain that you're going to review the basic concepts briefly so that everyone can build from the same knowledge base. Move as rapidly as possible toward more complex concepts.

you think of specific supporting details. As you outline and then expand on what you plan to say, use complete sentences rather than phrases at each step. Doing so gets you closer to your final form, and just as important, forces you to sharpen your thinking.

Box 87 presents a typical organizational outline for a speech, including suggestions for when you might need a clear transition between points. Use only a few of these suggestions—not all of them—or your speech will become so repetitive that no one will listen to it.

Organizational outline for an oral presentation **87**

Title: ______________________________

Topic: ______________________________

Specific purpose: ______________________________

Thesis statement: ______________________________

____

A. Introduction (followed by a clear transition to point 1 in the body)

B. Body

   1. Major point and specific supporting examples (followed by a clear transition from point 1 to point 2, perhaps with a brief reference to the introduction*)

   2. Major point and specific supporting examples (followed by a clear transition from point 2 to point 3, perhaps with a brief reference to point 1 and the introduction*)

   3. Major point and specific supporting examples (followed by a clear transition from point 2 to point 3, perhaps with a brief reference to points 1, 2, and the introduction*)

C. Conclusion

*Refer back to the introduction very sparingly, or your audience will become bored and lose interest.

Introducing yourself and your topic

All audience members ask themselves three questions when someone begins to speak: Who are you? What are you going to talk about? Why should I listen? To respond effectively to these unasked but very present questions without stating the obvious, try these suggestions:

- Grab your audience's attention with an interesting question, quotation, statistic, anecdote, compliment, or bit of background information. Even if someone has introduced you, briefly—and always modestly—mention your qualifications as a speaker about your topic.
- Explain briefly the organization of your talk. Give your audience a road map: Tell where you're starting, where you're going, and how you intend to get there, so the audience can know what to expect. This gives your listeners confidence that you won't waste their time. (As you revise your drafts, make sure that you deliver what you have promised.)

Following your road map

Listening to a speech is very different from reading an essay. Audiences for oral presentations generally need special help from the speaker in staying on track and following the speaker's line of reasoning. Here are some strategies to keep your listeners' minds from wandering and to make sure they are aware of where you—and they—are going.

- Signal clearly where you are on your road map by using words such as *first, second,* and *third*. Signal that you're discussing CAUSE AND EFFECT by using words such as *consequently, therefore,* and *furthermore,* the signposts of a coherent argument. Signal that you're telling a story or explaining a process by using locator words such as *before, then,* and *next*.
- Define unfamiliar terms and concepts, and follow up as soon as possible with strong examples, so that your audience can understand the new ideas you present.
- Comment on your own material. Tell the audience what you consider significant, memorable, or especially relevant, and why. Do so sparingly, however. If you overuse this strategy, you'll lose credibility and people will stop listening.
- Provide occasional summaries. Every so often, take a moment at a transition point to resume what you've covered and say how it relates to what's coming next. Doing this reassures your audience.

Wrapping up your speech

Use the conclusion of your speech to wrap up. You don't need to resolve every point you've made—after all, no one has all the answers to complex questions. Still, you need to demonstrate that you're in control of your material and aren't letting key points simply float away. Make an effort to end your speech reasonably and logically. To be successful, try these suggestions:

- Never let your voice volume fall or your clarity of pronunciation falter because the end is in sight.
- Signal the end with verbal cues ("In conclusion," "Finally") and body language (facial expressions, gestures). When you use these cues, make sure you are truly at the end of your speech. Never conclude more than once.
- Offer a fresh restatement of your main message; do not introduce new ideas at the last minute.
- Make a dramatic, decisive statement, cite a memorable quotation, or issue a challenge.

64d What type of language and tone are appropriate for oral presentations?

An oral presentation calls for the same awareness of language as your writing does. Review especially Chapters 18 through 20. For help with TONE, see 5d.

Here are some tips on use of language in oral presentations:

- Recognize the power of words. Dictionaries of quotations contain passages that you can read to appreciate or to analyze, spoken by powerful speakers such as Winston Churchill and Martin Luther King, Jr.
- Take care not to offend. Never use any word, phrase, or example that could offend your audience or people connected with them.
- Use GENDER-NEUTRAL LANGUAGE by avoiding sexist pronouns, nouns, and other words and expressions (20b).
- Use the ACTIVE VOICE (40g). The active voice is crucial in oral presentations because it helps listeners to grasp your point.
- Speak with dignity, not only in your choice of words but also in your body language, tone of voice, and dress.

DELIVERING AN ORAL PRESENTATION

64e How do I choose a presentation style?

Presentation style is the way you deliver your speech: You may memorize a prepared text, read your speech, map it, or speak without notes. As a student, you want to avoid speaking without notes until you have gained considerable experience giving speeches.

Memorizing your speech

Memorized speeches often sound unnatural. Unless you've mastered a memorized text well enough to recite it in a relaxed way, choose another presentation style. After all, no safety net exists if you forget a word or sentence. Fortunately, few academic situations call for pure memorization.

Reading your speech

Reading a speech aloud often bores your audience. Most listeners lose interest because burying your nose in sheets of paper creates an uncomfortable barrier between you and your audience. In addition, you may appear unfamiliar with your topic, unprepared, or insincere.

If you have no choice but to read your speech, practise enough so that you avoid speaking in a monotone voice. Few people can manage to listen to a speech for long if it is delivered without variations in tone of voice. In addition, try these tips:

- Memorize your words as much as possible so that you can look up to make frequent eye contact with your audience.
- Never hold the sheets of paper. Instead, place them on a podium—or even an inverted wastepaper basket on top of a table, if no podium is available.
- Keep your hands out of your pockets so that you can use them freely for gesturing.
- Turn your body—not just your head—to look at all members of your audience.

Mapping your speech

Relying on a "map" for your speech is an excellent choice. After you've written out your speech—or thought through every word of it—outline it. On a single page or on numbered index cards, write the key terms of each part of your speech. Use one colour of ink for each major point you want to make and a different colour for the examples and illustrations of each point. Use a highlighter to identify any material that you want to emphasize.

This method works only if you practise your presentation repeatedly to become thoroughly familiar with the major points and examples each key term signals you to recall. Always include information on the sources where you found your material, so that you can briefly mention them (and offer to give more details after your speech). Box 88 contains additional suggestions for preparing your note cards.

Speaking without notes

When you speak without notes, you not only must to master your content but also pace yourself so that you remain in control of the speech as it progresses to its conclusion. Unfortunately, unless you are highly experienced, you will tend to ramble, stray off the topic, or lose track of time when speaking without notes. No audience respects such a speaker.

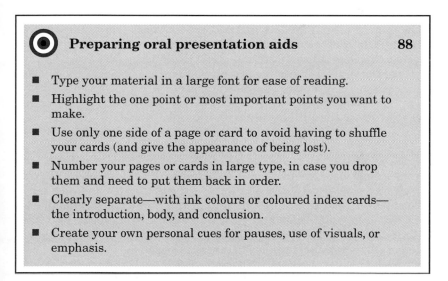

Preparing oral presentation aids **88**

- Type your material in a large font for ease of reading.
- Highlight the one point or most important points you want to make.
- Use only one side of a page or card to avoid having to shuffle your cards (and give the appearance of being lost).
- Number your pages or cards in large type, in case you drop them and need to put them back in order.
- Clearly separate—with ink colours or coloured index cards—the introduction, body, and conclusion.
- Create your own personal cues for pauses, use of visuals, or emphasis.

64f How do I vary my vocal delivery and use nonverbal communication?

Your voice is the focus of any oral presentation. If you're unsure of your voice's volume in a particular setting, speak briefly and then ask the audience if they can hear you. When you use a microphone, of course, you need to speak into it without raising your voice. If the sound system "screeches," you're getting electronic feedback, a problem you can solve by staying away from speaker units set up on the stage or around the room.

Articulate your words—speak slowly and deliberately—but not so slowly that your words have no rhythm or pace. Change the tone of your voice for emphasis and clarity. Pause every now and then to let a point sink in. Speak naturally but clearly.

Eye contact is your most important nonverbal communication tool; it communicates confidence and shows respect for your listeners. If you use a podium, wait until you're standing squarely behind it before beginning to speak. Smile or nod at your audience and make eye contact with them as you begin. To do this smoothly, you need to memorize your first few sentences.

Your body language either adds to or detracts from your overall message. Use appropriate facial expressions to mirror the emotions in your message. Gestures, if not overdone, contribute to your message by adding emphasis; they are best when they appear to be natural rather than forced or timed. When gestures aren't needed and you're unsure of where to place your hands, rest them on the podium—never scratch your head, dust off your clothing, or otherwise fidget. Step very slightly forward or backward from a microphone to indicate transitions in your message, but never sway from side to side.

64g How do I incorporate visual aids into my presentation?

Good visual aids make a speaker's ideas clear and understandable, but they cannot take the place of a well-prepared and rehearsed speech. Never show a visual of the points you're going to make and then read them aloud point by point—unless you use a PowerPoint animation to reveal each point separately as it comes up—or you'll lose the audience's attention quickly. Rather, save time by reinforcing your major points with illustrations or concrete images.

Well-prepared and well-delivered visuals add to your credibility and maintain an audience's attention. Number the sequence of your visuals so that you don't have to shuffle them by hand or "find" them on a projector. Always arrive early to double-check that a projector is working and in focus. For many types of visual aids you need to dim the lights, but never turn them off completely or you won't be able to see your notes, and your audience won't be able to take notes. To avoid PLAGIARISM, always include directly on the visual the DOCUMENTATION for any information that you've drawn from a source.

Here are various types of visual aids that you need to prepare and practise with in advance of a speech. Never combine one type of visual with others in a single speech. Your audience will sense that your material is too scattered for you to deliver a cohesive speech.

- **Slides of photographs, scientific material, etc.:** Always check that your slides are in the proper order and correctly placed (upright) in the projector. Turn off the projector or cover its lens when you don't need to use a slide. Keep the screen in one position—that is, try not to raise and lower it during your speech.
- **Overhead transparencies:** These are handy for when you want to write on the visual—for example, to illustrate a revision in progress or emphasize a point. If you can draw quickly and well, you can sketch a rough illustration from scratch on a blank transparency as your audience watches.
- **PowerPoint™:** This Microsoft product allows you to prepare slides on a computer and project them for your audience. Not every classroom is equipped to handle a computerized slide system, however, so find out what technology is available. You may need to bring your own laptop or submit a CD of your slides to a network administrator. If your classroom can't support PowerPoint, don't despair. Though the technology is impressive, other visual aids can work just as well. Finally, use PowerPoint only as an enhancement. Your information—spoken with clarity and authority—is the main attraction.
- **Posters:** Because posters are large, they can dramatize a point. Keep them covered until you're ready for them, or they'll lose their impact.
- **Dry-erase boards:** Because dry-erase colours are visually appealing, these boards are often preferable to chalkboards. Use them sparingly to emphasize an occasional technical word or to do a rough sketch when illustrating a process.
- **Handouts:** You can use handouts with any of the other visuals listed here. Audiences often appreciate being able to take away something tangible. Handouts are indispensable if you're conducting an interactive workshop and need your audience to participate in writing. Opinions vary about when to distribute them—in a packet before your speech, one by one as you need them, or at the end of your speech. If you hand them out in advance, people will read through them all as you speak. If you hand them out one by one, you need to ask someone to help when you're ready, so you can maintain your audience's attention. Handing them out

at the end works best when you want your listeners to have a record of your illustrations and other materials.

Visuals enhance a speech, but you should be able to give your presentation without them if the need arises. Bringing backup material can help you in a pinch. You might, for example, put key illustrations on transparencies in addition to in a PowerPoint file. If something does go wrong during your presentation, relax; it happens to everyone! Take a deep breath, apologize to the audience if necessary, and keep going. Here are some tips for using visuals:

- Make visuals large enough for the entire audience to see.
- Use simple layouts or drawings—nothing cluttered or overly complicated.
- Proofread your written visuals just as carefully as you would anything you write.
- Never use more than one or two visuals for each major point in the body of your speech.
- Practise with the visuals you plan to use; never let the mechanics of using visuals distract you from your audience or your speech.
- During your presentation, stay in eye contact with your audience; never turn away from your audience to read or look at a visual.

64h What can I do to practise for my presentation?

Good delivery requires practice. In preparing a speech, plan at least four complete run-throughs of your entire presentation, including visuals if you intend to use them. Time yourself and cut or expand material accordingly. Practise in front of a mirror or a friend. If possible, videotape yourself. As you watch yourself, notice your gestures. Do you look natural? Do you make nervous movements that you are not aware of as you speak?

If you suffer from stage fright—as almost everyone does—remember that the better prepared and rehearsed you are, the less frightened you will be. Your aim is to communicate, not perform. If you worry that your audience will see that you're nervous, read Box 89 for methods of overcoming physical signs of anxiety. The amazing truth is that once you're underway, the momentum of your presentation carries you onto another plane, and you forget to be nervous. Try it.

Overcoming anxiety in an oral presentation **89**

- **Pounding heart:** Don't worry. Studies show that absolutely no one else can hear it!
- **Trembling hands:** Rest them on the podium. If there is no podium, put your arms behind your back or use them to hold onto your outline or notes until the shaking stops. It always does once you're underway.
- **Shaky knees:** Stand behind the desk or podium. If there is no desk, step forward to emphasize a point. Walking slowly from one place to another can also help you get rid of nervous energy.
- **Dry throat and mouth:** Place water at the podium—or carry it up with you. Never hesitate to take an occasional sip, especially at a transition point.
- **Quavering voice:** Speaking louder can help until this disappears on its own, which it always does. The sooner you ignore the quaver, the faster it will stop.
- **Flushed face:** Although you might feel as if you're burning up, audiences don't notice. It always fades as you continue speaking.

65 WRITING UNDER PRESSURE

All writers, student and professional, sometimes find themselves under pressure to get words down on paper without losing their focus on a central message, their organization, and their control of vocabulary and grammar. This happens to journalists, for example, when they need to write a news story in a hurry to meet a deadline. It happens in the business world when a manager wants a report from a team member before the end of the day. And it happens to students when instructors require them to write an essay exam during class. Although many students resent the pressure of writing an essay exam under strict time limits, the reality is that doing so is practical preparation for the real world.

65a What strategies can I use to write essay exams?

Writing essay exams is like writing other essays, but with firm limitations on the time available. Therefore, you need to go through all the steps in the WRITING PROCESS, but at a highly stepped-up speed. Here are some time-tested strategies that students use to write essay exams under pressure.

STRATEGIES FOR WRITING ESSAY EXAMS

1. **Breathe.** Never begin writing immediately. Instead, take a deep breath and let it out slowly. Research shows that deliberate deep breathing is an effective way to relax and focus your thoughts.
2. **Read.** Read the test from beginning to end without skimming so that you understand the questions completely. If you have a choice among topics, and equal credit is given to each, select those topics you know the most about.
3. **Plan your time.** If the instructor asks three questions and indicates what percentage of your grade is allotted to each question, allocate your time to your greatest advantage. Jot down the total time available and divide it up to match the steps in the WRITING PROCESS; allot most of the time to drafting. Always allow time to reread and improve your writing after you have finished. Some—but definitely not all—instructors make allowances for the time limit and are less strict than usual about grammar, spelling, and other mechanical details.
4. **Underline cue words.** These words tell you what you must do in your essay. Look for words such as *analyze, classify,* and *criticize*. For example, your essay question might read as follows:
   - **Analyze** Socrates' discussion of "good life" and "good death." [Separate the concepts of "good life" and "good death" into parts and discuss each part.]
   - **Classify** the different stages of the digestive system in action. [Arrange the parts of the digestive system in groups based on their functions.]
   - **Criticize** the architectural function of the modern football stadium. [Give your opinion of the modern football stadium's architectural function.]

   Box 90 lists some common cue words with their meanings.

Some common cue words 90

CUE WORD	MEANING
ANALYZE	Separate into parts and discuss each.
CLASSIFY	Arrange in groups based on shared characteristics or functions.
COMPARE	Show similarities and differences.
CRITICIZE	Give your opinion and explain why you approve or disapprove of something.
DEFINE	Tell what a thing is to differentiate it from similar things.
DISCUSS	Consider in an organized way the various issues or elements involved.
EXPLAIN	Make clear a complex thing or process that needs to be illuminated or interpeted.
INTERPRET	Explain the meaning of something.
REVIEW	Evaluate or summarize critically.
SUMMARIZE	Lay out the major points.
SUPPORT	Argue in favour of a claim.

5. **Circle key content words.** Look for the key terms or major concepts in a statement or question. For example, your essay question might read as follows:
   - Compare and contrast a **book with its movie version.** [The key content words are *book with its movie version*.]
   - Justify the existence of **labour unions in a post-industrial economy.** [The key content words are *labour unions in a post-industrial economy*.]
   - Present evidence that **smoking** is a major **cause of lung cancer.** [The key content words are *smoking* and *cause of lung cancer*.]

6. As you begin writing, take a few minutes to **jot down your major ideas,** the **support** you'll give for each one, and the **order** you think best for presenting the ideas.
7. **Dive into the actual writing** and allow your notes to carry you along. Never get distracted from your time plan. If your instructor allows students to leave the room before class time is over, never assume that those people know more than you do. Even if no one but you remains in the room, keep working. The best writers are those who use every second available to write and polish.

   Trust me, I've been in that spot often and have never regretted working right up to the time limit.

TERMS GLOSSARY

This glossary defines important terms used in your *Quick Access Reference for Writers.* Terms printed throughout the book in SMALL CAPITAL LETTERS are defined here. Many of these glossary entries include parenthetical references to the handbook section(s) where the specific term is most fully discussed.

absolute phrase A phrase containing a subject and a participle that modifies an entire sentence: *The semester* [subject] *being* [present participle of *be*] *over, the campus looks deserted.* (39m)

abstract noun A noun that names things not knowable through the five senses: *idea, respect.* (39a)

action verb A verb that describes an action or occurrence done by or to the subject.

active voice An attribute of verbs showing that the action or condition expressed in the verb is done by the subject. It contrasts with the *passive voice,* which conveys that the action or condition of the verb is done *to* the subject. (40g)

adjective A word that describes or limits (modifies) a noun, a pronoun, or a word group functioning as a noun: *silly, three.* (39e, Ch. 43, 46b)

adjective clause A dependent clause also known as a *relative clause.* An adjective clause modifies a preceding noun or pronoun and begins with a relative word (such as *who, which, that,* or *where*) that relates the clause to the noun or pronoun it modifies. Also see *clause.* (39n)

adverb A word that describes or limits (modifies) verbs, adjectives, other adverbs, phrases, or clauses: *loudly, very, nevertheless, there.* (39f, Ch. 43, 46c)

adverb clause A dependent clause beginning with a subordinating conjunction that establishes the relationship in meaning between the adverb clause and its independent clause. An adverb clause modifies the independent clause's verb or the entire independent clause. Also see *clause, conjunction.* (Box 22, Ch. 43)

agreement The required match of number and person between a subject and verb (Ch. 41) or between a pronoun and antecedent (Ch. 42). A pronoun that expresses gender must match its antecedent in gender also.

analogy An explanation of the unfamiliar in terms of the familiar. Like a simile, an analogy compares things not normally associated with each other; but unlike a simile, an analogy does not use *like* or *as* in making the comparison (19e). Analogy is also a rhetorical strategy for developing paragraphs (8f).

analysis A process of critical thinking that divides a whole into its component parts in order to understand how the parts interrelate (Box 1, 26e). Sometimes called *division,* analysis is also a rhetorical strategy for developing paragraphs (8f).

antecedent The noun or pronoun to which a pronoun refers. (41f, Ch. 42)

antonym A word opposite in meaning to another word.

APA style Guidelines developed by the American Psychological Association (APA) for preparing and documenting papers. (Chs. 31 and 32)

appositive A word or group of words that renames a preceding noun or noun phrase: *my favourite month,* ***October.*** (39l, 50f)

argument A rhetorical attempt to convince others to agree with a position about a topic open to debate. (Ch. 10)

articles Included among *determiners* or *noun markers,* articles are the words *a, an,* and *the. A* and *an* are indefinite articles; *the* is a definite article. Also see *determiner.* (39e, Ch. 45, Box 69)

assertion A statement. In the process of developing a thesis statement, an assertion is a sentence that makes a statement and expresses a point of view about a topic. (5h)

audience The readers to whom a piece of writing is directed. (3b)

auxiliary verb Also known as a *helping verb,* an auxiliary verb is a form of *be, do, have, can, may, will,* and others, that combines with a main verb to help it express tense, mood, and voice. Also see *modal auxiliary verb.* (40c)

base form See *simple form.*

bibliography A list of information about sources. (23f, Chs. 29, 32, 34–36)

block style A common style of formatting business documents, in which paragraphs and other elements are not indented (37c, 63b). Contrast with *modified block style*.

brainstorming Listing all ideas that come to mind on a topic, and then grouping the ideas by patterns that emerge. (5g)

case The form of a noun or pronoun in a specific context that shows whether it is functioning as a subject, an object, or a possessive. In modern English, nouns change form in the possessive case only (*city* is the form for subjective and objective cases; *city's* is the possessive-case form). Also see *pronoun case.* (42k–t)

cause and effect The relationship between outcomes (effects) and the reasons for them (causes). Cause-and-effect analysis is a rhetorical strategy for developing paragraphs. (8f)

chronological order Also called *time order;* an arrangement of information according to time sequence; an organizing strategy for sentences, paragraphs, and longer pieces of writing. (8f)

citation Information to identify a source referred to in a piece of writing. Also see *documentation.* (Chs. 28, 31, 34a, 35a, 36a)

clause A group of words containing a subject and a predicate. A clause that delivers full meaning is called an *independent* (or *main*) *clause.* A clause that lacks full meaning by itself is called a *dependent* (or *subordinate*) *clause.* Also see *adjective clause, adverb clause, nonrestrictive element, noun clause, restrictive element.* (39n)

cliché An overused, worn-out phrase that has lost its capacity to communicate effectively: *flat as a pancake, ripe old age.* (19f)

climactic order Sometimes called *emphatic order,* climactic order is an arrangement of ideas or information from least important to most important. (8f)

clustering An invention technique based on thinking about a topic and its increasingly specific subdivisions; also known as *mapping* and *webbing.* (5g)

coherence The clear progression from one idea to another using transitional expressions, pronouns, selective repetition, and/or parallelism to make connections between ideas. (8e)

collective noun A noun that names a group of people or things: *family, committee.* (Box 36, 41h, 42e)

comma fault See *comma splice.*

comma splice The error that occurs when only a comma connects two independent clauses. (Ch. 12)

common noun A noun that names a general group, place, person, or thing: *dog, house.* (Box 46)

comparative The form of a descriptive adjective or adverb that expresses a different degree of intensity between two: *bluer, less blue; more easily, less easily.* Also see *positive, superlative.* (43e)

comparison and contrast A rhetorical strategy for organizing and developing paragraphs by discussing a subject's similarities (comparison) and differences (contrast). (8f)

complement An element after a verb that completes the predicate, such as a direct object after an action verb or a noun or adjective after a linking verb. Also see *object complement, subject complement, predicate adjective, predicate nominative.* (39l, Box 55)

complete predicate See *predicate.*

complete subject See *subject.*

complex sentence See *sentence types.*

compound-complex sentence See *sentence types.*

compound predicate See *predicate.*

compound sentence See *sentence types.*

compound subject See *subject.*

concrete noun A noun naming things that can be seen, touched, heard, smelled, or tasted: *smoke, sidewalk.* (Box 46)

conjunction A word that connects or otherwise establishes a relationship between two or more words, phrases, or clauses. Also see *coordinating conjunction, correlative conjunction,* and *subordinating conjunction.* (39h)

conjunctive adverb An adverb that creates a relationship, such as of addition, contrast, comparison, result, time, or emphasis, between words. (Box 50)

connotation Ideas implied by a word; connotations convey associations such as emotional overtones beyond a word's direct, explicit definition. (19b)

coordinate adjectives Two or more adjectives that equally modify a noun (***big, friendly*** *dog*). The order of coordinate adjectives can be changed without destroying meaning. Also see *cumulative adjectives.* (50e)

coordinating conjunction A conjunction that joins two or more grammatically equivalent structures: *and, or, for, nor, but, so, yet.* (Box 51)

coordination The use of grammatically equivalent forms to show a balance or sequence of ideas. (Box 51, 16a–16b)

correlative conjunction A pair of words that joins equivalent grammatical structures, including *both . . . and, either . . . or, neither . . . nor, not only . . . but also.* (39h)

count noun A noun that names items that can be counted: *radio, street, idea, fingernail.* (Box 46, 44a, 45a–45b)

critical response Formally, an essay summarizing a source's central point or main idea and then presenting the writer's synthesized reactions in response. (4b)

cumulative adjectives Adjectives that build up meaning from word to word as they get closer to the noun (***familiar rock*** *tunes*). The order of cumulative adjectives cannot be changed without destroying meaning. Also see *coordinate adjectives.* (50e)

dangling modifier A modifier that attaches its meaning illogically, either because it is closer to another noun or pronoun than to its true subject or because its true subject is not expressed in the sentence. (14e)

declarative sentence A sentence that makes a statement: *Sky diving is exciting.* Also see *exclamatory sentence, imperative sentence, interrogative sentence.*

definite article See *article.*

denotation The dictionary definition of a word. (19b)

dependent clause A clause that cannot stand alone as an independent grammatical unit; also called *subordinate clause.* Also see *adjective clause, adverb clause, noun clause.* (39n)

descriptive adjective An adjective that describes the condition or properties of the noun it modifies and (except for a very few, such as *dead* and *unique*) has comparative and superlative forms: *flat, flatter, flattest.*

descriptive adverb An adverb that describes the condition or properties of whatever it modifies and that has comparative and superlative forms: *happily, more happily, most happily.*

determiner A word or word group, traditionally identified as an *adjective,* that limits a noun by telling "how much" or "how many" about it. Also called *expressions of quantity, limiting adjectives,* or *noun markers.* (Box 49, 39e, 44b, Ch. 45)

diction Word choice. (19b)

direct discourse In writing, words that repeat speech or conversation exactly and so are enclosed in quotation marks. Also see *indirect discourse.* (13d)

direct object A noun or pronoun or group of words functioning as a noun that receives the action (completes the meaning) of a transitive verb. (39k)

direct question A sentence that asks a question and ends with a question mark: *Are you going?*

direct quotation See *quotation.*

discovery draft See *drafting.*

documentation The acknowledgment of someone else's words and ideas used in any piece of writing by giving full and accurate information about the person whose words were used and about where those words were found; for example, for a print source, documentation usually includes author name(s), title, place and date of publication, and related information. (Box 25, 23e, 26b, 26d, Box 39, Chs. 28–36)

documentation style Any of various systems for providing information about the source of words, information, and ideas quoted, paraphrased, or summarized from some source other than the writer. Documentation styles discussed in this handbook are MLA, APA, CM, CSE, and COS. (Box 25, 23e, 26b, Box 39, Chs. 28–36)

double negative A nonstandard negation using two negative modifiers rather than one. (43c)

draft See *drafting.*

drafting A part of the writing process in which writers compose ideas in sentences and paragraphs; the documents produced by drafting are often called *drafts.* A *discovery draft* is an early, rough draft. (6a)

edited Canadian English English language use that conforms to established rules of grammar, sentence structure, punctuation, and spelling; also called *standard English.* (19d)

editing A part of the writing process in which writers check a document for the technical correctness of its grammar, spelling, punctuation, and mechanics. (7d–7e, Box 30)

elliptical construction A sentence structure that deliberately omits words that are expressed elsewhere or words that can be inferred from the context.

essential element See *restrictive element.*

euphemism Language that attempts to blunt certain realities by speaking of them in "nice" or "tactful" words. (19g)

evidence Facts, data, examples, and opinions of others used to support assertions and conclusions. (10c, Box 16, 27b)

exclamation A word or words expressing strong feeling and ending in an exclamation point.

exclamatory sentence A sentence beginning with *What* or *How* that expresses strong feeling: *What a ridiculous statement!*

expletive The phrase *there is (are), there was (were), it is,* or *it was* at the beginning of a clause, changing structure and postponing the subject: *It is Mars that we hope to reach* (compare *We hope to reach Mars*).

faulty predication A grammatically illogical combination of subject and predicate. (16e)

first person See *person.*

freewriting Writing nonstop for a period of time to generate ideas by free association of thoughts. *Focused freewriting* may start with a set topic or may build on one sentence taken from earlier freewriting. (5e)

fused sentence See *run-on (run-together)* sentence.

future perfect progressive tense The form of the future perfect tense that describes an action or condition ongoing until some specific future time: *I will have been talking.*

future perfect tense The tense indicating that an action will have been completed or a condition will have ended by a specified point in the future: *I will have talked.*

future progressive tense The form of the future tense showing that a future action will continue for some time: *I will be talking.*

future tense The form of a verb, made with the simple form and either *shall* or *will,* expressing an action yet to be taken or a condition not yet experienced: *I will talk.*

gender Concerning languages, the classification of words as masculine, feminine, or neuter. In English, personal pronouns indicate gender in third-person singular: *he, him, his; she, her, hers; it, its, its.* A few nouns naming roles change form to show gender difference: *prince, princess,* for example. (20a)

gender-neutral language See *sexist language.*

gerund A present participle functioning as a noun: *Walking is good exercise.* Also see *verbal.*

gerund phrase A gerund, along with its modifiers, and/or object(s), which functions as a subject or an object. (39m)

graphics Especially in the context of documents created on a computer, images such as tables, graphs, charts, and diagrams (37f).

helping verb See *auxiliary verb.*

homonyms Words spelled differently that sound alike: *to, too, two.* (21d, Box 24)

idiom A word, phrase, or other construction that has a different meaning from its usual or literal meaning: *He lost his head. She hit the ceiling.*

illogical predication See *faulty predication.*

imperative mood The mood that expresses commands and direct requests, using the simple form of the verb and often implying but not expressing the subject, *you: Go.* (40f)

imperative sentence A sentence that gives a command: *Go to the corner and buy me a newspaper.*

indefinite article See *article, determiner.*

indefinite pronoun A pronoun, such as *all, anyone, each,* and others, that refers to a nonspecific person or thing. (39b, 41e, 42d)

independent clause A clause that can stand alone as an independent grammatical unit. (39n)

indicative mood The mood of verbs used for statements about real things or highly likely ones: *I think Grace is arriving today.* (40f)

indirect discourse Reported speech or conversation that does not use the exact structure of the original and so is not enclosed in quotation marks. (13d)

indirect object A noun or pronoun or group of words functioning as a noun that tells to whom or for whom the action expressed by a transitive verb was done. (39k)

indirect question A sentence that reports a question and ends with a period: *I asked if you are going.*

indirect quotation See *quotation.*

infinitive A verbal made of the simple form of a verb and usually, but not always, *to,* which functions as a noun, adjective, or adverb.

infinitive phrase An infinitive, its modifiers, and/or object, which functions as a noun, adjective, or adverb.

informal language Word choice that creates a tone appropriate for casual writing or speaking. (19d)

informative writing Writing that gives information and, when necessary, explains it; also known as *expository writing.* (5b, Ch. 9)

intensive pronoun A pronoun that ends in *-self* and that intensifies its antecedent: *Vida* ***himself*** *argued against it.* Also see *reflexive pronoun.* (Box 47)

interjection An emotion-conveying word that is treated as a sentence, starting with a capital letter and ending with an exclamation point or a period: *Oh! Ouch!* (39i, 55c)

interrogative pronoun A pronoun, such as *whose* or *what,* that implies a question: *Who called?* (Box 47)

interrogative sentence A sentence that asks a direct question: *Did you see that?*

intransitive verb A verb that does not take a direct object. (40a, Box 59)

invention techniques Ways of gathering ideas for writing. (5g)

inverted word order In contrast to standard order, the main verb or an auxiliary verb comes before the subject in inverted word order. Most questions and some exclamations use inverted word order. (17h, 46a)

irony Using words to imply the opposite of their usual meaning. (19e)

irregular verb A verb that forms the past tense and past participle in some way other than by adding *-ed* or *-d.* (40b, Box 60)

italics A slanting font used for titles of long works, certain names, foreign words, and terms, letters, and numbers referred to as such. (Ch. 59)

jargon Specialized vocabulary of a particular field or group that a general reader is unlikely to understand. (19g)

levels of formality The degree of formality of language, reflected by word choice and sentence structure. A highly formal level is used for ceremonial and other occasions when stylistic flourishes are appropriate. A medium level, which is neither too formal nor too casual, is acceptable for most academic writing. (19d)

limiting adjective See *determiner.*

linking verb A main verb that links a subject with a subject complement that renames or describes the subject. Linking verbs convey a state of being, relate to the senses, or indicate a condition. (Box 55, Box 59)

literal meaning What is stated by words. (2b)

logical fallacies Flaws in reasoning that lead to illogical statements. (10f)

main clause See *independent clause.*

main verb A verb that expresses action, occurrence, or state of being and that shows mood, tense, voice, number, and person.

mapping See *clustering.*

mechanics Conventions governing matters such as the use of capital letters, italics, abbreviations, and numbers. (Chs. 57–61)

metaphor A comparison implying similarity between two things; a metaphor does not use words such as *like* or *as,* which are used in a simile and which make a comparison explicit: *a mop of hair* (compare the simile *hair like a mop*). (19e)

misplaced modifier Describing or limiting words that are wrongly positioned in a sentence so that their message either is illogical or relates to the wrong word(s). (14a)

mixed construction A sentence that unintentionally changes from one grammatical structure to another, incompatible one, thus garbling meaning. (13e)

mixed metaphors Incongruously combined images. (19e)

MLA style Guidelines developed by the Modern Language Association (MLA) for preparing and documenting papers. (Chs. 28–30)

modal auxiliary verb A group of auxiliary verbs that add information such as a sense of needing, wanting, or having to do something or a sense of possibility, likelihood, obligation, permission, or ability. (Ch. 49)

modified block style A common style of formatting business documents, in which paragraphs are indented and the complimentary closing and signature begin halfway across the page. (63b)

modifier, modify A word or group of words functioning as an adjective or adverb to describe or limit (modify) another word or word group. (17g, Ch. 43)

mood The attribute of verbs showing a speaker's or writer's attitude toward the action by the way verbs are used. English has three moods: imperative, indicative, and subjunctive. Also see *imperative mood, indicative mood, subjunctive mood.* (40f)

noncount noun A noun that names "uncountable" things: *water, time.* (Box 46, 44a, 45a–45b)

nonessential element See *nonrestrictive element.*

nonrestrictive element A descriptive word, phrase, or dependent clause that provides information not essential to understanding the basic message of the element it modifies; it is therefore set off by commas. Also see *restrictive element.* (50f)

nonsexist language See *sexist language.*

nonstandard Language usage other than edited Canadian English. Also see *edited Canadian English.* (20d)

noun A word that names a person, place, thing, or idea. Nouns function as subjects, objects, or complements. (39a, 39k, 39l)

noun clause A dependent clause that functions as a subject, object, or complement. (39n)

noun complement See *complement.*

noun determiner See *determiner.*

noun phrase A noun along with its modifiers functioning as a subject, object, or complement. (39m)

number The attribute of some words indicating whether they refer to one (singular) or more than one (plural). (41a)

object A noun, pronoun, or group of words functioning as a noun or pronoun that receives the action of a verb (direct object); tells to whom or for whom something is done (indirect object); or completes the meaning of a preposition (object of a preposition). (39k)

object complement A noun or adjective renaming or describing a direct object after certain verbs, including *call, consider, name, elect,* and *think: I call* ***joggers*** [object] ***fanatics*** [object complement].

objective case The case of a noun or pronoun functioning as a direct or indirect object or as an object of a preposition or of a verbal. A few pronouns change form to show case (*him, her, whom*). Also see *case.* (42k–t)

paragraph A group of sentences that work together to develop a unit of thought. (8a)

paragraph development Use of specific, concrete details (RENNS) to support a generalization in a paragraph; rhetorical strategies for arranging and organizing paragraphs. (8d, 8f)

parallelism The use of equivalent grammatical forms or matching sentence structures to express equivalent ideas. (8e)

paraphrase A restatement of someone else's ideas in language and sentence structure different from that of the original. (26g)

parenthetical documentation See *parenthetical reference.*

parenthetical reference Information enclosed in parentheses following quoted, paraphrased, or summarized material from another source to alert readers to the use of the material from that source. Parenthetical references and a list of bibliographic information about each source used in a paper document the writer's use of sources. (Chs. 28–29 [MLA], Chs. 31–32 [APA], 36a [COS])

participipial phrase A phrase that contains a present participle or a past participle and any modifiers and that functions as an adjective. Also see *verbal.*

participle A verb form. See *past participle, present participle.*

passive construction See *passive voice.*

passive voice The form of a verb in which the subject is acted upon; if the subject is mentioned in the sentence, it usually appears as the object of the preposition *by: I was frightened by the thunder* (compare the active-voice version *The thunder frightened me*). The passive voice emphasizes the action, in contrast to the active voice, which emphasizes the doer of the action. (40g)

past participle The third principal part of a verb, formed in regular verbs by adding *-d,* or *-ed* to the simple form, as with the past tense. In irregular verbs, it often differs from the simple form and the past tense: *break, broke, broken.* (40b, Box 60)

past perfect progressive tense The past perfect tense form that describes an ongoing condition in the past that has been ended by something stated in the sentence: (*Before the curtains caught fire,*) *I had been talking.*

past perfect tense The tense that describes a condition or action that started in the past, continued for a while, and then ended in the past: *I had talked.*

past progressive tense The past tense form that shows the continuing nature of a past action: *I was talking.*

past-tense form The second principal part of a verb, in regular verbs formed by adding *-d* or *-ed* to the simple form. In irregular verbs, the past tense may change in several ways from the simple form. (40b)

perfect tenses The three tenses—the present perfect (*I have talked*), the past perfect (*I had talked*), and the future perfect (*I will have talked*)—that help to show complex time relationships between two clauses. (40e)

person The attribute of nouns and pronouns showing who or what acts or experiences an action. *First person* is the one speaking (*I, we*); *second person* is the one being spoken to (*you, you*); and third person is the person or thing spoken about (*he, she, it; they*). All nouns are third person.

personal pronoun A pronoun that refers to people or things: *I, you, them, it.*

persuasive writing Writing that seeks to convince the reader about a matter of opinion. (5b, Ch. 10)

phrasal verb A verb that combines with one or more prepositions to deliver its meaning: *ask out, look into.* (47b)

phrase A group of related words that does not contain a subject and predicate and thus cannot stand alone as an independent grammatical unit. A phrase can function as a noun, a verb, or a modifier. (39m)

plagiarism A writer's presenting another person's words or ideas without giving credit to that person. Documentation systems allow writers to give proper credit to sources in ways recognized by scholarly communities. Plagiarism is a serious offence, a form of intellectual dishonesty that can lead to course failure or expulsion. (Ch. 26, 62f)

planning An early part of the writing process in which writers gather ideas. When combined with shaping, planning is sometimes called *prewriting.* (Box 25, 22e)

plural See *number.*

positive The form of an adjective or adverb when no comparison is being expressed: *blue, easily.* Also see *comparative, superlative.* (43e)

possessive case The case of a noun or pronoun that shows ownership or possession. Also see *case.* (53a–53c)

predicate The part of a sentence that contains the verb and tells what the subject is doing or experiencing or what is being done to the subject. A *simple predicate* contains only the main verb and any auxiliary verb(s). A *complete predicate* contains the verb, its modifiers, objects, and other related words. A *compound predicate* contains two or more verbs and their objects and modifiers, if any. (39j)

predicate adjective An adjective used as a subject complement: *That tree is **leafy.***

predicate nominative A noun or pronoun used as a subject complement: *That tree is a **maple.***

prefix Letters added at the beginning of a root word to create a new word.

preposition A word that conveys a relationship, often of space or time, between the noun or pronoun following it and other words in the sentence. The noun or pronoun following a preposition is called its *object.* (39k, Ch. 47, 48a–b)

prepositional phrase A group of words beginning with a preposition and including a noun, which is called the object.

present participle A verb's *-ing* form. Used with auxiliary verbs, present participles function as main verbs (40b). Used without auxiliary verbs, present participles function as nouns or adjectives (39d).

present perfect progressive tense The present-perfect-tense form that describes something ongoing in the past that is likely to continue into the future: *I have been talking.*

present perfect tense The tense indicating that an action or its effects, begun or perhaps completed in the past, continue into the present: *I had talked.*

present progressive tense The present-tense form of the verb that indicates something taking place at the time it is written or spoken about: *I am talking.*

present tense The tense that describes what is happening, what is true at the moment, and what is consistently true. It uses the simple form (*I talk*) and the *-s* form in the third-person singular (*he, she, it talks*). (40b)

prewriting A term for all activities in the writing process before drafting. (5a)

primary sources "Firsthand" work: write-ups of experiments and observations by the researchers who conducted them; taped accounts, interviews, and newspaper accounts by direct observers; autobiographies, diaries, and journals; expressive works (poems, plays, fiction, essays); also known as *primary evidence.* Also see *secondary sources.* (22a, 23b)

principal parts Verb forms. (40b)

progressive forms Verb forms made, in all tenses, with the present participle and forms of the verb *be* as an auxiliary. Progressive forms show that an action, occurrence, or state of being is ongoing. (40e)

pronoun A word that takes the place of a noun and functions in the same ways that nouns do. Types of pronouns are demonstrative, indefinite, intensive, interrogative, personal, reciprocal, reflexive, and relative.

The word (or words) a pronoun replaces is called its antecedent. (39b, Ch. 42)

pronoun–antecedent agreement The match required between a pronoun and its antecedent in number and person, and for personal pronouns, in gender as well. (42a–e)

pronoun case The way a pronoun changes form to reflect its use as the agent of action (subjective case), the thing being acted upon (objective case), or the thing showing ownership (possessive case). (42k–t)

pronoun reference The relationship between a pronoun and its antecedent. (42f–j)

proofreading Reading a final draft to find and correct any spelling or mechanics mistakes, typing errors, or handwriting illegibility; the final step of the writing process. (7f)

proper adjective An adjective formed from a proper noun: *Victorian, Canadian.*

proper noun A noun that names specific people, places, or things; it is always capitalized: *Jim Carrey, Tim Horton's.*

purpose The goal or aim of a piece of writing: to express oneself, to provide information, to persuade, or to create a literary work. (5b)

quotation Repeating or reporting another person's words. *Direct quotation* repeats another's words exactly and encloses them in quotation marks. *Indirect quotation* reports another's words without quotation marks except around any words repeated exactly from the source. Both direct and indirect quotation require documentation of the source to avoid plagiarism. Also see *indirect discourse.* (13d, 26f, 54a–c)

reciprocal pronoun The pronouns *each other* and *one another,* referring to individual parts of a plural antecedent: *We respect* ***each other.***

References In many documentation styles, including APA, the title of a list of sources cited in a research paper or other written work. (Chs. 31, 32, 35, 36)

reflexive pronoun A pronoun that ends in *-self* and that reflects back to its antecedent: *They claim to support* ***themselves.***

regular verb A verb that forms its past tense and past participle by adding *-ed* or *-d* to the simple form. Most English verbs are regular. (40b)

relative adverb An adverb that introduces an adjective clause: *The lot **where I usually park my car** was full.* (39f)

relative clause See *adjective clause.*

relative pronoun A pronoun, such as *who, which, that, who, whom, whoever,* and a few others, that introduces an adjective clause or sometimes a noun clause. (Box 47)

restrictive clause A dependent clause that gives information necessary to the meaning of whatever it modifies. In contrast to a nonrestrictive clause, a restrictive clause is not set off with commas. (39n, 50f)

restrictive element A word, phrase, or dependent clause that provides information essential to the understanding of the element it modifies. In contrast to a nonrestrictive element, a restrictive element is not set off with commas. Also see *nonrestrictive element.* (50f)

revising, revision A part of the writing process in which writers evaluate their rough drafts and, on the basis of their assessments, rewrite by adding, cutting, replacing, moving, and often totally recasting material. (7a–7c, Box 10)

rhetoric The area of discourse that focuses on arrangement of ideas and choice of words as a reflection of the writer's purpose and sense of audience.

rhetorical strategies In writing, various techniques for presenting ideas to deliver a writer's intended message with clarity and impact. Reflecting typical patterns of human thought, rhetorical strategies include arrangements such as chronological and climactic order; stylistic techniques such as parallelism and planned repetition; and patterns for organizing and developing writing such as description and definition. (Ch. 8)

run-on (run-together) sentence The error of running independent clauses together without the required punctuation that marks them as complete units. (Ch. 12).

second person See *person.*

secondary source A source that reports, analyzes, discusses, reviews, or otherwise deals with the work of someone else, as opposed to a primary source, which is someone's original work or firsthand report. A reliable secondary source should be the work of a person with appropriate credentials, should appear in a respected publication or other medium, should be current, and should be well reasoned. (22a, 23b)

sentence See *sentence types.*

sentence fragment A portion of a sentence that is punctuated as though it were a complete sentence. (Ch. 11)

sentence types A grammatical classification of sentences by the kinds of clauses they contain. A *simple sentence* consists of one independent clause. A *complex sentence* contains one independent clause and one or more dependent clauses. A *compound-complex sentence* contains at least two independent clauses and one or more dependent clauses. A *compound sentence* contains two or more independent clauses joined by a coordinating conjunction. Sentences are also classified by their grammatical function; see *declarative sentence, exclamatory sentence, imperative sentence,* and *interrogative sentence.* (39o)

sexist language Language that unfairly or unnecessarily assigns roles or characteristics to people on the basis of gender. Language that avoids gender stereotyping is called *gender-neutral* or *nonsexist language.* (20b)

shift An unnecessary change in person, number, voice, tense, or other grammatical framework that makes a sentence unclear.

simile A comparison, using *like* or *as,* of otherwise dissimilar things. (19e)

simple form The form of the verb that shows action, occurrence, or state of being taking place in the present. It is used in the singular for first and second person and in the plural for first, second, and third person. It is also the first principal part of a verb. The simple form is also known as the *dictionary form* or *base form.* (40b)

simple predicate See *predicate.*

simple sentence See *sentence types.*

simple subject See *subject.*

simple tenses The present, past, and future tenses, which divide time into present, past, and future. (40e)

singular See *number.*

slang Coined words and new meanings for existing words, which quickly pass in and out of use; inappropriate for most academic writing. (19d)

source A book, article, document, other work, or person providing information.

split infinitive One or more words coming between the two words of an infinitive. (14c)

standard English See *edited Canadian English.*

standard word order The most common order for words in English sentences: The subject comes before the predicate. (17h, 46a)

subject The word or group of words in a sentence that acts, is acted upon, or is described by the verb. A *simple subject* includes only the noun or pronoun. A *complete subject* includes the noun or pronoun and all its modifiers. A *compound subject* includes two or more nouns or pronouns and their modifiers. (39j)

subject complement A noun or adjective that follows a linking verb, renaming or describing the subject of the sentence; also called a *predicate nominative.* (39l, 41h)

subjective case The case of the noun or pronoun functioning as subject. Also see *case.*

subject–verb agreement The required match between a subject and verb in expressing number and person. (Ch. 41)

subjunctive mood The verb mood that expresses wishes, recommendations, indirect requests, speculations, and conditional statements: *I wish you **were** here.* (40f)

subordinate clause See *dependent clause.*

subordinating conjunction A conjunction that introduces an adverbial clause and expresses a relationship between the idea in it and the idea in the independent clause. (16c, Box 52)

subordination The use of grammatical structures to reflect the relative importance of ideas. A sentence with logically subordinated information expresses the most important information in the independent clause and less important information in dependent clauses or phrases. (16c–16d)

suffix An ending added to a basic (root) word to change function or meaning.

summary An extraction of the main message or central point of a passage or other discourse; a critical thinking activity preceding synthesis. (4a, 26h)

superlative The form of an adjective or adverb that expresses comparison among three or more things: *bluest, least blue, most easily, least easily.* (43e)

synonym A word that is close in meaning to another word. (19a)

synthesis A component of critical thinking in which material that has been summarized, analyzed, and interpreted is connected to what is already known (one's prior knowledge). (4b, 22a)

tag question An inverted verb-pronoun combination, added to the end of a sentence and creating a question, that "asks" the audience to agree with the assertion in the first part of the sentence: *You know what a tag question is,* ***don't you?*** A tag question is set off from the rest of the sentence with a comma. (50h)

tag sentence See *tag question.*

tense The time at which the action of the verb occurs: in the present, the past, or the future. (40e)

tense sequence In sentences that have more than one clause, the accurate matching of verbs to reflect logical time relationships. (40e, Box 61)

thesis statement A statement of an essay's central theme that makes clear the main idea, the writer's purpose, the focus of the topic, and perhaps the organizational pattern. (5h, 7b)

third person See *person.*

tone The writer's attitude toward his or her material and reader, especially as reflected by word choice. (2b, 5d, 19g)

topic The subject of discourse.

topic sentence The sentence that expresses the main idea of a paragraph. (8c)

transition The connection of one idea to another in discourse. Useful strategies for creating transitions include transitional expressions, parallelism, and planned repetition of key words and phrases. (8e)

transitional expressions Words and phrases that signal connections among ideas and create coherence. (8e, Box 14)

transitive verb A verb that must be followed by a direct object. (39k, 40d)

unity The clear and logical relationship between the main idea of a paragraph and the evidence supporting the main idea. (Ch. 8)

unmarked infinitive A base verb functioning as an infinitive without the word *to* in front of it.

usage A customary way of using language. (Ch. 18, Usage Glossary)

verb A class of words that show action or occurrence or that describe a state of being. Verbs change form to show time (tense), attitude (mood), and role of the subject (voice). Verbs occur in the predicate of a clause and can be in verb phrases, which may consist of a main verb, any auxiliary verbs, and any modifiers. Verbs can be described as transitive or intransitive, depending on whether they take a direct object. (39c, Ch. 40)

verb phrase A main verb, along with any auxiliary verb(s) and any modifiers.

verbal A verb part functioning as a noun, adjective, or adverb. Verbals include infinitives, present participles (functioning as adjectives), gerunds (present participles functioning as nouns), and past participles. (39d)

verbal phrase A group of words that contains a verbal (an infinitive, participle, or gerund) and its modifiers. (39m)

voice An attribute of verbs showing whether the subject acts (active voice) or is acted upon (passive voice). (40g)

Works Cited In MLA documentation style, the title of a list of all sources cited in a research paper or other written work. (Ch. 29)

writing process Stages of writing in which a writer gathers and shapes ideas, organizes material, expresses those ideas in a rough draft, evaluates the draft and revises it, edits the writing for technical errors, and proofreads it for typographical accuracy and legibility. The stages often overlap. (Chs. 5–10)

writing situation Concerning a writing assignment, the assignment's topic, purpose, audience, and special requirements such as deadline and length. (5f)

INDEX

Note: Numbers in **bold** indicate main discussion; numbers in *italics* indicate definitions

A

E

J

K

L

M

N

P

W

Y